Stylistics

Jane Lugea · Brian Walker

Stylistics

Text, Cognition and Corpora

Jane Lugea
School of Arts, English and Languages
Queen's University Belfast
Belfast, UK

Brian Walker
School of Arts, English and Languages
Queen's University Belfast
Belfast, UK

ISBN 978-3-031-10421-3   ISBN 978-3-031-10422-0 (eBook)
https://doi.org/10.1007/978-3-031-10422-0

© The Editor(s) (if applicable) and The Author(s), under exclusive licence to Springer Nature Switzerland AG 2023

This work is subject to copyright. All rights are solely and exclusively licensed by the Publisher, whether the whole or part of the material is concerned, specifically the rights of translation, reprinting, reuse of illustrations, recitation, broadcasting, reproduction on microfilms or in any other physical way, and transmission or information storage and retrieval, electronic adaptation, computer software, or by similar or dissimilar methodology now known or hereafter developed.

The use of general descriptive names, registered names, trademarks, service marks, etc. in this publication does not imply, even in the absence of a specific statement, that such names are exempt from the relevant protective laws and regulations and therefore free for general use.

The publisher, the authors, and the editors are safe to assume that the advice and information in this book are believed to be true and accurate at the date of publication. Neither the publisher nor the authors or the editors give a warranty, expressed or implied, with respect to the material contained herein or for any errors or omissions that may have been made. The publisher remains neutral with regard to jurisdictional claims in published maps and institutional affiliations.

Cover illustration: © Daniel Liévano/Ikon Images

This Palgrave Macmillan imprint is published by the registered company Springer Nature Switzerland AG

The registered company address is: Gewerbestrasse 11, 6330 Cham, Switzerland

Acknowledgements

We would like to thank the many people who helped us to get this book ready for publication. Numerous friends and colleagues advised us and offered invaluable feedback on chapters. We would like to thank Jane Demmen, Lesley Jeffries, Dan McIntyre and Patricia Canning-Pask for giving up their time and lending us their expertise. We are grateful to Carolina Fernández-Quintanilla and Clara Neary for trialling some of the material and activities. Thanks are due to our anonymous reviewer, who provided constructive feedback that we believe improved the book. That said, any errors or anomalies are our own.

We would also like to thank the many staff at Palgrave for their help, support and infinite patience. We would particularly like to thank Cathy Scott, Helen van der Stelt, Helen Caunce, Paul Stevens, Bhavya Rattan and the rest of the team that helped us get this book published.

We would also like to thank Laurence Anthony, Sebastian Hoffmann, and Paul Rayson for their software, and for permission to use screenshots in our corpus activities. Special mention goes to screenwriter Paul Lavery and filmmaker Ken Loach for kind permission to use an extract from *I, Daniel Blake*, for which a donation was made to South Belfast Foodbank, in lieu of payment, at their request. We are grateful to the English department at Queen's University Belfast for financing some of the copyrighted works reproduced in this book.

The HUM19CUK corpus, which we refer to several times in the book, was constructed by a small team of people. Thanks to Francine Stradling, Hazel Price and Elliot Land for helping to make the corpus a reality.

Finally, we would like to thank friends and family, particularly our partners, for patiently suffering with us as we prepared this book.

About this book

In this book, our aim is to help you identify and interpret features that contribute towards the style of texts. With a primary focus on style in literary genres (prose fiction, poetry, drama), the following chapters present a toolkit for the analysis of style that incorporates **text**, **cognition** and **corpora**:

- **Text** is the main object of study in Stylistics and refers to a piece of discourse which stands on its own, but nevertheless relates to other texts (e.g. through authorship, genre, parody, etc.).
- **Cognition** refers to how readers process texts and the interaction between textual information and readers' minds.
- **Corpora** refers to incorporating methods, approaches and tools from Corpus Linguistics into stylistic enquiry to broaden, strengthen and motivate analyses. As we will discover in ▶ Chapter 1, corpora are large structured electronic compilations of texts.

Over the course of this book, we bring together these three pillars of contemporary Stylistics and provide the tools required to explicate the ways in which texts function and how we experience them.

◎ Focus boxes provide extra details about particular topics.

⤓ This book has **Electronic Supplementary Materials** hosted at chapter level on the book's webpage on the Palgrave and SpringerLink website: ▶ https://link.springer.com/book/9783031104237 Where relevant, readers are directed to those materials, which contain answers to activities and instructions for corpus KWIC-ies.

📄 Throughout this book, there will be **Activities** that encourage you to explore the concepts, models and frameworks we introduce. Where answers are not provided in this book, they are available for download from the book's webpage.

🖥 There will also be some **Corpus KWIC-ies** (we will explain the name later), which are short tasks aimed at developing familiarity with corpus methods. Instructions for KWIC-ies are found on the book's webpage.

The textbook provides arguably the first accessible introduction to what we believe are the three pillars of contemporary stylistic research: text, cognition and corpus. Throughout the book, we will show how these three pillars of Stylistics work together in the analysis of fiction. While the text has always been central to stylistic enquiry, the field has developed from formal approaches to texts to those that consider the role of cognition in interpreting texts and use corpora to lend empiricism and enhanced objectivity. These two main developments—cognition and corpora—have not been comprehensively elucidated for junior scholars of Stylistics. This textbook will demonstrate the possibilities afforded by an integrated approach which benefits from a) detailed textual analysis, b) consideration of cognitive processes in textual interpretation and c) use of corpus methodologies to enhance objectivity and empiricism in stylistic analysis. Cognitive and corpus approaches are sometimes seen as incompatible or divergent. However, in this book, we have taken the view that they are complementary, and necessarily so. We believe this combined approach encapsulates what contemporary Stylistics aims to achieve: evidence-based analyses of how texts achieve effects in their readers. The chapters in this book deal with analytical frameworks to provide readers with a toolkit for textual analysis, each informed by insights from the Cognitive Sciences and corpus methodologies.

Summary of Chapters

In ▶ Chapter 1, we start by introducing the notion of style before going on to describe how the three pillars of Stylistics (text, cognition and corpus) can be combined to understand how the style of a text is created. We introduce the important concepts of foregrounding and discourse structure, and outline key ideas from Cognitive and Corpus Linguistics.

We believe that a useful start in Stylistics is the idea that a text creates a 'world', as this metaphor helps to delineate the relationship between the text and its discourse context and emphasises the role of readers' cognition in creating an understanding of the text. Therefore, ▶ Chapter 2 provides a detailed summary of worlds-based approaches to Stylistics (Ryan 1991a, 1991b; Werth 1999; Gavins 2007). According to Text World Theory (TWT), discourse participants use a combination of textual cues and pre-existing knowledge to create a mental representation of discourse, known as a text-world. TWT draws on the Cognitive Sciences to provide a framework for analysing and diagramming discourse. We apply TWT to the opening paragraphs of *Tess of the D'Ubervilles*, revealing how the novel sets out its concern with social inequalities and immobility right from the outset, through its construction and elaboration of the text-world. Because TWT is impractical for analysing longer stretches of text, we suggest that a corpus can be used to find a 'way in' to a text, shedding light on a section of *Tess* for further, qualitative analysis. This is demonstrated by doing a text-internal analysis of the modal auxiliary verbs, which are key in the creation of modal-worlds. The chapter that used the most modal auxiliary verbs (when compared to other chapters in the novel) is then selected for further detailed text-world analysis. This combination of methods shows how the newlywed characters' use of modal-worlds informed their marital discussion and decision-making. Their modal-worlds are shaped by their society's gender norms, adding gender inequality to the class inequality identified as significant to the novel from the outset. Based on this innovative combination of corpus methods and TWT, we propose that this corpus-assisted method of data selection could be employed with other linguistic features and models.

▶ Chapter 3 synthesises a vast range of scholarship on narrative viewpoint including Short (1996) and Simpson (2000). Moreover, it offers a new way of thinking about *narrative, narration* and *story*, based on the discourse structures introduced in Chapters 1 and 2. We describe how, in the discourse-world, an author communicates to a reader through a *narrative* text. We define *narrative* as 'the *narration* of a *story*'. By integrating textual cues with pre-existing knowledge, readers form an impression of the text-world which includes the remaining two levels: (i) the *narration*; and (ii) the *story*. The *narration* is the discourse between the narrator and a narratee, the latter role visible to varying extents in different texts. Narrators tell the *story* from their viewpoint, embedding characters within it and have the option of presenting information from characters' viewpoints as well. Our framework is intended to crystalise how the discourse structure of narrative affects the roles of participants and enactors, and how it facilitates options for constructing viewpoint in narrative. The chapter continues with a discussion of the role of modality and evaluative language in narrative viewpoint using an example from Hemingway's *The Sun Also Rises* (TSAR). This author is known for his objective style, which appears void of narratorial subjectivity and evaluation. We investigate this commonly held assumption using corpus approaches. The corpus analysis shows that the narrator in TSAR uses comparatively fewer evaluative adverbs and adjectives, as well as modal auxiliary verbs. This finding lends empirical support for the intuitive assessment of the novel as having a clipped, journalistic style. We also show, through studying concordance lines, that some viewpoint indicators are *overused* in TSAR ('let's' and 'ought to' and question words) and that these are mainly found in characters' Direct Speech, not the narration itself. In this instance, the corpus method is used to a) confirm a preconceived hypothesis and b) provide a more nuanced understanding of subjectivity in Hemingway's novel. The use of corpus approaches here shows the interaction between intuitions and hypotheses. Intuitions about narrator style are used to form hypotheses about the text, which can be explored using corpus methods—in a way that would be extremely difficult manually—and supported by applying a model of viewpoint to uncover linguistic patterns in the text relevant to the narrative style.

▶ Chapter 4 picks up on the important distinction made between the narrative and the discourse attributed to characters, by exploring the different techniques available for presenting their speech, writing and thought (SW&TP). Drawing on the work of Leech and Short (2007: 261), we describe the different categories of SW&TP and illustrate them with examples drawn from Huddersfield, Utrecht, Middelburg Corpus of UK 19th century Fiction (HUM-19CUK). We demonstrate how SW&TP can be analysed using a corpus: first, by manually annotating the categories in Evelyn Waugh's short story 'Mr Loveday's little outing'; and second, by comparing it with the fiction section of the Lancaster SW&TP (LancFic). The manual annotation is guided by the model of SW&TP. The combination of stylistic framework and corpus approach enables an analysis that would have otherwise proven extremely difficult. The analysis is also aided by the comparison between a 'norm' of SW&TP in fiction and the text under investigation. The ability to make quantitative comparisons highlights differences between the target text and the norm that can then be followed-up qualitatively.

▶ Chapter 5 brings together models from Pragmatics and Conversation Analysis (CA) that, combined, help in the analysis of dialogue, particularly in

About this book

plays. The discussion in the chapter centres on an extract from the screenplay of *I, Daniel Blake,* a UK film produced in 2016. Using this extract, the chapter covers Gricean Conversational Implicature, Speech Acts, CA and (im)politeness, illustrating how these complementary models can be applied in tandem to understand the significance of character interactions both between them, and between the writer and reader. The corpus approach to the study of dialogue in a sitcom shows how the characters' dialogue can be compared against each other linguistically to reveal salient patterns of language usage that indicate a particular style feature of one of the main characters. This linguistic pattern is further analysed and made sense of using the pragmatic framework of (im)politeness. The case study shows the interplay between quantitative deviation within the text-world and deviation from our own intuitive sense of social norms in spoken communication. These deviations provide the necessary focus for further analysis using established stylistic frameworks.

In ► Chapter 6, we introduce the notions of character and characterisation and present a checklist for the analysis of characters in fiction derived from the work of Culpeper (2001) and informed by the work of Rimmon-Kenan (2003) and Pfister (1989). We develop Culpeper's (2001) model to demonstrate how it can be applied to characters in prose as well as plays. The chapter incorporates detailed analyses of characterisation in prose fiction to demonstrate this. We show how keywords can be used in the analysis of character in Shaw's *Pygmalion*. The keywords provide a focus for further analysis, which in turn depend on the cognitive stylistic model of characterisation. Indeed, the keywords are just a list of words until seen through the lens of the Cognitive Stylistic framework, emphasising the continued significance of the three pillars—text, cognition and corpus, throughout this book.

In ► Chapter 7, we show that the analysis of figurative language in fiction requires both textual and cognitive approaches and can be enhanced with corpus approaches. Our discussion of metaphor, metonymy and simile draws on the notion of Encyclopaedic Knowledge from Cognitive Grammar to help explain cross-domain mappings required for metaphor and simile, and within domain mappings for metonymy. The discussion of the analysis of figurative language is inspired by and combines ideas from Black (1955, 1977) and Richards (1936). The practical, step-by-step guide for the linguistic analysis of metaphor draws on and combines the work of Leech (1969), Miller (1993) and Steen (1999a, 1999b, 2009). Lakoff and Johnson's (1989) influential theory of conceptual metaphor is also incorporated into the analysis. The discussion of these steps incorporates ideas from Cognitive Grammar to help show how cross-domain mappings can be explicated. The chapter concludes with a discussion of corpus approaches that can help in the identification of source domains including semantic tagging, which is achieved using an automated tagging system that provides a window onto a text or corpus that could not be achieved manually.

► Chapter 8 summarises fifty years' work on mind style, defined as the accumulation of linguistic features which indicate a particular way of thinking in a character. It charts the lexico-grammatical features that are traditionally associated with mind style, as well as the inclusion of Pragmatics and cognitive approaches in research on fictional minds. The chapter finishes with an innovative combination of corpus methods with Cognitive Grammar, applying these tools to revisit a classic study of Benjy's mind style in Faulkner's *The Sound and The Fury*. Using new techniques to re-examine established understandings of a text illustrates Stylistics' dedication to methodological retrievability, rigour and replicability, practices encouraged throughout this book.

▶ Chapter 9 presents what is arguably the first review of the linguistics of Humour Studies for stylisticians. In this chapter, we explain how ambiguity, incongruities and their resolution are fundamental characteristics of humorous discourse before going on to introduce the General Theory of Verbal Humour (GTVH). Importantly, we illustrate the relevance of the GTVH to stylistic analysis. First of all, we demonstrate that the notion of script opposition can help in the analysis of irony. Second, we reorder the framework's list of Knowledge Resources (KRs) to emphasise how they contribute to a joke's construction at the level of text, discourse and cognition—organising principles in Stylistics. Last, we incorporate TWT into joke analysis by suggesting that the situation KR is better defined as the text-world of a joke, thereby including the co-text and context into the processing of humorous discourse. These modifications integrate GTVH into a Stylistics research paradigm. The chapter also incorporates concepts and models covered in earlier chapters to show how they apply to humorous discourse and, conversely, to demonstrate the role humour has in forging narrative voices, creating characters, and understanding their relationships. We finish the chapter by outlining some of the possible approaches to humour using corpus methods and illustrate how a corpus can be used to test the researcher's intuitions about normal language usage to help validate claims about incongruous or unexpected language use.

Throughout this textbook and others on the subject, the practice of *doing* Stylistics is often left as inferable from the examples under analysis. However, ▶ Chapter 10 makes the work of Stylistics explicit, by providing a useful guide to completing a project in Stylistics. This final chapter outlines the key principles of Stylistics and discusses the important notions of rigour, replicability and objectivity.

Summary of Corpus Approaches and Tools Used

Chapter	Corpus approach/method	Resource
1	KWIC concordances	*BNCweb*
2	Automated Parts of Speech (POS) or word class tagging; text-internal comparison, standard deviation	*CLAWS*
3	POS tagging; comparison of a text against a corpus that represents a 'norm'; key parts of speech/grammatical categories	*Wmatrix*

Chapter	Corpus approach/method	Resource
4	Corpus annotation using XML tags; wildcard searches; comparison against a corpus that represents a 'norm'	*LancFic corpus*
5	n-grams	*AntConc*
6	key words text-internal comparison	*AntConc*
7	semantic tagging, concordances	*Wmatrix*
8	Keywords and collocation	*AntConc and BNCweb*
9	Collocation via sorted concordances	*COCA*

Corpus Resources Used in This Book

The British National Corpus (BNC)
The British National Corpus (BNC) is an electronic collection of 100 million words of written (90%) and spoken (10%) British English from the 1990s. It can be accessed via BNCweb: ▶ http://bncweb.lancs.ac.uk/bncwebSignup

The Huddersfield, Utrecht, Middelburg Corpus of 19th Century UK novels (HUM-19CUK)
A 13-million-word corpus contain 100 nineteenth-century novels by 100 different UK authors, 50 male and 50 female.

The Contemporary Corpus of American English (COCA)
A 1-billion-word corpus of American English texts from 1990 to 2019. It includes text from spoken interactions, fiction, magazines, newspapers, academic journals, TV and movie scripts, and blogs.

AntConc
AntConc (Anthony 2022) free to download concordance software that enables the analysis of corpora and texts. Available at: ▶ https://www.laurenceanthony.net/software/antconc/

Wmatrix
Wmatrix (Rayson 2003, 2008, 2009) is a web-based tool for corpus analysis that incorporates standard corpus tools (like frequency lists, concordances and keyness analysis) with automated corpus annotation. It was developed by Paul Rayson at Lancaster University. On the Wmatrix home page ▶ http://ucrel.lancs.ac.uk/wmatrix/ there is useful information about the programme, including some helpful mini-tutorials ▶ http://ucrel.lancs.ac.uk/wmatrix/tutorial/

Project Gutenberg
A website with thousands of copyright-free, digitised books, including fiction and non-fiction in English and other languages. A useful source of texts for corpus studies. URL: ▶ https://www.gutenberg.org.

Contents

1	**Style: Text, Cognition and Corpora**	1
1.1	Introduction	2
1.2	Style	2
1.2.1	Stylistics	3
1.3	Text	9
1.3.1	Text: Discourse Structures of Poetry, Prose and Plays	10
1.4	Cognition	13
1.4.1	Cognitive Grammar	14
1.4.2	Schemas and Scripts	15
1.4.3	Reader Response	17
1.5	Corpora	18
1.5.1	What Is a Corpus?	18
1.5.2	Concordance and Collocation	20
1.5.3	Using Corpora to Check Our Intuitions	22
1.5.4	Using Corpora to Find an Analytical Focus	23
1.5.5	Corpora and Stylistic Analysis	25
1.6	**Chapter Summary**	26
References		27
2	**Worlds**	31
2.1	Introduction	32
2.2	**The Worlds of Fiction**	32
2.2.1	The Principle of Minimal Departure	32
2.2.2	Accessibility Between Worlds	33
2.2.3	The Worlds of Fiction Summary	36
2.3	**Text World Theory**	36
2.3.1	The Discourse-World	38
2.3.2	Building the Text-World	40
2.3.3	Advancing the Text-World	42
2.3.4	Modal-Worlds	44
2.3.5	World-Switching	46
2.3.6	The Relationships Between the Worlds and Interpreting Effects	50
2.4	**Corpus-Assisted Approaches to TWT**	51
2.4.1	Text-World Diagramming with a Computer	51
2.4.2	Using Corpus Approaches to Find a 'Way In'	51
2.4.3	Corpus-Assisted Text-World Analysis	54
2.5	**Conclusions**	57
References		58
3	**Point of View**	61
3.1	Introduction	62
3.2	Narrative	62
3.3	Narrators	63

3.3.1	Types of Narrator	64
3.4	**Point of View**	65
3.5	**Linguistic Cues for Point of View**	67
3.5.1	Temporal Point of View	68
3.5.2	Spatial Point of View	69
3.5.3	Point of View and Knowledge	71
3.5.4	Point of View and Modality	72
3.6	**Point of View Summary**	76
3.7	**Corpus Approaches and Point of View**	77
3.7.1	Investigating Hemingway's Handling of Viewpoint	77
3.8	**Conclusion**	81
References		83
4	**The Presentation of Speech, Writing and Thought**	87
4.1	**Introduction**	88
4.2	**What Is Speech, Writing and Thought Presentation?**	88
4.2.1	Thought Presentation	90
4.3	**Categories of Speech, Writing and Thought Presentation (SW&TP)**	90
4.3.1	Direct Speech (DS) Writing (DW) and Thought (DT)	91
4.3.2	Indirect Speech (IS) Writing (IW) and Thought (IT)	95
4.3.3	Free Indirect Speech (FIS), Writing (FIW) and Thought (FIT)	97
4.3.4	Narrator's Presentation of Speech, Writing and Thought Acts	99
4.3.5	Narrator's Presentation of Speech, Writing and Thought (NPS, NPW, NPT)	101
4.4	**Discourse Presentation and Faithfulness**	102
4.5	**Exploring Discourse Presentation Using Corpus Techniques**	103
4.5.1	Existing Corpus Research	104
4.5.2	Exploring DP in a Short Story Using Corpus Annotation	105
4.5.3	Using Annotation for Quantitative Analysis	106
4.5.4	Discussion of Results and Further Analysis	109
4.5.5	Summary of Case Study	110
4.6	**Conclusions**	111
References		112
5	**Fictional Dialogue**	115
5.1	**Introduction**	116
5.2	**Speech Acts**	118
5.2.1	Doing Things with Words	118
5.2.2	Choice of Words	119
5.2.3	Illocutionary Force Indicating Devices	120
5.2.4	Felicity Conditions	120
5.3	**Conversational Implicature**	121
5.3.1	Implicatures and Inferences	121
5.4	**Conversation Analysis**	124
5.4.1	Turn-Taking and Turn Allocation	124
5.4.2	Topic Control	125
5.4.3	Adjacency Pairs	125
5.4.4	Preferred/dispreferred Responses	126

5.4.5	Overlapping Talk and Interruptions	127
5.5	**Politeness and Impoliteness (Im/politeness)**	128
5.5.1	Face	128
5.5.2	Face Threatening Acts and Politeness Strategies	129
5.5.3	Impoliteness	132
5.5.4	Issues with (Im)politeness	134
5.6	**Corpus Approaches to Dialogue and Pragmatics**	136
5.6.1	Corpus Approaches and CA	136
5.6.2	Corpus Approaches and Pragmatics	136
5.6.3	Using n-grams to Find Pragmatic and Conversational Features	138
5.7	**Conclusions**	140
References		141
6	**Fictional Character**	145
6.1	**Thinking About Characters**	146
6.2	**Characters: In the Text or in the Mind?**	146
6.2.1	Humanising: Characters in the Mind	147
6.2.2	De-humanising: Characters in the Text	147
6.2.3	Humanising + De-humanising: Characters in the Text and Mind	148
6.2.4	Summary	149
6.3	**Textual Cues**	150
6.3.1	Character Names	150
6.3.2	Actions	150
6.3.3	Visual Features	151
6.3.4	Accent and Dialect	152
6.3.5	Paralinguistic Features	152
6.3.6	Syntax	153
6.3.7	Lexis	153
6.3.8	Conversational Structure	154
6.3.9	Conversational Implicature	154
6.3.10	(Im)Politeness	154
6.3.11	Context and Contrasts	155
6.3.12	Summary	155
6.4	**The Source of Character Cues**	156
6.4.1	The Character → Character Discourse Level	156
6.4.2	The Narrator → Narratee Discourse Level	157
6.4.3	The Author → Reader Discourse Level	158
6.5	**Working with Culpeper's Textual Cues on Prose Fiction**	159
6.6	**Using Corpus Tools to Analyse Characters in a Play**	163
6.6.1	Using AntConc to Explore Characters in Shaw's Pygmalion	163
6.6.2	Summary of Case Study	166
6.7	**Conclusions**	166
References		168
7	**Metaphorical Language**	171
7.1	**Introduction**	172
7.2	**Literal and Figurative (Non-literal) Language**	172

7.3	Encyclopaedic Knowledge, Concepts and Domains	173
7.4	**Metaphor: Text and Cognition**	174
7.4.1	Analysing Metaphor	175
7.4.2	Analysis of Non-Explicit Metaphor	180
7.5	**Metonymy**	185
7.5.1	Analysing Metonymy	186
7.5.2	Conceptual Metonymies	187
7.5.3	Metonymy and Point of View	188
7.6	**Simile**	189
7.6.1	Analysing Simile	190
7.7	**Metaphorical Language and Corpora**	193
7.7.1	Concordance Lines and Metaphor	193
7.7.2	Semantic Tags and Metaphor	195
7.8	**Taking Stock of Metaphorical Language**	196
References		198
8	**Mind Style**	201
8.1	Introduction	202
8.2	**Mind Style: Lexico-Grammatical Features**	203
8.2.1	Transitivity	204
8.2.2	Underlexicalisation	205
8.3	**Different Mind Styles**	207
8.4	**Mind Style in Interaction**	209
8.4.1	Cooperative Principle	210
8.4.2	Politeness	210
8.5	**Cognitive Approaches to Mind Style**	211
8.5.1	Schema Theory	212
8.5.2	Conceptual Metaphor Theory	213
8.6	**Reading Fictional Minds**	213
8.7	**Mind Style: Text, Corpus and Cognition**	215
8.8	**Summing up**	221
References		223
9	**Humour**	227
9.1	Introduction	228
9.1.1	Verbal Humour	228
9.1.2	Chapter Structure	228
9.2	**Verbal Humour: Ambiguity**	229
9.2.1	An Example of Punning from Prose Fiction	230
9.3	**Verbal Humour: Incongruity**	231
9.3.1	Incongruity and Resolution Theories	231
9.3.2	The General Theory of Verbal Humour (GTVH)	232
9.4	**Verbal Humour: Metaphor and Impoliteness**	237
9.4.1	Metaphorical Language and Humour	237
9.4.2	Impoliteness and Humour	239
9.5	**Irony**	240
9.5.1	Referential Irony	240

9.5.2	Verbal Irony	240
9.6	**Corpus Approaches to Humour**	243
9.6.1	Using a Corpus to Investigate 'Boasted'	244
9.7	**Conclusions**	246
References		247
10	**How to 'Do' Stylistics**	251
10.1	**Introduction**	252
10.2	**Research Design**	252
10.2.1	Selecting Texts and Analytical Frameworks: A Good 'Fit'	253
10.2.2	Research Questions	256
10.2.3	Data Selection	257
10.2.4	Using Corpus Approaches	258
10.3	**The Aims of Stylistic Analysis**	259
10.3.1	Identify Language Features	260
10.3.2	Describe Language Features	260
10.3.3	Interpretation	261
10.3.4	Supporting Interpretations: Corpora, Cognition and 'Real' Readers	263
10.4	**Writing a Stylistics Paper**	265
10.4.1	Preparation	265
10.4.2	Structure	265
10.5	**Summary**	269
References		270

Supplementary Information

References 276
Index 293

List of Figures

Fig. 1.1	The prototypical discourse structure for poetry (Short 1996: 39).	10
Fig. 1.2	The prototypical discourse structure for drama (Short 1996: 169).	11
Fig. 1.3	The prototypical discourse structure for prose fiction (Short 1996: 257).	12
Fig. 1.4	KWIC view of the first 30 concordances for 'style' in the BNC	21
Fig. 1.5	Three notions of saliency (Leech and Short, 2007; Leech, 2008)	25
Fig. 2.1	Split discourse-world of *Tess of the d'Urbervilles*	38
Fig. 2.2	A text-world diagram of the first two sentences of *Tess of the d'Urbervilles*	42
Fig. 2.3	An epistemic modal-world in *Tess of the d'Urbervilles*	45
Fig. 2.4	The enactor text-world in *Tess of the d'Urbervilles*	47
Fig. 2.5	Temporal world-switch in *Tess of the d'Urbervilles*	48
Fig. 2.6	Spatio-temporal world-switches in *Tess of the d'Urbervilles*	49
Fig. 2.7	Frequencies of modal auxiliary verbs per thousand words in *Tess* by chapter	54
Fig. 2.8	Modal-worlds in Angel and Tess' marital discussion.	55
Fig. 3.1	The first 20 concordances for 'let's' in TSAR.	81
Fig. 4.1	The prototypical situation for speech presentation	89
Fig. 4.2	Prototypical features of Direct Speech (DS) presentation.	93
Fig. 4.3	The speech, writing and thought presentation scale, narrator involvement and faithfulness (adapted from Leech and Short 2007: 261).	103
Fig. 5.1	Five super-strategies for dealing with a potential Face Threatening Act	130
Fig. 5.2	Concordance of 'I don't' in Sheldon's speech In S1 *TBBT*.	139
Fig. 6.1	Checklist of implicit character cues	155
Fig. 7.1	Source and target domains.	177
Fig. 7.2	Conceptual mappings between THORNY PLANT and LOVE	178
Fig. 7.3	Determining metaphorical language in 'drink life to the lees'.	181
Fig. 7.4	Source and target in 'I will drink life to the lees'	182
Fig. 7.5	Source and target analysis of 'drink', 'life' and 'lees'.	183
Fig. 7.6	Conceptual mappings between DRINK and LIFE	184
Fig. 7.7	Metonymic and metaphorical mappings	186
Fig. 7.8	Metonymic relationship between 'Kipling' and 'the works of Kipling'.	187
Fig. 7.9	Extract of a sorted concordance of 'love' from HUM19CUK	194
Fig. 7.10	Wmatrix concordance for semantic category M5: Flying and aircraft	195
Fig. 8.1	Benjy's use of the canonical action chain.	219
Fig. 8.2	A canonical construal of events described in extract 4	220

Fig. 8.3	Benjy [Maury]'s non-canonical construal of events in extract 4.	220
Fig. 10.1	How can I use corpus methods in my stylistic research?	259
Fig. 10.2	The stages of stylistic analysis	260
Fig. 10.3	Typical structure of a Stylistics paper	266

List of Tables

Table 2.1	Accessibility relations: the ways in which a text-world can relate to the real world.	34
Table 2.2	Transitivity processes and participants	43
Table 2.3	Three categories of modality and examples of their expression in English	46
Table 3.1	Linguistic cues for point of view	77
Table 3.2	Negative Key-POS in TSAR by comparison with USlit1920sSampler.	80
Table 3.3	Positive Key-POS in TSAR by comparison with USlit1920sSampler.	80
Table 4.1	The parallel clines of speech, writing and thought presentation	91
Table 4.2	Percentages of words under the four main categories of Discourse Presentation as a percentage of the total number of words in MLLO and LancFic.	108
Table 4.3	Speech presentation categories in MLLO and LancFic	108
Table 4.4	Number of words of DS as a percentage of the total DS per character and the number of turns	109
Table 5.1	Speech act categories (based on Searle 1976; Searle and Vanderveken 1985)	119
Table 5.2	Different ways to request a response	120
Table 5.3	Culpeper's strategies for positive and negative impoliteness	134
Table 6.1	Keywords for Eliza, Higgins and Pickering sorted by keyness (raw frequencies shown in brackets)	165
Table 7.1	Examples of conceptual metonymies	187
Table 7.2	The ten most frequent 'Anatomy and physiology' word types in the Jane Austen Corpus.	196
Table 8.1	Leech and Short's 1981/2007: 164–6) qualitative analysis of Benjy's mind style	216
Table 8.2	Benjy's positive and negative keywords.	217
Table 9.1	The Knowledge Resources (KRs) used in verbal humour, according to the GTVH (Attardo and Raskin 1991; Attardo 1997)	235
Table 9.2	Adjectives involved in the noun phrases following 'boasted a'	245
Table 10.1	The stylistic toolkit provided in this textbook.	254

List of Foci

Focus 1.1	The Levels of Language	7
Focus 1.2	Stylistics and Rhetoric	9
Focus 2.1	Deixis	39
Focus 3.1	Focalisation	65
Focus 3.2	Deictic projection and deictic shift theory	67
Focus 4.1	Text World Theory and Direct Discourse	94
Focus 4.2	Wildcards in Word	107
Focus 5.1	Grice's Co-operative Principle and Conversational Maxims	122
Focus 5.2	Brown and Levinson's Politeness Strategies (1987: 103–227)	131
Focus 7.1	Conceptual Metaphor Theory	175
Focus 7.2	Conventional, Creative, and Dead Metaphors	185
Focus 7.3	Synecdoche	189
Focus 10.1	Traps to avoid in stylistic research	268

Style: Text, Cognition and Corpora

Supplementary Information The online version contains supplementary material available at ▶ https://doi.org/10.1007/978-3-031-10422-0_1.

© The Author(s), under exclusive license to Springer Nature Switzerland AG 2023
J. Lugea and B. Walker, *Stylistics*,
https://doi.org/10.1007/978-3-031-10422-0_1

1.1 Introduction

In this chapter, we discuss the notion of **style** and the analytical approaches used by stylisticians to shed light on how style is created in texts. We then examine the three pillars of contemporary stylistics—**text, cognition** and **corpora**—and introduce some essential concepts that we will draw upon over the following chapters.

1.2 Style

Defining what is meant by 'style' is easier said than done because the term is widely used, both technically and non-technically, in many different contexts. Before reading on, readers might wish to explore the meaning(s) of style themselves by completing our first Corpus KWIC-ie.

> **Corpus KWIC-ie: Exploring Style in the BNC**
> Dictionary definitions are written based on experts' observations of how words are used in real texts and dictionary compilers (lexicographers) often turn to a corpus for this purpose. A corpus (pl. corpora) is a vast collection of texts, carefully compiled to represent a language or language variety. We will look at corpora in more detail later in this chapter. In this activity, we explore the use of 'style' by looking at occurrences of the word in the **British National Corpus** (BNC), which contains 100 million words of British English collected in 1991.
> *Instructions are on the book's webpage.*

Definitions of style provided by general English dictionaries show that the word is used in various areas of activity such as business, sport, architecture and fashion. The concordance lines for 'style' obtained from the BNC indicate a similar wide usage containing as they do reference to dozens of different styles (e.g. aggressive, parliamentary, Ontario, Gothic). In all arenas and in all its forms, style is a particular way of doing or being something. Style can be idiosyncratic (belonging to the individual) or belong to a group, movement, time period or institution. Importantly, as Wales (2011: 398) points out, style is distinctive; style distinguishes one thing (person, group, etc.) from another. Styles are, therefore, recognisable. For example, we can recognise `courier` and `comic` font styles even if we cannot describe in any detail which features distinguish one from the other.

Linguistic style is a particular way of doing things with language. It is how text producers (i.e. speakers and writers) use the resources of language available to them to convey their message. Linguistic style, then, is the sum of identifiable language choices manifest in a text made from the language system (either consciously or subconsciously) by the text producer (the speaker or writer). It is recognisable and distinctive; different writers and speakers have different ways of behaving linguistically.

Linguistic style can relate to an individual, to a text, part of a text or a group of texts (see Leech and Short 2007: 11; Wales 2011: 397). A speaker's persistent way of using language, including accent, lexis and morpho-syntactic structures, can shape what is known as their **idiolect**. Similarly, a novelist might (unconsciously) make linguistic choices that occur across every novel they write that amounts to a distinctive authorial style that is perceived by readers allowing them to distinguish the author from other writers. Individuals can also make distinctive language choices that identify them as belonging to a group (e.g. hip-hop artists). Language choices might also be constrained by convention relating to culturally recognised text categories (i.e. genre) such as recipes.

1.2.1 Stylistics

Stylistics is the study of style in text. It considers the language choices that text producers make over other possible choices and how these relate to what Leech and Short (2007: 12) call "artistic function" (cf. Jakobson's 'poetic function' discussed in ▶ Sect. 1.2.1.3 and Simpson and Carter's 'stylistic function' in ▶ Sect. 1.3). By **artistic function**, Leech and Short mean that stylistics is concerned with the linguistic choices in a text and their relationship to meaning and effects on the reader (see also Short 1996: 28, 331). So, as stylisticians, we are interested in language choices and their effects. In the rest of this section, we will consider three important concepts from which stylistics has grown that relate to choice and artistic function.

1.2.1.1 Defamiliarisation

In the early twentieth century, a group of scholars known as the Russian Formalists began to ask fundamental questions about what makes art *art* and, consequently, what makes literary texts *literary*. As their group moniker suggests, they were particularly concerned with the formal features that defined art and literature and differentiated them from non-artistic modes. Viktor Shklovsky, a founding member of the group, famously proposed, "[t]he device of art is the 'ostranenic' [defamiliarization] of things and the complication of form, which increases the duration and complexity of perception" (1917/2016: 80). Shklovsky went on to say that "the process of perception is its own end in art and must be prolonged" (1917/2016: 80), thus highlighting the cognitive work that defamiliarised forms evoke in the perceiver. The use of form (visual, aural or verbal) to 'defamiliarise' content became widely accepted as the defining characteristic of a work of art. Because literature uses language as its medium the Russian Formalists, and the Structuralist movement that followed them, investigated the ways in which literature 'defamiliarises' language.

The work of Roman Jakobson, a key contributor to the Formalist and Structuralist movements, paved the way for the emergence of Stylistics later in the twentieth century. In the 1930s, Roman Jakobson and his contemporary Nikolai Trubetzkoy coined the term 'markedness' to describe a linguistic form that is 'marked' or unusual in some respect. Clearly, this is a useful concept for identifying defamiliarisation in literary language. For Jakobson, a lexical choice such as 'bitch' is marked, whereas 'dog' is unmarked, because the former is more specific and loaded semantically. Word order can also be marked and is often found in poetry, where poetic license allows for unusual 'defamiliarising' syntax. For example, consider the closing lines of Keats' (1820) 'Ode to a Grecian Urn':

(i) When old age shall this generation waste,
Thou shalt remain, in midst of other woe
Than ours, a friend to man, to whom thou say'st,
"Beauty is truth, truth beauty",— that is all
Ye know on earth, and all ye need to know.

In Modern English, Subject-Verb-Object (SVO) is the typical clause structure. Therefore, an unmarked version of the first line of this extract would read:

Subject (S)	*Verb (V)*	*Object (O)*
When old age	shall waste	this generation

However, Keats separates the auxiliary verb 'shall' from the main verb 'waste' by inserting the direct object 'this generation' in between them, thus creating a marked Subject-Object-Verb (SOV) order. A consequence of this syntactic markedness is alliteration of the line-final words 'waste' and 'woe', and rhyme between the line-ending verbs 'waste' and 'say'st', both operating at the sound level of language. Postposing the verb 'waste' until the end of the line has an emphasising effect, stressing the effect of 'old age on this generation'. The marked syntax also provides a potential semantic ambiguity, where 'this generation' could be understood as the Subject of the main verb and so it is they who 'waste' (in the sense of 'squander') their older years. Haspelmath (2006) also points to the way Keats gives the poem's urn a voice and is responsible for the wise words quoted in the penultimate line (although see O'Rourke 1987 for the controversy surrounding this quotation). In this way, the poem displays 'situational markedness' because a talking urn is an unfamiliar departure from reality.

The concept of 'markedness' is helpful for understanding literature's defamiliarising effect, but nevertheless requires precision about how and why it is achieved. A stylistic analysis would aim to describe these features in detail and explain how they work and achieve an effect upon the reader/hearer. Stylistics provides the tools that can help achieve that analytical precision.

1.2.1.2 Foregrounding

Closely related to Defamiliarisation is linguistic 'foregrounding'. This concept emerged from the Prague school of Stylistics in the 1930s and describes where attention is drawn to a marked linguistic item, device or strategy. Derived from the Czech *aktualisace* (literally 'actualising'), foregrounding is a useful metaphor to describe the way, as in visual art, an element can be brought to the foreground to capture the viewer's attention. When an aspect of a text is foregrounded, the reader is encouraged to notice it, pay attention to its form and its possible meanings, thus 'deautomizing' the reading process (Mukařovsk 1958). Of course, as Leech (1985) points out, foregrounding may well be subjective (markedness is in the eye of the beholder!) but there is empirical evidence to support its psychological effects (see, e.g., van Peer 1986; van Peer et al. 2007).

Linguistic foregrounding can be achieved through strategies, such as **deviation** and repetition. Much like markedness, deviation is a departure from a linguistic norm and can occur at any language level (see Focus 1.2). Deviation can be internal and external (Levin 1965). **External deviation** is when the language of a text departs from the norms of a language system in general. We saw an example of this in Keats' poem in (i) above, where the first line of the stanza deviated from the syntactic norm of English. **Internal deviation** is a language feature that is at odds with a norm that is established within a text. An example given by Levin (1965: 228) would be where a poem established a pattern of rhyme and then breaks the pattern with a "non-rhyme".

Additionally, any linguistic element of a text can be repeated to produce foregrounding effects. A special type of repetition is **parallelism**, where linguistic patterns are repeated but with some slight variation within the pattern; this invites comparison and a connection of either equivalence or contrast to be made (see Leech 1969: 67). A famous and often quoted example of parallelism is at the opening of Dickens' *A Tale of Two Cities*:

(ii) It was the best of times, it was the worst of times, it was the age of wisdom, it was the age of foolishness, it was the epoch of belief, it was the epoch of incredulity, it was the season of Light, it was the season of Darkness, it was the spring of hope, it was the winter of despair, ...

The example above exemplifies syntactic parallelism. There are a series of cleft clauses, where 'it' (a dummy subject) is followed by a form of 'be' (in this case 'was') and then a noun phrase (NP). Each NP consists of the definite article ('the') followed by a head noun which is post-modified by a prepositional phrase (PP). Each PP consists of the preposition 'of' followed by a noun. There is also semantic parallelism whereby each parallel pair of clauses forms an antonymic relationship ('best' versus 'worst') to create a series of paradoxical statements.

Poetry tends to experiment with and break linguistic conventions more so than any other literary genre and is often abound with foregrounding devices. This is demonstrated by Heine's poem 'A Woman', which is the focus of Activity 1.1.

Activity 1.1: Foregrounding in a Poem

Read 'A Woman' and identify any occurrences of parallelism and deviation. Make a note of the linguistic levels that any such foregrounding devices operate on. Do this task before reading our answer below the poem.

'A Woman'
Each loved the other beyond belief;
She lived by her wits and he was a thief.
He played the Fool and fooled the crowd;
She sprawled on the bed and laughed aloud. The days ticked by with joy and with jest;
At night she swooned upon his breast.
When the policeman came, the skies all cloud,
She thought it funny and laughed aloud. He sent her a letter, 'Oh come to me,
By day and by night I long for thee.
Love is forever, that's what we vowed.'
She shook her head and laughed aloud. At six in the morning they hung him high
-For fooling and thieving he had to die.
At seven o'clock he lay stiff in his shroud;
And she quaffed red wine and laughed aloud.

      Heinrich Heine (1797–1856) Translated by Dannie Abse (2015).

To help you complete this task, go to the book's webpage where we provide further examples of parallelism and deviation.

The poem contains various examples of parallelism. First, the poem uses a structure of rhyming couplets in each four-line stanza (or 'quatrain'), so there is parallelism at the phonological level of language. This structure, known as 'heroic couplet', is common in traditional English verse and is achieved by paired repetition of vowel sounds. Within the rhyming scheme of this poem, the same vowel sound is repeated in the third and fourth line of each quatrain. Second, the verb phrase (VP) 'laughed aloud' is repeated at the end of the last line in each stanza. This repetition is part of a larger repeated grammatical structure on every fourth line: [PRONOUN] [VP1] [CONJUNCTION] [VP2]. All elements of the structure are repeated apart from VP1 which varies. So, all last lines state that the woman did something and then laughed aloud. The something described in each VP1 is a carefree action. In the first stanza, the action fits with the couple's renegade relationship but, as the poem progresses and each stanza describes the downfall of her partner, the VP1 actions and repeated laughter become less appropriate.

Focus 1.1: The Levels of Language

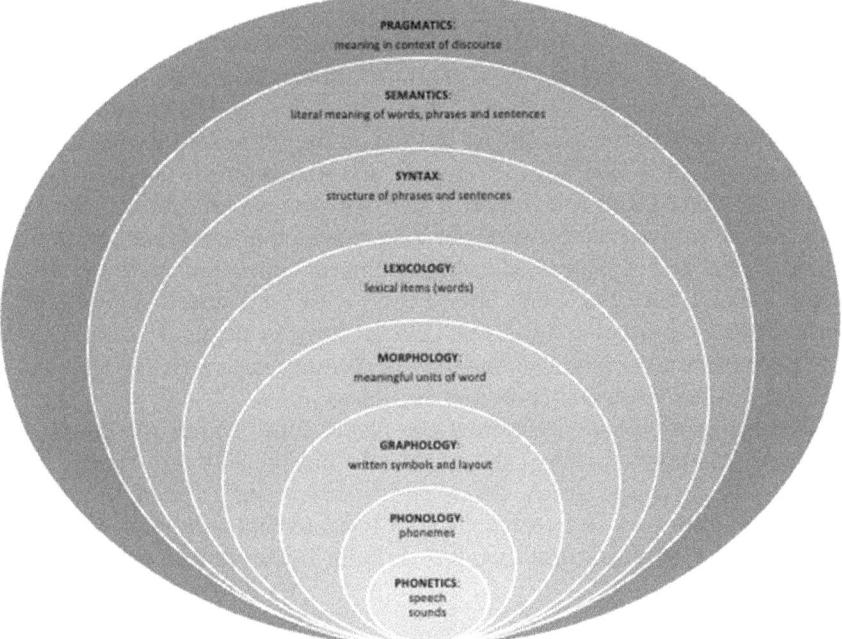

Language operates across several 'levels' which, although interconnected, can be studied more or less separately in linguistics. **Phonetics** studies the production of sounds using articulatory organs in the body, the transmission of sounds through acoustics and their perception when heard. Closely related is **phonology**, which examines **phonemes**—the meaningful sounds of a language system. **Graphology** is the study of written symbols (e.g. punctuation), typeface (e.g. capitalisation and font) and layout (e.g. spacing, line length and paragraphing). **Morphology** is concerned with the smallest units of meaning in language, **morphemes**, that combine to create words. **Lexicology** is the study of words, although linguists prefer the term **lexical item** to 'word'. This is because lexical meaning can be expressed in structures that are a size of a single morpheme (e.g. 'rise'), multiple morphemes (e.g. 'riser') or complex multi-word units (e.g. 'early risers'). The lexical item, 'early risers', contains two words: the adjective 'early', and the noun 'risers'; the latter being composed of a root morpheme derived from the verb 'rise', converted to a noun with the derivational morpheme '-er', and made plural with the morpheme 's' as a suffix. The study of grammatical structure in phrases and sentences is **Syntax**. When the literal meaning of words, phrases and sentences is studied, this is **Semantics**, but when meaning is considered in relation to the context in which it used, this is **Pragmatics**. All of these levels of language are of importance to Stylistics because they have a bearing on style. Because Stylistics usually studies written texts, phonetics and phonology are arguably the least important but are still useful when considering how speech is captured in writing (e.g. accent and **eye dialect**), dialogue in plays, and how written discourse might be spoken.

The rhyme structure, while an example of parallelism, is arguably not an example of foregrounding since rhyming couplets are a poetic convention and therefore not unexpected. However, the rhyme invites the reader to understand this as a traditional love poem, but it becomes apparent that this couple's love is not conventional, or at least not entirely mutual. This is achieved through a combination of the syntactic parallelism described above and semantic deviation, whereby the semantic content of the parallel structure becomes increasingly at odds with the semantic content of the stanza they close and deviates from the norms expected of a love poem. Certainly, the repetition of 'laughed out loud' serves to emphasise and foreground that particular action, and we can draw a connection of equivalence between the VP1 actions that emphasise the woman's continued carefree behaviour. Additionally, internal deviation occurs in the very last line, which (unlike the other lines) begins with 'And' and therefore breaks a pattern set in the preceding lines. This deviation marks the final line as a closure to the poem's narrative and emphasising the iterative nature of the woman's actions, and that her behaviour continues regardless.

When expectations are frustrated, the reader must search for meaning—in the case of this poem, between the sad events and the woman's marked behaviour. The reading experience is, therefore, 'defamiliarised', forcing the reader to do some cognitive work to try to reconcile inconsistencies in the text. It is this defamiliarisation that encourages engagement with literature and produces enjoyment in readers.

1.2.1.3 Poetic Function

In his later work, Jakobson (1960) identified six main functions or purposes of language, one of which is the **poetic function**: the use of language in such a way that it calls attention to the linguistic process and form by taking familiar forms and using them in a marked fashion, focusing "on the message for its own sake" (1960: 356). Clearly, the poetic function of language is the result of the foregrounding process and achieved through devices such as deviation, repetition and parallelism. Importantly for stylisticians, Jakobson was clear that the poetic function was not the sole property of literary language (see also Cook 1994: 29). You do not have to look too far to find other discourse types putting the poetic function to use, from informal conversations to advertising campaigns. Consider, for example, the tagline for a French brand of bottled water:

> L'Evian, Live young

The slogan involves parallelism at the phonological level of language, which only works if it is pronounced with a French accent. Consequently, the parallelism invites semantic associations to be drawn between the water, its youth-giving properties and French language and culture in general. The short text creates a **homophonic pun** (for more on puns, see ▶ Chapter 9) and invites the consumer to 'try on' a French identity, thus engaging them at a personal level with the brand.

Jakobson underlined that the poetic function is found in all kinds of discourse, saying "[t]his function cannot be productively studied out of touch with the general problems of language, and, on the other hand, the scrutiny of language requires a thorough consideration of its poetic function" (1960: 356). Jakobson was, therefore, adamant that linguistic creativity could not be studied without an understanding of language in general and that our understanding of language in general could be enhanced by understanding linguistic creativity. His work sought to bring linguistics and literary studies together in a mutually productive way because, as he pointed out, "[a] linguist deaf to the poetic functions of language and a literary scholar indifferent to linguistics are flagrant anachronisms' (1960: 377). It is from Jakobson's call for interdisciplinarity that Stylistics emerged (e.g. Fowler 1986/1996) and continues to flourish.

Focus 1.2: Stylistics and Rhetoric

Rhetoric is a classical subject and an important precursor to Stylistics. It is the ancient study of artful and persuasive language, with origins in Greece in the fifth century BC. Aristotle's *Poetics* is considered the first major work in the West to describe the art of language. In *Rhetoric*, he describes three modes of persuasion, *logos*, *pathos* and *ethos*, which appeal to reason, emotions and emphasise the authority or credibility of the text producer, respectively. Rhetoric does not distinguish between literary and non-literary language but focuses on how—regardless of discourse type—language can be used to influence effectively. In this book, we sometimes use the term 'rhetorical aims' or 'rhetorical effects' to refer to the way a writer or their text may persuade their readers or audience. We also use terminology with origins in the study of Rhetoric, which has explored the meaningful effects of language forms for many centuries. Where possible we point out these roots and relevant sources, but limits on space prevent us from providing a detailed account of Rhetoric's influence on Stylistics.

For an overview of the relevance of Rhetoric to Stylistics, see Burke (2014); for a discussion of the differences between the disciplines, see Fahnestock (2016).

1.3 Text

In Linguistics, a text is a single coherent stretch of naturally occurring spoken or written language, such as an interview, speech, email or advertisement. For stylisticians, the text is central to stylistic endeavour and the focus of analysis. This is because style is a property of the text and results from patterned linguistic features. Our particular focus in this book is the style of written 'literary' texts (i.e. poems, plays and prose fiction). The analysis of style in any text requires (as the formalists were keen to show) an appreciation of the linguistic forms and structures that make up a text, but also consideration of context in which the text occurs since this can influence and shape textual form and meaning. Stylistics, therefore, comprises more than formalist descriptions of texts; it considers literature as discourse (see, e.g., Cook 1994) and recognises the role of the analyst, as a reader, in interpreting style. Consequently, style is a property of the text that results from linguistic choices, as well as an understanding arrived at by the reader. As Carter and Simpson point out, "[t]he assignment of meaning or stylistic function to a formal category in the language remains an interpretative act" (1989: 5). The stylistician's toolkit has, therefore, expanded to include context-sensitive approaches to language that consider not just the text but the communicative context, goals and functions of literary texts. And, as we will see later in this chapter, because style can also be shared by many texts, such as texts belonging to the same genre (e.g. plays) or literary movement (e.g. the Beat poets), or by the same author (i.e. authorial style), the stylistician's toolkit also incorporates approaches and methods from Corpus Linguistics.

Nowadays, an understanding of literature as discourse (Fowler 1986; Cook 1994; Hall 2015) is fundamental to stylistic enquiry. Fowler (1996/1986: 130) views "texts as *discourses*" (original emphasis); that is, "interactions between speakers and addressees who might be real, implied or fictional". We discuss this in more detail below where we explore discourses and their structures in fictional texts.

1.3.1 Text: Discourse Structures of Poetry, Prose and Plays

With any communication the text is both the message communicated between discourse participants and the artefact to which style belongs. Synchronous, face-to-face interaction is often understood to be the prototypical discourse situation in human communication. Other ways of interacting are possible, of course, including asynchronous written communication. In his seminal introduction to Stylistics, Short (1996) suggests that literary texts (poems, plays, prose fiction) are the written communicative message between author and reader. Of the three main literary genres, poetry is most like face-to-face communication where an addresser (the poet) addresses an addressee (the reader), albeit asynchronously (Short 1996: 39). For example, if we consider the poem 'The Woman', which we discussed above, the poet (Heinrich Heine) addresses the many readers who encounter this text.[1] Short sets out the prototypical structure for this discourse situation, between poet and reader, in a diagram which we reproduce in ◘ Fig. 1.1.

Short (1996) goes on to explain how the simple discourse structure shown in ◘ Fig. 1.1 can become more complex if the author is distinct from the 'voice' delivering the words (i.e. a poetic persona), or if the implied addressee is distinct from the reader. For example, in Edwin Brock's (1977) 'Song of the Battery Hen', a battery hen apparently addresses the reader, and in Keats' 'Ode to a Grecian Urn' the poet apparently addresses an urn! In such cases, the diagram shown in

◘ **Fig. 1.1** The prototypical discourse structure for poetry (Short 1996: 39)

◘ Fig. 1.1 becomes more complex since it must incorporate participants other than the author and the reader. The form that such diagrams might take is shown in ◘ Fig. 1.2, which is also the prototypical structure for drama.

In drama, prototypically, there are two levels of discourse (Short 1996) where the primary level is the communication between the playwright and reader/audience, and the secondary, embedded level is the communication between characters in the play. The playwright may communicate apparently directly with the readers (but not the audience) via stage directions.[2] However, the playwright mainly conveys a message (or story) to the reader or audience indirectly via the interactions between characters in the play. The character dialogue contributes to most of our understanding of the story, the characters themselves and their relationships. Because the discourse between characters is embedded in the discourse between the playwright and reader/audience, the character dialogue might be attributable to the characters but can also be understood as originating from the playwright and may, therefore, be conveying messages on behalf of the playwright (e.g. a social critique).

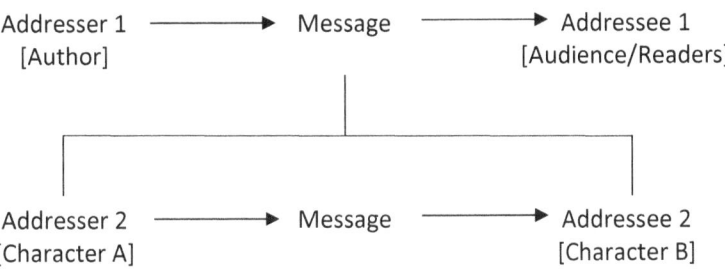

◘ **Fig. 1.2** The prototypical discourse structure for drama (Short 1996: 169)

In texts that have one or more narrator (prototypically prose fiction[3]) the discourse situation is more complex, because the basic discourse structure has at least three levels and six participants (although, cf. Chatman 1978: 151; Rimmon-Kenan 1983: 86–89; Toolan 2001: 76–80). As ◘ Fig. 1.3 shows, the discourse structure for texts with a narrator includes a narrator-narratee level of discourse "intervening" (Short 1996: 257) between the author-reader and character-character levels.

While there has been much discussion about the existence and nature of the narrator in fictional narratives, there is some agreement that readers tend to imagine that a story is told by a person or voice who is saying the words in the story (Bortolussi and Dixon 2003: 60) and relating various aspects of the story world to readers. The narrator-narratee discourse level acknowledges this by showing that the voice telling the story can be distinct from the author, and that the person that the storyteller is talking to (the narratee) can be distinct from the real reader.

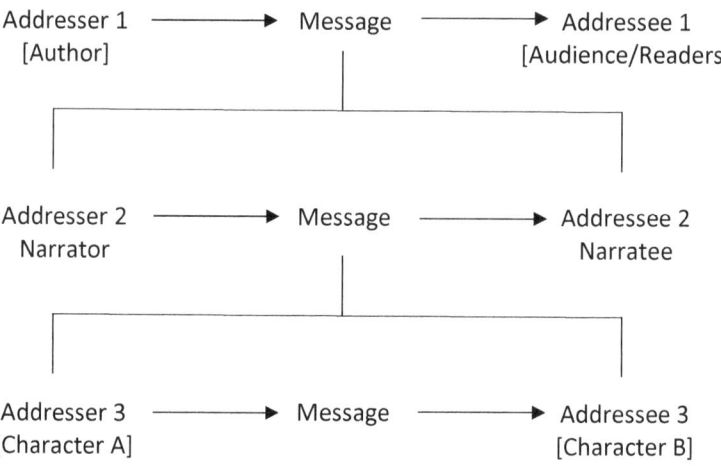

■ Fig. 1.3 The prototypical discourse structure for prose fiction (Short 1996: 257)

It must be remembered that ■ Figs. 1.1, 1.2 and 1.3 are simplified schematic representations of the possible discourse structures of poetry, drama and prose. For instance, they exclude discourse levels relating to what are often referred to as the implied author and the implied reader: the author and reader that are implied by the text and that are different from the real author and reader (see Chatman 1978: 151; Leech and Short 2007: 209–210; Rimmon-Kenan 1983: 87–88; Toolan 2001: 76–77). Also, it is possible for the participants in the models to function as one, which is known as collapsing of discourse levels (Leech and Short 2007: 211). For example, the reader might feel that they are also the narratee in the discourse.

In general, considering the discourse structure of any text under analysis is useful for identifying how and where meaning is conveyed. As we will see throughout this book, appreciating author and reader as participants of a discourse within which are embedded other discourses is crucial to the analysis of literary (and other) texts.

Activity 1.2: Discourse Structure
i. Select a poem, play or prose text that is familiar to you and diagram the discourse structure, considering the following:
   a. Who is the author and is s/he distinct from the 'speaking voice' in the text (playwright, characters, poetic persona or narrator)?
   b. Does the text specify an addressee(s) somehow and is she/he/it distinct from the real reader?
   c. Who are the characters and who do they address?
ii. Do you think the discourse structure is typical of your chosen genre?

iii. Are any of the participants involved in more than one level of discourse? For example, does a character or narrator address the reader?
iv. How does the discourse structure affect the meaning or the message of the literary text?

 We provide a discussion for this task on the book's webpage.

1.4 Cognition

We have established that, in stylistics, the text is of prime importance for meaning. However, meaning does not happen in a vacuum and a text only becomes alive, becomes discourse, when it is read and engaged with. In ▶ Sect. 1.1, we discussed how the origin of Stylistics lies in the Formalist understanding of literary language being language that calls attention to itself and, in doing so, foregrounds an aspect of the text. Note the extent to which these claims deal with cognition. Cognition describes the complex set of mental processes involved in dealing with information and experience, including 'perception, memory, attention, problem-solving, language, thinking, and imagery' (Tsur 2002: 281). Understanding cognition helps us understand how textual meanings are activated and arrived at by readers. Cognition plays a major part in reading literature and insights from the cognitive sciences have increasingly influenced research in language, literature and, consequently, stylistics.

Scholars from a wide range of disciplines—including Psychology, Anthropology, Sociology, Neuroscience and Linguistics—try to describe mental processes, and their work constitutes the broad field of the cognitive sciences. More specifically, Cognitive Linguistics explores the meaning-making process involved in all kinds of discourse. A basic assumption in Cognitive Linguistics is that "meaning is an inseparable part of language study" (Dancygier 2017: 1) and meaning is best described with reference to the conceptual mechanisms that language users employ in its creation. Central to Cognitive Linguistics is the idea that meaning is embodied, recognising the role the human body plays in experience, including linguistic experience. This will become clear when we explore, for example, how perspective is created in fictional language based on our bodily experience of physical space (▶ Chapter 3), or how metaphors often involve considering an abstract concept—such as life—in terms of a more tangible, physical experience such as a journey (▶ Chapter 7). Langacker (2014) points out that its attention to meaning makes Cognitive Linguistics particularly suitable for literary-linguistic analysis and interpretation.

Cognitive Stylistics (also known as Cognitive Poetics—see Wales 2001; Stockwell 2002: 60) aims to describe how texts work in the minds of readers, how readers process and interpret texts, and helps us explain the poetic 'effects' on readers' minds—the final stage of meaning-making. In an early account of Cognitive Stylistics, Semino and Culpeper (2002: p. ix) assert:

> Traditional stylistic analysis [...] tends to make use of linguistic theories or frameworks in order to explain or predict interpretation. What is new about cognitive stylistics is the way in which linguistic analysis is systematically based on theories that relate linguistic choices to cognitive structures and processes. This provides more systematic and explicit accounts of the relationship between texts on the one hand and responses and interpretations on the other.

The twenty-first century has seen cognitive approaches to stylistic research become mainstream and this book aims to integrate them into an accessible toolkit for stylistic enquiry.

In their account of Cognitive Linguistics, Evans and Green (2006) distinguish between Cognitive Grammar and Cognitive Semantics. **Cognitive Grammar** describes an approach to grammar that is less 'rule-based' than other grammars of language, and instead considers units of language as constructions that are stored in memory. Langacker's (2008) version of Cognitive Grammar has had the greatest influence on work in stylistics and a necessarily brief introduction is provided in ▶ Sect. 1.4.1. **Cognitive Semantics** deals with how language users conceptualise language meaning using categories, scripts and schemas, and conceptual metaphors. In ▶ Sect. 1.4.2, we provide an overview of scripts and schemas because they inform our understanding of literary reading generally and are relevant to various chapters throughout. We look at social categories in connection to our understanding of how we conceptualise characters in ▶ Chapter 6, while conceptual metaphors are discussed to in ▶ Chapter 7.

1.4.1 Cognitive Grammar

Langacker's Cognitive Grammar (CG) is underscored by the basic principle that "grammar is meaningful" (2008: 3). Any given speech community (e.g. speakers of a certain language or language variety) have a set of resources for expressing themselves, called "conventional linguistic units" (Langacker 2008: 222). Through the repeated use of a form with a certain meaning, the pairing between form and meaning becomes entrenched, and common elements across individual instances of use are 'schematized' (i.e. abstracted) until this abstract concept becomes a 'conventional linguistic unit'. Viewing language units and habits in this way is useful for stylistics because it helps to explain how, when literary language deviates from a norm, it ruptures any relevant 'conventional linguistic units' and the associated meaning, requiring readers to seek out alternative meanings.

Another concept from CG which is important for Stylistics is **construal**. According to Langacker, construal is "our manifest ability to perceive and portray the same situation in alternate ways" (Langacker 2008: 55) and, as Taylor (2002: 11) notes, "the very wording we choose in order to linguistically encode a situation rests on the manner in which the situation has been mentally construed". Construal, therefore, relates to the importance of choice in linguistic expression and in forging stylistic patterns, as discussed in ▶ Sect. 1.1. Drawing on Langacker (2008) and Verhagen (2007), Nuttall (2018) describes six dimensions of construal:

i. **Specificity**—the level of detail used to describe something.
ii. **Focusing**—what is selected for description.
iii. **Prominence**—which elements are brought to our attention.
iv. **Perspective**—where something is viewed from.
v. **Scanning**—how a situation unfolds in space and time.
vi. **Action chains**—how objects and entities move through space and impact on one another.

These dimensions of construal are labels for particular language choices, their functions and effects. There is some overlap between these six dimensions (e.g. focussing can lead to prominence), and with some of the concepts we have already discussed (e.g. focussing and prominence relate to foregrounding). We will also be making connections between these dimensions and the topics we cover in subsequent chapters in this book: in ▶ Chapter 3, we will see that perspective and scanning can encode of point of view, and in ▶ Chapter 8 that action chains, specificity and focus can be involved in the linguistic creation of fictional mind styles.

1.4.2 Schemas and Scripts

Reading literature is a complex interactive process between text and cognition. Cognitive psychologists distinguish between two ways our minds can process information: (i) **bottom-up processing** describes the influence of external stimuli on our perception (e.g. text, temperature, smell); while (ii) **top-down processing** describes how pre-existing knowledge, understandings and expectations are called on to interpret and organise incoming information. Text contains features which convey conventionally held meanings and invites bottom-up processing on behalf of the reader. However, when the individual reader interprets and processes incoming textual information, she uses her pool of experience to flesh it out and fully understand and engage with the text, leading to an individual interpretation. In practice, both kinds of processing occur simultaneously, although some texts may require more top-down cognitive effort than others (Culpeper 2002), which is another way of stating Shklovsky's (1917/2016) assertion that literature 'prolongs' the act of perception. In this short section, we provide a brief overview of **Schema Theory** which is key for the description of top-down processes (i.e. those that involve the activation of previously held information).

A **schema** (pluralised as schemata) is an "organized packet of information about the world, events, or people, stored in long-term memory" (Eysenck and Keane 2002: 531). Although the concept can be traced back to the Gestalt psychologists of the 1930s (e.g. Bartlett 1932), interest in it was renewed in the latter half of the last century, as scholars tried to describe how humans process discourse. They realised, of course, that discourse processing inevitably involves knowledge about the world, and that such knowledge is stored in convenient packages (i.e. schemata). Schematic knowledge is required for readers to understand much of what they read.

Activity 1.3: Schematic Knowledge

Read this complete vignette by Ernest Hemingway. What do you know about 'Young Buckley' and the narrator telling the story? Give as much detail as you can. Now think about how you derived those details. Do this task before reading our answer below.

> We were in a garden at Mons. Young Buckley came in with his patrol from across the river. The first German I saw climbed up over the garden wall. We waited till he got one leg over and then potted him. He had so much equipment on and looked awfully surprised and fell down into the garden. Then three more came over further down the wall. We shot them. They all came just like that.

In Our Time (Hemingway, 1926: Ch4)

Even if your literary or historical knowledge does not help you process the discourse (Mons is a village in Belgium that saw one of the major battles of the First World War; Hemingway's prose is often set in wars of that period), the use of a term such as 'patrol' is likely to trigger schematic knowledge of the military and might help you interpret 'Young Buckley' as being a soldier. Using 'triggers' to evoke schematically stored, shared knowledge means we can communicate efficiently. As Cook (1994: 13) suggests, "[t]his mental ability to 'read in' details is particularly relevant to literary narrative, in which readers are given points of reference and left to fill in the gaps 'from imagination'". Thus, schemata are crucial for processing all discourses, but have a particular import for literary reading.

An important point to note is that schemata are created through our ongoing interaction with the world and thus socially and personally determined. For example, 'sandcastles' might activate a 'beach' schema which entails other associations (the sea, ice cream, summer), but the precise details might vary according to your personal or cultural particularities. Beachgoers in the British Isles might include donkey rides and piers in their beach schema, while a Spanish person might expect *chiringuitos* (beach bars). Therefore, Schema Theory helps to explain how different readers can arrive at different interpretations of the same text, as the schematic knowledge they call upon will be dependent on their personal and cultural experience.

Psychologists, such as Bartlett (1932) and Schank (1986), recognised that schemata can change and be reorganised. Cook (1994) went further by proposing that certain discourses are **schema-refreshing**. That is, through their content or form, they challenge our pre-existing knowledge and evoke some change in our understanding of the world (this idea is supported by empirical research using real readers carried out by Miall and Kuiken 1999). Although Cook provides examples of how literary texts can be schema refreshing, he makes it clear that other discourses can also challenge and update our schemata (e.g. Stephen Hawking's popular science writing proposes new ways of thinking about the nature of time). Conversely, literary texts can also reinforce or add to existing schematic knowledge. For example, the social etiquette found in Jane Austen's novels may uphold and contribute to our schema for social norms governing behaviour.

Closely related to the concept of schema is a **script**, which refers more specifically to the structured knowledge we gather through repeated "sequences of events in a particular context" (Schank and Abelson 1977: 41). The example Schank and Abelson elaborate is the 'restaurant script', whereby a chain of events can be expected (entering, ordering, eating, exiting) as well as specific roles (e.g. customer, waiter, cook) and possible results (customer is sated). Although this script may vary for different cultures or types of restaurants, a restaurant script has an important impact on language production and understanding. It means, for example, that when a waiter greets you and asks "Inside or outside?" you can interpret this to refer to where you would like to be seated, thanks to your knowledge of the sequencing of events in a restaurant script. Schank and Abelson elaborate on how our knowledge of scripts influences how stories are told and interpreted using the following example: "While giving his order to the waiter at Mamma Leone's one evening, Spillane was approached by the owner, a notorious Mafia figure" (Schank and Abelson 1977: 37). The 'while'-clause introduces an action (ordering) and a role (the waiter) that pertains to our restaurant script. Note that the latter is introduced through definite reference 'the', indicating the certainty with which this script is introduced. These textual clues mean that although the word 'restaurant' is not mentioned, we can infer that the proper noun 'Mamma Leone's' is the name of the restaurant. By the activation of the restaurant script through textual cues, the reader 'fills in' much of the background details.

As well as the experience of literary reading in general and its schema-refreshing potential, over the course of this book we will see that scripts and schemata are important for understanding text-worlds (▶ Chapter 2), viewpoint (▶ Chapter 3), characterisation (▶ Chapter 6), mind style (▶ Chapter 8) and humour (▶ Chapter 9).

1.4.3 Reader Response

Although not covered in this book, a further important dimension of cognition is reader response to texts. As we have discussed, literary meaning is the product of linguistic choices made by the author, which lead to effects on the reader. While the text is of prime importance, the reader's interaction with the text is also essential. However, Stylistics has traditionally tended to treat the 'reader' as an abstract concept, or analysts have identified themselves as the 'reader' and thus recognised their reading as an individual and subjective process (see, e.g., Gavins 2016a). In the past, cognitive approaches to Stylistics have been criticised for not carrying out empirical study to verify its principles (see, e.g., Miall 2006: 3). However, the use of real readers' insights is on the rise in stylistic research (see, e.g., Whiteley and Canning 2017) whereby responses from real readers are used to ascertain the effects of textual choices made by the author.

1.5 Corpora

Corpora is the third pillar of contemporary Stylistics and refers to the combination of Stylistics with approaches, methods and tools from Corpus Linguistics. **Corpus Stylistics**, as it is now usually known, involves investigating style using electronic collections of texts known as corpora (**corpus** is the singular form) and specialised computer software. Since the pioneering work of, for example, Burrows (1986, 1987) and Louw (1989), Corpus Stylistics has become progressively more popular not least because analytical opportunities corpus approaches offer. As Widdowson (2008) points out:

> Stylistics claims to provide linguistic substantiation for the interpretation of literary texts. Since corpus analysis is par excellence a means of revealing textual features in precise detail, it seems reasonable to suppose that it must be relevant to the stylistic enterprise.
>
> Widdowson (2008: 293)

Widdowson leaves little doubt about the usefulness of corpus approaches to Stylistics and his comments hint at the important ability of computers to systematically work through whole texts quantitatively in whatever way the software enables. In this section, we will provide a brief overview of some of the important concepts associated with corpora and how they can be used for stylistic analysis. We will start by first establishing what a corpus is.

1.5.1 What Is a Corpus?

McEnery and Wilson (2001) define a corpus as follows:

> a finite body of text, sampled to be maximally representative of a particular variety of a language, and which can be stored and manipulated using a computer
>
> McEnery and Wilson (2001: 73)

McEnery and Wilson's first defining feature is that a corpus has a finite size. The size of a corpus is typically measured in the number of words (or tokens) it contains. The size can be predetermined, and then enough texts (or extracts of texts) are collected to achieve that size. Alternatively, the texts that will comprise the corpus can be decided upon first and the size of the corpus is the number of words that results. Either way, once built, corpora tend to be fixed in size.[4] Corpora vary considerably in size but tend to be very large. For example, the British National Corpus (BNC) of 1990s spoken and written British English contains 100 million words, while the more recent corpus of Global Web-Based English (GloWbE) is 1.9 billion words in size.

The second, crucial, defining characteristic of a corpus is that it is a representative **sample** of a **variety of language** (such as a national or regional variety). Language varieties tend to be delimited by combinations of non-linguistic parameters, such as geographical location (country, region, town); time period (Early Modern 1500–1700); mode/medium of communication (spoken, written, a form of computer-mediated communication); domain (social context or setting); genre (novels, newspaper editorials); or author. When building a corpus, the aim is to collect enough samples of the language variety to represent its entirety. In social sciences, the entirety of whatever it is being researched is usually referred to as the **population**. So, a corpus is a sample of language data that aims to represent the population it was drawn from. However, no matter how big a corpus is, it might contain only a small selection of the language population that is being researched. This is particularly true for corpora that aim to represent national varieties of language and demonstrates why sampling is important. For example, the British National Corpus (BNC), which we met in the corpus KWIC-ie at the start of the chapter, aims to represent 1990s British English (BrE) with 10 million words of transcribed spoken data and 90 million words of written data. Clearly, collecting every instance of spoken and written language for a whole country for any time period is impossible. The BNC, therefore, aims to be a representative sample of 1990s BrE by containing numerous examples of spoken data from a variety of different contexts (e.g. casual conversations, business meetings), and written data from many different written genres (e.g. prose fiction, letters, print news stories). Sampling is still important even if a corpus aims to represent a more narrowly defined language variety. For example, say you wanted to build a corpus representing British prose fiction 1800–1899, it would still be impossible to collect every single text. Activity 1.4 invites you to consider some of the problems you might encounter in constructing such a corpus.

Note, though, that where the language variety under investigation is very constrained then sampling might not be necessary to build a corpus. For example, Fischer-Starcke (2010) and Hori (2004) bring together the output of a single author (Jane Austen and Charles Dickens, respectively) to answer questions concerning authorial style. Such specialised corpora comprise a finite amount of data that can be collected in its entirety. The sample is, therefore, equal to the population.

The idea of a corpus, in theory at least, is to collect enough examples of a language variety to represent the entirety of that language variety. Creating a corpus that aims to be a representative sample is important because it means you can make generalisations about the population from which you drew your sample. The better your sample the more reliable your generalisations will be.

The final part of McEnery and Wilson's definition is that corpora are stored on a computer in a format that allows computer programs can recognise and process the individual words in the corpus. This means that corpus data must be **machine readable** and so excludes scanned copies of texts that are stored in, for example, JPEG, PDF or PNG format.

Activity 1.4: Building a Corpus

How would you go about building a corpus that represents British prose fiction 1800–1899?

How would you start such a task? What problems do you think you would encounter? What types of text would you collect, how many and by which authors? Would you collect whole texts or small extracts? Think about these questions and draft out a design for such a corpus.

⬇ *Now, go to the book's webpage where we provide details of the Huddersfield Utrecht Middelburg corpus of 19th Century British prose fiction (HUM19CUK). Compare your design with the design of this corpus. Do you agree with the decisions the designers made?*

It is worth mentioning that you do not need a corpus to do Corpus Stylistics. Numerous studies apply corpus methods and tools to a single text. For example, Culpeper (2002, 2009), Archer and Bousfield (2010) and McIntyre (2010) all use corpus tools to make text internal comparisons to investigate characters in individual dramatic texts (*Romeo and Juliet*, *King Lear* and *Reservoir Dogs*, respectively). Similarly, Hoover (1999) uses corpus tools to analyse William Golding's *The Inheritors*, and Walker (2010, 2012) analyses Julian Barnes' novel *Talking It Over*. Each of these studies sub-divide the text into smaller components and make comparisons between those components. For example, the speech of one character in a play is compared against the combined speech of all the other characters. We will show how this works in ▶ Chapter 6 when we examine the characters in Shaw's *Pygmalion*.

1.5.2 Concordance and Collocation

Corpus research is assisted by the outputs of computer software (e.g. *Wordsmith Tools*; *AntConc*, *Wmatrix*) designed to process large quantities of texts in various ways. Indeed, without such tools, the investigation of the textual data in a corpus, especially very large corpora, would be practically impossible. Most corpus tools can calculate (absolute and relative) frequencies of every word in a corpus, and these can be a useful starting point in the analysis of style. Below, we summarise two other important functions that corpus tools typically perform under the headings: **concordance** and **collocation**

1.5.2.1 Concordance

If you completed our corpus KWIC-ie on 'style' in the BNC, then you will have already encountered concordance lines. Hopefully, the activity will have demonstrated that concordances are listings of all the occurrences of an item (typically a word or short phrase) in a corpus along with some of the surrounding **co-text,**

Style: Text, Cognition and Corpora

Left context	Node	Right context
cheese, curds, butter and suchlike — yogurt, traditional Cornish	style	! — washed down with water rather than ale. In addition
e a little more than 10 minutes to achieve this amazing sculptured	style	!' Colette's old perm had almost grown out and the
. 'And I'm quite sure that you are exactly my	style	!' he added smoothly, removing the champagne glass from her
chniques and mental disciplines (including not least a good arguing	style	!)' She was once very close to death, in
TOO! So start shopping the new way soon — it says	style	! 20% OFF YOUR 1ST ORDER CALL FREE FOR YOUR CATALOGUE
out that his client was exclusively tied to The Sun. Such	style	! And such a change from that of Leo Beenhakker, the
the Knavesmire to enjoy a day of top class racing in champagne	style	! And they could strike it rich! We've teamed-up with
went well with thallium? Curried things? Chicken Dopiaza Thallium	Style	! But she wouldn't eat curry, would she? Anyway
a signature model impose another player's personality on my own	style	! Created by Charlie Miller in Scotland; Make-up by Janet Miller
BOBS SLEEK CHIC SO LONG Short, bleached cut with swirls of	style	! Early example of nose-art displayed on a Maurice Farman Short
competitors and won the race in what was to become true Alcock	style	! For this look, the wig was given a weave and
hide AND want to impress your friends, fake it in fabulous	style	! In the capital there's a magnificent parade of roughly caparisoned
Day in January is celebrated all over India and in the grandest	style	! INDIE 14 November 1992 Psalm Enchanted Evening! On The Road
this new 'cart' is an amalgam of nearly every pop	style	! Large curls stacked high on the crown for maximum effect Sweet!
soft fringe by Sean Hanna Klownz went over the top with this	style	! Oh dear me! Tell you what would be a good
Yes er! I like that woman I think she's got	style	! She I know. [unclear] if you can wear that top
the worst dressed woman in the world. She's got some	style	! Something fast. Something with style? Something [pause] somet
have to see. But if you do [pause] buy me something with	style	! Their special moisturising formula ensures great condition, too. If
in shades of Fiery Auburn or Golden Bronze to really liven your	style	! This style is the very height of fashion!' '
!' Ellie retorted. 'No shop girl could afford this	style	" (Fowler 1977: 103 – 13; Fowler 1986:
1981, 1986). The result is an alien "mind	style	" (preface) for undergraduates and sixth-formers. Blake's aim
" . This book is intended as a "basic guide to	style	" (see below); It will be particularly important for
minorities; * religious sub-cultures; * identifiable sub-culture "life	style	"), there is no matching entry for "Literature and
entry for "Applied linguistics" (which cross-refers readers to "	style	"). As part of the drive to restore party unity
ideological and political work, and neglect of the building of party	style	", "early eighteenth-century style" , "euphuistic style"
school of writing, or some combination of these: "epistolary	style	", "euphuistic style" , "the style of Victorian
bination of these: "epistolary style" , "early eighteenth-century	style	", "the style of Victorian novels" , etc.
epistolary style" , "early eighteenth-century style" , "euphuistic	style	", a "common language of the people" , "
lectures, he stressed the need in poetry for a "common	style	", a "new regime in politics" and a new
linked to the sense of a new departure, a "new	style	

■ **Fig. 1.4** KWIC view of the first 30 concordances for 'style' in the BNC

i.e. the text around the word or phrase of interest. Concordances are useful for looking for linguistic patterns that a word or phrase is involved in, and examining concordances is a crucial step in any corpus analysis. ■ Figure 1.4 shows the first 30 concordances for 'style' in the BNC, and these help to show some of the different uses and meanings of 'style'. The format of the concordances in ■ Fig. 1.4 is known as Key Word in Context, or **KWIC** (hence our choice of 'corpus KWICies' to name our corpus exercises). The term 'KWIC' was coined by H.P. Luhn (1960) and refers to concordances where the search item (the keyword in Luhn's terminology) is displayed in the centre of the screen with some co-text either side. The use of Key Word in the KWIC acronym refers to the item being searched for <u>and not</u> statistical keywords, which we introduce below. Some tools (including the web interface to the BNC we used in our KWIC-ie) allow concordances to be sorted alphabetically by the words occurring to the left or the right of the search item and this can be of considerable help when exploring patterns in the data. The corpus KWIC-ie demonstrated this with 'style'.

1.5.2.2 Collocation

The term '**collocation**' was coined by J.R. Firth (1957) and refers to the habitual or frequent tendency for a word to co-occur with a particular word or set of words. The **collocates** of a word are the words that frequently co-occur with it. Firth's idea was that the frequent collocates of a word can add to its meaning ("meaning by 'collocation'", Firth 1957: 194). Indeed, Firth famously said "you shall know a word by the company it keeps" (1957: 179).

While Firth's notion of collocation suggests that some words have a tendency to frequently, or habitually co-occur with others, such tendencies can be difficult to assess. Corpora and computer tools can help to explore the collocational behaviour of words in real language data in ways that were unavailable to Firth. One way is to manually examine sorted concordance lines to identify patterns of co-occurrence to provide a systematic and complete assessment of a word's immediate collocates. However, as with the case of 'style' in the BNC (see the first corpus KWIC-ie), when there are thousands of concordance lines, this can be rather daunting. Some computer tools can also calculate collocates automatically based on absolute frequencies of collocates or different statistical calculations that measure strength of attraction between words or whether the co-occurrence is a chance happening. These sorts of statistical calculations evaluate collocation within a specified span of the word under investigation, or '**node word**' (Sinclair et al. 2004: 10). For example, the span recommended by Sinclair (2004) is four words before and after the node word, so nine words in total (for more discussion of this, see Sinclair et al. 2004: 35). Even when collocates are calculated automatically, though, making sense of the results still requires manual investigation, usually by returning to concordance lines where creating data-driven categories can sometimes help to make sense of any collocational patterns.

1.5.3 Using Corpora to Check Our Intuitions

The corpus KWIC-ie on 'style' demonstrated that we can use large collections of text to explore how units of meaning (such as words) are used in texts. Using evidence from large quantities of data to help ascertain and describe the different uses and meanings of words and phrases is one way in which corpora can be used (by, for example, dictionary writers). The KWIC-ie also demonstrated the availability and accessibility of readymade corpora for such investigations. Stylisticians can, therefore, also make of use of such corpora in similar ways, for example as a reference point to provide evidence for intuitions we might have about language choices in a text.

Bill Louw, a pioneer of this approach, showed how concordance lines from large corpora can reveal observable patterns in word usage that can help to support claims and intuitions, and explain reader reactions (Louw 1989, 1993, 2008). For example, Louw (1993) uses COBUILD, another large corpus of British English texts, to support his intuition that the word 'utterly', in Larkin's poem 'First Sight', hints at "the myriad cruelties of the world" (Louw 1993: 161). Louw shows that in the corpus 'utterly' usually co-occurs with 'bad' things, such as 'devastating' and 'wrecked' and, adopting some of Firth's ideas (introduced above), suggests the term **semantic prosody** for when a word is "imbued" with an "aura of meaning" by the words it usually co-occurs with (Louw 1993: 157). Although Louw's notion of semantic prosody has been widely critiqued (see, e.g., Hunston 2007), we can notice that large corpora nevertheless allow us to explore patterns of co-occurrence that can support the discussion of connotations and intuitions that are rooted in data.

Louw (1993) also suggests that combinations of words or phrases that intuitively seem unusual—a "collocative clash" (Louw 1993: 157)—can be explored using corpora. Such 'clashes' are a type of deviation, where the word combination seems at odds with what we would normally expect. Large corpora can help support such intuitions. Louw illustrates this idea using the phrase 'bent on self-improvement' from David Lodge's novel *Small World*. Louw argues that the phrase is ironic, and that the irony is created because the usual right-hand collocates for the phrase 'bent on' (which include 'destroying', 'harrying', 'mayhem') are negative; 'self-improvement' is positive and therefore deviates from that pattern of negativity (see ▶ Chapter 9 for further discussion of irony).

Large, ready-made, corpora can, therefore, be used by stylisticians to provide a yardstick or a 'norm' against which language use in the text under investigation can be compared. Comparison is key to discerning style and corpora provide a way to do this.

1.5.4 Using Corpora to Find an Analytical Focus

Louw's approach to testing language use in a text, which we introduced above, depended on his own language intuitions to decide what is marked and foregrounded (see ▶ Sect. 1.2.1 above) and then seek support from a corpus. With this type of corpus approach, the text is typically being analysed manually and a corpus is being used to help support and/or explain the analyst's intuitions and inform the analysis. The corpora used are often large, ready-made corpora, chosen for their suitability to potentially explain language intuitions, acting as a reference point for what 'normally' happens in a particular language or language variety.

This sort of manual approach—where foci for analysis are selected based on what is foregrounded in a text—can be a problem when dealing with a larger text. Indeed, carrying out a stylistic analysis of a longer text using any of the frameworks discussed in this book would be a serious and time-consuming endeavour. Leech and Short (2007: 2) make this point, saying "[…] linguistic techniques are more readily adapted to the miniature exegesis of a lyric poem, than to the examination of a full-scale novel". They go on to say:

> […] the effects of prose style, and their sources in the language, are often more unobtrusive than those of poetic language. While a condensed poetic metaphor, or a metrical pattern, will jump to the attention as something which distinguishes the language of poetry from everyday language, the distinguishing features of prose style tend to become detectable over longer stretches of text, and to be demonstrable ultimately only in quantitative terms. […] In prose, the problem of how to select - what sample passages, what features to study - is more acute, and the incompleteness of even the most detailed analysis more apparent.
>
> Leech and Short (2007: 2)

Leech and Short make the points that assessing prose style is a quantitative undertaking and selecting shorter passages for more detailed analysis is a problem. Corpus linguistic tools can help to address these points by providing frequency information (e.g. word frequency) for a text, and by finding a focus (or a 'way in') for further detailed analysis via principled quantitative means. One such way is by textual comparison and the associated concept of **keyness**, which can suggest linguistic items or locations in a text for further analysis.

1.5.4.1 Keyness

It is perhaps the computer's ability to perform comparisons, and the associated concept of statistical keyness, that has proved so productive over recent years. Keyness is determined via quantitative comparison and is the identification of textual elements (usually word-forms) that are statistically salient in one text or corpus when compared with another text or corpus. Such comparisons can be carried out using corpus tools. Mike Scott and his corpus analysis software, *Wordsmith Tools* (Scott 2020) have made keyness analysis popular, in particular **keywords**.

Keywords are statistically salient words in a text or corpus. A list of keywords is a list of all words in a text or corpus that occur more (or less) frequently than they do in a comparison or reference corpus. As the name suggests, keyword comparisons occur at the word level, where all the word-forms and corresponding frequencies from the text or corpus under investigation (sometimes known as the **target**), are compared with the word-forms and corresponding frequencies from a **reference corpus**. This produces a list of words that are statistically over-represented (**positive keywords**) or under-represented (**negative keywords**) in the target text or corpus.

The notion of keyness extends beyond single word-form comparisons. *WordSmith Tools* (Scott 2020), for example, can search for key differences in repeated strings of words, known as key-clusters (see, e.g., Mahlberg 2007), and *WMatrix* (Rayson 2009) can calculate key grammatical parts of speech (**Key-POS**) and semantic categories (**Key Concepts**) due to its ability to automatically assign words and phrases in texts to grammatical and semantic groups.

1.5.4.2 Keyness and Foregrounding

Leech and Short's observation (2007: 2), cited above, that prose style is less obtrusive than "poetic language" and "detectable over longer stretches of text" relates to foregrounding theory and the notion of psychological prominence (or what is noticeable). With keyness analysis, the principle that is generally accepted is that elements of a text that are highlighted as being statistically deviant (and therefore statistically salient) are worthy of further analysis on the basis that they might be interpretatively relevant. Keywords (as well as Key POS and Key concepts) can be said to be statistically deviant and statistically salient because their relative frequencies differ significantly from those in a reference corpus. According to Scott and Tribble (2006: 55–56), keyness is "[…] a quality words may have in a given text or set of texts, suggesting that they are important […]". However, not all key items will be interpretatively important, so it is up to the analyst to discover whether statistical salience relates to interpretative salience. This point is made by Leech and Short (2007: 41) and Leech (2008: 163) who describe three notions of saliency which relate to foregrounding; these are shown in ◘ Fig. 1.5.

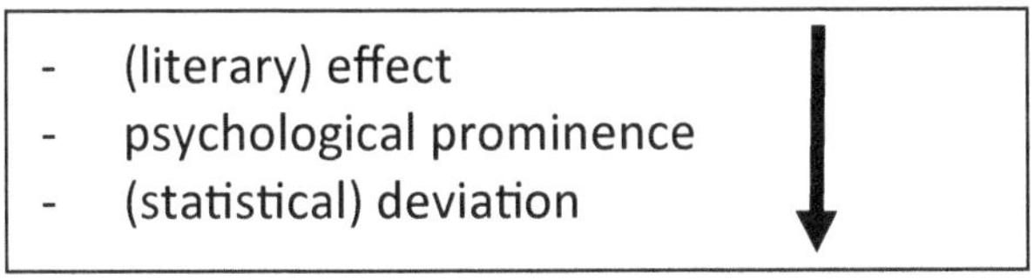

```
- (literary) effect
- psychological prominence
- (statistical) deviation     ↓
```

Fig. 1.5 Three notions of saliency (Leech and Short, 2007; Leech, 2008)

As Leech (2008) explains, the arrow in ◘ Fig. 1.5 indicates that all instances of foregrounding have interpretative relevance, are psychologically prominent, and are (statistically) deviant. Foregrounding, then, is noticeable deviation for literary effect. However, Leech (2008) goes on to explain that the arrow in ◘ Fig. 1.5 only works in one direction and so the opposite relationship does not apply. So not all (statistically) deviant items are psychologically prominent and not instances of foregrounding. This is important for keyness because while all key items are statistically deviant, they are not necessarily psychologically prominent and not necessarily relevant to our understanding and/or interpretation of the text. Therefore, keyness does not necessarily equate to foregrounding in the sense posited by the Prague School scholars (discussed in ▶ Sect. 1.2.1.2). Instead, keyness suggests what is worth examining more closely (see Leech 2008: 163–164; see also McIntyre 2010: 181). When key items do, on closer inspection, prove to be interpretatively relevant, it is more likely that they occupy what Van Peer (1986: 69) refers to as the middle ground. Here, foreground and background, rather than being binary divisions, operate on a cline (see Douthwaite 2000: 191) with the middle ground being the parts of a text that are less noticeable than the foregrounded ones but contribute (albeit, perhaps to a lesser extent) interpretatively and to readers' responses to texts. Corpus outputs and their analysis can, therefore, be important for cognitive approaches to Stylistics because they potentially provide evidence for readers' reactions to texts.

1.5.5 Corpora and Stylistic Analysis

Short (2011: 35) points out that "[...] an important aspect of stylistics is being systematic", and corpus tools can certainly help with the systematicity, particularly when analysing lengthy texts. However, while searches and lists of frequencies, collocates and keywords can be achieved systematically by a computer, it should be remembered that this is *not* a stylistic analysis. Frequency lists and keywords are virtually meaningless without further (human) analysis. Therefore, as Ho (2011) points out, Corpus Stylistics must always incorporate interpretative elements:

> [...] 'corpus stylistics' is not purely a quantitative study of literature. Rather, it is still a qualitative stylistic approach to the study of language of literature, combined with or supported by corpus-based quantitative methods and technology.
>
> Ho (2011: 10)

Ho reminds us that when embarking on a corpus stylistic analysis, the focus should be the general goal of Stylistics, i.e. explaining our understanding and response to a text (Leech and Short 2007: 289). Corpus Stylistics is, therefore, not just about counting language features, which computers are very good at, but also looking at the computer-generated results, and using analytical frameworks or models from other areas of Linguistics to make sense of the results.

1.6 Chapter Summary

Style is linguistic behaviour. It is the culmination of (conscious or subconscious) language choices in a text made by the text producer. It is recognisable and distinctive with different writers and speakers having different styles. Stylistics is the study of style in text. It examines the language choices that text producers make over other possible choices and how these choices relate to **artistic function** (Leech and Short 2007: 12), **poetic function** (Jakobson 1960: 356), **stylistic function** (Carter and Simpson 1989: 5) or **rhetorical effect** (Focus 1.1). Stylistics, then, is concerned with the relationship between linguistic choices and meaning and their (artistic, poetic, stylistic or rhetorical) effects on the reader. Importantly, Stylistics involves both linguistic description and interpretation of effects based on that description. In this chapter, we introduced the three pillars of contemporary Stylistics that combine to facilitate description and interpretation: **text**, **cognition** and **corpora**. Text is central to Stylistics and the focus of analysis because style results from patterned linguistic features in the text. Cognition helps us understand and explain how textual meanings and effects are activated and arrived at by readers. Corpora refers to investigating style using large electronic collections of texts and/or specialised computer software. Over the course of this book, we will introduce a toolkit for stylistic analysis that helps analysts to describe the linguistic features of a text and offer an interpretation of their meanings and effects. In doing so, we will bring together the three pillars of Stylistics and show how the combination of text, cognition and corpora is essential for successful stylistic enquiry.

- **Further Reading**

For a detailed discussion of style, see Leech and Short (2007: Chapter 1).
For more detailed discussions of Cognitive Grammar and its applicability to Stylistics, see Stockwell (2002), Harrison et al. (2014), Harrison (2017), Nuttall (2018), Giovanelli and Harrison (2018).
For a book-length introduction to Corpus Stylistics see McIntyre and Walker (2019).
On the poetic function of internet memes see Lugea (2020).

- **Notes**
1. Because 'The Woman' is a modern translation of a German poem the discourse structure diagram could also include the translator, Abse, to reflect his intermediatory influence on the message, which is significant for any translated discourse.

2. These messages can, to some extent, be related indirectly to the audience via the performance and staging of the play but will inevitably incorporate the actor's/director's interpretation of the information.
3. See McIntyre (2006) for a convincing account of narrative intervention in plays.
4. The exception is what are known as monitor corpora which are added to on a regular basis. For example, the COBUILD corpus started out in the 1980s at around 22 million words. By the 1990s, it had increased to 220 million. It is now around 4.5 billion words.

References

Abse, D., ed. 2015. *Favourite Love Poems*. London: Pavillion Books.
Archer, D. and Bousfield, D. 2010. 'See Better, Lear'? See Lear Better! A Corpus-Based Pragma-Stylistic Investigation of Shakespeare's *King Lear*. In *Language and Style*, eds. D. McIntyre, and B. Busse, 183–203. Basingstoke: Palgrave.
Bartlett, F. C. 1932. *Remembering*. Cambridge: Cambridge University Press.
Bortolussi, M. and Dixon, P. 2003. *Psychonarratology: Foundations for the Empirical Study of Literary Response*. Cambridge: Cambridge University Press.
Brock, E. 1977. *Song of the Battery Hen: Selected Poems, 1959–75*. London: Secker and Warburg.
Burke, M. 2014. Rhetoric and Poetics: The Classical Heritage of Stylistics. In *The Routledge Handbook of Stylistics*, ed. M. Burke, 11–30. London and New York: Routledge.
Burrows, J. F. 1986. Modal Verbs and Moral Principles: An Aspect of Jane Austen's Style. *Literary and Linguistic Computing* 1,1: 9–23.
Burrows, J. F. 1987. *Computation into Criticism. A Study of Jane Austen's Novels and an Experiment in Method*. Oxford: Clarendon.
Carter, R. and Simpson, P. 1989. Introduction. In *Language, Discourse and Literature: An Introductory Reader in Discourse Stylistics*, eds. R. Carter and P. Simpson, 1–21. London and New York: Routledge.
Chatman, S. 1978. *Story and Discourse: Narrative Structure in Fiction and Film*. Ithaca: Cornell University Press.
Cook, G. 1994. *Discourse and Literature*. Oxford: Oxford University Press.
Culpeper, J. 2002. Computers, Language and Characterisation: An Analysis of Six Characters in Romeo and Juliet. In *Conversation in Life and in Literature: Papers from the ASLA Symposium, Association Suedoise de Linguistique Appliquee (ASLA)*, 15, eds. U. Melander-Marttala, C. Ostman, and M. Kytö, 11–30. Universitetstryckeriet: Uppsala.
Culpeper, J. 2009. Keyness: Words, Parts-of-Speech and Semantic Categories in the Character-Talk of Shakespeare's Romeo and Juliet. *International Journal of Corpus Linguistics* 14, 1: 29–59.
Dancygier, B. (ed.). 2017. *The Cambridge Handbook of Cognitive Linguistics*. Cambridge: Cambridge University Press.
Douthwaite, J. 2000. *Towards a Linguistic Theory of Foregrounding*. Alessandria: Edizioni dell'Orso.
Evans, V. and Green, M. 2006. *Cognitive Linguistics: An Introduction*. Edinburgh: Edinburgh University Press.
Eysenck, M. W. and Keane, M. 2002. *Cognitive Psychology: A Student's Handbook*. London: Routledge.
Fahnestock, J. 2016. Rhetorical Stylistics. *Language and Literature* 14, 3: 215–230.
Firth, J. R. 1957. *Papers in Linguistics, 1934–1951*. Oxford: Oxford University Press.
Fischer-Starke, B. 2010. *Corpus Linguistics in Literary Analysis*. London: Continuum
Fowler, R. 1986/1996. *Linguistic Criticism*. 2nd ed. Oxford: Oxford University Press.
Gavins, J. 2016a. Text-Worlds. In *The Bloomsbury Companion to Stylistics*, ed. V. Sotirova, 444–457. London and New York: Bloomsbury.

Gavins, J. 2016b. Stylistic Interanimation and Apophatic Poetics in Jacob Polley's 'Hide and Seek'. In *World-Building: Discourse in the Mind. Advances in Stylistics*, eds. J. Gavins and E. Lahey, 277–292. London and New York: Bloomsbury.

Giovanelli, M. and Harrison, C. 2018. *Cognitive Grammar in Stylistics*. London and New York: Bloomsbury.

Hall, G. 2015. *Literature in Language Education*. 2nd ed. New York: Palgrave Macmillan.

Harrison, C. 2017. *Cognitive Grammar in Contemporary Fiction*. Amsterdam: John Benjamins.

Harrison, C., Nuttall, L., Stockwell, P. and Yuan, W., eds. 2014. *Cognitive Grammar in Literature*. Amsterdam and Philadelphia: John Benjamins.

Haspelmath, M. 2006. Against Markedness (and What to Replace It with). *Journal of Linguistics* 42, 1: 25–70.

Hemingway, E. 1926. Chapter III. In *In Our Time*. London: Jonathan Cape.

Ho, Y. 2011. *Corpus Stylistics in Principles and Practice: A Stylistic Exploration of John Fowles' The Magus*. London: Continuum

Hoover, D. L. 1999. *Language and Style in "The Inheritors"*. Lanham: University Press of America.

Hori, M. 2004. *Investigating Dickens' Style: A Collocational Analysis*. Basingstoke: Palgrave Macmillan

Hunston, S. 2007. Semantic Prosody Revisited. *International Journal of Corpus Linguistics* 12, 2: 249–268.

Jakobson, R. 1960. Closing Statement: Linguistics and Poetics. In *Style in Language*, ed. T. A. Sebeok, 350–377. Cambridge, MA: MIT Press. ▶ https://monoskop.org/images/8/84/Jakobson_Roman_1960_Closing_statement_Linguistics_and_Poetics.pdf (Last accessed 19th September 2017).

Keats, J. 1820. *Lamia and Other Poems*. London: Taylor and Hessey.

Langacker, R. W. 2008. *Cognitive Grammar: A Basic Introduction*. Oxford: Oxford University Press.

Langacker, R. W. 2014. Foreword. In *Cognitive Grammar in Literature*, eds. C. Harrison, L. Nuttall, P. Stockwell and W. Yuan, xiii–xiv. Amsterdam and Philadelphia: John Benjamins.

Leech, G. 1969. *A Linguistic Guide to English Poetry*. Harlow, UK: Pearson Education.

Leech, G. 1985. Stylistics. In *Discourse and Literature: New Approaches to the Analysis of Literary Genres*, ed. T. A. van Dijk, 39–58. Amsterdam and Philadelphia: John Benjamins.

Leech, G. 2008. *Language in Literature: Style and Foregrounding*. London and New York: Routledge.

Leech, G. and Short, M. 2007. *Style in Fiction: A Linguistic Introduction to English Fictional Prose*. 2nd ed. London and New York: Longman.

Levin, S. R. 1965. Internal and External Deviation in Poetry. *Word* 21, 2: 225–237.

Louw, W. E. 1989. Subroutines in the Integration of Language and Literature. In *Literature and the Learner: Methodological Approaches*, ed. R. Carter. London: Pergamon.

Louw, W.E. 1993. Irony in the Text or Insincerity in the Writer? The Diagnostic Potential of Semantic Prosodies. In *Text and Technology*, eds. M. Baker, G. Francis, and E. Tognini-Bonelli. Amsterdam and Philadelphia: John Benjamins.

Louw, B. 2008. Consolidating Empirical Method in Data-Assisted Stylistics: Towards a Corpus-Attested Glossary of Literary Terms. In *Directions in Empirical Literary Studies*, eds. S. Zyngier, M. Bortlussi, A. Chesnokova, and J. Auracher, 243–264. Amsterdam and Philadelphia: John Benjamins.

Lugea, J. 2020. The pragma-stylistics of 'image macro' internet memes. In *Contemporary Media Stylistics*, eds. H. Ringrow and S. Pihlaja, 81–106. London and New York: Bloomsbury Academic.

Luhn, H. P. 1960. Key Word-in-Context Index for Technical Literature (KWIC Index). *American Documentation* 11, 4: 288–295.

Mahlberg M. 2007. Clusters, Key Clusters and Local Textual Functions in Dickens. *Corpora* 2, 1: 1–31.

McEnery, T. and Wilson, A. 2001. *Corpus Linguistics*. 2nd ed. Edinburgh: Edinburgh University Press.

McIntyre, D. 2006. *Point of View in Plays: A Cognitive Stylistic Approach to Viewpoint in Drama and other Text-Types*. Amsterdam and Philadelphia: John Benjamins.

McIntyre, D. 2010. Dialogue and Characterization in Quentin Tarantino's Reservoir Dogs: A Corpus Stylistic Analysis. In *Language and Style*, eds. D. McIntyre and B. Busse, 162–182. Basingstoke: Palgrave.

McIntyre, D. and Walker, B. 2011. Discourse Presentation in Early Modern English Writing: A Preliminary Corpus-Based Investigation. *International Journal of Corpus Linguistics* 16, 1: 101–130.

Miall, D. S. 2006. Experimental approaches to reader responses to literature. In *New Directions in Aesthetics, Creativity, and the Arts* eds. P. Locher, C. Martindale, and L. Dorfman, 175–188. Amityville, NY: Baywood Press.

Miall, D. S. and Kuikan, D. 1999. What Is Literariness? Three Components of Literary Reading. *Discourse Processes* 28: 121–138.

Mukařovsk, J. 1958. Standard Language and Poetic Language. In *A Prague School Reader on Aesthetics, Literary Structure and Style*, ed. Trans. P. L. Garvin. Washington, DC: Georgetown University Press.

Nuttall, L. 2018. *Mind Style and Cognitive Grammar: Language and World View in Speculative Fiction*. London and New York: Bloomsbury.

O'Rourke, J. 1987. Persona and Voice in Keats' Ode to a Grecian Urn. *Studies in Romanticism* 26, 1: 27–48.

Rayson, P. 2009. *Wmatrix: A Web-Based Corpus Processing Environment*. Computing Department, Lancaster University. ▶ http://ucrel.lancs.ac.uk/wmatrix/

Rimmon-Kenan, S. 1983. *Narrative Fiction*. London: Methuen.

Schank, R. C. 1986. *Explanation Patterns: Understanding Mechanically and Creatively*. Hillsdale, NJ: Erlbaum.

Schank, R. C. and Abelson, R. P. 1977. *Scripts, Plans, Goals and Understanding: An Inquiry into Human Knowledge Structures*. Hillsdale, NJ: Lawrence Erlbaum.

Scott, M. 2020. *WordSmith Tools Version 8*. Stroud: Lexical Analysis Software.

Scott, M. and Tribble, C. 2006. *Key Words and Corpus Analysis in Language Education*. Amsterdam and Philadelphia: John Benjamins.

Semino, E. and Culpeper, J., eds. 2002. Foreward. In *Cognitive Stylistics: Language and Cognition in Text Analysis*, ix–xvi. Amsterdam and Philadelphia: John Benjamins.

Shklovsky, V. 1917/2016. Art as Device. In *Viktor Shklovsky: A Reader*, ed. A. Berlina, 73–96. London and New York: Bloomsbury Academic.

Short, M. 1996. *Exploring the Language of Poems, Plays and Prose*. Harlow: Longman.

Sinclair, J. 2004. *Trust the Text: Language, Corpus and Discourse*. London: Routledge.

Stockwell, P. 2002. *Cognitive Poetics: An Introduction*. London and New York: Routledge.

Taylor, J. R. 2002. *Cognitive Grammar*. Oxford: Oxford University Press.

Toolan, M. 2001. *Narrative: A Critical Linguistic Introduction*. 2nd ed. London: Routledge.

Tsur, R. 2002. Aspects of Cognitive Poetics. In *Cognitive Stylistics: Language and Cognition in Text Analysis*, eds. E. Semino and J. Culpeper, 279–318. Amsterdam and Philadelphia: John Benjamins.

van Peer, W. 1986. *Stylistics and Psychology: Investigations of Foregrounding*. London: CroomHelm.

van Peer, W., Hakemulder, J., and Zyngier, S. 2007. Lines on feeling: Foregrounding, aesthetics and meaning. *Language and Literature*, 16, 2: 197–213.

Verhagen, A. 2007. Construal and perspectivization. In *The Oxford Handbook of Cognitive Linguistics*, eds. D. Geeraerts and H. Cuyckens, 48–81. Oxford: Oxford University Press.

Wales, K. 2011. *A Dictionary of Stylistics*. Harlow, UK: Pearson Education Ltd.

Walker, B. 2010. WMatrix, Key Concepts and the Narrators in Julian Barnes's Talking It Over. In *Language and Style*, eds. D. McIntyre and B. Busse, 364–387. Basingstoke: Palgrave.

Walker, B. 2012. *Character and Characterisation in Julian Barnes's Talking It Over: A Corpus Stylistic Analysis*. Unpublished PhD thesis: Lancaster University.

Whiteley, S. and P. Canning, eds. 2017. Special Issue: Stylistic Approaches to Reader Response Research. *Language and Literature* 26, 2: 71–187.

Widdowson, H. G. 2008. The Novel Features of Text. Corpus Analysis and Stylistics. In *Language, People, Numbers: Corpus Stylistics and Society*, eds. A. Gerbig and O. Mason, 293–304. Amsterdam: Rodopi.

Worlds

Supplementary Information The online version contains supplementary material available at ▶ https://doi.org/10.1007/978-3-031-10422-0_2.

© The Author(s), under exclusive license to Springer Nature Switzerland AG 2023
J. Lugea and B. Walker, *Stylistics*,
https://doi.org/10.1007/978-3-031-10422-0_2

2.1 Introduction

What is fiction? What happens in your mind when you read fiction, or engage in any kind of discourse? For some scholars, the answer to these questions is a 'world'. The 'worlds' metaphor has been adopted by scholars in various disciplines including Philosophy (e.g. Lewis 1973, 1986), Linguistics (e.g. De Beaugrande 1980; Werth 1999) and Literary Studies (e.g. Ryan 1991a, b) to describe alternative states of affairs, whether they are represented or imagined in discourse. This chapter explores the two main ways that scholars have used the 'world' metaphor to describe a text.

i. First, how the world created by a fictional text can relate to the real world in particular ways (known as **accessibility relations**), which can be particularly useful for describing how readers relate to fiction and the effects it can bring about.
ii. Second, how textual information and context combine to create a coherent mental representation of the discourse in the minds of participants (i.e. a text-world).

These two worlds-based approaches to fictional discourse structure the chapter. ▶ Section 2.2 outlines how fictional worlds relate to the real world, while ▶ Sect. 2.3 covers Text World Theory, providing a detailed account of the textual features and cognitive operations involved in world creation. Because a whole text (e.g. a novel) is too much for a detailed text-world analysis, in ▶ Sect. 2.4 we outline how corpus approaches can provide a principled method for selecting an extract for further qualitative analysis.

2.2 The Worlds of Fiction

Fiction is, by definition, imagined and often untrue. How is it, then, that it has the power to evoke real-world effects, such as tears and laughter in readers? In order to account for this paradox and explain fiction's 'truth value', literary scholars have borrowed the *possible world* concept from philosophers (Lewis 1973; Rescher 1979). Using this approach, literary texts can be understood as advancing statements that may not be true in this world but contribute to the creation of a **possible world** in which they *can* be considered true. In this section, we discuss and summarise the work of literary scholar and narratologist Marie-Laure Ryan (1991a, b) and her application of possible worlds theory to fiction. We adapt some of the terms she uses for coherence with other worlds theories discussed later in this chapter[1]; crucially, we refer to the world created by the text as a **text-world**.

2.2.1 The Principle of Minimal Departure

Ryan (1980, 1991a, b) proposes the '**principle of minimal departure**', which claims that readers assume the text-world is like the real world, deviating only if there are textual indications to the contrary. For example, the principle of minimal departure describes how readers of *Harry Potter* might assume that the roles and activities in the fictional school, Hogwarts, are similar to those of real-world public boarding schools, until discrepancies arise such as the fictional game of 'quidditch'. Readers only depart from their expectations when the text does. Although not alluded to by Ryan, Schema Theory (which we introduced in ▶ Sect. 1.3.2) supports the principle of minimal departure insofar as readers' schematic knowledge can help to process and understand information from the text even if it deviates from expectations. As strange and impossible as the flying game of quidditch is, it fits within a schema of public schools where competitive team sports are played. Readers' schematic knowledge about public school life may help with understanding and coherence of the unusual aspects of the *Harry Potter* text-world.

2.2.2 Accessibility Between Worlds

As Semino (1997: 8) observes, "the ability to project worlds that are somehow alternative to the 'real' world is often presented as a crucial property of literary texts". Readers can assume similarities between the real world and the text-world, but we can also appreciate when they differ. Ryan (1991a, b) proposes a list of the ways in which the real world can differ from the text-world, which she calls a taxonomy of '**accessibility relations**'. An adapted version of her list is found in ◘ Table 2.1, ranging from more fundamental and physical accessibility relations (A) to more abstract and conceptual accessibility relations (I).

If a text-world matches the real world by having the same objects (*B*/same inventory) with the same characteristics (*A*/properties), the result is a very realistic text-world, such as an autobiography. However, if a text uses a fictional narrator to tell an otherwise true story, the text-world includes a person that the real world does not, meaning that the accessibility relation '*B*/same inventory' has been relaxed. If the author takes a bit more creative licence with a realistic story by adding fictional characters to the narrative, *B*/same inventory is replaced by *C*/expanded inventory. For example, the Sherlock Holmes stories are set in a London that has the same properties as the London of the time and were based on a real crime-solving doctor (upholding *A*/properties) but include fictional characters (replacing *B*/same inventory with *C*/expanded inventory). Accessibility relations A, B and C are the most basic in relating fiction to reality.

The result of breaking relations D to I is a much more 'unreal' text. The text-world is incompatible with the real world in terms of *D*/chronology if the events take place in the future or if time passes in an irregular manner, as in science fiction. When *E*/natural laws are broken, it means that events in the text-world indicate it is not subject to the same laws of nature. For example, in Kafka's novella *Metamorphosis* the lead character, a salesman, morphs into an insect, breaking *E*/natural laws. However, the relation *F*/taxonomy is upheld, as both salesmen and insects are species that can be found in the real world. Texts that tend to break *F*/taxonomy are found in science fiction or fantasy genres, which often include invented creatures, aliens or monsters.

■ **Table 2.1** Accessibility relations: the ways in which a text-world can relate to the real world

Category	Description
A/properties	**Identity of properties:** text-world is accessible from real world if the objects have the same properties, including events and locations
B/same inventory	**Identity of inventory:** text-world is accessible from real world if they are furnished by the same objects and members
C/expanded inventory	**Compatibility of inventory:** text-world is accessible from real world if text-world's inventory includes all the members of the real world, as well as some native members
D/chronology	**Chronological compatibility:** text-world is accessible from real world if it takes place in the past or present and time passes in the same way; the future cannot be judged as compatible as it has not happened/may not happen
E/natural laws	**Physical compatibility:** text-world is accessible from real world if they share natural laws e.g. gravity
F/taxonomy	**Taxonomic compatibility:** text-world is accessible from real world if both worlds contain the same species, and the species are characterised by the same properties. (F usually follows from E, but sometimes taxonomic and physical compatibility can be separated (see Ryan 1991b)
G/logic	**Logical compatibility:** text-world is accessible from real world if both worlds respect the principles of 'noncontradiction and excluded middle' (see ▶ Sect. 2.2)
H/analytical	**Analytical compatibility:** text-world is accessible from real world if they share analytic truths, i.e. if objects designated by the same words have the same essential properties
I/linguistic	**Linguistic compatibility:** text-world is accessible from real world if the language by which text-world is described can be understood

Adapted from Ryan (1991a, b)

When a text departs from *G*/logic, it is breaking fundamental laws of logic which entail that a statement cannot be true and untrue at the same time (the **principles of 'non-contradiction and excluded middle'**).[2] In Flann O'Brien's novel *The Third Policeman*, the narrator describes a box which, "…reminded me forcibly, strange and foolish as it may seem, of something I did not understand and had never even heard of" (2007: 284). *G*/logic is broken here as it is impossible to be both reminded and to have never heard of something; this logical incompatibility is found throughout the novel and is typical of postmodern and absurd styles (Gavins 2001, 2013; Vassilopoulou 2008).

The Third Policeman also breaks *H*/analytical truths, as the concepts designated by familiar words do not have familiar properties. In one scene, the narrator describes at length:

a house which astonished me [...] it did nothing to reconcile itself with the shape of an ordinary house [...] I seemed to see the front and the back simultaneously from my position approaching what should have been the side.

O'Brien (2007: 266)

The narrative description continues in a similar way, defying a conceptualisation of any conceivable house. While breaking *H*/analytical truths entails breaking the relationship between words and their referents, *I*/linguistic compatibility relates to the use of language that is not understood in the real world, as in nonsense literature (see, e.g., Lewis Carroll's poem 'Jabberwocky') or the invented languages of fantasy fiction (such as Dothraki in *Game of Thrones*).

Activity 2.1: Fictional Worlds and Their Accessibility Relations

Consider how the text-world of the following popular fictional texts relates to the real world, in terms of Ryan's eight 'accessibility relations'. (Where relevant, either the written or audiovisual text can be considered.)

	The Handmaid's Tale	*Ghostbusters*	*Lord of the Rings*	*Dreams from My Father* (Barack Obama's self-penned memoir)
A/properties				
B/inventory				
C/expanded inventory				
D/chronology				
E/natural laws				
F/taxonomy				
G/logic				
H/analytical				
I/linguistic				
Genre:				

a. Put a plus (+) next to the accessibility relations that are upheld in the text-world and a minus (−) next to those which are broken.
b. Sometimes the answer may not be as straightforward as + / −. In these cases, note how and why.
c. Make a note of the genre of each text in the final row. Do you think each text breaks accessibility relations typical of their genre? Can you think of other texts from the same genre that break the same accessibility relations?

Suggested answers can be found on the book's webpage. To find out more about the relationship between accessibility relations and genres, see Ryan (1991a: 9).

2.2.3 The Worlds of Fiction Summary

In this section, we have discussed how several theories and principles from Philosophy and Logic can prove useful for considering:
a. what fiction is (a world);
b. how and why fiction can be conceived of as real (i.e. its **truth-value**);
c. how readers conceive of the fictional world as similar to the real world, unless told otherwise (**the principle of minimal departure**);
d. how the fictional world can suspend real-world norms in patterned ways (**accessibility relations**); and
e. how logic that applies to the real world can be suspended for and in fiction (by breaking **the principles of non-contradiction and excluded middle**)

Equipped with these concepts, the researcher can consider fictional texts in their entirety as whole objects in relation to the real world, and chart their differences in principled ways.

An analysis of how a text ruptures real-world norms in terms of its accessibility relations can be extremely useful for explaining how it fits in a certain genre, or has a certain overall effect. For example, the reception of *The Third Policeman* as absurd can be explained by the fact that while the text-world appears to be the same as the real world in terms of the most fundamental accessibility relations it is different in terms of many others. So, fictional characters (*C*/expanded inventory) are recognisable as our species (*F*/taxonomy) that speak a common language (*I*/language) and the story is set in the recent past (*D*/chronology). However, in contrast, events are both true and false *(G*/logic), the narrator's analysis of a house is not a house as we know it (*H*/analytical), and bicycles and humans start to merge (*E*/natural laws and *A*/properties). Against a background of familiarity, then, these differences are even more salient and, as the story progresses, the text-world becomes increasingly strange. When it is revealed in the final pages that the narrator has been dead for most of the book, we realise why the fictional world became so strange: the majority of the action occurs in the after-life (further breaking *E*/natural laws and *A*/properties). We realise that only after the narrator's death that the logical and analytical rules of reality were relaxed. This demonstrates that even within one text, there can be various worlds governed by different rules.

2.3 Text World Theory

The philosophical and narratological accounts, summarised above, only go so far in describing how fiction creates worlds; crucially, they do not account for the fundamental role of *language* in world creation. Text World Theory (TWT) proposes that language and cognition work together to create mental representations of discourse known as text-worlds (Werth 1995, 1999; Gavins 2007; Gavins and Lahey 2016). TWT aims to describe the text-worlds created by different kinds of discourse, from spoken interactions to reading any text. TWT offers a framework

Worlds

for both describing the processes involved in text-world creation and diagramming the discourse. Over the rest of this section, we demonstrate the processes involved in constructing a text-world diagram and creating a mental representation of the text using the opening paragraphs of Hardy's *Tess of the d'Urbervilles: A Pure Woman* (see Activity 2.2).

Activity 2.2: Tess of the d'Urbervilles: A Pure Woman
Read the following extract in preparation for the explication of Text World Theory.

1) On an evening in the latter part of May, a middle-aged man was walking homeward from Shaston to the village of Marlott, in the adjoining Vale of Blakemore, or Blackmoor. 2) The pair of legs that carried him were rickety, and there was a bias in his gait which inclined him somewhat to the left of a straight line. 3) He occasionally gave a smart nod, as if in confirmation of some opinion, though he was not thinking of anything in particular. 4) An empty egg-basket was slung upon his arm, the nap of his hat was ruffled, a patch being quite worn away at its brim where his thumb came in taking it off. 5) Presently, he was met by an elderly parson astride on a grey mare, who, as he rode, hummed a wandering tune.

6) 'Good night t'ee,' said the man with the basket.

7) 'Good night, Sir John,' said the parson.

8) The pedestrian, after another pace or two, halted, and turned round.

9) 'Now, sir, begging your pardon; we met last market-day on this road about this time, and I said 'Good night,' and you made reply 'Good night, Sir John,' as now.'

10) 'I did,' said the parson.

11) 'And once before that—near a month ago.'

12) 'I may have.'

13) 'Then what might your meaning be in calling me 'Sir John' these different times, when I be plain Jack Durbeyfield, the haggler?'

14) The parson rode a step or two nearer.

15) 'It was only my whim,' he said; and, after a moment's hesitation: 'It was on account of a discovery I made some little time ago, whilst I was hunting up pedigrees for the new county history. 16) I am Parson Tringham, the antiquary,

of Stagfoot Lane. 17) Don't you really know, Durbeyfield, that you are the lineal representative of the ancient and knightly family of the d'Urbervilles, who derive their descent from Sir Pagan d'Urberville, that renowned knight who came from Normandy with William the Conqueror, as appears by Battle Abbey Roll?'

18) 'Never heard it before, sir!'

19) 'Well it's true. 20) Throw up your chin a moment, so that I may catch the profile of your face better. 21) Yes, that's the d'Urberville nose and chin—a little debased. [...] 22) Aye, there have been generations of Sir Johns among you, and if knighthood were hereditary [...] you would be Sir John now.'

23) 'Ye don't say so!'

24) 'In short,' concluded the parson, decisively smacking his leg with his switch, 'there's hardly such another family in England.'

25) 'Daze my eyes, and isn't there?' said Durbeyfield. 'And here have I been knocking about, year after year, from pillar to post, as if I was no more than the commonest feller in the parish…

2.3.1 The Discourse-World

Before examining the text itself, TWT considers the **discourse-world**, which refers to the context of discourse production and reception. This includes the **discourse participants**, their physical environment(s), as well as any personal knowledge and experience they use to understand the discourse. In face-to-face interaction, the discourse-world is shared, as participants occupy the same space, at the same time. However, since Thomas Hardy wrote *Tess of the d'Urbervilles* (hereafter *Tess*) in 1891 in southwest England, his spatio-temporal location differs from that of his readers, creating a **split discourse-world** (◘ Fig. 2.1).

◘ **Fig. 2.1** Split discourse-world of *Tess of the d'Urbervilles*

For every new reading, a new discourse-world is created according to the unique contextual features captured in the diagram (participants, time, location). There are also many important features the diagram cannot capture, including the discourse participants' personal, socio-cultural and historical contexts. For example, many features could influence how you process this text and build the text-world, such as your familiarity with this novel, Victorian literature, or the rural English setting. Because the discourse-world is different for each reading, TWT inherently acknowledges that each reading experience is unique, dependent on the individual set of experiences that the reader brings to the text.

Focus 2.1: Deixis

The term 'deixis' comes from the Greek for 'show'. Deixis is an aspect of language which links referents (people, places, things, events) to a subjective viewpoint, known as the '**deictic centre**'. In other words, rather than simply naming these referents in language, deictic markers 'point' to them from the speaker's particular viewpoint. As such, deixis is incredibly important for understanding how text-worlds and point-of-view are created through language. Deixis is expressed through a range of linguistic forms, including tense markers, demonstrative pronouns and adverbs. There are three core categories of deixis:

1. **Temporal deixis:** relates events to the current time, using tense (past, present or future) and temporal adverbs (e.g. *now, back then, yesterday, today, the day after tomorrow*).
2. **Spatial deixis:** relates entities to the speaker's physical location, using demonstrative pronouns (e.g. *this/that*), demonstrative determiners (*this* woman/*that* man) and spatial adverbs (e.g. *here, there, over the page*) and even spatial deictic verbs (e.g. *come* indicates movement towards a deictic centre).
3. **Person deixis:** relates people, objects and actions to a personal viewpoint, using pronouns (e.g. *I, you*) and determiners (e.g. *my, his, our*).

The key thing to notice about the examples listed above is that their meaning changes according to their context of use. This is because deixis creates a link between a referent and its context. The kind of link that the deictic marker creates is constant (e.g. *my* always relates an object to a speaker in a relationship of possession), but the speaker and the referent are variable (e.g. *my book* will mean something different when I say it and when you say it). Because we have to look at the context to decode its meaning, deixis is a vital clue to understanding and analysing viewpoints, relationships and world-building.

Read more: see Levinson (1983) for a comprehensive account of deixis.

Activity 2.3: Try Analysing Deixis Yourself

Allison, W. M. and Kirk, W. 1936. The Diamond Dick. In *Detective Picture Stories*, Vol. 1, No. 1. New York: Comics Magazine Co. Inc, page 4.

a. Identify the personal, spatial and temporal deictic markers in the Direct Speech in the cartoon (i.e. the linguistic features which point to aspects of the context).
b. The dialogue in this cartoon uses a lot more deictic reference than definite reference (see ▶ Sect. 2.3.2), especially compared to the narrative prose in Activity 2.2. Why do you think that might be?

 Our answers are on the book's webpage

2.3.2 Building the Text-World

TWT advances **'the principle of text-driveness'** (Werth 1999) to describe how discourse participants only call to mind the knowledge and experience that is relevant for processing the ongoing discourse. The mental representation, the **text-world**, arises as a result of language use and is jointly negotiated by discourse participants (e.g. author and reader). It is dynamic, being continually updated as the discourse progresses. Through **world-building information** provided by the text, the text-world is furnished with a location and a timeframe and populated with objects and **enactors** (people). The term enactors is used instead of 'characters' as TWT is also applicable to non-fictional discourse.

World-building is largely achieved through the linguistic system of **reference**, expressions that refer to entities, time or space. The opening sentence of *Tess* establishes key world-building information through **definite reference**, using proper nouns and noun phrases to specify an enactor ('a middle-aged man'), the text-world's time ('an evening in the latter part of May') and location ('from Shaston to the village of Marlott'). Although these placenames are invented by Hardy, his use of the definite article suggests a real place. Opening a fictional world in this way (known as *in media res*) assumes it is a given reality (see also ▶ Sect. 3.4.4).

While definite reference *names* text-world features, **deictic reference** *points* to them, indicating their relationship to a subjective viewpoint, known as a **deictic centre** (see Focus 2.1). It is almost impossible to find a sentence without **deixis**. The second sentence from the opening of *Tess* illustrates the ubiquity of this aspect of language and its contribution to world-building:

> 2) The pair of legs that <u>carried him were</u> rickety, and there <u>was</u> a bias in <u>his</u> gait which <u>inclined him</u> somewhat <u>to the left</u> of a straight line (emphasis added).

Now, in addition to knowing the events take place in May, the past tense temporal deictic markers (*carried, were, was, inclined*), which are typical of narrative prose, indicate it was a May in the past. The second sentence adds to spatial world-building with the prepositional phrase 'to the left', an inherently deictic expression as it implies there is a deictic centre from which the right or left can be viewed. However, it is not clear whether the 'left' relates to the perspective of 'the middle-aged man' or the narrator (we discuss point-of-view in ▶ Chapter 3). Through the use of the third-person pronouns (*his, him*), the narrator and the character are established as distinct **enactors**. With all this referential information in the first two sentences of *Tess*, the reader begins to construct a picture of the discourse and therefore a text-world.

A simplified version of the emergent text-world is found in ◘ Fig. 2.2, which builds on and includes the discourse-world box from ◘ Fig. 2.1. By keeping the discourse-world in the diagram, ◘ Fig. 2.2 reminds us that discourse-world features shape the text-world and the bidirectional arrow indicates this interactive relationship. The world-building information discussed thus far is captured at the top of the text-world box: **time**, **location**, **objects** and **enactors**. For our understanding of the text-world of *Tess*, we rely on a narrator who is not a discourse-world participant, but an enactor in the text-world, so this is an **enactor accessible text-world**, not directly available to discourse-world participants. Alternatively, when a member of the discourse-world establishes a text-world (e.g. in face-to-face conversation or in an autobiography), this is called a **discourse participant accessible text-world**. Therefore, the concept of accessibility (▶ Sect. 2.2) also has significance for TWT, as it helps to delineate who has access to the different worlds, or on whom we rely for our understanding of them. In the case of *Tess*, readers rely on the narrator, an enactor, to help in creating the text-world.

World-building information can be elaborated through verbal processes (Gavins 2007: 36–52), for which TWT draws on Halliday's (1994) **transitivity** model, which is summarised in ◘ Table 2.2. **Existential processes** identify the existence of something, often using a 'dummy subject' as in "there was a bias in his

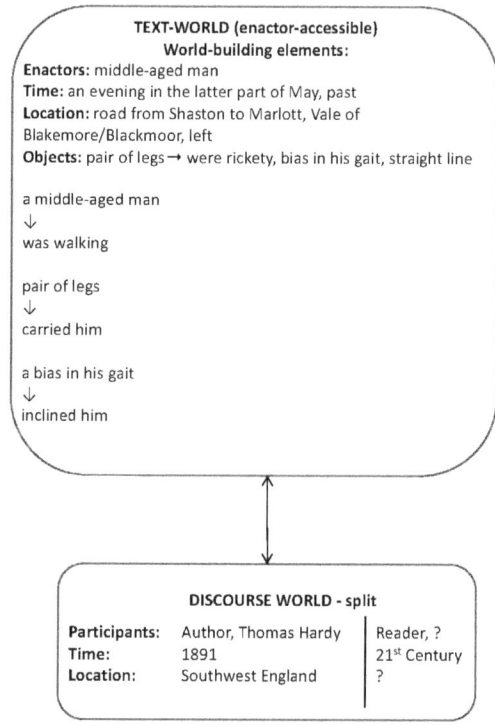

Fig. 2.2 A text-world diagram of the first two sentences of *Tess of the d'Urbervilles*

gait". These process types help to populate the text-world with enactors and objects and describe the scene. Furthermore, entities in the text-world can be described using **relational processes**, which relate an entity (either an enactor or an object) to its attributes, possessions or circumstances, as in "legs [...] were rickety". Typically, these are realised by the verb 'be' and further describe the world-building features. These world-building relational processes are included in the diagram using a horizontal arrow to indicate that the entity is being described in further detail, e.g. "pair of legs → were rickety" (◘ Fig. 2.2).

All of the world-building information that can be extracted from the novel's first two sentences is included at the top of the diagram in ◘ Fig. 2.2. Representing the information this way illustrates the opening's focus on the location, direction and manner of the middle-aged man's movement.

2.3.3 Advancing the Text-World

In principle, and in diagramming practice, text-world theorists (Werth 1999; Gavins 2007; Gavins and Lahey 2016) make a distinction between world-building information and **function-advancing propositions**, which are the clauses that advance the ac-

Table 2.2 Transitivity processes and participants

Process type	Description	Participants and other entities	Example
Material process	Process of doing, usually concrete, physical actions	Actor, Goal	*A pair of legs* (Actor) *carried* (material process) *him* (Goal)
Behavioural process	Process of physiological behaviour	Behaver, Behaviour, Range	*He* (Behaver) *occasionally gave* (behaviour process) *a smart nod* (Range)
Mental process	Process of thinking or feeling	Senser, Phenomenon	*He* (Senser) *was not thinking* (mental process) *of anything in particular* (Phenomenon)
Verbal process	Process of communication	Sayer, Receiver and Verbiage	*'Good night t'ee,'* (Verbiage) *said* (verbal process) *the man with the basket* (Sayer)
Relational process	Process of relating two concepts, in terms of: (i) Attribution (ii) Identification	(i) Attributive: Carrier, Attribute (ii) Identifying: Identified and Identifier	*His legs* (Carrier) *were* (attributive relational process) *rickety* (Attribute) *I* (Identified) *am* (identifying relational process) *Parson Tringham* (Identifier)
Existential process	Process of existing (e.g. *there is…*)	Existent	*There was* (existential process) *a bias in his gait* (Existent)

Simplified from Halliday and Matthiessen (2014: 311) and Thompson (1996: 102)

tion. Function-advancing is typically expressed by Halliday's **material processes**, which are verbs that describe something happening or being done and have a responsible actor. Function-advancing is represented in the text-world diagram using vertical arrows between the actor and the process and, space-permitting, is listed below the world-building information in the text-world diagram, as depicted in ◘ Fig. 2.2.

Diagramming the text in this way helps to highlight that, in these first two sentences, the middle-aged man is only referred to specifically in the first clause, after which it his body parts and their idiosyncrasies that become actors ('pair of legs', 'gait') in material processes ('carried', 'inclined') affecting him. The character's physique and movement are subtle yet significant cues for creating an impression of the text-world, and more specifically, the enactor's character (► Chapter 6).

A text-world analysis of the first two sentences of *Tess* has revealed the textual features that contribute to building the text-world, its temporal and spatial parameters, and most significantly the enactor whose character has been developed using existential and relational processes. Because TWT draws on Hallidayan processes and lays bare which actors are responsible for which actions, it has also been possible to identify an emergent pattern in the way the man is represented: his physical characteristics act upon him.

2.3.4 Modal-Worlds

The third sentence in the extract (Activity 2.2) continues the focus on the middle-aged man's physicality:

> 3) He occasionally gave a smart nod, as if in confirmation of some opinion, though he was not thinking of anything in particular.

This time the narrator describes how the character's outward physical behaviour *could* be perceived, contrasting appearances with the vacuous contents of the character's inner thoughts! In TWT, only propositions that are verifiable as true by participants or by enactors can be included in the text-world. A speaker's attitude towards the truth-value of a proposition is expressed through the modal system in language. Any information that is called into doubt through the use of **modality** is stored at a remove from the text-world in a modal-world (Gavins 2005, 2007). Before discussing how this can be incorporated into our analysis of *Tess*, we outline modality in general.

TWT uses three core kinds of modality: epistemic, boulomaic and deontic (◘ Table 2.2). As Nuyts observes, these three modal categories indicate, "the extent to which the speaker (or another person in descriptive cases) is committed to the state of affairs" (2005: 17). **Epistemic modality** is the expression of speaker confidence in the truth-value of the proposition, whether small or great. Lyons (1977: 808–809) points out that even if a speaker expresses absolute certainty, their use of modality suggests there is the possibility of doubt. With **deontic modality**, the proposition is expressed as an obligation; this still constitutes modality because the implication is that it is not (yet) a reality. Deontic modality is closely related to epistemic modality and even shares some forms of expression. For example, the auxiliary verb *must* can express doubt in some contexts or obligation in others. **Boulomaic modality** is the speaker's expression of desire towards the truth-value of the proposition, which again entails that it is not (yet) true. Boulomaic modality is less grammaticalised, meaning it is less part of the grammar of English than the other modal categories and is not expressed using modal auxiliary verbs. The three kinds of modality and examples of how they can be expressed are found in ◘ Table 2.3. Note, though, that these modal categories and their forms of expression are not exhaustive, or even fully agreed upon by linguists, as modality can be tricky to classify and to delineate from other systems (Jesperson 1924; Palmer 1990).

Wherever commitment towards a proposition is called into doubt, the information cannot be included directly in the text-world and is, instead, held in a **modal world** (see Gavins 2005, 2007). So, when in *Tess* the narrator tells us that the middle-aged man "gave a smart nod, as if [...]", the use of the comparative structure 'as if' introduces a hypothetical proposition and the contents of the proposition are called into doubt. Therefore, rather than being stored in the text-world, they create an **epistemic modal world**, as shown in ◘ Fig. 2.3.

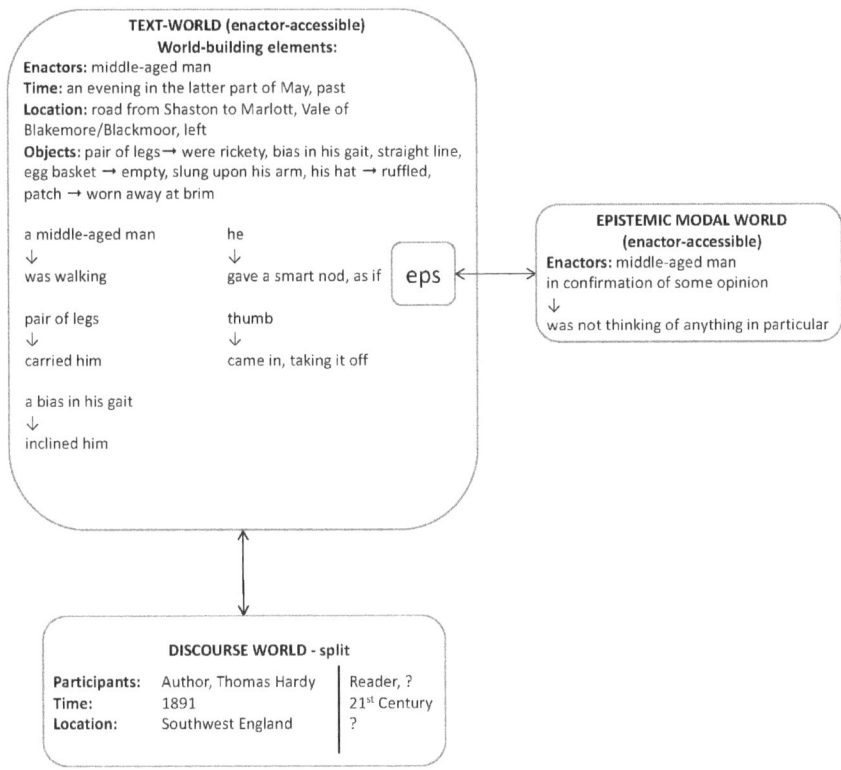

◘ **Fig. 2.3** An epistemic modal-world in *Tess of the d'Urbervilles*

Gavins (2005) proposes that epistemic modal-worlds are created by a wide range of features, including hypothetical and conditional constructions (e.g. "if.."), as well as some Speech and Thought Presentation categories[3] (see ► Chapter 4). Following Gavins, the epistemic modal world in ◘ Fig. 2.3 includes the narrator's suggestion of a possible interpretation for the man's nod, as well as the presentation of his thoughts. While we have simply integrated negation (e.g. '*not* thinking') into the epistemic modal world in ◘ Fig. 2.3, some TWT scholars have suggested different ways of diagramming negation (e.g. Hidalgo-Down-

■ **Table 2.3** Three categories of modality and examples of their expression in English

Modality: *The expression of speaker commitment towards a state of affairs*

	Epistemic	Deontic	Boulomaic
Lexical verbs	*think, know, remember, wonder, suppose…*	*better*	*hope, wish, dream, regret…*
Auxiliary verbs	*can, could, may, must, might, would, shall, should*	*must, should, shall, ought to, have to*	–
Adverbs	*possibly, maybe, probably, definitely…*	*necessarily*	*hopefully, regretfully*
Adjectival construction	to be + *sure, certain, possible, (un) likely, doubtful…*	to be + *obligatory, necessary, mandatory…*	to be + *hopeful*
Participial constructions	to be + *supposed, assumed that*	to be + *obliged, required that…*	to be + *hoped that*

ing 2000a, b, 2003; Lugea 2016a; Gavins 2016b). We adopt a different method in ▶ Sect. 2.4.3, where our aim is to illustrate the important effect of negation on that text-world.

Although the epistemic modal-world triggered by 'as if' entails a brief departure from the text-world, we return to the main text-world when the narrator continues (in sentence 4) describing the character's appearance:

> 4) An empty egg-basket was slung upon his arm, the nap of his hat was ruffled, a patch being quite worn away at its brim where his thumb came in taking it off.

With this description, the text-world is fleshed out with further world-building information (see ■ Fig. 2.3). Again, the narrator focuses on the man's body parts ('arm', 'thumb') and their effect on his person and dress. This is a man whose physical reality has taken a toll on his appearance.

2.3.5 World-Switching

The text-world is further developed in sentence 5 with the arrival of a new enactor, an "elderly parson astride on a gray mare". The two characters then greet one another and begin to converse, their speech presented directly in the narration (▶ Chapter 4), with the parson using florid Standard English and the middle-aged man employing the non-standard features of his West Country dialect (sentences 6 to 25). Text-world theorists have approached Direct Speech in various ways; some have noted that its use in narrative prose entails a change from past to present tense (Werth 1999), while others that it involves a change in person deixis from the narrating voice to first person 'I' of the character (Gavins 2007; Cruikshank and Lahey 2010). However, a central tenet of TWT is that each 'world' is subject to the same rules (Werth 1999), so if discourse participants like you and I are said to create shared mental representations of the discourse, then so too should characters (Lugea 2013, 2016a, b). In other words, just as we create a text-world of *Tess* as we engage with the discourse, so too do the novel's characters as they engage in discourse with each other. By this approach, when the elderly parson and the middle-aged man converse, they create an **enactor text-world**, embedded within the main text-world. Their discourse informs our understanding of the main text-world, helping us elaborate our mental representation of the characters and their situations. As the narrative switches back and forth between narration and Direct Speech, so too does our mental representation, between the main text-world and the enactor text-world. ◘ Figure 2.4 demonstrates how this can be diagrammed. From ◘ Fig. 2.4 onwards, the diagrams omit function-advancing information to save space and to give a more general illustration of the world-building and the relationships between worlds.

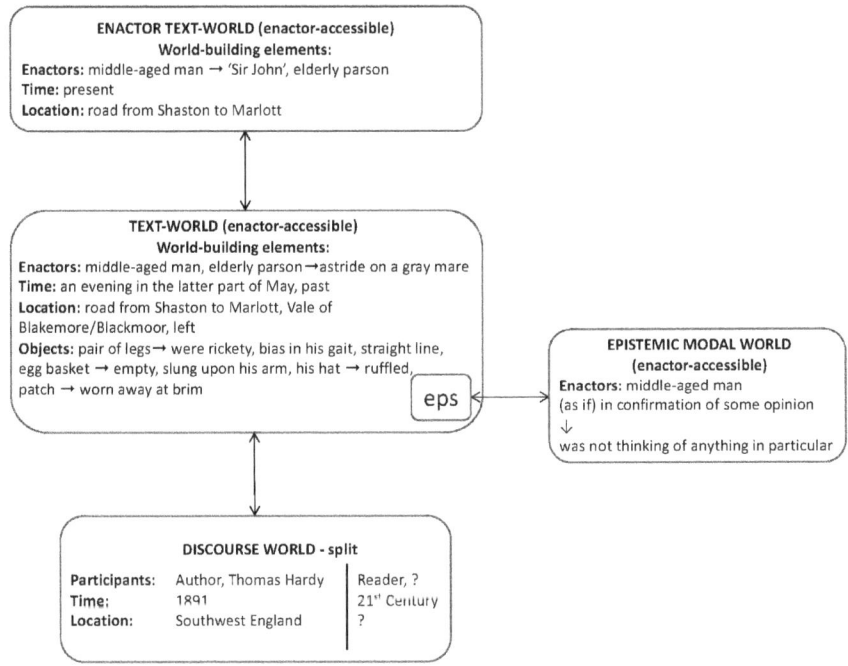

◘ **Fig. 2.4** The enactor text-world in *Tess of the d'Urbervilles*

The enactor text-world is in the enactors' present time. They greet one another, with the parson addressing the man with the basket using the honorific 'Sir' in front of his name, a marker of respect. The honorific is at odds with the picture of the character elaborated thus far, one of physical hardship and humble means. This anomaly is noticed by the middle-aged man himself, as he stops walking and turns around to ask the man on horseback why he has addressed him as 'Sir John' every time they have met on this road in the past, when in reality he is 'plain Jack Durbeyfield the haggler'. In the early course of this conversation, the middle-aged man (Sir John or plain Jack) has switched from their present discursive context to refer to past interactions, a switch initiated by the enactor's use of past tense and temporal adverb:

> 9) "we met last market-day on this road about this time"

Because the temporal coordinates have changed, a temporal world-switch is created. A **world-switch** is an alteration in the time and/or location of a text-world; the information exists at the same level of accessibility as the world from which it was initiated, but the events pertain to different deictic coordinates. In this case, the location is roughly the same, as the enactors have met regularly on this particular road, but at times in the past. The middle-aged man points out how the parson's past and present use of 'Sir John' is incongruous with his actual social standing. In labelling himself 'plain Jack Durbeyfield', the enactor adds to our understanding of the text-world by self-identifying his humble social standing (Jack is a common name for the more formal John). The **temporal world-switch** between past encounters and the present encounter is represented in ◘ Fig. 2.5.

The information provided using Direct Speech in the enactor text-world feeds into readerly[4] understandings of the main text-world in the centre of ◘ Fig. 2.5; we update our mental representation of the enactors, their past encounters and learn that the parson's repeated use of the honorific 'Sir John' is deemed inappropriate by the humble addressee. The parson's initial response as to why he used this address form is 'It was only my whim', a relational process describing his naming strategy as insignificant. However, he goes on to elaborate a fuller reason for his use of the honorific with reference to an historical account of plain Jack's aristocratic heritage as a d'Urberville, not a Durbeyfield. First, the parson explains his own identity further, an 'antiquary', who has researched the county his-

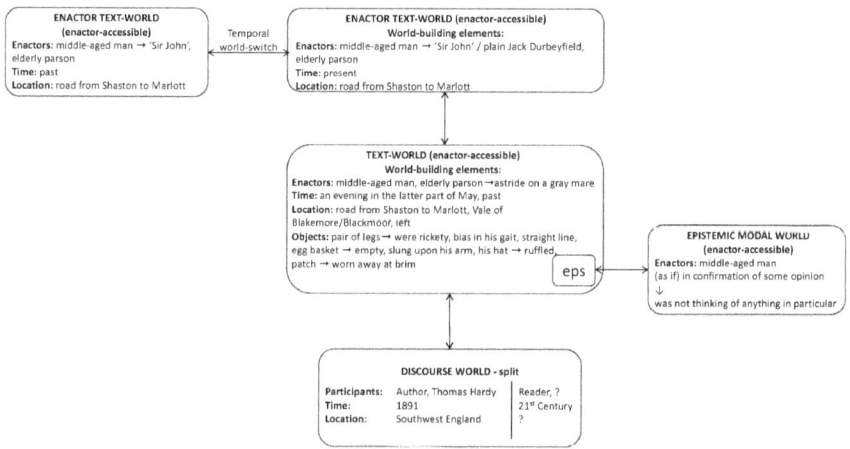

◘ **Fig. 2.5** Temporal world-switch in *Tess of the d'Urbervilles*

tory. This statement creates a brief temporal world-switch to the recent past, presumably in a different spatial location from their roadside conversation. The parson describes his recent discovery pertaining to the man's descendance from Sir Pagan d'Urberville, a knight who accompanied William the Conqueror crossing from Normandy. Although the date of this past event is not explicitly stated, an historically savvy reader might infer that it is 1066, the date of the Norman conquest of England. Thus, a further **spatio-temporal world-switch** is created to 1066 and events subsequent to the d'Urberville's arrival in England. These additional two world-switches, which deviate from the spatial and temporal coordinates of the enactor text-world, are depicted in ◘ Fig. 2.6.

The text-world diagram in ◘ Fig. 2.6, although complex, displays the text-world in such a way that we can begin to understand something of the narrative structure of the opening of this novel. In the main text-world (centre of ◘ Fig. 2.6), the narrator provides an initial characterisation of the unnamed 'middle-aged man' by foregrounding the wear and tear of his physical existence upon his person; this was expressed through the focus on his body parts in the world-building information and through the use of body parts as actors in material processes carried out on himself. In other words, he was a victim of his own physical experience. An almost humorous contrast is created—and illustrated in ◘ Fig. 2.6—between the man's outward behaviour in the text-world (regular firm nods) and the limited possibilities of his inner thoughts in the epistemic modal-world. The very fact that the narrator has access to the character's thoughts, and indeed presents them in this ironic contrast, suggests that the narrator is evaluating—or at least encouraging the reader to evaluate—the man as a simple person. Textual indications of the man's low social class are found in references to his humble attire in the text-world ('empty egg basket', 'ruffled and worn hat')

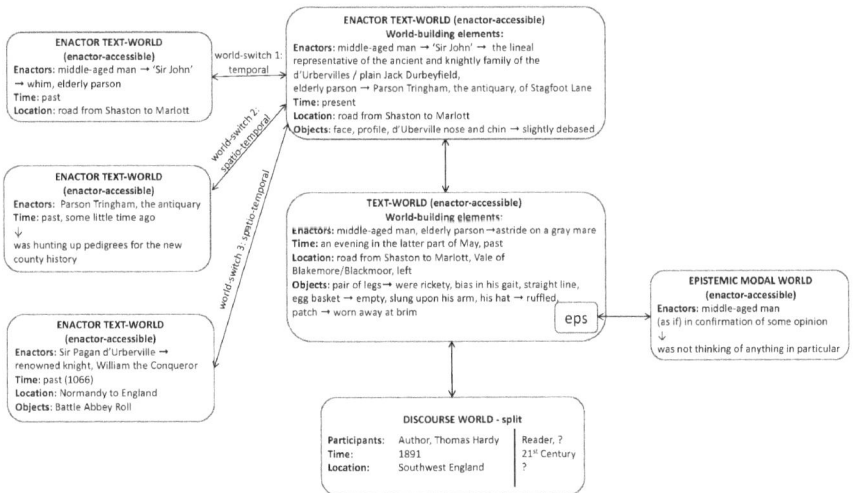

◘ **Fig. 2.6** Spatio-temporal world-switches in *Tess of the d'Urbervilles*

2

and, in the enactor text-world, his use of regional dialect, which contrasts with the parson's formal Standard English. The reader is encouraged to understand why the character would be perplexed at being called 'Sir John' by the parson (whom he incidentally addresses as 'sir'), when to all outward appearances, and by his own and the narrator's judgements, he is simply plain Jack Durbeyfield.

All of this is very much at odds with what transpires from the parson's contribution to the enactor text-world, which involves two spatio-temporal world-switches in his attempt to explain why he addressed Jack Durbeyfield as 'Sir John'. In world-switch 3 (◘ Fig. 2.6), we are told the history of the noble d'Urberville, a Norman knight from whom Jack descends. Switching back to the enactor text-world, the parson asks Jack to lift his chin and show his facial profile, developing the earlier focus on the poor man's physical appearance in the initial text-world. The parson affirms, 'Yes, that's the d'Urberville nose and chin—a little debased', and in doing so brings together the depiction of the lowly Jack Durbeyfield in the present with the representation of his noble ancestry in the past. Once again, the contrast between alternative representations of the man are possible sources of humour in the text (see ▶ Chapter 9).

2.3.6 The Relationships Between the Worlds and Interpreting Effects

It is striking that, in his (fictional) historical account of the d'Urbervilles, the parson refers to real historical events, people and objects (the Norman conquest, William the Conqueror and the Battle Abbey Roll). As such, world-switch 3 appeals to the reader's discourse-world knowledge to flesh out their understanding of the d'Urberville's past in the text-world. In ▶ Sect. 2.2 of this chapter, we saw how Ryan's taxonomy of accessibility relations provided a list of ways in which a fictional text-world could be accessible from the discourse-world. In the case of *Tess*, references to real historical events increase the accessibility of *A*/properties. The reference to William the Conqueror, an enactor who has a real **counterpart** in the discourse-world, means the relation *B*/same inventory is upheld (although the text-world does contain enactors who are fictional, relaxing *C*/expanded inventory). As well as incorporating elements of the discourse-world, the text-world of this novel continues to uphold all of the remaining accessibility relations, which could explain, at least in part, its classification as 'realism' by some literary critics (although see Widdowson [1999] for a critique of this position on Hardy's prose).

Hardy himself rejected realism as a literary genre, observing in his notes at the time of writing *Tess*: "Art is a disproportioning—(i.e. distorting, throwing out of proportion)—of realities, to show more clearly the features that matter in those realities [...] Hence, 'realism' is not Art" (1984: 239). Hardy's adherence to core accessibility relations (*A*/properties and *B*/same inventory) lends the novel some realism, yet Hardy's view of art is evident in the findings of the text-world analysis in this section. Hardy's commitment to 'disproportioning' is visible in how he foregrounds the man's physical 'features that matter' and depicts him as a victim of his low social standing. Furthermore, by foregrounding the physical effects of hardship on the man and juxtaposing it with the parson's lofty story about his ancestral nobility, the reader is reminded of the stark social class divide, visible across the divisions between the worlds that make up this text. The opening sets the scene for the novel as a whole, where Jack Darbeyfield's delusions of grandeur lead to the further demise of his family and the tragic life of his daughter, Tess.

2.4 Corpus-Assisted Approaches to TWT

In this section, we discuss how computer tools and corpus approaches can support a TWT analysis.

2.4.1 Text-World Diagramming with a Computer

Computer software can help with the difficult task of text-world diagramming. Although it is impossible to capture a discourse participant's mental representation in full, computer software can represent the multi-dimensional and layered nature of text-worlds better than a two-dimensional page. Two freely available diagramming tools are Visual Understanding Environment (VUE) and Worldbuilder 1.0. VUE was adopted by Lugea (2016a, c) to diagram fifty-two versions of the same story to investigate differences in spoken narrative styles (the diagrams can be downloaded from the book's website (2016a) and viewed using VUE). Worldbuilder is an online text-world annotation and diagramming tool developed by stylisticians and computer scientists at University of Huddersfield. Both tools have also been used in forensic text-world analyses of witness statements from, for example, the Meredith Kercher murder trial (Ho et al. 2018, 2019) and the Hillsborough disaster inquiry (Canning et al. 2021). This shows that diagramming complex discourse carries practical potential for legal professionals to help them visualise complex cases and evaluate contrasting witness accounts.

2.4.2 Using Corpus Approaches to Find a 'Way In'

Following our qualitative text-world analysis of the opening of *Tess* (▶ Sect. 2.3), we suggested that the opening paragraph establishes class division and social inequality as main themes in the novel as a whole. Although diagramming software can help, TWT is impractical for analysing longer stretches of text, let alone a whole novel. Corpus tools can provide principled *quantitative* means for finding a 'way in' to longer texts (Leech and Short 2007: 2) for further detailed *qualitative* analysis. Such an approach is demonstrated in this section using the whole of *Tess*.

According to TWT, modal expressions create modal-worlds (▶ Sect. 2.3.4). It is possible that parts of a text that use a lot of modality have interpretative significance. A reasonable research aim, therefore, is to identify a part of *Tess* which

features a lot of modality and investigate it further using a qualitative TWT analysis. In order to proceed, however, we first need to clarify:
1. What is meant by 'part' of the novel?
2. What constitutes a 'norm' for modal frequency?
3. What counts as 'a lot' of modality?

To answer question (1), we reasoned that chapters, being textually complete and coherent components of a novel, and which might feasibly be analysed using TWT, make sensible parts to divide the novel into. For question (2), we decided that a 'norm' for modal frequency can be based on the **mean** number of modal expressions in each chapter, calculated by finding the total number of modal expressions in the novel and dividing by the number of chapters (59 chapters in *Tess*). The result, the mean number of modal expressions per chapter, is a **text internal norm** (i.e. a norm established by the text itself, and not by some external measure). To answer question (3), we calculated how much each chapter deviates from the text internal norm using a statistical measure called **standard deviation**, which we explain further below.

As outlined in ▶ Sect. 2.3.4, modality is a slippery phenomenon and is realised by a wide range of features, sometimes making it difficult to distinguish from non-modal expressions, such as tense. Nonetheless, the English modal auxiliary verbs (see ◘ Table 2.2) *are* easily identifiable using a grammatical parts-of-speech **(POS) tagger**. POS tagging automatically identifies and labels grammatical categories in texts. Such tagging software adds a code, or tag, to each word in a text, identifying its grammatical part of speech based on a pre-defined list of grammatical categories known as a **tagset**. We used the *CLAWS4* grammatical tagger (freely available online) to produce a tagged version of the novel. The opening from *Tess* below demonstrates how, after tagging, every word is followed by an underscore and a code denoting its grammatical category:

> On_II an_AT1 evening_NNT1 in_II the_AT latter_DA part_NN1 of_IO May_NPM1 a_AT1 middle-aged_JJ man_NN1 was_VBDZ walking_VVG homeward_JJ from_II Shaston_NP1 to_II the_AT village_NN1 of_IO Marlott_NP1 ,_, in_II the_AT adjoining_JJ Vale_NN1 of_IO Blakemore_NP1 ,_, or_CC Blackmoor_NP1 ._.

The standard tagset currently used by CLAWS4 (known as C7) contains over 160 tags providing detailed grammatical information about the word forms making up a text. The meaning of each tag in the set can be found on the CLAWS website. We can see from the extract that CLAWS4 has tagged 'on' as _II which is the code for a preposition, 'an' as _AT1 which is the code for a singular (denoted by '1') article, and 'evening' as _NNT1 which is the code for a singular temporal noun, and so on. The tagging system allows for different types of general grammatical categories such as nouns and verbs, with tags for different types of the same general category all starting with the same letter (e.g. all noun tags start with 'N'; all verb tags start with 'V'). So 'evening' is tagged as one particular type of noun and 'May' (also on the first line) is tagged as another: a singular month noun. The latter example shows that CLAWS4 is able to differentiate between the use of the form 'may' to denote a month and its use as a modal auxiliary verb, which is very useful for our task.

Once a text is POS tagged, the researcher can easily search the tags for grammatical categories. In order to establish the number of modal auxiliary verbs in the novel, we simply counted the number of occurrences of the tags denoting modal auxiliary verb forms (_VM and _VMK in the CLAWS4 tagset). Counting can be achieved by opening the tagged novel in a text processing package (e.g. *Microsoft Word*) and using the search facility to search for all occurrences of _VM (note: this search will also find occurrences of _VMK). Our search found 2201 modal verbs across the whole novel of 150,335 words. The mean average frequency of modal verbs per 1000 words (‰) is, therefore:

$$2201/150,335 \times 1000 = 14.64.$$

Our next step was to split the tagged version of the novel into its constituent (59) chapters (a laborious task) and then for each chapter to count (i) the total number of words and (ii) the number of modal auxiliary verbs. We then calculated the per thousand frequency of the modal verbs in each chapter (= frequency/number of words in the chapter × 1000). We needed to calculate per thousand frequencies because this allows comparison between the chapters which are different sizes. We used per thousand rather than per cent in order to avoid very small numbers.

Our next step was to evaluate the differences in frequencies of modal auxiliary verbs in each chapter against the mean frequency for the whole novel. For this we used **standard deviation** (SD) which measures the variance from the mean value of a set of numbers and is a useful way in which to assess which numbers in a set are unusually high or low. There are any number of books and websites that explain SD in more detail than we have space to do here, one of which we list in our online resources section below. We calculated the SD for our modal verbs in *Tess* in *Microsoft Excel* using the 'stdev' function[5] (also available in *Apache Open Office*), which conveniently performs the calculation for you. The value produced was 4.68. What this means is that the ‰ frequency of modal verbs in the majority of chapters in *Tess* deviates from the mean frequency no more than plus or minus 4.68. So, the ‰ frequency of modal verbs in most of the chapters is between 19.05 (14.37 + 4.68) and 9.68 (14.37 − 4.68). So, we can say that a normal ‰ frequency of modal verbs in *Tess* is between 19.05 and 9.68, i.e. within plus or minus one standard deviation of the mean frequency.

Having established the SD we can then say that any frequencies that are more than plus or minus one standard deviation from the mean (i.e. >19.05 or <9.68) are unusually high or low, any frequencies that are more than plus or minus two standard deviations from the mean (i.e. >23.73 or <5.00) are very unusually high or low. This method provides a principled and quantifiable means to answer question 3 above: what constitutes 'a little' or 'a lot of' modality?

The ‰ modal auxiliary verb frequencies in *Tess* per chapter are shown in the bar chart in ◘ Fig. 2.7. The chart includes trend lines indicating the mean ‰ value of modal verbs in the novel, and the values for: the mean + 1 standard deviation; −1 standard deviation; +2 standard deviations; and −2 standard deviations. From the graph, we can see that Chapters 36 and 48 have very unusually high ‰ frequencies of modal verbs while Chapter 59 has a very unusually low frequency (there is just one modal auxiliary verb in that chapter). The graph makes

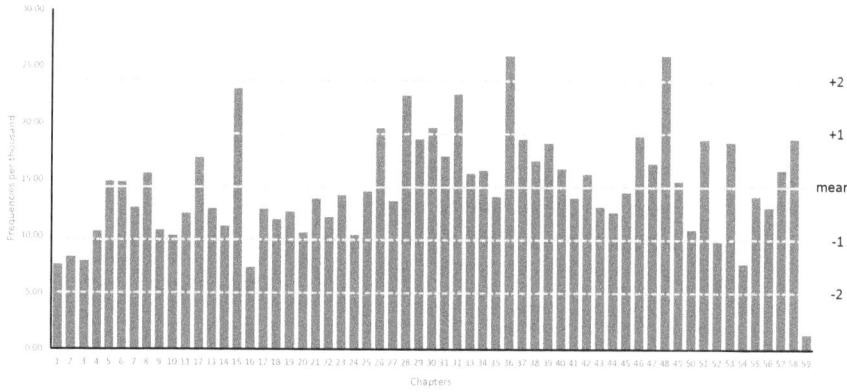

☐ **Fig. 2.7** Frequencies of modal auxiliary verbs per thousand words in *Tess* by chapter

it clear which chapters are quantitatively salient in terms of their use of modal auxiliary verbs and provides the researcher with justification for choosing a part of the text for qualitative analysis. In ▶ Sect. 2.4.3, we examine Chapter 36, where modal auxiliary verbs are overused the most in the novel.

2.4.3 Corpus-Assisted Text-World Analysis

For the reader, Chapter 36 is a particularly powerful chapter, so the fact that it has statistical salience supports this impression and gives additional impetus for further qualitative analysis. Following a sensuous—but chaste—courtship, the poor milkmaid Tess Darbeyfield marries Angel Clare, a minister's son. On their wedding night, Tess confides to her new husband that she was raped by her previous employer and gave birth to a child who died. Despite the fact they are deeply in love, Angel cannot see past this news because she is not 'pure' to him anymore. Chapter 36 begins the morning after, as the couple deal with the fallout in which Tess is wrought with anguish and Angel is cold, unforgiving and taking the moral high ground. Angel states his position to Tess:

> "I thought – any man <u>would</u> have thought – that by giving up all ambition to win a wife with social standing, with fortune, with knowledge of the world, I <u>should</u> secure rustic innocence as surely as I <u>should</u> secure pink cheeks, but – However, I am no man to reproach you, and I <u>will</u> not."
> Tess felt his position so entirely that the remainder had not been needed.

The modal auxiliaries *would* and *should* mark the belief held by Angel (and he thinks, 'any man') that in foregoing social value in his bride, he deserved chastity. With the incomplete sentence, he stops short of calling her unchaste and claims he 'will not' reproach her, implying that it may be possible (for some men). Tess understands the implication, so he manages to denigrate her while assuming a position of social and moral superiority, normalising it as one of 'any man'. Angel's socially determined expectations of womanhood (a product of a patriarchal and classist system) create an epistemic modal-world, a belief, which he feels is violated by Tess' revelation. All this is notwithstanding the cruel injustice in further punishing and, therefore, revictimising Tess.

As they attempt to figure out how to proceed, the newlyweds advance their contrasting thoughts, wishes and obligations, which explains the high density of modality in Chapter 36. Because modal auxiliaries feature heavily in their dialogue, we base the following analysis on their Direct Speech in Chapter 36. ◘ Figure 2.8 presents a distilled depiction of the modal-worlds created by Tess and Angel in their dialogue.

As discussed in ▶ Sect. 2.3.1, the discourse-world features are shaped by the reader's context; the text-world has moved to Chapter 36's post-marital breakdown. Because we focus on modal auxiliary verbs used by the enactors in Direct Speech, they all emanate from the enactor text-world (▶ Sect. 2.3.5). Tess claims she did not intend to trap Angel in marriage because she thought divorce was a possibility, albeit one she did not want; he says it is not legal in their case. Tess

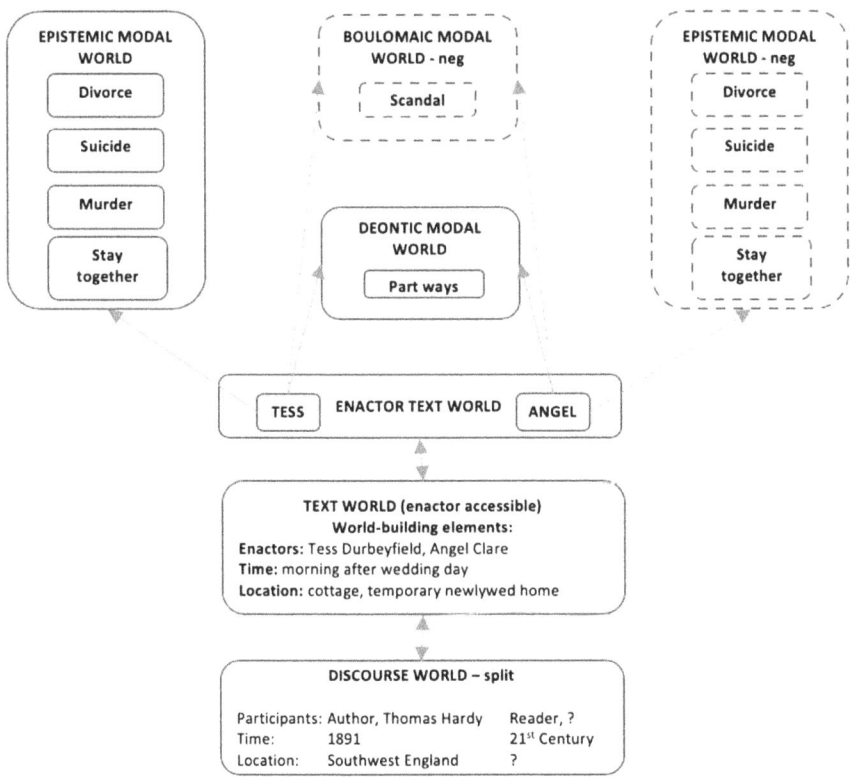

◘ Fig. 2.8 Modal-worlds in Angel and Tess' marital discussion

says she contemplated suicide after confiding in him and, when Angel dismisses it as a possibility, she suggests that he kill her himself, which he also refuses. All of Tess' suggestions (divorce, suicide, murder) are held in her epistemic modal-world and, because they are ruled out by Angel, in his negated epistemic modal-world. The distance between their epistemic modal-worlds represents their opposing views on possible steps forward (◘ Fig. 2.8).

Angel insists, however, on staying together in the cottage for a few days to avoid a scandal, a social threat they both fear and an unwanted consequence of all the other possibilities discussed, represented in their shared negated boulomaic modal-world (◘ Fig. 2.8). During their impasse, he chastises her for overdoing it in the kitchen:

> "You are not my servant; you are my wife."
> She raised her eyes, and brightened somewhat. "I may think myself that—indeed?" she murmured.
> "You *may* think so, Tess! You are."

Tess' use of modal auxiliary 'may' emphasise her belief in the marriage. Of course, we might also consider how 'may' can have a deontic reading, whereby Tess seeks Angel's permission on her self-identity. After three torturous days, he decides that, because the truth might come to light later, he 'cannot' stay in the marriage, captured in his negated epistemic modal-world (◘ Fig. 2.8). Unable to argue, Tess finally proposes that they 'should' part ways depicted in the shared deontic modal-world (◘ Fig. 2.8). As this is the only outcome that they both agree on, it alters the course of their relationship and seals Tess' tragic fate.

For reasons of space, it has not been possible to consider or reproduce all the modal auxiliaries in Chapter 36, nor all their possible interpretations. However, in our analysis so far, we introduced the epistemic modal-world in which Angel believes femininity to be impingent on chastity which is so strong that it overcomes his feelings towards his new wife. Angel's belief system is supported by Victorian social norms and accepted unquestioningly by Tess. Subsequently, using the diagram to summarise the data, we have demonstrated how the modal-worlds evoked by the enactors cohere and diverge, influencing their decision-making and changing the course of events in the novel (◘ Fig. 2.8). Socio-political forces in the text-world influence their use of modal-worlds and their choices about how to proceed in the text-world. Thus, the characters in *Tess* are shaped by the socio political morals of the time. Tess is not only a victim of her poverty, like her father, but also her gender.

This section has demonstrated how, when a corpus approach is employed to identify where a particular feature of interest is over/under-used in a text, the researcher then has a principled means to select an extract for more detailed, qualitative analysis. While we have applied this process to modal auxiliary verbs and explored them using modal-worlds of TWT, the same corpus-assisted method of data selection could be employed with other linguistic features and models.

2.5 Conclusions

We realise we have started this book by considering the biggest and most complex questions, how fiction creates a 'world'. But by doing so, we hope to have provided an overview of how discourse is constructed. An ambitious model, TWT aims to account for the contextual features surrounding discourse, and their effect on discourse processing, as well as a huge variety of textual features which contribute to building and developing mental representations of discourse. For this reason, it cannot practically be fully applied to whole novels or long texts. We have demonstrated, though, how a corpus analysis of a long text can identify where features of interest are over/under-used, providing a 'way in' for the more detailed analysis TWT entails.

TWT can be combined with Ryan's taxonomy of accessibility relations (▶ Sect. 2.2) to gain a better understanding of how the fictional text-world differs from reality and how this relates to literary genre and effect (Hidalgo-Downing 2000a; Vassilopoulou 2008; Lugea 2013). TWT helps in understanding discourse structure and how the discourse relates to reality, in understanding how a fictional world is built, advanced and can be broken into component spatio-temporal and modal-worlds. However, other stylistic details may be lost in the process of capturing all this, for which models outlined elsewhere in this textbook may be more applicable.

We encourage our readers to try text-world analysis for themselves, although a few cautionary words might make this a more rewarding process. Text-world diagramming is a way of illustrating, in as simple a way as possible, the very complex elements involved in processing discourse. As such, diagramming inevitably loses some of the details, and the written analysis that goes alongside a diagram is paramount. We recommend using the text-world diagram, first, as a way to explore the text and to find patterns and, second, as a tool to illustrate the points you eventually want to make about the text. Sometimes, simplified diagrams that do not include *all* the information may be the best way to summarise your analysis of longer stretches of text (e.g. ◘ Figure 2.8). Even without the diagraming, TWT nevertheless provides useful terms for describing how readers process discourse, which will be employed in the remainder of this book.

- **Further Reading**

For a comprehensive introduction to Text World Theory:
Gavins, J. 2016a. Text-Worlds. In *The Bloomsbury Companion to Stylistics*, ed. V. Sotirova, 444–457. London and New York: Bloomsbury.
Gavins, J. 2007. *Text World Theory: An Introduction*. Edinburgh: Edinburgh University Press.

For an accessible introduction to possible worlds:
Ryan, M. L. 2012. Possible Worlds. In Hühn, Peter et al., eds. *The Living Handbook of Narratology*. ▶ http://www.lhn.uni-hamburg.de/article/possible-worlds (Last accessed: 2nd October 2017).

- **Resources**

Possible worlds: ▶ http://www.lhn.uni-hamburg.de/article/possible-worlds.
Deixis: ▶ http://linguistics.oxfordre.com/view/10.1093/acrefore/9780199384655.001.0001/acrefore-9780199384655-e-213.
Text-World Theory: ▶ https://textworldtheory.org.
Standard deviation: ▶ https://www.mathsisfun.com/data/standard-deviation.html.
CLAWS Tagger: ▶ http://ucrel-api.lancaster.ac.uk/claws/free.html.
Up to 100,000 words can be entered and tagged online. Texts such as *Tess* that are greater than 100,000 words need to be split into smaller chunks before tagging.
CLAWS is also available via *Wmatrix* (Rayson 2009).
Alternative POS tagger: *TagAnt* - ▶ https://www.laurenceanthony.net/software/tagant/.

- **Notes**

1. Ryan (1991a, 1991b) calls the real world the Actual World, which is equivalent to the discourse-world in Text-World Theory (Werth 1999). Ryan's Text Actual World (TAW) is the equivalent of the text-world in Text-World Theory, meaning the world created by the text.
2. More precisely, when there are two contradictory propositions, they cannot be both true at the same time and in the same sense (principle of non-contradiction), and when one is true the other must be false (principle of excluded middle).
3. For an alternative approach TWT and speech presentation, see Lugea (2016a)
4. 'Readerly' originates from Barthes (lisible = legible) and means texts that are not demanding on the reader that the reader can sit back and enjoy (generally nineteenth-century realism). According to Barthes, there are also writerly texts (scriptable)—generally modernist texts—which are supposed to give a heightened sense of pleasure. In cognitive stylistics, readerly refers to reader's cognition, and a readerly understanding is an understanding based on Text + Cognition.
5. Microsoft Office online support explains how to use this function.

References

Canning, P., Ho, Y. and Bartl, S. 2021. Worlds of Evidence: Visualising Patterns in Witness Statements in the Aftermath of the Hillsborough Football Stadium Disaster. *English Text Construction* 14, 1: 25–67.

Cruikshank, T. and Lahey, E. 2010. Building the Stages of Drama: Towards a Text World Theory Account of Dramatic Play-Texts. *Journal of Literary Semantics* 39, 1: 67–91.

De Beaugrande, R. A. 1980. *Text, Discourse and Process. Advances in Discourse Processes*, Vol. IV, ed. R. O. Freedle. Norwood, NJ: Ablex Publishing.

Gavins, J. 2001. The Absurd Worlds of Billy Pilgrim. In *Poetics, Linguistics and History: Discourses of War and Conflict*, eds. I. Biermann and A. Combrink, 402–16. Potchefstroom: Potchefstroom University Press.

Gavins, J. 2005. (Re)thinking Modality: A Text-World Perspective. *Journal of Literary Semantics* 34, 2: 79–93.

Gavins, J. 2007. *Text World Theory: An Introduction*. Edinburgh: Edinburgh University Press.

Gavins, J. 2013. *Reading the Absurd*. Edinburgh: Edinburgh University Press.
Gavins, J. 2016a. Text-Worlds. In *The Bloomsbury Companion to Stylistics*, ed. V. Sotirova, 444–457. London and New York: Bloomsbury.
Gavins, J. 2016b. Stylistic Interanimation and Apophatic Poetics in Jacob Polley's 'Hide and Seek'. In *World-Building: Discourse in the Mind. Advances in Stylistics*, eds. J. Gavins and E. Lahey, 277–292. London and New York: Bloomsbury.
Gavins, J. and Lahey, E., eds. 2016. *World-Building: Discourse in the Mind. Advances in Stylistics*. London and New York: Bloomsbury.
Halliday, M.A.K. 1994. *An Introduction to Functional Grammar*. 2nd ed. London: Arnold.
Halliday, M. A. K., & Matthiessen, C. M. I. M. 2014. *Halliday's Introduction to Functional Grammar*, 4th ed. London and New York: Routledge.
Hardy, T. 1984. *The Life and Work of Thomas Hardy*, ed. M. Millgate. Houndmills, Basingstoke: Macmillan.
Hidalgo-Downing, L. 2000a. Negation, Text Worlds and Discourse: The Pragmatics of Fiction. Advances in *Discourse Processes series*. Vol. 66. Stamford, CT: Ablex Publishing.
Hidalgo-Downing, L. 2000b. Negation in Discourse: A Text World Approach to Joseph Heller's Catch-22. *Language and Literature* 9, 3: 215–239.
Hidalgo Downing, L. 2003. Negation as a Stylistic Feature in Joseph Heller's Catch-22: A Corpus Study. *Style* 37, 3: 318–341.
Ho, Y., Lugea, J., McIntyre, D., Wang, J. and Xu, Z. 2018. Projecting (Un)certainty: A Text-World Analysis of Three Statements from the Meredith Kercher Murder Case. *English Text Construction* 11, 2: 285–316.
Ho, Y., Lugea, J., McIntyre, D., Wang, J. and Xu, Z. 2019.Text-World Annotation and Visualization for Crime Narrative Reconstruction. *Digital Scholarship in the Humanities* 34, 2: 310–334.
Jesperson, O. 1924. *The Philosophy of Grammar*. London: Allen & Unwin.
Leech, G. and Short, M. 2007. *Style in Fiction: A Linguistic Introduction to English Fictional Prose*. 2nd ed. London and New York: Longman.
Levinson, S. C. 1983. *Pragmatics*. Cambridge Textbooks in Linguistics. Cambridge: Cambridge University Press
Lewis, D. 1973. Possible Worlds. In *Counterfactuals*, 84–91. Cambridge, MA: Harvard University Press.
Lewis, D. 1986. *On the Plurality of Worlds*. Oxford: Basil Blackwell.
Lugea, J. 2016a. *World-Building in Spanish and English Spoken Narratives. Advances in Stylistics series*. London and New York: Bloomsbury. ▶ https://www.bloomsburyonlineresources.com/world-building-in-spanish-and-english-spoken-narratives.
Lugea, J. 2016b. Code-Switching in the Text-World of a Multilingual Play: The Senile Mind Style in You and Me. In *World Building: Discourse in the Mind*, eds. J. Gavins and E. Lahey, 221–140. London and New York: Bloomsbury.
Lugea, J. 2016c. A Text-World Account of Temporal World-Building Strategies in Spanish and English Spoken Narratives. In *Analysing Discourse Strategies in Social and Cognitive Interaction: Multimodal and Cross-Linguistic Perspectives*, eds. M. Romano and D. Porto Requejo, 245–272. Amsterdam and Philadelphia: John Benjamins.
Lugea, J. 2013. Embedded Dialogue and Dreams: The Worlds and Accessibility Relations of Inception. *Language and Literature* 22, 2: 133–153.
Lyons, J. 1977. *Semantics*, Vol. 1 & 2. Cambridge: Cambridge University Press.
Nuyts, J. 2005. Modality: Overview and Linguistic Issues. In *The Expression of Modality*, ed. W. Frawley, 1–26. Berlin: Mouton DeGruyter.
O'Brien, F. 2007. *The Complete Novels*. New York: Knopf.
Palmer, F. R. 1990. *Modality and the English Modals*. 2nd ed. New York and London: Routledge.
Rayson, P. 2009. *Wmatrix: A Web-Based Corpus Processing Environment*. Computing Department, Lancaster University. ▶ http://ucrel.lancs.ac.uk/wmatrix/.
Rescher, N. 1979. The Ontology of the Possible. In *The Possible and the Actual*, ed. M. J. Loux, 166–181. Ithaca, NY and London: Cornell University Press.
Ryan, M. L. 1980. Fiction, Non-Factuals, and the Principle of Minimal Departure. *Poetics*, 403–422.

Ryan, M. L. 1991a. Possible Worlds and Accessibility Relations: A Semantic Typology of Fiction. *Poetics Today* 12, 3: 553–576.

Ryan, M. L. 1991b. *Possible Worlds, Artificial Intelligence and Narrative Theory.* Bloomington: University of Indiana Press.

Ryan, M. L. 2012. Possible Worlds. In Hühn, Peter et al., eds. *The Living Handbook of Narratology.* ▶ http://www.lhn.uni-hamburg.de/article/possible-worlds (Last accessed: 2nd October 2017).

Semino, E. 1997. Language and World Creation in Poems and Other Texts. London and New York: Longman.

Thompson, G. 1996. Voices in the Text: Discourse Perspectives on Language Reports. *Applied Linguistics* 17, 4: 501–530.

Vassilopoulou, K. 2008. Possible Worlds in the Theatre of the Absurd. In *The State of Stylistics*, ed. G. Watson, 157–176. Amsterdam and New York: Rodopi.

Werth, P. 1995. How to build a world (in a lot less than six days, using only what's in your head). In *New Essays in Deixis: Discourse, Narrative, Literature*, ed. K. Green, 49–80. Amsterdam: Rodopi.

Werth, P. 1999. *Text Worlds: Representing Conceptual Space in Discourse.* London: Longman.

Widdowson, P. 1999. Hardy and Critical Theory. In *The Cambridge Companion to Thomas Hardy*, ed. D. Kramer, 73–92. Cambridge: Cambridge University Press.

3

Point of View

Supplementary Information The online version contains supplementary material available at ▶ https://doi.org/10.1007/978-3-031-10422-0_3.

© The Author(s), under exclusive license to Springer Nature Switzerland AG 2023
J. Lugea and B. Walker, *Stylistics*,
https://doi.org/10.1007/978-3-031-10422-0_3

3.1 Introduction

In the last chapter, we explored how discourse in general—and fiction in particular—stimulates the creation of text-worlds in our minds. In this chapter, we consider the view we are offered of the fictional world and whose (i.e. which enactor in the text-world) view that is. This chapter, then, concerns point of view in texts, in particular prose fiction. Point of view in narrative is one of the most widely discussed subjects in Narratology (the science of narrative) and Stylistics and this is largely because prose fiction comprises a three-tiered discourse structure (▶ Sect. 1.3.1). Central to this structure is the narrator, who—although possible in poetry and drama—is fundamental to prose fiction.

Our discussion of point of view starts by looking at what is meant by narrative (▶ Sect. 3.2). Following that, we go on to look at narration and different types of narrators (▶ Sect. 3.3). Then, synthesising a vast body of scholarship, we provide an overview of the textual cues that can be used to identify and analyse point of view (▶ Sect. 3.4). Such is the complexity of the topic, our aim (following Short 1996) is to provide a usable checklist of features for the analysis of viewpoint. In the final section of this chapter, we explore how corpus methods can be used to look at point of view in prose fiction.

3.2 Narrative

Narrative is central to a diverse range of texts including drama, comic strip, jokes, as well as some poems and song lyrics. We might also think of the oral tradition of storytelling, including those we tell in naturally occurring conversation. But what is narrative? To answer that question, consider the following scenario:

(i) *Someone asks you to tell them how you came to study Stylistics. You respond by telling your story about your journey to Stylistics from wherever you deem to be the starting point.*

Your response forms a discourse between you and your addressee(s). The series of events that you select is the **story**, your telling of the story is the **narration**, and the discursive interaction is the **narrative**. Applying the terms, we introduced in the previous chapter; this narrative discourse would create a discourse participant accessible text-world (▶ Sect. 2.3.2).

Narrative, then, is a combination of story (what is told) and narration (the telling of the story) (Genette 1980: 25–27). This distinction between story and narration originates from Russian Formalism and was developed by French Structuralists in the early twentieth century. Notably, Tzvetan Todorov, who uses the terms *histoire* (story) and *discours* (which is equivalent to narration) proposed the following:

> […] the literary work has two aspects: it is at the same time a story [histoire] and a discourse [discours]. It is story, in the sense that it evokes a certain reality […]. But the work is at the same time discourse […]. At this level, it is not the events reported which count but the manner in which the narrator makes them known to us.
>
> Todorov ([1966] 1980: 5)

Although other scholars have developed more complex typologies (e.g. Genette 1980; Bal 1997; Rimmon-Kenan 1983), Todorov's two-way distinction has been widely adopted and echoed within narratology (e.g. Chatman 1978; Prince 2001). An important aspect of Todorov's idea is that *discours*/narration is the manner in which story events are related to the hearer/reader. That is, it is the way in which the story is told. To illustrate that point, consider this scenario which follows on from (i) above:

(ii) *A day or two later, the person to whom you told your 'how I came to study Stylistics' story goes on to tell your story to someone else.*

In (ii), your story is re-told by your addressee and while the events (we will assume) remain largely the same, the telling (the narration) will inevitably change because the identity of the narrator has changed. One obvious change is that when you told your story, you were both the narrator of and an enactor (a character) in the story, and consequently, you will have used first-person pronouns to describe your actions. However, the new narrator will use third-person pronouns to describe your actions. The re-narration will, therefore, present the story from a different point of view, and this will affect, for example, deixis (which we introduced in ▶ Chapter 2) and the way in which enactors, actions and objects in the story are described. So the first important distinction to bear in mind is between the story, the telling of it (narration) and the discursive interaction between the storyteller and readers/listeners (narrative). Next we explore the identity that the storyteller or author adopts in the narration, i.e. the narrator.

3.3 Narrators

Narratologists broadly agree that in fictional narratives the words of the text are attributable to a narrator (Fludernik 1993; Margolin 1983, 1990). According to Bortolussi and Dixon (2002: 68–69), whose work combines Cognitive Psychology with Narratology, readers use textual cues to build a mental representation of the narrator and to construct the narrator and narratee as participants in a kind of conversation. This constructed fictional interaction varies in its elaboration in different texts. For example, in epistolary novels, where letters are addressed to a named recipient who is clearly not the reader, readers might feel like onlookers or overhearers. With other types of novels, however, readers may feel like the addressees of the narrator, a situation which causes the reader to adopt the role of narratee. Consider the following extract from *Lolita* in which the paedophile Humbert lusts after the 12-year-old girl with whom he lodges:

(1) As she bent her brown curls over the desk at which I was sitting, Humbert the Hoarse put his arm around her in a miserable imitation of blood-relationship; and still studying, somewhat shortsightedly, the piece of paper she held, my innocent little visitor slowly sank to a half-sitting position upon my knee. Her adorable profile, parted lips, warm hair were some three inches from my bared eyetooth; and I felt the heat of her limbs through her rough tomboy clothes.

All at once I knew I could kiss her throat or the wick of her mouth with perfect impunity. I knew she would let me do so, and even close her eyes as Hollywood teaches. A double vanilla with hot fudge - hardly more unusual than that. I cannot tell my learned reader (whose eyebrows, I suspect, have by now traveled all the way to the back of his bald head), I cannot tell him how the knowledge came to me; perhaps my ape-ear had unconsciously caught some slight change in the rhythm of her respiration - for now she was not really looking at my scribble, but waiting with curiosity and composure - oh, my limpid nymphet! - for the glamorous lodger to do what he was dying to do.

Nabokov (1955)

The narrator of (1), Humbert, relates an encounter with Lolita that excited him, addressing 'my learned reader' directly. In doing so, the reader is nominated to take on the role of narratee, as though in 'conversation' with the narrator. However, we are sure most readers would agree that the role is not a comfortable one. While some of the attributes Humbert assigns to his narratee may be inaccurate ('his bald head'), being cast in the role of addressee in conversation with a paedophile revealing his inner-most thoughts and desires is unsettling to say the least. Despite any reader resistance to the role, it is impossible to avoid unless you put the book down. This example demonstrates that the narrator/narratee roles that are constructed, assigned and adopted in fictional narrative can potentially have powerful effects on the reader.

3.3.1 Types of Narrator

Important textual cues for the construction of narrators by readers are personal pronouns (e.g. 'I', 'you', 'he'/'she') to refer to participants in the discourse. Narrators are often defined based on the pronouns they use (first-person, third-person and, less often, second-person). Genette (1980), who was dissatisfied with this pronoun-based taxonomy, proposed the following categories based on the position of the narrator in relation to the story:
(a) **heterodiegetic**—(hetero is Greek for 'different') the narrator is not also a character in the story so tells the story from an external perspective;
(b) **homodiegetic**—(homo is Greek for 'same'; diegesis is Greek for narrative) the narrator is also a character in the story, so tells the story from an internal perspective.

Whether a narrator is heterodiegetic or homodiegetic has a profound influence on point of view choices. Heterodiegetic narrators are often (but not always) omniscient, which means they have unrestricted knowledge about the story world including, for example, what characters can perceive (see, hear, smell, touch and taste), what they are thinking, and what motivates their actions. For instance, thinking back to our discussion of the opening of *Tess of the D'Urbervilles* in ▶ Chapter 2, the narrator is (i) heterodiegetic because she/he does not use first-person pronouns and is not a character in the story, and (ii) omniscient because she/he has access to the characters thoughts.

Homodiegetic narrators tend not to have the power of omniscience; their view of the story world is restricted to their own perceptions and thoughts. For example, in extract (1), Humbert, who is a homodiegetic narrator because he is also a character in the story he is telling, can only imagine what Lolita is thinking and desiring and we (the readers) can only take his word for it. On this basis, a general assumption is that homodiegetic narrators are less reliable than omniscient heterodiegetic narrators because their account of the story is subjective (i.e. related to an individual narrator/character in the text) and 'restricted' (O'Neill 1994). Omniscient narrators are usually taken to be reliable, authoritative and truthful. These assumptions, however, are sometimes exploited in fiction to mislead the reader and to create particular effects.

As we have seen, narrative can be formulated as 'story' (what is told) plus 'narration' (the way it is told). The way of telling a story is contingent on the narrator's position to the story (whether they were part of the action or remote to it), the extent of their knowledge, and whether they are evaluative, subjective or objective. These are all indicated by the language used in the narration and concern point of view.

Focus 3.1: Focalisation

Genette (1980: 186) distinguishes between "who speaks" in narrative (the narrator) and "who sees" (later reformulated as "who perceives" [Genette 1988: 162]). He proposed focalisation as an alternative term for 'point of view', suggesting that when the narrator only presents information or knowledge pertinent to a particular character, including their thoughts and feelings (Genette 1980: 189–190), the narrative is focalised. An omniscient narration is one with no focalisation (nonfocalised or zero focalisation) and in such narrations the narrator 'says more than any of the characters knows' (Genette 1980: 189).

Although Genette (1980) uses focalisation synonymously with 'point of view', it refers to a particular phenomenon where the text invites readers to perceive the text-world through the senses and consciousness of a character. It, therefore, recognises narrators and characters as occupants of different parts of a narrative (for discussion of this, see Chatman 1986: 194–195). While the meaning and status of focalisation have been discussed extensively, reinterpreted and criticised (e.g. Chatman 1986; McIntyre 2006; Phelan 2001; Simpson 1993), it remains an important idea (and term) in Narratology (see, e.g., Rimmon-Kenan 1983; Bal 1997), which has been adopted into other frameworks (e.g. Simpson 1993).

3.4 Point of View

Before reading on about point of view, try doing the following corpus KWIC-ie that investigates the use of the phrase 'point of view' in the BNC.

> **Corpus KWIC-ie: Point of View in the BNC**
> How is the phrase 'point of view' used and what does it mean? Using the British National Corpus (BNC), investigate 'point of view'.
> Does the corpus search help to identify different meanings of 'point of view'?
>
> ⬇ *Instructions on how to do the search can be found on the book's webpage.*

As the Corpus KWIC-ie on 'point of view' illustrates, even though the phrase 'point of view' literally refers to the visual sense and the position from which seeing occurs, both of which are physical phenomena, it is typically used figuratively in a non-visual, non-physical sense to mean ways in which something is conceptualised (manifesting as attitudes, opinions and beliefs). Indeed, this is the meaning that dictionaries tend to list first. Similarly, when we talk about point of view in fiction, we mean both visual and non-visual (figurative) perspectives. It is partly for this reason that Chatman (1990) divides point of view into perceptual (relating to the senses and position of perceiving) and conceptual (relating to, for example, beliefs and attitudes).

Narrative texts contain information that gives an impression of who or what is telling the story and the (perceptual/conceptual) point of view they are telling the story from. The text invites us to experience the text-world from that point of view which it can do along various dimensions, including:

- Time—the text can position us in time, so that we share the same temporal viewpoint as an enactor.
- Space—the text can create the impression that we are sensing (seeing, hearing, etc.) the text-world from the point of view of an enactor thus positioning us spatially with that enactor (a narrator or character).
- Knowledge—the text can create a viewpoint that is certain/uncertain about aspects of the text-world or makes assumptions about what other discourse participants or enactors know/do not know.
- Attitude—we might experience the text-world via the opinions, attitudes and evaluations of an enactor, and this may present a particular ideological position.

To summarise, the text creates an impression of a narrator and the position from which they tell the story: either inside (homodiegetic) or outside (heterodiegetic). This positioning is fundamental to other aspects of point of view. The text also creates impressions about the point of view being taken to aspects of the story along different dimensions, including time, space, knowledge and attitudes. Point of view analysis concerns investigating linguistic cues that are likely to create an impression of point of view in all its types. In the following section, we will examine some of the linguistic cues to point of view in more detail, drawing on a broad spectrum of scholarship.

👁 **Focus 3.2: Deictic projection and deictic shift theory**
In ▶ Chapter 2 (Focus 2.2), we described deixis as the way language links textual referents to the context of discourse production, known as the **deictic centre** (Levinson 1983: 64) or **origo** (Bühler 2011 [1934]). More specifically, a deictic centre is the reference point to which deictic expressions are anchored (along dimensions of space, time, person and society) and from which they are to be interpreted and understood. Recall that deixis is contextual and therefore deictic expressions (sometimes referred to as deictics) do not have fixed referents; what they refer to depends on the context in which they are used. A basic distinction that can be drawn with deictic expressions is that they express position near to (**proximal**) or away from (**distal**) the speaker.

Deictic projection refers to our ability to assume "the spatiotemporal location of the addressee" when "separated in space and time" (Lyons 1977: 579), meaning that we can mentally shift our deictic centre and experience things from the other person's point of view. According to Bühler (2011 [1934]), deictic projection also occurs in imaginary situations, including narrative. In narratives, deictic expressions are associated with an imaginary observer (a narrator or character in a text) in what Bühler calls *Deixis am Phantasma* or imagination-oriented deixis (Bühler 2011: 140). This type of deixis, which utilises the same deictic expressions used in face-to-face interactions, leads the reader into "the realm of constructive imagination" and guides them around the "phantasy product" where they can "see and hear what can be seen and heard there" (Bühler 2011: 140). Importantly, in imagination-oriented deixis, the deictic centre is transferred to the imaginary observer (narrator or character in the story).

Deictic Shift Theory (DST), developed by academics at University at Buffalo (see, e.g., Duchan et al. 1995), builds on the idea of deictic projection. DST aims to explain how readers become immersed in texts and take up different points of view or cognitive positions within the story world. A **deictic shift** refers to our capacity to take up imagined positions, understand deictic expressions and shift our deictic centre to one in an imagined text-world using textual information.
Useful introductions to and analyses using DST can be found in:
- Stockwell (2002)—which includes an analysis of prose fiction and a poem.
- McIntyre (2006)—which focuses on play texts and provides a detailed critique of the theory and proposes some developments, which are demonstrated via an extended analysis of a play.

3.5 Linguistic Cues for Point of View

Narrators and point of view are inferred from the language choices in the text and are constructed via a combination of text and cognition. The textual cues for point of view we discuss here follow the work of Fowler (1996), Short (1996) and Simpson (1993). We start with cues that relate to time and space, which include markers of deixis (see ▶ Chapter 2, Focus 2.1; see also Focus 3.2 on Deictic Shift Theory) and language that indicates perception. We then move on to language that indicates point of view in relation to knowledge (given and new information). Then, following Simpson (1993) and Fowler (1986), we discuss point of view indicators relating to modality (briefly introduced in ▶ Chapter 2).

3.5.1 Temporal Point of View

When a scene or event is described in discourse, its temporal relation to the moment of speaking or writing is encoded through temporal deixis, mainly via tense. Past tense, the most common in fictional narrative, indicates that the narrated events are prior to the moment of narration. Temporal deixis is also marked by some time adverbs (e.g. 'now', 'soon', 'later', 'recently', 'yesterday', 'today', 'tomorrow') and noun phrases (e.g. 'last year', 'this week', 'next month'). What makes these terms deictic is that their referents can only be understood if you know the temporal viewpoint from which they are uttered. Readers interpret the temporal deictic markers in texts to understand the temporal relationship between the moment of reading, the moment of narrating, and the time the narrated events and actions took place (see Focus 3.2).

 Activity 3.1: Deictic Projection Through Time
Imagine you arrive at a shop door to find this sign stuck to the locked door.
- What time will the shopkeeper be back?
- Why does this message fail to help you infer what time the shopkeeper will return?

Our answer can be found on the book's webpage.

Consider again extract (1) from *Lolita*, Humbert uses the past tense to describe the encounter with Lolita (e.g. "she bent", "I was sitting"), placing the event temporally before the moment of narrating and the moment of reading. Notice, though, that the narrator then switches to the present tense ("I cannot tell", "I suspect") to address "my learned reader". Typically, the present tense is used in face-to-face interaction, so its use here is likely to cue the reader to create a "mental representation" (Bortolussi and Dixon 2003) of this narration as a conversation. Although Humbert switches back to the past tense to continue to describe the encounter with Lolita, his use of the proximal temporal deictic adverb 'now' ("for now she was [...] waiting with curiosity and composure [...]") is at odds with the past tense. The effect of this deviation is to further draw the reader in to sharing an uncomfortable viewpoint (or deictic centre; see Focus 3.2) with the narrator at the moment of his lustful behaviour. Temporal cues, then, may not only serve temporal functions in narrative, but can also be used to create proximal or distal psychological viewpoint effects (Lugea 2016b).

3.5.2 Spatial Point of View

Textual cues relating to space and spatial relationships between objects, people and places are important for creating the impression of a perceiver (whether narrator or character) and their perceiving position (Fowler 1996: 162; Bortolussi and Dixon 2003: 184–188). Spatial deixis is of key importance for inferring point of view (Short 1996: 269–271), because it links the physical setting with the position from which it is seen. It is expressed through demonstrative pronouns/determiners (e.g. 'this', 'that', 'these', 'those'), some adverbs (e.g. 'here', 'there') and certain verbs (e.g. 'come', 'go', 'bring', 'take'). In extract (1), the homodiegetic narrator Humbert states that Lolita 'came' into the room, indicated that the direction of movement is towards his deictic centre as both narrator and character.

Spatial viewpoint can also be indicated non-deictically by naming features of the fictional world, linking those features and indicating spatial relations between them. This can be achieved by the use of other adverbs of space (e.g. 'north', 'south', 'up', 'down', 'above', 'below', 'behind', 'forward', 'backward', 'left', 'right') and prepositions (e.g. 'in', 'at', 'on') and prepositional phrases (e.g. 'in front of'). We can see these non-deictic cues at work in extract (1) to position Lolita in relation to Humbert ("over the desk", "upon my knee", "three inches from"). Fowler (1996) proposes that the use of prepositions and adverbs to order and sequence information can indicate the way they are perceived from a certain vantage point. He goes on to say that such descriptions "do not simply refer to locations, they also relate them", so the sequencing of information can imply a starting point for viewing and "a chain of perceptions moving from that position" (Fowler 1996: 164; see also Short 1996: 275–276).

Within Cognitive Grammar (CG) this 'chaining of perceptions', where elements of a scene are described in a contiguous series (like a moving film shot), is known as 'sequential scanning' (Langacker 1987; Stockwell 2002; Giovanelli and Harrison 2018). Schematic knowledge of spatial arrangements is important for the interpretation of sequencing and is indicated by what Short (1996) calls "schema-oriented language", which refers to "choosing to describe only what could be seen from a particular position" (Short 1996: 264). For example, consider the following extract from the prologue of the novel, *All the Beggars Riding*:

(2) Late May, a Thursday, the morning. Early morning, say six or half six, but the sunlight is already pouring in, through the curtainless window set high in the slope of the roof, over the narrow bed and the sheets and the bare boards of the floor, flooding the room and everything in it, so that everything feels lit from inside.

Caldwell (2013: 1)

Activity 3.2: Spatial Point of View
Before reading on, consider the following question: Where would you place the perceiving eye—outside the room or inside the room?

The prepositions used to describe the direction of the light rays indicate that the perceiving eye is inside the room because the light pours 'in' and makes everything feel 'lit from inside'; note that the special viewpoint entails a sensory one too, where the perceiver's proximity to the rays means their light is *felt* (▶ Sect. 3.5.2.1). Furthermore, our **schematic knowledge** of houses and rooms tells us that the best-place to identify that a window is 'curtainless' is if you are looking at it from inside. The **sequencing of events** is also important for viewpoint. Notice that the description of the sunlight entering the room starts from the window, where the sunlight enters, over the bed and then down to the floor. The viewing position of this **sequential scanning** is not, for example, under the sheets peering through them, but away from the bed, observing the room and "everything in it".[1]

3.5.2.1 Verbs of Perception

As previous scholars have demonstrated (Short 1996: 288–289; Fowler 1996: 172; Uspensky 1973), point of view can also be indicated by verbs of perception and cognition. Uspensky (1973) uses the term ***verba sentiendi*** (derived from Latin for feel, perceive) to describe verbs that indicate a character's sensory experiences (see, hear, taste, touch, smell), feelings and thoughts, and give apparent perceptual access to a character. Note also that nominal forms such as, for example, 'gaze' and 'view' and reference to sensory organs can indicate acts of perception. When presented with such information in a text, a reader may attribute perceptual knowledge to the perceiver (narrator or character), known as perceptual attribution (Bortolussi and Dixon 2003: 188–189). In this way, verbs of perception can also be important indicators of a spatial viewpoint. As mentioned above, the narrator of Example (2) uses 'feel' to a refer to physical sensation that could only be experienced from a position within the room.

3.5.3 Point of View and Knowledge

According to Fowler (1996) (see also Uspensky, 1973), texts make assumptions about 'who knows what', and such assumptions present the text-world from a particular point of view. Information that the speaker/narrator assumes the addressee to know is referred to as **given**, whereas information that is not shared is **new** (Prince 1981; Short 1996). Information is said to be given if it has already been mentioned in the discourse (anaphora) or if the speaker/narrator assumes that the named entity is known universally (e.g. 'the sun', 'the moon', 'the sky') or is culturally established ('the immortal bard'; 'the Eiffel Tower'). One way in which the text can indicate assumptions about given and new information is through definite and indefinite reference, a topic we introduced in ▶ Chapter 2 (▶ Sect. 2.3.2) in relation to text-world-building.

Definite reference can be signalled by the definite article 'the', as well as personal pronouns (e.g. 'our') and demonstrative pronouns (e.g. 'this', 'that') in English. Looking at extract (2), in the opening sentence, 'the' pre-modifies 'sunlight' and 'curtainless window', suggesting that the information has already been introduced in the discourse or is accessible because it is shared or common knowledge. However, because the extract is taken from the beginning of the novel and this is the first mention of these referents, this is new information for the reader. Therefore, as we saw with *Tess* (which we discussed in ▶ Chapter 2, ▶ Sect. 2.3.2), the definite reference at the start of the narrative signals that it begins *in media res*. In this situation, the narrator appears to assume that information is shared with the reader, and this can draw us into the narrator's perspective and, as Short (1996: 267) remarks, encourage us "to feel intimately involved with what is going on from the beginning of a story".

Zubin and Hewitt (1995: 135), two scholars who worked on Deictic Shift Theory (see Focus 3.2), also suggest that definite reference has the potential to foreground or individuate objects in a scene. According to Ehlich (1982: 325), this can have a 'focussing' effect and direct an addressee's "attention towards a specific item which is part of the respective deictic space". Zubin and Hewitt (1995: 133) also note that readers see definite reference from the point of view of the narrator or character in the story. We can observe these effects in (2), where the definite reference brings the 'sunlight' and arguably the 'window' into focus and draws the reader into a shared viewpoint with the narrator.

In English, **indefinite reference** is marked through the use of the indefinite article 'a/an', or indefinite pronouns (e.g. someone). Indefinite reference indicates that the speaker/writer assumes the information being introduced is 'new', previously unknown, suggesting a particular viewpoint. For example, in an extensive study of dementia fiction, Lugea (2022) found that the forgetfulness of characters with dementia is often depicted through marked use of indefinite reference. For instance, in Bernlef's (1988) novel, *Out of Mind*, the homodiegetic narrator, Maarten, has dementia and describes his wife as follows: "An older woman, her brown hair pinned up wearing a black high-necked dress. (She is as complete as you could wish the image of a person to be.)". Maarten's wife Vera is already well-known to readers at this stage in the novel and, obviously, to Maarten. His use of the indefinite article 'an' suggests the limits of his memory at this point, inviting the reader to share in his viewpoint where the woman in front of him is unknown. It is interesting that despite the fact she appears 'new' to him, her image inspires feelings of satisfaction in him ('complete as you could wish'). Lugea (2022) also found that indefinite pronouns (e.g. someone, somewhere, something, everywhere, nowhere) were statistically over-represented in a corpus of dementia fiction when compared against a reference corpus providing further evidence that indefinite reference is key to representing knowledge, or its limitations, in narrative.

3.5.4 Point of View and Modality

We now turn to an aspect of point of view that relates to authoritativeness, attitude and opinion. This type of point of view, according to Uspensky (1973: 8), is "manifested on the level we may designate as ideological or evaluative", and has been referred to in different terms, including conceptual (Chatman 1978), psychological (Rimmon-Kenan 1983) and ideological (Fowler 1996) viewpoint. Similarly, the term 'stance' has also been used to describe the encoding of "personal feelings, attitudes, value judgements, or assessments" in texts (Biber et al. 1999: 966). Our choice of the term 'modality' follows Fowler (1996: 78–79) who uses the term to refer to various sorts of value judgments and personal feelings and attitudes in a text. As Fowler (1996: 166) explains, modality is:

> […] the means by which people express their degree of commitment to the truth of the propositions they utter, and their views on the desirability or otherwise of the states of affairs referred to.

Our discussion of modality draws on Simpson (1993), who builds on Fowler's (1986, 1996) and Uspensky's (1973) taxonomies of narrative viewpoint and incorporates the three kinds of modality (which we outlined in ▶ Chapter 2): epistemic, buolomaic and deontic. According to Simpson's (1993) framework, modal expressions indicate the attitude taken by narrators towards the story and story elements they narrate. **Epistemic** is to do with commitment to truth (uncertainty/certainty), **deontic** is to do with obligation and necessity, and **buolomaic** relates to wants and desires. To take into account Fowler's broad view of modality, which includes 'views on desirability' (see the quotation above), we add **evaluation** to Simpson's model.

3.5.4.1 Doubt and Uncertainty

Doubt and uncertainty can be suggested by modal auxiliary verbs (e.g. 'might', 'could'), verbs of perception ('think', 'believe') and so-called words of estrangement (Uspensky 1973: 75). The latter include adverbs, such as 'evidently' 'apparently', 'say' and 'almost', as well as "comparative structures which have some basis in human perception" (Simpson 1993: 53) such as 'it looked as if', 'it seemed', 'it appeared to be'. Such 'words of estrangement' suggest conscious attempts at processing incoming information, and, as Fowler (1996) notes, a narrator's difficulty in understanding and describing the fictional world, resulting in a sense of bewilderment and uncertainty in the narrator. Consequently, this can bring into question the reliability of the narration. Extract (3) is from Samuel Beckett's (1955) novel *Molloy*, which is a first-person, homodiegetic narration that contains many of these features:

(3) And suddenly I remembered my name, Molloy. My name is Molloy, I cried, all of a sudden, now I remember. Nothing compelled me to give this information, but I gave it, hoping to please, I suppose. They let me keep my hat on, I don't know why. Is it your mother's name? said the sergeant, it must have been a sergeant. Molloy, I cried, my name is Molloy. Is that your mother's name? said the sergeant. Yes, I said, now I remember. And your mother? said the sergeant. I didn't follow. Is your mother's name Molloy too? said the sergeant. I thought it over. Your mother, said the sergeant, is your mother's—Let me think! I cried. At least I imagine that's how it was. Take your time, said the sergeant. Was mother's name Molloy? Very likely. Her name must be Molloy too, I said.

Beckett (1955)

The epistemic lexical verbs of perception ('remember', 'suppose', 'know', 'imagine') foreground the narrator's uncertainty and the cognitive efforts he makes to provide basic information, including his name and identity. The epistemic modal adverb 'likely' and the modal auxiliary verb 'must' (used twice in this extract) express epistemic modality, as they articulate a strong belief about the truth of the propositional content. However, even if a speaker uses epistemic markers to express certainty, they inevitably introduce the possibility that the propositional contents may not be true and highlight their processing of this fact (Lyons 1977: 809). The numerous markers of epistemic modality may incline readers not to trust the narrator's judgement and contribute to the impression that Malloy is an unreliable narrator (for more on unreliable narrators, see Nunning 2015; D'hoker and Martens 2008).

3.5.4.2 Obligation, Necessity and Desire

According to Simpson (1993: 52), narrators can indicate their viewpoint on how events should unfold or how they hope for them to be through deontic and boulomaic modal expressions. Consider the following extract from *The Great Gatsby*, narrated by a character in the novel, Nick:

(4) When I came back from the East last autumn I felt that I wanted the world to be in uniform and at a sort of moral attention forever; I wanted no more riotous excursions with privileged glimpses into the human heart. Only Gatsby, the man who gives his name to this book, was exempt from my reaction—Gatsby who represented everything for which I have an unaffected scorn.

Fitzgerald (1925/2004: 2)

As would be expected from a homodiegetic narrator, he expresses an attitudinal viewpoint, using the *verba sentiendi* 'felt', and repeating the boulomaic lexical verb 'wanted'. His attitude is used to make a distinction between the protagonist, Gatsby, and what he represents, for which Nick expresses 'scorn'. The next section discusses how these kinds of evaluations also index viewpoint.

3.5.4.3 Evaluation

Evaluative adjectives and adverbs, mark the speaker/narrator's opinion and attitude concerning something (cf. Short [1996] value-laden expressions). A basic distinction can be made between positive and negative polarity (e.g. good versus bad). Consider the following extract from the beginning of *Uncle Tom's Cabin*:

> (5) Late in the afternoon of a chilly day in February, two gentlemen were sitting alone over their wine, in a well-furnished dining parlor, in the town of P——, in Kentucky. There were no servants present, and the gentlemen, with chairs closely approaching, seemed to be discussing some subject with great earnestness.
>
> For convenience sake, we have said, hitherto, two gentlemen. One of the parties, however, when critically examined, did not seem, strictly speaking, to come under the species. He was a short, thick-set man, with coarse, commonplace features, and that swaggering air of pretension which marks a low man who is trying to elbow his way upward in the world.
>
> Beecher Stowe (1852: 1)

The narrator shows an attitudinal point of view towards the characters and events described. Although the narrator uses the first-person plural pronoun 'we' to refer to his/her existence, she/he does not have a character role in the story and is, therefore, heterodiegetic. But also notice how the narrator gives away his/her viewpoint through subjective descriptions of the characters, with *verba sentiendi* 'seemed', and evaluative adjectives ('thickset', 'swaggering') and evaluative adverbs (e.g. 'critically', 'strictly'). Taken together, these features create subjective descriptions of the characters, suggesting that they are 'critically examined' from the narrator's viewpoint, which readers are invited to share through the use of the inclusive pronoun 'we'.

It transpires that the characters described in (5) are slave traders in Kentucky, USA, and their dialogue in this scene revolves around one man 'buying' a slave from the other. This might explain why the narrator questions whether the term 'gentleman', a socially deictic marker of respect, is a suitable term for the morally corrupt character. The linguistic choices provide an external attitudinal stance that is strongly critical towards the slave-trading characters which readers are invited to share, illustrating how an ideological point of view can be expressed at the narrator discourse level that differs from the ideologies espoused by characters. Indeed, *Uncle Tom's Cabin* was a best-selling anti-slavery novel in the nineteenth century that offered a strong social critique of the slave-trade via the narrator's subjective evaluation of the characters in the novel and is said to have played a significant role in changing public attitudes towards slavery. Although the narration encodes a strong sense of the narrator's point of view, heterodiegetic narrators are often characterised as reliable, a possible reason for the narrative being so persuasive. Therefore, analysing narrative point of view is crucial for understanding the attitudinal position a writer takes on the story content and the potential rhetorical or persuasive effects it has on readers.

3.5.4.4 A Lack of Modality

When the narrator makes limited use of modal expressions and instead makes unmodalised categorical assertions about events the effect is a neutral or objective point of view. In such cases, there is "straightforward physical description with little attempt at psychological development" and "subjective evaluation" is withheld (Simpson 1993: 55), so there appears to be no subject filtering the information. For example, consider the following extract from a short story, 'The Lottery':

(6) The people of the village began to gather in the square, between the post office and the bank, around ten o'clock; in some towns there were so many people that the lottery took two days and had to be started on June 26th. But in this village, where there were only about three hundred people, the whole lottery took less than two hours, so it could begin at ten o'clock in the morning and still be through in time to allow the villagers to get home for noon dinner.

Jackson (1948/2019: np)

In this fictional story, 'the lottery' refers to the village tradition of stoning randomly selected families to death. With its lack of evaluative and attitudinal markers, the narration in 'The Lottery' lends an objectivity which at first conceals the true 'game' to the reader and, once it is revealed, contrasts with the abhorrent ritual, adding to the disturbing effect. Simpson (1993: 55) remarks on "the often startling effect created when this mode is used to narrate events to which emotional involvement is normally attached".

As you might imagine (and as Simpson acknowledges), narratives where a first-person (homodiegetic) narrator narrates a story that they are part of without expressing any attitudinal point of view are quite rare. A notable exception is Hemingway, who is known for his clipped, journalistic style, which pervades even when he uses homodiegetic narrators, as the following excerpt from *The Sun Also Rises* demonstrates.

(7) The taxi went up the hill, passed the lighted square, then on into the dark, still climbing, then levelled out onto a dark street behind St. Etienne du Mont, went smoothly down the asphalt, passed the trees and the standing bus at the Place de la Contrescarpe, then turned onto the cobbles of the Rue Mouttetard. ... The street was torn up and men were working on the car-tracks by the light of acetylene flares. Brett's face was white and the long line of her neck showed in the bright light of the flares. The street was dark again and I kissed her. Our lips were tight together and then she turned away and pressed against the corner of the seat, as far away as she could get. Her head was down.

Hemingway (1926/1962: 25)

Notice that the narrator describes his love interest, Brett, with little to no evaluation, but in the same chronological, physical 'sequential scanning' descriptions that he uses for the Paris landmarks visible from their taxi. Even though he is moved to kiss her, his action is appended to a description of the street, using the coordinating conjunction 'and' as if they were of equal importance. There are no attitudinal warning signs for his actions nor indication of his motivations; instead, the reader must try to deduce his feelings from the stark descriptions, which has its own beauty as a minimal style. A lack of evaluation and presentation of feelings is a hallmark of Hemingway's style. It is important to note, however, that this objective style is not constant throughout *The Sun Also Rises*, as it may be difficult and even undesirable to maintain. The same chapter ends with Brett leaving the narrator's apartment, kissing him goodbye and the narrator's psychological viewpoint comes to the fore:

> (8) I felt like hell again. It is awfully easy to be hard-boiled about everything in the daytime, but at night it is another thing.
>
> Hemingway (1926/1962: 34)

The *verba sentiendi* 'felt' and the evaluation 'awfully easy' present the narrator's feelings and evaluative opinion and, because they serve as a sudden departure from the non-modalised style of the narrative, provide an internal deviation that makes the power of the feeling stronger.

3.6 Point of View Summary

◘ Table 3.1 provides a summary of the ways in which the text can position you as a reader in relation to time, space and so on, along with examples of linguistic indicators.

  Activity 3.3: Untouchable
Analyse the linguistic cues for point of view in the following short extract from Mulk Raj Anand's novel *Untouchable*.
Context: In 1930s India, Bakha (a so-called 'untouchable') has gone to the house of Charat Singh (a Havildar, or army sergeant) to collect a hockey stick that Charat has promised to give him. This scene is inside the house:

> He followed Charat Singh with his gaze, curiously amazed.
> The Havildar opened a door by the side of his room and disappeared for a moment. Then he came out with an almost brand-new hockey stick which must have been used only once.
>
> Anand (1947 [1935]: 89)

  Our answer is on the book's webpage.

◘ Table 3.1 Linguistic cues for point of view

Point of view effect	Linguistic forms
Temporal position	Tense, time adverbs (e.g. *now, soon, later, recently, yesterday, today, tomorrow*) and noun phrases (e.g. *last year, this week, next month*)
Spatial position	Demonstrative pronouns/determiners (e.g. *this, that, these, those*), deictic adverbs (e.g. *here, there*), adverbs of space (e.g. *north, south, up, down, above, below, behind, forward, backward, left, right*), prepositions (e.g. *in, at, on*) and prepositional phrases and certain verbs (e.g. *come, go, bring, take*)
Assumed knowledge	Definite/indefinite articles (*the, a, an*), personal pronouns (e.g. *our*) and demonstrative pronouns (e.g. *this, that*)
Doubt/certainty	Modal auxiliary verbs: *can, could, may, might* Verbs of perception: *feel, think, seem, appear, look, say* Adverbs: *possibly, certainly, evidently, apparently, almost* Comparative structures: *as if, as though, looked like* Adjectival expressions: *it is possible that...*
Obligation and necessity	Modal auxiliary verbs: *must, should* Semi-modal verbs: *ought to, got to, have to* Adjectival expressions: *it it obligatory...*
Desire and want	Verbs: *wish, want, desire* Adverbs: *hopefully*
Assessment, judgement, evaluation	Adjectives: *good/bad; beautiful/ugly; right/wrong* Adverbs: *stupidly/cleverly; sadly/happily; carefully/clumsily*

3.7 Corpus Approaches and Point of View

As we have seen in this chapter, viewpoint in texts is signalled by a variety of linguistic forms, and scholars have provided lists of the sorts of word forms that signal different points of view. These lists can be used to provide search terms for corpus exploration of point of view in texts. Moreover, a text or corpus that is annotated for Parts of Speech (POS) using the CLAWS tagger (which we met in ► Chapter 2) enables searches for classes of words relating to point of view (e.g. adjectives, adverbs) rather than individual words. In this section, we use a small case study to show how POS annotation and corpus comparison at the level of grammatical class can reveal authorial style in relation to point of view.

3.7.1 Investigating Hemingway's Handling of Viewpoint

During our discussion of point of view in this chapter, we noted, with reference to Hemingway, that the way in which an author handles viewpoint can be one feature of their style. This point is made by Simpson (1993), who says:

[…] much of the 'feel' of a text is attributable to the type of point of view it exhibits, and, furthermore, sufficient generalizations can be made about the ways in which writers consistently draw on particular points of view.

Simpson (1993: 46)

In our discussion of Hemingway's *The Sun Also Rises* in ▶ Sect. 3.3.3.4, we noted that Hemingway was known for an objective style because he uses few modal verbs and *verba sentiendi*. We also noticed that this style feature and this way of handling point of view fluctuated across the novel. One way to assess the style of the novel with regard to its handling of point of view is to compare the novel against a collection of other novels by contemporaneous writers using our checklist of lexical features of point of view. Using corpus tools, it is possible to compare the Hemingway text against other texts and see whether such lexical features are used more or less by Hemingway when compared to his contemporaries. This can be accomplished provided we have:

(i) an electronic version of *The Sun Also Rises* (TSAR) and
(ii) an electronic **reference corpus** that brings together the works of other authors against which we can compare TSAR.

3.7.1.1 A Suitable Reference Corpus

Deciding what the reference corpus should consist of requires deciding what the corpus is aiming to represent. In general terms, the more restricted the comparison corpus is, the more straightforward it is to construct. So, if our reference contained only the novels of William Faulkner, then the corpus would contain nineteen texts. Notice though that the more restricted the corpus is, the more restricted are the questions you can answer from the comparison. So, comparing TSAR with Faulkner's novels will only tell you about the linguistic differences (and similarities) between TSAR and, you guessed it, Faulkner's novels. Your research objectives and questions should, therefore, inform your corpus building. So, if you want to know how TSAR compares against novels in general, then building a corpus of Faulkner's novels is going to offer little help in fulfilling that research goal. Likewise, if you wanted to know how TSAR compares with Faulkner's work, then a corpus of general fiction is not going to be useful. We can see then that research objectives need to be matched by a suitable corpus.

Our overall aim is to assess the subjectivity/objectivity of Hemingway's writing in TSAR. To address that aim we are going to use our knowledge of the linguistic indicators of point of view that relate to modality and see if these are used more or less in TSAR when compared against novels written by Hemingway's contemporaries. In particular, we want to assess whether the frequencies of evaluative adverbs and adjectives and modal forms (mainly modal auxiliary verbs) are unusually high or low in TSAR when compared against other novels published in the same decade (1920s).

To achieve our research aims, we built a corpus of Hemingway's contemporaries writing in the 1920s. Our corpus contains 10,000-word chunks randomly selected from 80 different novels each by a different author, all published between

1920 and 1929, inclusive. The resulting corpus, which we named USlit1920sSampler, contains an 800,000-word sample of writing published during the same decade by a broad spread of US writers.

3.7.1.2 Key-POS and Viewpoint Indicators

Using *Wmatrix* we compared TSAR against our USlit1920sSampler corpus. *Wmatrix* (Rayson 2009) is a web-based corpus analysis tool which incorporates the CLAWS grammatical parts of speech (POS) tagger, (which we used in ▶ Chapter 2), and a semantic tagger. Users upload plain, unformatted .txt versions of the text (or corpus) they want to analyse to the *Wmatrix* server using a web interface, and during the upload process the text is organised and quantified in three different ways:

1) Lexically—frequency lists of all the words in a text are generated.
2) Grammatically—using CLAWS (Garside 1987; Leech, Garside and Bryant 1994; Garside 1996; and Garside and Smith 1997) POS tagger every word is coded according to the grammatical category it belongs. Frequency lists based on grammatical groupings of words are then generated.
3) Semantically—all the words in the uploaded text (or corpus) are assigned a semantic tag using semantic analysis software called USAS (Wilson and Thomas 1997). Frequency lists based on the semantic groupings of words are then generated.

As in ▶ Chapter 2, our focus here is on grammatical categories. We compared the frequencies of POS categories in TSAR against those in the USlit1920sSampler. *Wmatrix* can perform keyness comparisons not only at the word level (to produce keywords), but also at the levels of grammar (Key-POS) and semantics (key concepts). The grammatical and semantic quantification performed by *Wmatrix* by counting the word forms within each grammatical or semantic grouping based on the tags it automatically assigns and the number of words within a group decides the group's ranking. By making the comparison we wanted to determine which grammatical categories are statistically over-and under-represented in TSAR (positive Key-POS and negative Key-POS, respectively). Then, from those lists, we want to see if any categories match up with point of view indicators summarised in ◘ Table 3.1 above. We focus on modal auxiliary verbs (which have the CLAWS code _VM), adjectives (codes beginning with _JJ) and adverbs (codes that begin with _R). We start by looking at under-represented categories.

The rationale is that if TSAR has a clipped style where the narrator withholds subjective evaluations and opinions, then there should be fewer modal verbs and fewer evaluative adjectives and adverbs, and this might manifest as general under-use.

The results shown in ◘ Table 3.2 show that there is indeed under-use of grammatical categories that align with point of view indicators. So, while the narrator in TSAR undoubtedly uses adverbs, adjectives and modal auxiliary verbs, he uses comparatively fewer. This finding lends support for the intuitive assessment about the novel having a clipped, journalistic style. However, these results are only part of the story, and we move now to the positive Key-POS categories.

◘ Table 3.2 Negative Key-POS in TSAR by comparison with USlit1920sSampler

POS	Freq. TSAR (%)	Freq. 1920s (%)	LL
JJ—general adjective (e.g. *good, big, nice*)	3062 (4.70)	45995 (5.74)	122.44
RR—general adverb (e.g. *always, only, rather*)	1620 (2.49)	25542 (3.19)	101.65
RGR—comparative degree adverb (e.g. *more*)	7 (0.01)	548 (0.07)	46.81
JJR—comparative adjective (e.g. *better, older, stronger*)	42 (0.06)	1285 (0.16)	45.62
VM—modal auxiliary (e.g. *would, could*)	920 (1.41)	13750 (1.72)	34.90
RGT—superlative degree adverb (e.g. *most*)	4 (0.01)	346 (0.04)	31.09
RRR—comparative adverb (e.g. *better, higher, faster*)	55 (0.08)	1294 (0.16)	27.30
JJT—superlative adjective (e.g. *best, greatest, oldest*)	31 (0.05)	679 (0.08)	11.85

◘ Table 3.3 Positive Key-POS in TSAR by comparison with USlit1920sSampler

POS	Freq. TSAR (%)	Freq. 1920s (%)	LL
RP: prep. adverb particle (e.g. *out, down*)	553 (0.85)	3550 (0.44)	172.29
VM21: modal phrase (e.g. *let's*)	68 (0.1)	78 (0.01)	162.34
RG: degree adverb (e.g. *very, so, quite*)	491 (0.75)	4005 (0.5)	66.13
RRQ: wh-adverb (e.g. *how, why*)	313 (0.48)	2532 (0.32)	43.76
VMK: modal catenative (e.g. *ought to*)	42 (0.06)	191 (0.02)	27.35

The statistically over-used Key-POS categories that relate to textual cues for point of view are shown in ◘ Table 3.3. We can see from the table that some categories are over-used in TSAR. This, at first sight, runs counter to intuitions about the novel. However, we should remember that results from keyness comparisons are a starting point for further analysis rather than an endpoint. Concordances can assist with further analysis.

Looking first at the RP category, this relates to spatial point of view so is not relevant to attitude and opinions of the narrator. The VM21 category only contains 68 occurrences of 'let's'. The concordances show that every instance of this short phrase falls within quotation marks and so it is part of direct speech and therefore occurring at the character-character discourse level. The first 20 concordances are shown in ◘ Fig. 3.1 for illustrative purposes.

It is the same story for the VMK category which contains 34 occurrences of 'ought to' and eight of 'used to'. All instances of the former and five of the latter are part of character's direct speech. Similarly, RRQ ('how', 'why", 'where'

Point of View

Oh , well , " I said , "	let 's	go to Senlis . " " Do n't
? " " No , not now . " "	Let 's	get out of here . She 's
you do n't . " " Well ,	let 's	shut up about it . " " I
or a minute . " " Good .	Let 's	get something else to eat
" " Yes . " " Come on .	Let 's	go and eat . " " There 's
t , is there ? Come on ,	let 's	go back to the cafe . " "
you know I love you . " "	Let 's	not talk . Talking 's all
't I say so ? I am . " "	Let 's	have a drink , then . The
s is to enjoy them . " "	Let 's	enjoy a little more of the
seen arrow wounds ? " "	Let 's	have a look at them . " T
Brett said . " Come on .	Let 's	get out of this . " " Hav
right , " said Brett . "	Let 's	have one . " " Sommelier
music stopped again . "	Let 's	go over . " Brett started
y father . " " Come on .	Let 's	dance , " Brett said . We
drummer sang softly . "	Let 's	go , " said Brett . " You
id . " " Well , anyway ,	let 's	eat , " said Bill . " Unl
stories . " " Go on . " "	Let 's	eat . " We went down-stair
make any difference . Only	let 's	not get daunted . Suppose
" Her bags fell on me .	Let 's	go in and see Brett . I s
and ? " " I say , Brett ,	let 's	turn in early . " " Do n'
ring them right up . " "	Let 's	find Bill . " " I want to
bus ride . " " Come on .	Let 's	go over to the Iruna and

◘ Fig. 3.1 The first 20 concordances for 'let's' in TSAR

and 'when') relates mainly to questions asked by characters in direct speech. The RG category, which relates to emphasis (e.g. 'very'), is a mixture of narrator and character discourse and would require further analysis, possibly to see what is being emphasised and by whom. Therefore, these overused categories mainly concern the character-character discourse level rather than the narrator-narratee and do not provide much insight into the style and POV of the narrator.

3.8 Conclusion

In this chapter, we have seen how prose fiction is not simply a story but also a telling of that story, a narration which entails a viewpoint. Authors can use language to manipulate viewpoint effects, creating distinct points of view, shifts in points of view and merged points of view. Narrative is a complex of choices concerning who is telling the story, from which viewpoint, and how viewpoints may merge or contrast for meaningful effects. Even if the viewpoint(s) provided by authors seem relatively uncomplicated, they often grant us a different perspective from our own and immersion in another viewpoint is one of the most pleasurable—and sometimes uncomfortable or unsettling—aspects of fictional reading.

It is worth bearing in mind that most of the work on viewpoint in the last century has been dedicated to fictional prose, because it is the most obvious place to find interesting and complex narrative viewpoints. As a result, many of the models and concepts advanced by researchers and summarised here are designed specifically for the analysis of viewpoint in prose fiction. Nonetheless, there is analytical potential in researching viewpoint in other fictional discourses. For example, Semino (1997) discusses how viewpoint is operational in poetry, and Dancygier and Vandelanotte (2017) look at comics and memes. McIntyre (2004, 2006) demonstrates how point of view can be detected in plays, pointing to stage directions and the use of a chorus, amongst other strategies.

Our corpus analysis of viewpoint in Hemingway's novel revealed that, while subjective viewpoint was comparatively uncommon in that text, he did attribute it to characters in their dialogue. Therefore, it is important to understand that different strategies might be used by the author at different levels of discourse. The next chapter continues examining textual choices and effects in prose fiction but moves on to consider how writers present the speech, writing and thoughts of characters. This is linked to viewpoint because it involves the incorporation of different 'voices' in a text.

- **Further Reading**

In the interests of clarity, this chapter focuses on equipping readers with terminology to describe textual indicators of viewpoint. We have chosen to avoid the complex terminology for the different kinds of narrators in prose. For useful overviews of narrator taxonomies, readers are directed to the following:

Neary (2014) provides a useful summary of the taxonomies of viewpoint, modality and narrators advanced by Uspensky, Fowler and Simpson.

McIntyre (2006: 18–56) provides an extensive and evaluative overview of key research on narrative viewpoint, including focalisation and deixis.

For corpus approaches to point of view:

Yufang Ho (2011) provides a book-length analysis of two editions/versions of the same novel, *The Magus* by John Fowles. ▶ Chapter 6 deals with using with corpus tools to investigate Point of View in the novels.

Reiko Ikeo (2016) uses frequent multi-word sequences (or n-grams) to explore the viewpoints of the protagonists in DH Lawrence's *Lady Chatterley's Lover*.

- **Resources**

Wmatrix (Rayson 2009): see the *Wmatrix* website for more details, ▶ https://ucrel.lancs.ac.uk/wmatrix/.

USlit1920sSampler: 800, 000 words of prose from US novels published in the 1920s.

- **Notes**
1. The description of the sunlight as if it were a visibly moving liquid ('pouring', 'flooding') is an example of 'fictive motion' (Talmy 1996; Matlock 2017) and emphasises the perceptual experience of someone within the room.

References

Anand, H. R. 1947 [1935]. *Untouchable: A Novel*. London: Hutchinson International Authors.
Bal, M. 1997. *Narratology*. 2nd ed. Toronto: University of Toronto Press.
Beckett, S. 1955. *Molloy*. Trans. by P. Bowles. New York: Grove Press.
Beecher Stowe, H. 1852. *Uncle Tom's Cabin*. Boston: John P. Jewett.
Bernlef, J. 1988. *Out of Mind*. Trans. by A. Dixon. London and Boston: Faber and Faber.
Biber, D., Johansson, S., Leech, G., Conrad, S., and Finegan, E. 1999. *The Longman Grammar of Spoken and Written English*. London: Longman.
Bortolussi, M. and Dixon, P. 2002. *Psychonarratology: Foundations for the empirical study of literary response*.
Bortolussi, M. and Dixon, P. 2003. *Psychonarratology: Foundations for the Empirical Study of Literary Response*. Cambridge and New York: Cambridge University Press.
Bühler, K. 2011 [1934]. *Theory of Language: The Representational Function of Language*. Trans. by D. F. Goodwin. Amsterdam: John Benjamins.
Caldwell, L. 2013. *All the Beggars Riding*. London: Faber and Faber.
Chatman, S. 1978. *Story and Discourse: Narrative Structure in Fiction and Film*. Ithaca: Cornell University Press.
Chatman, S. 1986. Characters and Narrators: Filter, Center, Slant, and Interest Focus. *Poetics Today* 7, 2: 189–204.
Chatman, S. 1990. *Coming to Terms: The Rhetoric of Narrative in Fiction and in Film*. Ithaca, NY: Cornell University Press.
Dancygier, B. and Vandelanotte, L. 2017. Viewpoint Phenomena in Multimodal Communication. *Cognitive Linguistics* 28, 371–380.
D'hoker, E. and Martens, G. eds. 2008. *Narrative Unreliability in the Twentieth-Century First-Person Novel*. Berlin: Walter De Gruyter.
Duchan, J. F., Bruder, G. A. and Hewitt, l. E. eds. 1995. *Deixis in Narrative: A Cognitive Science Perspective*. Hillsdale: Lawrence Erlbaum Associates.
Ehlich, K. 1982. Anaphora and Deixis: Same, Similar, or Different? In *Speech, Place and Action: Studies in Deixis and Related Topics*, eds. R. J. Jarvella and W. Klein, 315–338. New York: John Wiley & Sons.
Fitzgerald, F. S. 1925/2004. *The Great Gatsby*. New York and London: Scribner.
Fludernik, M. 1993. *The Fictions of Language and the Languages of Fiction: The Linguistic Representation of Speech and Consciousness*. London: Routledge.
Fowler, R. 1986/1996. *Linguistic* Criticism. 2nd ed. Oxford: Oxford University Press.
Garside, R. 1987. The CLAWS Word-Tagging System. In *The Computational Analysis of English: A Corpus-based Approach*, eds. R. Garside, G. Leech, and G. Sampson, 30–41. London: Longman.
Garside, R. 1996. The Robust Tagging of Unrestricted Text: The BNC Experience. In *Using Corpora for Language Research: Studies in the Honour of Geoffrey Leech*, eds. J. Thomas and M. Short, 167–180. London: Longman.
Garside, R. and Smith, N. 1997. A Hybrid Grammatical Tagger: CLAWS4. In *Corpus Annotation: Linguistic Information from Computer Text Corpora*, eds. R. Garside, G. Leech, and A. McEnery, 102–121. London: Longman.
Genette, G. 1980. *Narrative Discourse: An Essay in Method*. Trans. J. E. Lewin. Ithaca, NY: Cornell University Press.
Genette, G. 1988. *Narrative Discourse Revisited*. Trans. J. E. Lewin. Ithaca, NY: Cornell University Press.
Giovanelli, M. and Harrison, C. 2018. *Cognitive Grammar in Stylistics*. London and New York: Bloomsbury.
Hemingway, E. 1926/1962. The Sun Also Rises. In *Three Novels of Ernest Hemingway*, 3–247. New York: Charles Schribner's Sons.
Ho, Y. 2011. *Corpus Stylistics in Principles and Practice: A Stylistic Exploration of John Fowles' The Magus*. London: Continuum.

Ikeo, R. 2016. An analysis of viewpoints by the use of frequent multi-word sequences in DH Lawrence's Lady Chatterley's Lover. *Language and Literature* 25, 2: 159–184.
Jackson, S. 1948/2019. The Lottery. *The New Yorker*, 26th June 1948. ▶ https://www.newyorker.com/magazine/1948/06/26/the-lottery (Last accessed: 21st February 2019).
Langacker, R. W. 1987. Foundations of Cognitive Grammar, Vol. 1: *Theoretical Prerequisites*. Stanford: Stanford University Press.
Leech, G., Garside, R. and Bryant, M. 1994. CLAWS4: The Tagging of the British National Corpus. In *Proceedings of the 15th International Conference on Computational Linguistics (COLING 94)*, Kyoto, Japan, 622–628.
Levinson, S. C. 1983. *Pragmatics*. Cambridge and New York: Cambridge University Press.
Lugea, J. 2016a. Code-switching in the text-world of a multilingual play: The senile mind style in You and Me. In *World Building: Discourse in the Mind*, eds. J. Gavins and E. Lahey, 221–240. London and New York: Bloomsbury.
Lugea, J. 2016b. 'A text-world account of temporal world-building strategies in Spanish and English spoken narratives. In *Analysing Discourse Strategies in Social and Cognitive Interaction: Multimodal and Cross-linguistic Perspectives*, eds. M. Romano and D. Porto Requejo, 245–272. Amsterdam: John Benjamins.
Lugea, J. 2022. Dementia Mind Styles in Contemporary Narrative Fiction. *Language and Literature* 31, 2: 168-195.
Lyons, J. 1977. *Semantics*, Vol. 1 & 2. Cambridge: Cambridge University Press.
Margolin, U. 1983. Characterization in Narrative: Some Theoretical Prolegomena. *Neophilologus* 67: 1–14.
Margolin, U. 1990. Individuals in Narrative Worlds: An Ontological Perspective. *Poetics Today* 11, 4: 843–871.
Matlock, T. 2017. Metaphor, Simulation and Fictive Motion. In *The Cambridge Handbook of Cognitive Linguistics*, ed. B. Dancygier, 477–490. Cambridge: Cambridge University Press.
McIntyre, D. 2004. Point of View and Drama: A Socio-Pragmatic Analysis of Dennis Potter's Brimstone and Treacle. *Language and Literature* 13, 2: 139–160.
McIntyre, D. 2006. *Point of View in Plays: A Cognitive Stylistic Approach to Viewpoint in Drama and other Text-Types*. Amsterdam and Philadelphia: John Benjamins.
Nabokov, V. 1955. *Lolita*. New York: Vintage International.
Neary, C. 2014. Stylistics, Point of View and Modality. In *The Routledge Handbook of Stylistics*, ed. M. Burke, 175–190. London: Routledge.
Nünning, V. ed. 2015. *Unreliable Narration and Trustworthiness: Intermedial and Interdisciplinary Perspectives*. Berlin: DeGruyter.
O'Neill, P. 1994. *Fictions of Discourse: Reading Narrative Theory*. University of Toronto Press.
Phelan, J. 2001. Why Narrators Can Be Focalizers and Why It Matters. In *New Perspectives on Narrative Perspective*, eds. W. van Peer and S. Chatman, 51–64. New York: State University of New York Press.
Prince, G. 1981. Understanding Narrative. *Studies in 20th Century Literature* 6, 1: 37–50.
Prince, G. 2001. A point of view on point of view or refocusing focalization. In *New Perspectives on Narrative Perspective*, eds. W. van Peer and S. Chatman, 43–50. State University of New York Press: New York.
Rayson, P. 2009. *Wmatrix: A Web-Based Corpus Processing Environment*. Computing Department, Lancaster University. ▶ http://ucrel.lancs.ac.uk/wmatrix/
Rimmon-Kenan, S. 1983. *Narrative Fiction*. London: Methuen.
Semino, E. 1997. *Language and World Creation in Poems and Other Texts*. London and New York: Longman.
Short M 1996. *Exploring the Language of Poems, Plays and Prose*. Harlow: Longman.
Simpson, P. 1993. *Language, Ideology and Point of View*. London and New York: Routledge.
Stockwell, P. 2002. *Cognitive Poetics: An Introduction*. London and New York: Routledge.
Talmy, L. 1996. Fictive motion in language and "ception". In *Language and space*, eds. P. Bloom, M. A. Peterson, L. Nadel, and M. F. Garrett, 211–276. Cambridge, MA: MIT Press.
Todorov, T. 1966. Les Catégories du récit littéraire. *Communications* 8: 125–151.

References

Uspensky, B. 1973. *A Poetics of Composition: The Structure of the Artistic Text and Typology of a Compositional Form*. In Trans. V. Zavarin and S. Wittig. Berkeley: University of California Press.

Wilson, A. and Thomas, J. A. 1997. Semantic Annotation. In *Corpus Annotation: Linguistic Information from Computer Text Corpora*, eds. R. Garside, G. Leech, and A. McEnery, 53–65. Longman, London.

Zubin, S. A. and Hewitt, L. E. 1995. The Deictic Center: A Theory of Deixis in Narrative. In *Deixis in Narrative: A Cognitive Science Perspective*, eds. J. F. Duchan, G. A. Bruder, and L. E. Hewitt, 129–155. Hillside NJ: Lawrence Erlbaum Associates.

The Presentation of Speech, Writing and Thought

Supplementary Information The online version contains supplementary material available at ▶ https://doi.org/10.1007/978-3-031-10422-0_4.

© The Author(s), under exclusive license to Springer Nature Switzerland AG 2023
J. Lugea and B. Walker, *Stylistics*,
https://doi.org/10.1007/978-3-031-10422-0_4

4.1 Introduction

In this chapter, we turn our attention to the presentation of speech, thought and writing in a text—or **Discourse Presentation** as it is also known. The presentation of what characters or other people said, wrote or thought is an essential component of both fiction and non-fiction. Try recounting any personal event to another party without including what you or someone else said or what you were thinking at the time, and it is likely that you will find it is both quite difficult to do and that your story (which will contain only actions) is not particularly interesting. This is because the inclusion of the words and thoughts of characters or people in a text serves several purposes such as progressing the narrative by providing motivations or explanations for actions. Discourse Presentation also offers different perspectives on events and actions and therefore has close links with **point of view** (the topic of our last chapter). It can also provide character information, which is something we discuss further in ▶ Chapter 6.

The model of Discourse Presentation we describe in this chapter is based on Short (2012), which is a development of the original model introduced by Leech and Short (2007 [1981]). The model has been extensively researched and refined over several years through corpus-based projects and Semino and Short's (2004) book-length report of the findings from that research provides a detailed survey of the different Discourse Presentation categories. We owe much of our discussion below to that comprehensive account.

In this chapter, we will first explain what is meant by Discourse Presentation and then present a description of the model using examples mainly drawn from the HUM19UK corpus of nineteenth-century novels. We will then demonstrate one way in which corpus methods can be used in the analysis of speech, writing and thought in prose fiction. Throughout our discussions in this chapter, we use the terms **Discourse Presentation** and **Speech, Writing and Thought Presentation** interchangeably, along with their respective abbreviations **DP** and **SW&TP**. Also, following Semino and Short (2004) and Short (2012), we use the term 'presentation' in preference to 'report' or 'representation' (see Focus 4.1).

4.2 What Is Speech, Writing and Thought Presentation?

Prototypically, Speech, Writing and Thought Presentation refers to a situation where a person presents the speech, writing or thought of another person or themselves sometime after the original words were spoken, written or thought. Discourse Presentation, therefore, combines two discourse situations:
i. the **anterior discourse** (i.e. a discourse happening earlier or before in time) where the original words were spoken, written or thought; and
ii. the **posterior discourse** (i.e. a discourse coming later in time or after the original, anterior, discourse), where the presentation of the speech, writing or thought takes place.

◨ Figure 4.1 presents a summary of the prototypical relationship between anterior and posterior discourse using the presentation of speech (inspired by events in Chapter 34 of Jane Austen's *Pride and Prejudice*). In ◨ Fig. 4.1, the anterior discourse situation is a conversation between A and B, while the posterior discourse situation, which occurs later in time, is a conversation between B and C. In the posterior discourse, B tells C what A said by inserting some of the words spoken by A into their own discourse. The result is that a small part of A's discourse has been appropriated into and framed by B's discourse both structurally and evaluatively. The structural framing includes reference to who spoke ('she'), a reporting verb form ('said') and quotation marks. The evaluative framing is achieved by a prepositional phrase ('without a flicker of emotion'), which contains B's attitudinal assessment of A (therefore encoding B's point of view). The framing of A's words and that they are a faithful rendering of what was originally said are two of the many choices open to B because, as we will see in this chapter, the presentation of speech, writing and thought can take a variety of different forms, each involving the words and structures used in the original, anterior discourse to different extents.

Discourse Presentation, therefore, provides readers or hearers with (limited) access to an anterior discourse via the mediating person/entity (the presenter) that presents the discourse. In non-fiction, such as news report, the presenter tends to be the writer/text producer who communicates with us directly, typically presenting the spoken and written words (and sometimes thoughts) of (real) people and institutions. In fiction, however, a narrator is constructed as the presenter of what characters in the story apparently said, wrote and thought. We say 'apparently' because in prose fiction there is no anterior discourse; rather, speech, writing and thought presentation creates the illusion of an anterior discourse presented to us via a narrator. Readers must use textual cues to attribute discourse to either the narrator or a character (on this point, see Bortolussi and Dixon 2002: 223).

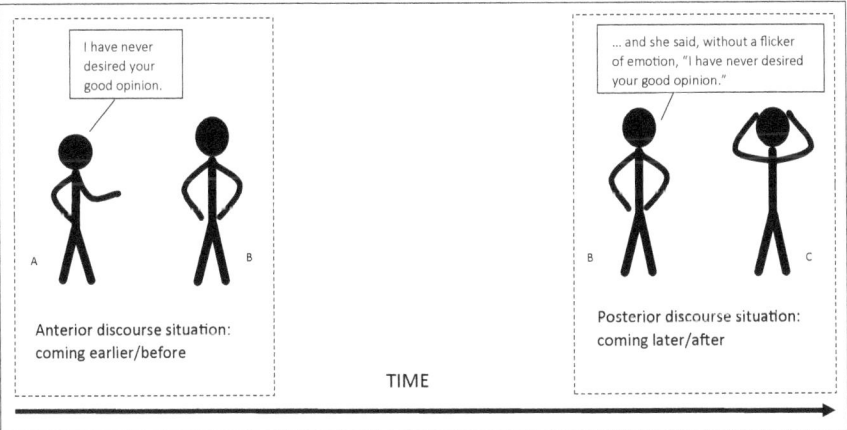

◨ **Fig. 4.1** The prototypical situation for speech presentation

In this chapter, we concentrate on prose fiction and so our discussion will be of narrators and characters. Remember, though, that the model we present is extremely relevant to non-fiction. Any presentation of other people's discourse is an act of mediation and, as Sternberg (1982: 145) points out "to mediate is to frame, and to frame is to interfere and exploit". There are numerous framing choices open to anyone presenting another person's discourse and therefore numerous ways of interfering and exploiting the original discourse to produce different effects.

4.2.1 Thought Presentation

Before we move on to describing the model of Discourse Presentation, it is worth highlighting the special status of thought presentation. As we mentioned above, Speech, Writing and Thought Presentation is often referred to collectively as Discourse Presentation (see Semino and Short 2004: 2), where 'discourse' refers to a 'connected series of utterances by which meaning is communicated' (*OED online*). Note, though, that thought is rather different from speech and writing. For one thing, communication of meaning between people via thought is currently impossible in the real world (although it can happen in fictional worlds). Furthermore, it is debatable whether thoughts count as utterances or are composed of words, phrases and sentences. We can perhaps see thought as discourse with oneself; as inner self-communication, where thoughts have meaning to the thinker and sometimes manifest in ways that can be verbalised and presented to others. In fiction, we can be given apparent access to character thoughts via the narrator in a variety of different ways, and the study of thought and fictional minds has been the focus of several scholars (see, e.g., Cohn 1978; Fludernik 1993; Rundquist 2014; Short 2007; Sotirova 2004).

4.3 Categories of Speech, Writing and Thought Presentation (SW&TP)

The model we introduce in this chapter, which is summarised in ◘ Table 4.1, provides a framework for the analysis of Discourse Presentation in texts. It comprises three parallel clines for speech, writing and thought, which are ordered according to the extent the narrator is involved in presenting the discourse of a character and the amount of access we have to the original. Each continuum in the model ranges from the categories (at the bottom of the table) where the involvement of the narrator is greatest, to the categories (at the top) where the character apparently has maximum involvement. Anything lying in between these two extremes is a combination, in varying proportions, of character and narrator discourses. Moving upwards through the categories in ◘ Table 4.1 coincides with a gradual transition in viewpoint, shifting from the **point of view** of the narrator, to that of the character.

Note that Semino and Short (2004) and Short (2012) use the term 'presentation' in preference to the terms 'report' or 'representation' which are used (sometimes interchangeably) in earlier versions of the model (e.g. Leech and Short 2007 [1981]). 'Presentation' is the preferred term because it makes no prior assumptions about the existence of any match/mismatch between the anterior discourse.

The Presentation of Speech, Writing and Thought

Table 4.1 The parallel clines of speech, writing and thought presentation

Speech presentation		Writing presentation		Thought presentation	
(F)DS	(Free) Direct Speech	(F)DW	(Free) Direct Writing	(F)DT	(Free) Direct Thought
FIS	Free Indirect Speech	FIW	Free Indirect Writing	FIT	Free Indirect Thought
IS	Indirect Speech	IW	Indirect Writing	IT	Indirect Thought
NPSA	Narrator's Presentation of a Speech Act	NPWA	Narrator's Presentation of a Writing Act	NPTA	Narrator's Presentation of a Thought Act
NPS	Narrator's Presentation of Speech	NPW	Narrator's Presentation of Writing	NPT	Narrator's Presentation of Thought

Also, in prose fiction the anterior discourse is an illusion created by the author who relates the imagined discourse of characters to the reader via a narrator; this makes the notions of report and representation redundant.

Corpus KWIC-ie: Describing Formal Features of Discourse Presentation

It is likely that some of the categories in the model will look familiar (e.g. Direct Speech). This CORPUS KWIC-ie task aims to test your knowledge of Discourse Presentation against evidence from real data.

Without looking at our examples below, your task is to set out a list of formal linguistic features that describe both **Direct** and **Indirect** presentation of speech using a combination of your own knowledge and evidence from the fiction section of the BNC.

1. Make a list of the linguistic features of **Direct** *and* **Indirect** Speech presentation.
2. **Now,** use the BNC to find examples of both Direct and Indirect Speech presentation (instructions on how to do the search can be found online). Use these examples to help inform your list of linguistic features.

Do the examples you obtain from the corpus search suggest features that you did not think of (or vice versa)?

When you look at your examples from the corpus, keep in mind some of the linguistic features of **point of view** from the previous chapter such as deixis and pronouns. Also consider clausal structure and verb tense.

Comprehensive guidance and discussion for this task can be found on the book's webpage. We provide a summary of the features below but do this task first before reading on.

4.3.1 Direct Speech (DS) Writing (DW) and Thought (DT)

We will start by setting out the formal attributes of Direct Speech, Writing and Thought presentation, using examples drawn from the HUM19UK corpus of nineteenth-century fiction which we introduced in ▶ Chapter 1. We will then move on to consider the possible effects of direct Discourse Presentation. Consider the following six examples extracted from the HUM19UK corpus:

(1) "My dear fellow, I congratulate you most warmly," he said. "It is the finest portrait of modern times. Mr. Gray, come over and look at yourself."

Oscar Wilde: *A Picture of Dorian Gray*

(2) "Try and come soon," she wrote to her sister.

Mona Caird: *The Daughters of Danaus*

(3) "Let the world think, and say what it likes," she thought, "I need not, and I will not care."

Julia Kavanagh: *Rachel Gray: A Tale Founded on Fact*

(4) "How long the days are now!" Jack says presently…

Elizabeth Brandon: *Red as a Rose is She*

(5) "Your threats of violence are lost on me, I can take care of myself," said Mervyn, haughtily.

Joseph Sheridan Le Fanu: *The House by the Church-Yard*

(6) He wrote accordingly on a blank leaf – "Mr. Septimus Luker, Middlesex-place, Lambeth, London."

Wilkie Collins: *The Moonstone*

The examples demonstrate that, syntactically, direct forms of Discourse Presentation are typically formed of two clauses: the independent **reported clause** which contains the original discourse enclosed in quotation marks, and the dependent **reporting clause** which contains the words of the narrator. Other terms for reporting clauses include 'quotative' (Crystal 2008).

Our corpus examples also show that within the reported clause verb tense, pronouns and deictic markers (we introduced deixis in Chapters 2 and 3) are appropriate to the original (anterior) discourse situation and reflect the character's point of view and **deictic centre**. The reporting clause can come after or before the reported clause, or in medial position which means in between two reported clauses, as in examples (1) and (3). Prototypically, reporting clauses contain an indication of the speaker, writer or thinker (via a name or pronoun) and a reporting verb. As examples (1), (2) and (3) show, the verb form used may signal the mode of the original discourse (e.g. 'said', 'wrote', 'thought') and the verb tense is appropriate to the narrator-narratee discourse (posterior discourse), so is typically past tense. However, Example (4) demonstrates that use of the present tense is also possible. Additionally, the reporting clause may include information concerning the manner of production. For example, in (5) this is achieved with the adverb 'haughtily' (we return to this aspect of reporting clauses in ▶ Sect. 4.3.2.2).

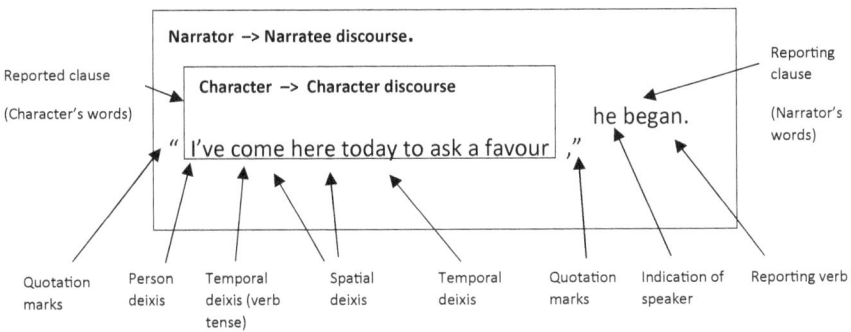

Fig. 4.2 Prototypical features of Direct Speech (DS) presentation

The prototypical formal features of direct Discourse Presentation are summarised in Fig. 4.2 using a short extract of speech presentation from Elisabeth Gaskill's novel, *Wives and Daughters*.

4.3.1.1 Possible Effects

One effect of direct Discourse Presentation can be, as Short (1996: 293) notes, to bring characters' words to the foreground. This is especially true of Direct Thought (DT) which presents mental action as though it is lexically and syntactically akin to spoken and written discourse. The linguistic status of thought is debatable but direct presentation nevertheless creates the impression of cognitive activity that is, according to Semino and Short (2004: 118) "highly conscious" and "deliberate". As Example (3) shows, such conscious and deliberate thoughts can be part of "internal, self-addressed speech" (Semino and Short 2004: 118), where characters appear to be in conversation with themselves (cf. "quoted monologue", Cohn 1978). Additionally, Leech and Short (2007: 274–276) state that direct thought can coincide with intensified emotional states, rising passions or moments of clarity. This is supported by Busse's corpus research of nineteenth-century fiction, which showed that DT occurs in moments of "heightened intensity" (Busse 2010: 270).

4.3.1.2 Free Direct Forms of Speech, Writing and Thought

Reporting clauses can be omitted from direct forms of Discourse Presentation resulting in Free Direct Speech (FDS), Writing (FDW) and Thought (FDT). For example, consider the following short extract from Dicken's *Pickwick Papers*:

(7)
    "Muzzle!" said the magistrate.
    Muzzle was an undersized footman, with a long body and short legs.
    "Muzzle!"
    "Yes, your Worship."
    "Place a chair, and leave the room."
    "Yes, your Worship."

"Now, ma'am, will you state your business?" said the magistrate.
"It is of a very painful kind, Sir," said Miss Witherfield.

Charles Dickens: *The Pickwick Papers*

In (7), some of the Direct Speech presentation is not accompanied by a reporting clause so we experience only the words of the characters without any extra narratorial comment (cf. "zero-quotative", Crystal 2008). Different turns and speakers are nevertheless discernible in the text because of the following textual cues:

- graphology—a new line for each turn and speaker;
- sequencing of turns—which makes it possible to work out who is speaking;
- terms of address (social deixis)—Muzzle addresses magistrate as 'your worship'.

Interactions that are uninterrupted by the narrator can have the effect of the exchange appearing more dramatised and *perhaps* more rapid than other exchanges around it (see also Leech and Short 2007: 259 for a discussion of FDS in *Bleak House*). However, the following example from Claire Kilroy's novel, *All Names Have Been Changed*, demonstrates that direct presentation can also be *free* by virtue of not including reporting clauses or quotation marks:

(8)   Glynn crumpled before the teenager in a gesture of feudal submission, clawing the clotted fluid from his face as if it burned. 'State a ya', the young fella pronounced in lofty judgement over the writer's bent back. The rest of the youths laughed and congratulated one another on the calibre of the joke. <u>Nice one, deadly, your man's a fucken spa</u>.

Kilroy (2009: 166–167; emphasis added)

The underlined section in (8) is, in our opinion, Direct Speech, because of the use of 'your' (deictic marker for person), present tense form of 'be' and non-standard spelling ('fucken'), which aims to reproduce the accent of the original speaker (or speakers). With free direct discourse, therefore, the reader must interpret markers in the dialogue in order to be able to assign the speech to a speaker, which may require closer attention to the text, more cognitive effort, and could lead to bewilderment and slowed reading.

◉ Focus 4.1: Text World Theory and Direct Discourse

What happens to the text-world when characters use direct discourse?

Werth (1999: 221) suggests that direct forms of Discourse Presentation produce a temporal world-switch triggered by the change in tense from the narrative, which is typically past tense, to character dialogue, which is typically present tense. Alternatively, Gavins (2007: 50) and Cruikshank and Lahey (2010: 70) suggest that the switch from narrative to character dialogue creates a personal world-switch.

Lugea (2013), however, points out problems with both approaches. Werth's view fails to consider present tense narratives, where no temporal shift is triggered between narrative and character dialogue, and, perhaps more seriously, does not address play texts which consist mostly of character dialogue and any stage directions are typically present tense anyway. Text World Theory was designed to be applied to all kinds of discourse, so it should treat direct discourse the same, whether it is used in a present or past tense narrative, or in a play. The issue with the view that each instance of direct discourse creates a personal world-switch is that it does not fit into the Text World Theory framework. TWT stipulates that (a) all discourse participants jointly create a text-world and (b) 'sub-worlds consist of the very same elements in the very same kind of patterns as text-worlds' (Werth 1999: 353). What this means is that enactors' discourse must obey the same rules as participants' discourse and, as such, character discourse must generate a character text-world (see Lugea 2013: 138–139). This is the approach we take in ▶ Chapter 2, Sect. 2.35, 'World-switching'.

4.3.2 Indirect Speech (IS) Writing (IW) and Thought (IT)

Indirect speech, writing and thought presentation merge the discourse of the original speaker, writer or thinker with that of the narrator and therefore present a blend of points of view. Consequently, indirect forms do not faithfully present the original words and structures used in the anterior discourse but, instead, render only the propositional content (or meaning). The following examples (from HUM19UK) aim to demonstrate some of the formal attributes of indirect speech, writing and thought presentation (all emphasis added):

(9) **Ellis said** that she would see whether her trunk were ready.
Fanny Burney: *The Wanderer*

(10) **Amy wrote** that she would be at home at eleven tomorrow evening.
George Gissing: *New Grub Street*

(11) **Lady Carbury thought** that she was nearly eaten up already, but said nothing.
Anthony Trollope: *The Way We Live Now*

The examples above show the prototypical features for indirect Discourse Presentation: a reported clause (underlined) which is syntactically **subordinate** to reporting clause (bold font); an (optional) subordinating conjunction, *that*, and no quotation marks. Additionally, in the reported clause, verb tense, pronouns and deixis relate to the narrator-narratee discourse (and therefore the narrator's deictic centre) rather than to the character-character discourse. We can also note from the examples that the reported clause comes after the reporting clause, and that both clauses are **finite** (i.e. verbs are marked for tense). These features are common to Indirect Speech, Writing and Thought. However, as the following examples demonstrate, variations on this prototypical structure are possible (all emphasis added):

(12) Frances **told her** to come again, whenever she was lonesome or wanted advice about anything.
Willa Cather: *My Antonia*

(13) After some consideration the duke assented, and, **promising** <u>to return on the following day and report what had occurred</u> he took his leave.

William Harrison Ainsworth: *Windsor Castle*

(14) On the evening of his arrival **he asked** <u>how far we were from the nearest town, and whether we knew of any Italian gentlemen who might happen to be settled there.</u>

Wilkie Collins: *The Woman in White*

(15) He palpitated at **the thought** <u>that she had fled to him in her trouble as he had fled to her in his.</u>

Thomas Hardy: *Jude the Obscure*

In examples (12) and (13), the subordinated reported clauses (underlined) are to-infinitive clauses. We can also notice in (13) that the reporting verb form ('promising') is non-finite. Example (14) demonstrates that reported clauses can also be wh-clauses. Notice that the questions are presented as statements whereas in the original discourse it is likely they were interrogatives. Example (15) shows that noun phrases can act as reporting clauses and that relative clauses modifying a head noun can act as reported clauses.

4.3.2.1 Possible Effects

With indirect forms the original discourse is filtered through the narrator (or person presenting the discourse). This creates a blend of anterior and posterior discourses that may contain the evaluations and judgements of the narrator. Also, because indirect forms only present the propositional content of the original discourse and not the original words verbatim, the narrator has more freedom of choice in how to present the original discourse. Indirect forms, therefore, place us more in the hands of the narrator than direct forms which results in a shift in point of view to that of the narrator. With IS and IW this shift causes the reader to be distanced from the original discourse and from the person/character that produced it. The original content, therefore, becomes backgrounded. With Indirect Thought[1] (IT), however, we are still gaining access to a character's thoughts, and any such access brings us closer to the character, which has the opposite effect to IS and IW. Additionally, Leech and Short (2007) note that IT can more readily be seen as a norm for thought presentation[2] because thoughts, while having meaning and content, are not necessarily lexically and syntactically complete structures and so there are no actual original words to present. Therefore, as Leech and Short (2007: 277) go on to say, Indirect Thought might be "perceived" as less "artificial". On a similar note, Semino and Short (2004: 128) comment that IT is more "understated" and "less dramatic" than Direct Thought.

 Activity 4.1: Transpose Direct Speech into Indirect Speech

Test out your knowledge of indirect forms of Discourse Presentation by transposing (i.e. translating) the Direct Speech we used in ◘ Fig. 4.2 into Indirect Speech: "I've come here today to ask a favour," he began.

 We give our answer on the book's webpage.

4.3.2.2 Reporting 'Clauses'

So far, in our discussion we have used the term 'reporting clause' to refer to the words that introduce both direct and indirect Discourse Presentation. However, Example (15) demonstrates that reporting clauses are sometimes not actually clauses (see Thompson 1996: 524). For that reason, other terms have been suggested including 'signal' (Thompson 1996), 'reporting device' (Semino and Short 2004: 38) and 'frame' (Sternberg 1982). Whatever term is adopted, it is important to note that the words and structures that introduce direct and indirect Discourse Presentation are NOT themselves part of the original discourse; they are part of the narrator-narratee discourse and 'belong' to the narrator. These reporting signals/devices/frames are, nevertheless, an important aspect of Discourse Presentation because of the extra information they provide about the original (anterior) discourse situation, including:

- mode of discourse indicated, for example, via reporting verbs (e.g. 'said', 'thought', 'wrote');
- who spoke, thought, wrote (i.e. attribution);
- speech act label (e.g. 'promised', 'threatened');
- manner of articulation indicated, for example, via choice of verbs (e.g. 'whispered'), adverbs (e.g. 'hoarsely'), noun phrases (e.g. 'the hoarsely whispered reply');
- emotive states indicated, for example, by adverbs (e.g. 'angrily', 'lovingly').

The mediating presence of a narrator is textually created via reporting signals/devices/frames and the information they provide relates to the narrator's point of view. For example, consider the reporting clauses that accompany the speech presentation in the following examples and think about the attitudinal information they convey:

(16) 'I think it extremely likely,' <u>replied Nicholas, in a quiet manner</u>.
'Oh, you do, do you?' <u>sneered Squeers</u>. 'Maybe you know he has?'
Charles Dickens: Nicholas Nickleby

(17) I curtly requested her to hold her tongue.
Charlotte Brontë: Villette

The choice of reporting verb ('sneered'), adverb ('curtly') and adverbial ('in a quiet manner') provides additional, evaluative information about the manner of production of the original discourse. These evaluative choices concern the attitude being taken by the original speaker, and/or the attitude of the narrator towards the original speaker/writer/thinker. Such choices are important because, as (16) and (17) help to show, they can guide how the reader evaluates characters and narrators (Thompson 1996: 507, 522).

4.3.3 Free Indirect Speech (FIS), Writing (FIW) and Thought (FIT)

Free Indirect Speech, Writing and Thought sit between direct and indirect forms of Discourse Presentation and combine narrator and character discourses, but nevertheless tend to be anchored to the narrator's deictic centre and point of view. Unlike indirect forms, Free Indirect Discourse Presentation is 'free' from reporting clauses and has no stable set of formal features, which makes it notoriously difficult to pin down. Typically, though, verb tense and pronouns are, as with indirect forms, appropriate to the narrator, while other features, such as lexis (e.g. dialect, colloquialisms), terms of address, discourse markers (e.g. 'Oh'), punctuation (e.g. exclamation marks) and syntax (e.g. incomplete sentences) are, as with direct forms, appropriate to the character. Sometimes, it is not clear whose point of view is being presented and consequently evaluative language and other markers of subjectivity can relate to either the narrator or character. In the following scene from *Northanger Abbey*, the protagonist Catherine is conversing with General Tilney, whose Free Indirect Speech is underlined in the extract:

(18) The general's good humour increased. **Why**, as he had such rooms, <u>he thought</u> it would be simple not to make use of them; but, **upon his honour**, <u>he believed</u> there might be more comfort in rooms of only half their size. Mr. Allen's house, <u>he was sure</u>, must be exactly of the true size for rational happiness.

Jane Austen: *Northanger Abbey*

Discourse markers (highlighted in bold) suggest it is the general's spoken discourse being presented, and the use of 'he thought', 'he believed', 'he was sure' (underlined) present the general's opinion and are not the narrator's reporting clauses. We can see this more clearly if we transpose the FIS into DS: 'Why, as I have such rooms, I think it would be simple not to make use of them; but, upon my honour, I believe there might be more comfort in rooms of only half their size. Mr. Allen's house, I am sure, must be exactly of the true size for rational happiness'.

We can look at the co-text for help to identify free indirect forms, examining whether some other form of Discourse Presentation occurs immediately before or after. For example, this Free Indirect Thought (underlined) is preceded by reference to cognitive activity (in bold):

(19) Hetta retired from her seat on the sofa, and when her mother again went upstairs **she turned it all over in her mind**. <u>Could it be right that she should marry one man when she loved another? Could it be right that she should marry at all, for the sake of doing good to her family?</u>

Anthony Trollope: *The Way We Live Now*

The description of her turning 'it all over in her mind' establishes a situation in which the subsequent questions can be interpreted as the questions she thought to herself, represented in FIT (underlined). As we would expect in Indirect Thought, verb forms ('could', 'loved',) and pronouns ('she', 'her') are from the point of view of the narrator, while the questions are presented in interrogative mood appropriate to the character.

4.3.3.1 Possible Effects

There has been plenty of discussion about the effects of Free Indirect Discourse in fiction (e.g. Bray 2007a, b; Cohn 1978; Fludernik 1993; Sotirova 2004) and some in non-fiction (see, e.g., Jeffries 2010). According to Semino and Short (2004: 83–85), Free Indirect Speech (FIS) distances the reader from the original discourse and can indicate the narrator's evaluative point of view towards the discourse and/or the character that produced it (see also Short 1996: 308; Leech and Short 2007: 268–270). Such distancing and point of view effects may lead to irony and sometimes humour. Free Indirect Thought (FIT), however, has the opposite effect; it brings us closer to characters by providing access to their thoughts, which may lead to a sense of intimacy and reader empathy (Semino and Short 2004: 124; see also Short 1996: 315). Semino and Short (2004: 123) also note that FIT presents character thoughts "in a dramatic and immediate way, but without the more obvious artificiality of (F)DT". On a similar vein, Cohn (1978) says that FIT (Cohn uses the term 'narrated monologue') merges the words of the narrator with the verbalised thoughts of a character in a way that suspends characters' thoughts "on the threshold of verbalization in a manner that cannot be achieved by direct quotation". She goes on to say that this merging lends stretches of FIT an ambiguity and a sense of "now-you-see-it, now-you-don't" which has a "special fascination" and is "one reason why so many writers prefer the less direct technique" (1978: 103).

 Activity 4.2: Identify the Discourse Presentation
In the following two extracts from novels, identify the Discourse Presentation.

> *(Context: Erica has received a letter from Brian)*
> … she tore open the envelope with trembling hands … He asked her to think it all over once more, he had gone away too hastily. If she could change her mind, could see any possible hope for the future, would she write to him? If he heard nothing from her, he would understand what the silence meant.
>
> Edna Lyall: *We Two*

> I noticed my serious friend's precious publications huddled together on a table in a corner. Had she chanced to look into them?-I asked. Yes-and they had not interested her. Would she allow me to read a few passages of the deepest interest, which had probably escaped her eye? No, not now-she had other things to think of.
>
> Willkie Collins: *The Moonstone*

 Our answers are on the book's webpage.

4.3.4 Narrator's Presentation of Speech, Writing and Thought Acts

Narrator's Presentation of Speech Acts, Writing Acts and Thought Acts (NPSA/NPWA/NPTA)[3] is even more indirect than the forms we discussed above because they do not even present the propositional content of original discourse but only a summary. Typically, these DP categories take the form of a reporting verb followed by a noun phrase or prepositional phrase. These formal attributes are demonstrated in the following examples (DP underlined):

(20) All chatted, and laughed, and eyed each other's dresses, and <u>gossiped about each other's husbands and servants</u> ...

Charles Kingsley: *Westward Ho!*

(21) <u>So I wrote a brief farewell</u> to Dr. Chéron

Amelia Ann Blandford Edwards: *In the Days of My Youth*

(22) <u>she enumerated to herself all the diseases incident to the climate, and the danger of the voyage</u>.

Amelia Alderson Opie: *Adeline Mowbray*

In (20), the speech verb 'gossiped' is followed by a prepositional phrase (starting with 'about') which gives an indication of the topics of conversation (note that the use of the verb 'gossip' is suggestive of the narrator's evaluation of the original discourse). In (21), the topic is contained in a noun phrase that is the direct object of the writing verb 'wrote'. Example (22), which is structurally similar, probably presents a reflexive (i.e. directed back to the thinker) silent act that was not articulated and therefore an example of NRTA (see Semino and Short 2004: 130). The examples show that, unlike IS/IW/IT which has a two-clause structure, NPSA/NPWA/NPTA are typically one clause. The information relating to the content of the original discourse and the reporting verb (or similar) are therefore not in separate clauses, which means the reporting verb (the signal/device/frame) becomes part of the Discourse Presentation. NPSA/NPWA/NPTA are, therefore, squarely in the realm of the narrator; the original discourse is presented from the narrator's point of view and the narrator (or text producer) is in control of the lexical choices used to summarise the original discourse.

This category of DP also includes the following sorts of examples; in each case, consider what we are told about the original discourse:

(23) He greeted me in his usual quiet, unaffected way ...

Ann Bronte. *Agnes Grey*

(24) He turned round, and apologised confusedly.

Sarah Grand: *The Heavenly Twins*

Both examples comprise a reporting verb and an indication of manner of articulation. Notice, however, that the verbs used indicate the essence of what was said without the sorts of summaries we saw in examples (21) and (22). Instead, the reporting verbs label the speech act performed in the original discourse, indicate the force of what was said (we talk more about speech acts in ▶ Chapter 5) and hint at the possible content of the original discourse. For example, the use of the speech verb 'greet' in (23) might lead us infer a range of possible utterances, such as 'hello', 'good morning', 'how are you?'. Similarly, in (24), 'apologise' provides a summary of the original discourse from which we might infer utterances, such as 'I'm sorry' or 'I beg your pardon'.

4.3.4.1 Possible Effects

With NPSA, NPWA and NPTA, the narrator apparently controls the presentation of discourse and chooses the lexis to summarise the original words in terms of both reporting verb and content. The content of the original discourse is backgrounded, and attention is focused on the discourse act. We are, therefore, placed at a further distance from the original discourse. With NPSA and NPWA, this can have the effect of distancing us from the character's point of view. NPTA, however, has the opposite effect and can bring us closer to a character's viewpoint. This point is made by Leech and Short (2007), who say:

> [a] writer who decides to let us know the thoughts of a character at all, even by the mere use of thought act reporting, is inviting us to see things from the character's point of view.
>
> Leech and Short (2007 [1981]: 271)

4.3.5 Narrator's Presentation of Speech, Writing and Thought (NPS,[4] NPW, NPT)

Narrator's Presentation of Speech/Writing/Thought are the most minimal forms of Discourse Presentation, where none of the propositional content of the original discourse is presented.[5] What we learn about the discourse is completely through the narrator's choice of reporting verb. McHale (1978: 258), who uses the term "diegetic summary", describes this phenomenon as "bare report that a speech event has occurred, without any specification of what was said or how". The underlined sections of the following extracts illustrate NPS, NPW and NPT. In each case, readers may wish to consider what they can infer about the original discourse.

(25) He spoke for a minute or two with Richard Carstone, not seated, but standing...
Charles Dickens: *Bleak House*

(26) He wrote for about half an hour, then replaced the document in the pigeon-hole, and locked the cabinet.
Mary Elizabeth Braddon: *Lady Audley's Secret*

(27) Lady Carbury went from the door of her son's room to her own chamber, and there sat thinking through the greater part of the night.
Anthony Trollope: *The Way We Live Now*

In the extracts, the reporting verbs indicate that discourse occurred, but we are not given access to the words that were used or the propositional content. In (25), for example, all we are told is that a character spoke with another character, but we are not given any hint of anything that was said. With these forms, then, there is only the reporting verb (or similar signal/device/frame), which is chosen by the narrator, and these alone provide information about the original discourse.

4.3.5.1 Possible Effects

With NPS, NPW and NPT, the narrator is apparently in complete control of the presentation of discourse, and we are furthest away from the original speaker/writer/thinker and their words. The distancing effect is demonstrated particularly well in Example (25) where the NPS positions us as onlookers, distanced from the characters and their discourse and not privy to the content of the conversation. This can also be true of NPT whereby we are told a character is thinking but not given access to the thoughts, as in Example (27).

 Activity 4.3: NPS and Point of View
Consider these two short extracts from novels containing NPS:

> (a) *[Harker, a solicitor who is visiting Dracula on business, is staying in Dracula's castle in the Carpathian Mountains and finds that he has been locked in his rooms.]*
> Then I ran to the window and cried to them. They looked up at me stupidly and pointed, but just then the "hetman" of the Szgany came out, and seeing them pointing to my window, said something, at which they laughed. Henceforth no effort of mine, no piteous cry or agonised entreaty, would make them even look at me. They resolutely turned away.
> Bram Stoker: *Dracula*
> (b) She fixed her black eyes steadily on him, her lips moved slightly, and she said something in French. What it was, no one knew; but Legree's face became perfectly demoniacal in its expression, as she spoke.
> Harriet Beecher Stowe: *Uncle Tom's Cabin*

In each case identify the speech presentation and then describe how it helps to indicate point of view.

 Our answers can be found on the book's webpage.

4.4 Discourse Presentation and Faithfulness

The Discourse Presentation categories and their typical effects are summarised in ◘ Fig. 4.3. The figure shows that direct forms tend to bring us closer to the original discourse, the person (or character) who produced it and their point of view. Moving down the cline, away from the direct presentation categories, distances the reader from the original discourse and brings us closer to the narrator and their point of view, with the narrator having more involvement with the mediation of the original discourse.

Each category of Discourse Presentation also carries with it different assumptions about its **faithfulness** to the original discourse. Direct forms of DP are usually said to be the most faithful because they apparently offer a **verbatim** rendering the words and syntactic structures of the anterior discourse. Indirect forms

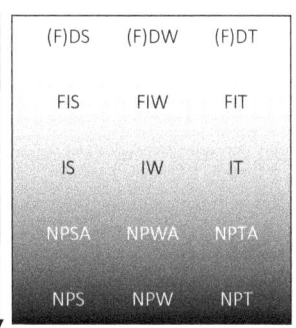

Fig. 4.3 The speech, writing and thought presentation scale, narrator involvement and faithfulness (adapted from Leech and Short 2007: 261)

are less faithful than direct forms because they do not present the original words and structures of anterior discourse but the **propositional content** (i.e. the meaning expressed). Free indirect forms combine narrator and character discourse in a manner that makes separating anterior from posterior discourse difficult. For that reason, faithfulness to the original discourse is unclear and ambiguous, which might be particularly important in non-fiction. The least direct forms—NPSA/NPWA/NPTA and NPV/NPW/NPT—are the least faithful since, at best, they only present a summary of the original discourse and not any of the original words or propositional content, with the narrator being in complete control of the language used.

While in fiction faithfulness to the original is not a concern (not least because there is no anterior discourse to be faithful to), in non-fiction the notion of faithfulness can be extremely important (e.g. see Short et al. 2002). In certain contexts, such as academic writing, the practice and expectation are that quoted words faithfully present the original discourse. However, in other contexts (e.g. newspaper headlines), direct forms do not guarantee faithfulness to the original (e.g. see Ikeo 2009, 2012; Short 1988). Similarly, while the use of indirect forms might suggest propositional faithfulness, it does not guarantee it. Expressing the proposition of an utterance using different words and structures can (subtly) alter meaning which can be of critical importance in, for example, news report (e.g. see Walker and Kapenko-Seccombe 2017).

4.5 Exploring Discourse Presentation Using Corpus Techniques

In this section, we explore how corpus approaches can be used in the analysis of Discourse Presentation in prose fiction. We will first consider some of the existing research in this area and then present a case study which analyses SW&TP in a short story. Our methodological focus in this section is on corpus annotation, which is the process of adding labels (or tags) directly to corpus data to encode the functions that sections of data are performing. So, for example, tags can be added to corpus data to indicate where different categories of Discourse Presentation occur. Adding tags is rather like using a highlighting pen to mark up a paper copy of a text. The difference is that electronic labels can be used by computer tools to quantify whatever has been labelled, but do not interfere with the text because computer tools can be instructed to ignore them.

4.5.1 Existing Corpus Research

The model of Discourse Presentation we introduced in this chapter was developed over several years via corpus research at Lancaster University. The research project used the Lancaster SW&TP Written Corpus, which contains a total of 260,000 words, made up of 2000-word samples of serious and popular prose fiction, tabloid and broadsheet news journalism, and biography and autobiography, all from the twentieth century (see Semino and Short 2004). The corpus approach adopted for the project was to manually add annotation the corpus for different categories of Discourse Presentation (we explain this process in more detail below) and by doing so account for all the data. In this way, existing categories from the original Leech and Short (2007 [1981]) model were re-assessed and new categories developed. The work also established quantitative norms for the different types of DP in fiction and non-fiction.

The technique of annotating corpus data means that all instances of all categories of Discourse Presentation are accounted for. An alternative option is to search a corpus for examples of Discourse Presentation. However, this means that findings are limited to the structural forms of Discourse Presentation that it is possible to search for. This procedure is adopted by Jucker (2006) in his investigation of DP in news discourse, and means, for example, that he does not analyse Free Indirect Discourse because this is only apparent by its co-text. Similarly, Ruano (2018), who investigates the presentation of Direct Thought in Dickens' novels, searches for forms of the verb 'think' (i.e. 'thinks', 'thought') using the corpus software, *Wordsmith Tools* (Scott 2020). While Ruano's choice of search term is (perhaps) intuitively obvious, it is also justified by Semino and Short's (2004) findings which showed, through a systematic tagging of data, that 'think' is the most used thought-reporting verb.

The approaches adopted by Jucker (2006) and Ruano (2018) can reveal informative patterns of usage of Discourse Presentation but, of course, the results can only tell you about the words/phrases you have searched for. As Ruano acknowledges, any patterns of Direct Thought found from a search of 'think' can only tell you about Direct Thought when accompanied by a reporting clause containing a form of the verb 'think'. It cannot tell you about items NOT searched for (although you might be able formulate hypotheses based on findings). So other patterns of thought presentation associated with other reporting verbs (or other linguistic forms used to introduce thought) might well be waiting to be discovered.

4.5.2 Exploring DP in a Short Story Using Corpus Annotation

We now move on to demonstrating how corpus annotation can be used in an analysis of Speech Writing and Thought Presentation in a short story by Evelyn Waugh called 'Mr. Loveday's little outing' (comprising approximately 2600 words). The aim of this small-scale study is to investigate the connections between Discourse Presentation in the story and:
i. point of view (see ▶ Chapter 3), including the strategies adopted by the writers to handle the point of view and to manipulate the reader; and
ii. characterisation (see ▶ Chapter 6).

While this study uses corpus approaches, the main thrust of the analysis is manual whereby the short story was manually analysed for Discourse Presentation. The results of the analysis, however, were recorded in the text. To achieve this, we used an electronic version of the short story and added a series of codes to mark off the different categories of Discourse Presentation each time they occurred in the story—a process known as annotation. The codes were of our own design but in the format of eXtensible Markup Language (XML). We describe and explain the codes in the next section.

Although this case study uses just one text rather than a corpus of texts, it demonstrates how the use of corpus techniques (i.e. manual annotation) can be used to document the analysis of texts and to help calculate frequencies arising from the analysis. Furthermore, by adopting a similar technique to Semino and Short (2004), we can compare frequencies of Discourse Presentation categories in the short story against the frequencies from the Lancaster SW&TP corpus thus demonstrating how previous corpus research can provide a yardstick for comparison which can inform the discussion of results.

'Mr. Loveday's little outing' (hereafter MLLO) is a third-person/heterodiegetic narrative. Lady Moping and daughter, Angela, visit an asylum where (husband and father) Lord Moping is a long-term resident. During the visit, Angela meets and talks to a doctor and Mr. Loveday. The latter is acting as Lord Moping's secretary but is also an inmate who was detained there 35 years ago after strangling to death a young woman. He appears to be completely sane, however, and both Angela and her mother mistake him for a warder. After the visit, Angela makes it her mission to secure Mr Loveday's release because she feels that his continued incarceration is unfair. After much letter writing she eventually accomplishes her goal. However, there is a surprising and tragic end to the tale, which we will not disclose here just in case you wish to read the story. That the ending is a surprise is partly due to the strategic use of Discourse Presentation in the story.

4.5.2.1 Annotating Texts for Discourse Presentation

We manually annotated the text within Microsoft *Word* (other text editing software can be used for this task). We adopted a similar system of annotation to that used in the Lancaster SW&TP Corpus, as described in Semino and Short

(2004: 26–39) and McIntyre et al. (2004). Every occurrence of Discourse Presentation was enclosed in what are referred to as tags, which are labels that are manually typed into the text to identify different categories of DP. As well as DP, we also tagged reporting clauses (clausal and non-clausal reporting structures that signal or frame DP) and stretches of narration. In this way, every part of the story was annotated as the following example from the very beginning of the text demonstrates:

<dptag cat="DS">'You will not find your father greatly changed,'</dptag>
<dptag cat="NRS"> remarked Lady Moping, </dptag>
<dptag cat="N"> as the car turned into the gates of the County Asylum.</dptag>
<dptag cat="DS">'Will he be wearing a uniform?'</dptag>
<dptag cat="NRS"> asked Angela.</dptag>
<dptag cat="DS">'No, dear, of course not. He is receiving the very best attention.'</dptag>

The annotation we used follows XML format which consists of start and end tags. **Start tags** comprise a 'name' (or identifier), which can be made up of any combination of letters and numbers (but not spaces), bounded by a left and right angle bracket (<>). We named our tags 'dptag'. Start tags can optionally contain **attributes**, which consist of a name (made up of alpha-numeric characters but not spaces), followed by an equals sign and then the attribute value, which can be any combination of alpha-numeric characters (including spaces) enclosed in either single or double quotation marks (but not a mixture of both). Our 'dptag' contained one attribute, which we called 'cat', to identify the category of Discourse Presentation (or otherwise). For example, we used 'DS' to mark Direct Speech. The 'NRS' category marks Narrator's Reporting Structures, which are reporting clauses and other non-clausal reporting signals/devices/frames. The 'N' category marks narration. **End tags** comprise the tag name enclosed in angle brackets with a forward slash (/) immediately following the left angle bracket. Together, the manually added start and end tags enclose sections of data, and this data becomes the content of the tags. See McIntyre and Walker (2019: 86–97) for more information about corpus annotation.

4.5.3 Using Annotation for Quantitative Analysis

Using the annotated the text, we ascertained (i) the numbers of occurrences of each DP category and (ii) the number of words in the story that belonged to each category. We achieved (i) using the 'Find' facility in Microsoft *Word* and simply searched for particular attributes within the start tags. So, to find the number of instances of Direct Speech in the story we searched for the following:

<dtag cat="DS">

We achieved (ii) also using the 'Find' facility in *Word*, but this time we utilised the wildcard search function, which allows for patterns to be searched for in the data. Once the 'Use wildcards' option is ticked, certain characters take on special meaning. For example, the question mark takes on the special meaning of 'any character'. Focus 4.2 sets out some of the wildcard characters in *Word* and their special meanings.

Focus 4.2: Wildcards in Word

?Any character.
*Zero or more occurrences.
[-]A range of characters, e.g. [A-Z] means any uppercase character in the range a to z inclusive; [0-9] means any number character.
<At the start of a word.
>At the end of a word.
\Cancel special meaning of character.

If we wanted to search for sections of text marked as Direct Speech (DS) then, using wildcards, the following search pattern will find those sections:

\<dtag cat="DS"\ >?*\</dtag\>

The search looks for any text (denoted by **?***) in between tags where the attribute contains 'DS'. The backslashes (\) tell the search to ignore the special meaning of the angle brackets (see Focus 4.2). The quotation marks used both in the text and in the search must be 'smart quotes', which differentiate between opening and closing quotation marks (i.e. " ...") rather than 'straight quotes' (i.e. " ... "); otherwise, the search will not work correctly. Using the 'Highlight all items found in main document' option in *Word*, all occurrences of DS in the text are highlighted and quantified. These results can then be copied and pasted into another document for further analysis.

One of the reasons for annotating the story for Discourse Presentation and narration is to find out what proportions of the story are made up of characters' speech, writing and thought. So, for example, we can find out whether most of the story is made up of narration or Discourse Presentation. ◘ Table 4.2 shows the composition of MLLO, and from it we can see that just over half of the story is some form of speech presentation, while around 42% of the text is narration. Just 3.8% of the story is either writing or thought presentation. The remaining 1.3% of the story received portmanteau tags (see Semino and Short, 2004) which mark ambiguous sections of text that cannot be assigned to just one category.

Looking at the results, we might wonder whether the proportions of Discourse Presentation and narration are 'normal' or marked. One way to assess our results is via comparison with what we might call a norm. For this purpose, the fiction section of the Lancaster SW&TP (Hereafter LancFic) makes a suitable point of reference (i.e. a reference corpus). ◘ Table 4.2 includes figures from LancFic (see Semino and Short 2004: 59) and shows that the speech presenta-

Table 4.2 Percentages of words under the four main categories of Discourse Presentation as a percentage of the total number of words in MLLO and LancFic

SW&TP Category	MLLO %	LancFic %
Narration	42.6	45.04
Speech	52.5	31.59
Writing	1.4	0.63
Thought	2.3	19.20
Portmanteau	1.2	3.54
Total	100	100

MLLO % = Number of words in discourse category as a percentage of the total number of words in the short story
LancFic % = Number of words in discourse category as a percentage of the total number of words the fiction section of the SW&TP corpus

Table 4.3 Speech presentation categories in MLLO and LancFic

	Occurrences (%)	
Category	MLLO	LancFic
(F)DS	61 (86)	1569 (74.5)
FIS	0 (0)	57 (2.7)
IS	0 (0)	117 (5.5)
NPSA	2 (2.8)	251 (12.0)
NPS	8 (11.2)	111 (5.3)
Total	71 (100)	2105 (100)

tion in MLLO is markedly higher than the reference corpus (in fact 66% higher), while the thought presentation is strikingly lower (about 88% lower). If we take LancFic as representing some sort of norm, then MLLO seems to contain a lot of speech presentation, but not very much thought presentation. These two 'abnormal' frequencies can provide a focus for further analysis whereby we can consider the reasons for these proportions of speech and thought presentation and their effects. As Short (1996: 291) notes, "we should be on the look-out for authors using speech and thought presentation for tactical or strategic purposes".

For the purposes of this discussion, we will only look at on speech presentation. Table 4.3 shows the different speech categories used in the story and their frequencies. The figures show that Direct Speech is by far the most frequent category, making up 86% of the (71) occurrences of speech presentation in the story. This figure is somewhat higher than the 74.5% in LancFic. This suggests that

◘ **Table 4.4** Number of words of DS as a percentage of the total DS per character and the number of turns

Character	Words (%)	Occurrences	Words/occurrence
The Doctor	432 (33.0)	13	33.2
Mr. Loveday	347 (26.5)	8	43.4
Lord Moping	203 (15.5)	7	29.0
Lady Moping	177 (13.5)	14	12.6
Angela	151 (11.5)	19	7.9
Total	1310 (100)	61	

% = number of words spoken by the character as DS as a percentage of the total amount of DS in the story
Occurrences = the number of occurrences of DS per character

Waugh favours Direct Speech presentation in the story which means, by and large, we get to hear directly from characters in the story and experience the fictional world from their point of view.

Having ascertained that Direct Speech is the prevalent form of speech presentation in the story, we can now look at which characters we hear from directly and in what amounts. ◘ Table 4.4 shows the number of words presented in direct form for each character.

4.5.4 Discussion of Results and Further Analysis

◘ Table 4.4 shows that in the story the reader experiences more speech in direct form originating from the doctor than from any other character in the story. Seven of the doctor's turns provide information about Mr Loveday from which we learn about Loveday's character (known as *other-presentation*—see ▶ Chapter 6). The doctor provides a lengthy inventory of Loveday's talents which include playing billiards, conjuring, mending gramophones of other patients, acting as a valet and helping with crossword puzzles. On top of that, the doctor describes him as 'invaluable' and says that 'everybody loves him' and that he 'has a way with even the most troublesome' patients. The only reason that the doctor is reluctant to pursue Mr Loveday's release is that he is 'far too useful' to the asylum staff. These words of explicit character presentation apparently come straight from the doctor's mouth and present information about Mr Loveday from the doctor's point of view without any extra input from the narrator (via, for example, reporting clauses). The doctor's descriptions present to the reader a physically and mentally skilful person who selflessly devotes himself to the care and assistance of others. The evaluations and the evaluative language used are in the DS and therefore 'belong' to the doctor. When asked why Mr. Loveday is in the asylum, the doctor provides the following explanation:

Well, it is <u>rather</u> sad: When he was a <u>very</u> young man he killed somebody - a young woman quite unknown to him, whom he knocked off her bicycle and then throttled. He gave himself up <u>immediately</u> afterwards and has been here ever since.
Waugh (1967; emphasis added)

The murder committed by Mr. Loveday over thirty-five years ago is presented to us from the doctor's point of view and is (i) downplayed by the doctor's subjective, evaluative language (underlined), which mitigates the horror of the murder; and (ii) offset against his many sane acts during twenty years of selfless service to other inmates. Consequently, the doctor seems to imply that Mr. Loveday is not a habitually violent or murderous person.

The character with the second highest total of DS attributed to him in the story is Mr. Loveday (see ◘ Table 4.4). Through this DS we find out about Mr. Loveday through self-presentation (see ▶ Chapter 6). For example, in each of the occurrences of Direct Speech when he is talking to Lord Moping's daughter, Angela, he calls her 'miss' showing his respectful nature and positioning himself socially lower than her (i.e. social deixis). Additionally, he twice refers to and evaluates his fellow inmates of the asylum as 'poor crazed people', which displays his sympathy as well as suggesting that he can judge their mental states and does not consider himself to be the same as them. He also shows empathy by presenting what he considers to be the feelings of some of the other inmates (via *verba sentiendi* including 'think' and 'feel'), and their emotional states (e.g. 'fond'). That he acknowledges the feelings of other people potentially operates against a schema we might associate with murderers and the criminally insane.

The combination of Direct Speech attributed to the doctor and Mr Loveday and the combination of POV indicators and character cues (see ▶ Chapter 6) encourage us to assess Mr Loveday as a useful, helpful, caring, gentle person. This, however, turns out to be a 'smokescreen' orchestrated by the author to give the reader a shock at the end of the story. We can also note that the relatively small amount of thought presentation in the story is strategic because it means that the author does not allow us inside the head of Mr Loveday. Instead, we only get access to his words in the form of Direct Speech presentation, which indicates to us (and the characters in the story) that he is lucid and sane. From the perspective of Text World Theory (see ▶ Chapter 2), the proliferation of Direct Speech in the story creates a lot of action at the level of the enactor text-world, meaning that it is enactors' speech that plays a large part in fleshing out our text-world representation.

4.5.5 Summary of Case Study

Our analysis of a short story using corpus methods demonstrates the benefits of annotating texts and corpora electronically for linguistic categories, in this case Discourse Presentation. It also demonstrates how other corpora (in this case the Lancaster SW&TP corpus) can be used as a comparison for assessing frequencies. Our method was to first electronically annotate a text using the model of SW&TP

outlined in this chapter, which means we performed a rigorous and systematic qualitative analysis, the results of which we recorded in the data using tags. We then used those annotations to provide quantitative information about Discourse Presentation in the short story. These quantitative results provided us with a general overview of the patterns of DP in the story and, when compared against frequencies in a reference corpus acting as a 'norm', indicated which types of DP (speech, writing or thought) were under- or over-used. The annotation helped us to look more closely at which categories of DP were prevalent, in this case DS, and then which characters had most DS attributed to them. This quantitative strand of analysis provided a focus for further qualitative analysis of the DS of the doctor and Mr Loveday, which was guided and constrained by a framework of point of view (► Chapter 3) and characterisation (see ► Chapter 6). The analysis highlighted textual evidence of Mr Loveday's sympathy and empathy which were matched by the doctor's descriptions. Our method, therefore, alternates between detailed and systematic qualitative and quantitative analyses, using one to inform the other.

4.6 Conclusions

In this chapter, we described different forms of discourse presentation in fiction based on the model originally proposed by Leech and Short (2007 [1981]). Although we concentrated on fictional prose, the model has been tested out on other genres (see Semino and Short 2004), applied to spoken data (see McIntyre et al. 2004) and used in Critical Stylistics (see, e.g., Jeffries 2010, Ch10). Our discussion in this chapter was largely informed by the findings reported in Semino and Short (2004).

Discourse Presentation is a textual phenomenon, but one which has profound effects on the reader. From a Text World Theory perspective, DP is world-building information from which readers construct mental representations of enactors in the text-world. Direct Discourse Presentation triggers an enactor text-world and discourse between enactors helps us to elaborate our mental representation of characters and our understanding of the main text-world. DP gives us apparent access to discourse between characters via a narrator. This allows readers to experience characters' words and thoughts and see the text-world through their eyes and consciousness, and also helps to create the presence of a narrator who apparently presents the discourse. DP is, therefore, important for point of view (► Chapter 3) and (looking forward to ► Chapter 6) characterisation.

In our next chapter, we remain at the character-character level of discourse, but concentrate on dialogue in drama where, prototypically, there is no intervening narrator.

- **Further Reading**

Semino and Short (2004) reports of a substantial corpus linguistic study of Discourse Presentation that is based on the Leech and Short model.

Thompson (1996) presents a different model of DP that is also based on corpus research.

For more on Discourse Presentation and text-worlds, see Lugea (2013).

Rundquist (2014) examines the notion of Free Indirect Style and, using Woolf's *To the Lighthouse*, argues for the integration of formal thought presentation categories into cognitive approaches to analysing fictional consciousness.

For more on using corpus annotation, see McIntyre and Walker (2011), who apply Leech and Short's model to a small corpus of Early Modern English.

- **Resources**

The British National Corpus (BNC): ▶ http://corpora.lancs.ac.uk/BNCweb/
HUM19CUK: A corpus of nineteenth century novels.
LancFic: The Lancaster University fiction corpus; this corpus can be found on the Oxford Text Archive (OTA); ▶ https://ota.bodleian.ox.ac.uk/repository/xmlui/

- **Notes**

1. IT is also known as 'reported inner speech' (Genette 1980: 176) and 'psycho-narration' (Cohn 1978).
2. Leech and Short's intuition is supported by the corpus research reported in Semino and Short (2004).
3. Thompson (1996) uses the category name 'summary' for this type of DP.
4. Note: Semino and Short (2004) refer to NPS as Narrator's Representation of Voice and abbreviate it to NV while Short (2012) uses the label Narrator's Presentation of Voice (NPV). Here we adopt a slightly different label to maintain consistency across categories and clines.
5. Thompson (1996: 518) refers to this category as 'omission'.

References

Bortolussi, M. and Dixon, P. 2002. *Psychonarratology: Foundations for the Empirical Study of Literary Response*.

Bray, J. 2007a. The Effects of Free Indirect Discourse: Empathy Revisited. In *Contemporary Stylistics*, eds. M. Lambrou and P. Stockwell, 56–67. London: Continuum.

Bray, J. 2007b. The "Dual Voice" of Free Indirect Discourse: A Reading Experiment. *Language and Literature* 16, 1: 37–52.

Busse, B. 2010. *Speech, Writing and Thought Presentation in a Corpus of Nineteenth-Century English Narrative Fiction*. Bern: University of Bern.

Cohn, D. H. 1978. *Transparent Minds: Narrative Modes for Presenting Consciousness in Fiction*. Princeton University Press.

Cruikshank, T. and Lahey, E. 2010. Building the Stages of Drama: Towards a Text World Theory Account of Dramatic Play-Texts. *Journal of Literary Semantics* 39, 1: 67–91.

Crystal, D. 2008. *Dictionary of Linguistics and Phonetics*. John Wiley & Sons, Incorporated.

Fludernik, M. 1993. *The Fictions of Language and the Languages of Fiction: The Linguistic Representation of Speech and Consciousness*. London: Routledge.

Gavins, J. 2007. *Text World Theory: An Introduction*. Edinburgh: Edinburgh University Press.

Genette, G. 1980. *Narrative Discourse: An Essay in Method*. Trans. J. E. Lewin. Ithaca, NY: Cornell University Press.

Ikeo, R. 2009. An Elaboration of Faithfulness Claims in Direct Writing. *Journal of Pragmatics* 41: 999–1016.

Ikeo, R. 2012. Misleading Speech Report in the Media with a Special Reference to an Australian Defamation Case. *Journal of Pragmatics* 44: 1183–1205.

Jucker, A. H. 2006. 'But 'tis Believed That …': Speech and Thought Presentation in Early English Newspapers. In *News Discourse in Early Modern Britain. Selected Papers of CHINED 2004*, ed. N. Brownlees, 105–125. Bern: Peter Lang.

Kilroy, C. 2009. *All Names Have Been Changed*. London: Faber and Faber.

Leech, G. and Short, M. 2007. *Style in Fiction: A Linguistic Introduction to English Fictional Prose*. 2nd ed. London and New York: Longman.

Lugea, J. 2013. Embedded Dialogue and Dreams: The Worlds and Accessibility Relations of Inception. *Language and Literature* 22, 2: 133–153.

McHale, B. 1978. Free Indirect Discourse A Survey of Recent Accounts. *PTL A Journal for Descriptive Poetics and Theory of Literature* 3: 248–287.

McIntyre, D. and Walker, B. 2011. Discourse Presentation in Early Modern English Writing: A Preliminary Corpus-Based Investigation. *International Journal of Corpus Linguistics* 16, 1: 101–130.

McIntyre, D. and Walker, B. 2019. *Corpus Stylistics: Theory and Practice*. Edinburgh: Edinburgh University Press.

McIntyre, D., Bellard-Thomson, C., Heywood, J., McEnery, A., Semino, E. and Short, M. 2004. Investigating the Presentation of Speech, Writing and Thought in Spoken British English: A Corpus-Based Approach. *ICAME Journal* 28: 49–76.

Ruano, P. 2018. A Corpus-Based Approach to Charles Dickens's Use of Direct Thought Presentation. *Corpora* 13, 3: 319–345.

Rundquist, E. 2014. How Is Mrs Ramsay thinking? The Semantic Effects of Consciousness Presentation Categories Within Free Indirect Style. *Language and Literature* 23, 2: 159–174.

Scott, M. 2020. *WordSmith Tools version 8*. Stroud: Lexical Analysis Software.

Semino, E. and Short, M. 2004. *Corpus Stylistics: Speech, Writing and Thought Presentation in a Corpus of English Writing*. London: Routledge.

Short, M. 1988. Speech Presentation, the Novel and the Press. In *The Taming of the Text*, ed. W. van Peer. London: Routledge.

Short, M. 1996. *Exploring the Language of Poems, Plays and Prose*. Harlow: Longman.

Short, M. 2007. Thought Presentation Twenty-Five Years on. *Style* 41, 2: 227–257.

Short, M. 2012. Discourse Presentation of Speech (and Writing but not Thought) Summary. *Language and Literature* 21, 1: 18–32.

Short, M., Semino, E. and Wynne, M. 2002. Revisiting the Notion of Faithfulness in Discourse Presentation Using a Corpus Approach. *Language and Literature* 11, 4: 325–355.

Sotirova, V. 2004. Connectives in Free Indirect Style: Continuity or Shift? *Language and Literature* 13, 3: 216–234.

Sternberg, M. 1982. Proteus in Quotation-Land: Mimesis and the Forms of Reported Discourse. *Poetics Today* 3, 2: 107–156.

Thompson, G. 1996. Voices in the Text: Discourse Perspectives on Language Reports. *Applied Linguistics* 17, 4: 501–530.

Walker, B. and Karpenko-Seccombe, T. 2017. Speech Presentation and Summary in the BBC News Online Coverage of a Russian TV Interview with Vladimir Putin. *CADAAD Journal* 9, 2: 79–96.

Waugh, E. 1967. Mr. Loveday's Little Outing. In *The Penguin Book of English Short Stories*, ed. C. Dolley, 293–301. Harmondsworth, Middlesex, England: Penguin Books Ltd.

Werth, P. 1999. *Text Worlds: Representing Conceptual Space in Discourse*. London: Longman.

Fictional Dialogue

Supplementary Information The online version contains supplementary material available at ▶ https://doi.org/10.1007/978-3-031-10422-0_5.

© The Author(s), under exclusive license to Springer Nature Switzerland AG 2023
J. Lugea and B. Walker, *Stylistics*,
https://doi.org/10.1007/978-3-031-10422-0_5

5.1 Introduction

In ▶ Chapter 4, we explored ways in which the speech, writing and thought of characters is presented in prose fiction apparently via narrators. In this chapter, we continue to look at discourse between characters but this time we focus on dramatic texts (such as plays) where, prototypically, character-character discourse is not filtered through a narrator. This is because (as we saw in ▶ Chapter 1) dramatic texts usually comprise just two levels of discourse: that between the author and reader, and that between characters. Drama is therefore mainly fictional dialogue,[1] where character interactions provide information about the characters and their relationships, advance the action and may carry discourse level messages from the author to the reader. Thus, dialogue can, on the one hand, tell us about the characters and their characteristics and, on the other, carry messages to the audience on behalf of the writer. While fictional dialogue is scripted and unspontaneous, which distinguishes it from natural spoken language, authors nonetheless intuitively draw on their knowledge of real spoken interactions to create realistic, and sometimes deviant, dialogue between characters. This chapter demonstrates how models and frameworks which are typically used by linguists to analyse real-life interactions can be applied to the study of fictional texts.

Of particular importance for the stylistic analysis of drama has been the application of Pragmatics,[2] which is an area of Linguistics that explores how conversational participants derive meanings from utterances using the linguistic forms, contextual information and other (background) knowledge and resources. Many of the concepts and frameworks developed in Pragmatics for the analysis of real interactions are useful for the analysis of fictional interaction. In fact, because dramatic dialogue is scripted, it can be assumed that any deviations from the pragmatic norms of conversation are interpretatively significant.

Throughout this chapter, we will draw on the following extract of dialogue from the opening of the film *I, Daniel Blake* set in Newcastle-upon-Tyne (a city in the Northeast of England) in 2016. Daniel is a construction worker who is seeking financial help from the government because he suffered a heart attack while at work, and almost fell from scaffolding. Consequently, he is unable to work. This interaction is with Amanda, who works for an outsourced agency appointed to assess people's eligibility for financial support (often referred to as 'benefits'). For ease of reference, we have numbered the characters' 'turns':

1. ASSESSOR Good morning, Mr Blake. My name's Amanda. I've got a couple of questions here for you today to establish your eligibility for Employment Support Allowance. It won't take up much of your time. Could I just ask firstly, can you walk more than 50 metres unassisted by any other person?
2. DANIEL: Yes.
3. ASSESSOR: Okay. Can you raise either arm as if to put something in your top pocket?
4. DANIEL: I filled this in already on your 52-page form.
5. ASSESSOR: Yes. I can see that you have, but unfortunately I couldn't make out what you had said there.
6. DANIEL: (Sighs) Yes.

Fictional Dialogue

7. ASSESSOR: ... Can you raise either arm to the top of your head as if you are putting on a hat?
8. DANIEL: I've told you, there's nothing wrong with me arms and legs.
9. ASSESSOR: Could you just answer the question, please.
10. DANIEL: Well, you've got me medical records. Can we just talk about me heart?
11. ASSESSOR: Do you think you could just answer these questions?
12. DANIEL: Okay.
13. ASSESSOR: So, is that a 'yes' that you can put a hat on your head?
14. DANIEL: Yes.
15. ASSESSOR: Okay, that's great... Can you press a button such as a telephone keypad?
16. DANIEL: Well, there's nought wrong with me fingers either. I mean, we're getting farther and farther away from me heart.
17. ASSESSOR: If we could just keep to these questions, thank you. Do you have any significant difficulty conveying a simple message to strangers?
18. DANIEL: Yes! Yes, it's me fuckin' heart! I'm trying to tell you but you'll not listen!
19. ASSESSOR: Mr Blake, if you continue to speak to us like that, that's not going to be very helpful for your assessment. If you could just answer the question, please.
20. DANIEL: Yes (sighing).
21. ASSESSOR: Okay... Do you ever experience any loss of control leading to extensive evacuation of the bowel?
22. DANIEL: No, but I can't guarantee there won't be a first if we don't get to the point!
23. ASSESSOR: Can you complete a simple task as setting an alarm clock?
24. DANIEL: (sighs) Jesus, yes. Can I ask you a question? Are you medically qualified?
25. ASSESSOR: I'm a healthcare professional appointed by the Department of Work and Pensions to carry out assessments for Employment Support Allowance.
26. DANIEL: But there was a bloke out in the waiting room, he says that you work for an American company.
27. ASSESSOR: Our company has been appointed by the government.
28. DANIEL: Are you a nurse? Are you a doctor?
29. ASSESSOR: I'm a healthcare professional.
30. DANIEL: Listen. I've had a major heart attack. I nearly fell off the scaffolding. I want to get back to work too. Now please, can we talk about me heart, forget about me arse, that works a dream.

The interaction in the extract above can be understood in terms of Brown and Yule's distinction between transactional and interactional language. **Transactional language** is used to 'transfer information'/ 'transmission of factual or propositional information' (Brown and Yule 1983: 2), and **interactional language** is used to 'express social relations and personal attitudes' (Brown and Yule 1983: 1).

Many interactions tend to use a combination of both. In the extract, the Assessor's list of set questions conforms to transactional language. For Daniel, the questions are irrelevant because he knows the medical issue preventing him from working. Consequently, he tries various techniques to move the conversation from one that is simply transactional to one that addresses the issues pertinent to him as an individual. However, the Assessor has **institutional power** in this interaction, including the power to decide on Daniel's eligibility for state financial support. Over the course of this chapter, we will discuss, using concepts and theories from Pragmatics and Conversation Analysis (CA), how these institutional roles influence the characters' interaction and the structure of the conversation.

Over the rest of this chapter, we will refer to the extract above from *I, Daniel Blake* as *I,DB*.

5.2 Speech Acts

As we go about our daily lives, we have goals (e.g. cooking dinner; buying goods) some of which can be achieved largely through physical action, while others require some form of communication and therefore language. Achieving goals using language requires choosing words that are most likely, under the circumstances you find yourself in, to achieve your goal.

5.2.1 Doing Things with Words

The idea that goals can be accomplished through language was famously expounded by Austin (1962), who said that utterances/sentences have a performative aspect where language use can achieve or perform actions. Indeed, sometimes our primary purpose of using language is to bring about some sort of action. For example, in Turn 1 of *I,DB*, the Assessor outlines her goal: to obtain answers to set questions to assess Daniel's eligibility for Employment Support Allowance. That we perform actions via words is, according to Austin, the difference between "doing something rather than merely saying something" (Austin 1979: 235). Austin suggested that utterances can be divided into three separate acts, exemplified here with Turn 9 from *I,DB*:

Locutionary: The production of meaningful words that conform to the rules of a language. e.g. 'Could you just answer the question, please'
Illocutionary: The act being performed by producing the words. e.g. A request that Daniel answer the question.
Perlocutionary: The effect or consequence of the locutionary and illocutionary acts. e.g. Daniel eventually answers the question (in Turn 14).

When we produce **locutions**, they have intended meanings (**illocutionary force**) and perform intended acts (**illocutionary acts**), also known as **speech acts** (Searle 1969, 1976). These acts have labels such as 'praising', 'promising', 'predicting' and, as we saw in Turn 9, 'requesting'. Building on the work of Austin (and others), Searle places illocutionary/speech acts into five groups, summarised in ◘ Table 5.1.

◘ **Table 5.1** Speech act categories (based on Searle 1976; Searle and Vanderveken 1985)

Category	Action	Examples of acts
Representatives (also known as Assertives)	Represent the world by asserting what is, was or will be	*stating, announcing, predicting, concluding*
Directives	Make addressee do something	*ordering, commanding, requesting*
Commissives	Make a commitment to perform an action	*promising, pledging, offering, vowing, threatening*
Expressives	Express point of view, attitudes, feelings about things	*praising, accusing, congratulating, thanking*
Declarations	Make something the case by saying that it is the case	*resigning, naming, appointing, dismissing, sentencing*

5.2.2 Choice of Words

When it comes to performing speech acts, we make language choices which are often driven by the context we find ourselves in. Therefore, illocutionary acts can be performed using a variety of different locutions and the content of an utterance does not predict its illocutionary force and vice versa. That means, for example, to request a response we can use different locutions that perform different illocutionary acts. To account for this, Searle (1969, 1976) makes a distinction between **Direct Speech Acts** (DSA), where the locution matches the illocution, and **Indirect Speech Acts** (ISA), where the locution and illocution do not match. For example, the Assessor's locution 'Could you answer the question?' (Turn 9) performs the speech act of requesting (a response), but a direct request for a response would be 'answer the question'. The Assessor instead issues a request for information concerning Daniel's *ability* to answer the question ('could you…'), and this performs the act of requesting an action. It is, therefore, an Indirect Speech Act. The ISA is successful because Daniel does not interpret it as referring to his ability but recognises the illocutionary force behind it and eventually satisfies her request by answering the question, resulting in the desired perlocutionary effect (Turn 14). Indirectness can also involve a speaker producing one type of speech act (e.g. a representative) to perform another (e.g. a directive). For example, the Assessor could have used the speech act of stating (e.g. 'I would love you to answer the question'), or threatening (e.g. 'If you don't answer the question now, I'll terminate the interview'). Indeed, the Assessor does the latter in Turn 19. Some of the possibilities for this type of indirectness are shown in ◘ Table 5.2.

Table 5.2 Different ways to request a response

Locutionary Act	Locution type	Speech Act	Category
Will you please answer me?	Interrogative	Requesting	Directive
Answer me!	Imperative	Ordering	Directive
I think you should answer me	Declarative	Stating	Representative
I request that you answer me	Declarative	Stating	Representative
You didn't answer the question	Declarative	Stating	Representative

5.2.3 Illocutionary Force Indicating Devices

Illocutionary Force Indicating Devices (IFIDs) refer to elements of the locution that indicate the illocutionary force. IFIDs include performative verbs (e.g. 'promise', 'apologise', 'warn') and the structure of the utterance (declarative, imperative, interrogative). As we have seen, though, there is no one-to-one match between IFID and illocutionary force. So, for example, a declarative could function as a request.

5.2.4 Felicity Conditions

Felicity conditions are the conditions that need to be met for a speech act to be successful (Austin 1962; Searle 1969). Although they vary depending on the kind of speech act being performed (Searle 1969), in general for a speech act to be felicitous, the speaker and hearer must recognise and understand their roles and the context in which the utterance is made. For instance, for a medical declaration to be made (a performative speech act), the right 'preparatory conditions' should be in place; that is, the person declaring has the appropriate medical qualifications. It is because Daniel has these expectations of the interaction in I,DB that he questions the Assessor's qualifications, the 'preparatory conditions' he sees as necessary for her decision on his eligibility for state aid. On the other hand, the Assessor understands her role differently. She needs only sincere answers from Daniel, 'sincerity' being another felicity condition for a speech act to be successful.

According to Leech (2014: 77) decoding Indirect Speech Acts relates to felicity conditions. One of the (usual) felicity conditions of a question is that the asker intends to fill a gap in their knowledge. However, asking whether someone has the ability to answer is unlikely to be filling a knowledge gap because (under typical circumstances) the speaker will already know the answer, as the Assessor does in Turn 9. The hearer infers the question is performing some other function, i.e. a request to address the question. Interlocutors usually aim to achieve goals while maintaining social harmony, which can involve careful management of conversational maxims and our interlocutor's face (Sects. 5.3 and 5.5).

Activity 5.1: Direct and Indirect Speech Acts

Looking at Extract 1, find locutions which seem to express Indirect Speech Acts, i.e. their literal meaning seems to differ from their intended meaning. For each locution:
a. identify the Direct Speech Act, i.e. what is the locution literally doing? (see ◘ Table 5.1 for categories);
b. identify the Indirect Speech Act, i.e. what is the intended illocutionary force? (see ◘ Table 5.1 for categories); and
c. look at subsequent turns in the dialogue for a perlocutionary effect, i.e. an outcome.

 Our answers to these questions are provided on the book's webpage.

5.3 Conversational Implicature

Speech Act Theory accounts for how goals can be achieved via communication directly or indirectly. Indirect Speech Acts require the hearer to decode the illocutionary force. However, Speech Act Theory lacks a means to explain *how* we arrive at the intended illocutionary force, especially when it is expressed indirectly. In this section, we briefly introduce Grice's (1975, 1978) influential Co-operative Principle, which attempts to explain the rules that govern conversation and how we draw inferences when those rules are broken. We go on to demonstrate, with reference to *I,DB*, how to go about a Gricean analysis of a text and to show the possible stylistic effects.

5.3.1 Implicatures and Inferences

Our discussion of Indirect Speech Acts introduced the idea that sometimes what we say and what we mean are different. Grice tried to explain *how* utterances can communicate meanings that are different from the semantic or literal meanings of the words uttered. He suggests the verb *implicate* for verbal action that creates meaning beyond what is said and coins the term *implicature* for that meaning. At the heart of Grice's discussion of conversational implicature is the Cooperative Principle (hereafter CP), which is an attempt to describe our shared expectations about how conversation should progress. Within the CP are four categories of **maxims** (rules) which shape co-operative conversational contributions: **Quantity**, **Quality**, **Relation** and **Manner**. Although phrased as imperatives, the CP and associated maxims are not commands to conduct conversation in a certain way but try to capture language users' shared expectations. For a full account, see Focus 5.1.

> **Focus 5.1: Grice's Co-operative Principle and Conversational Maxims**

The Co-operative Principle (CP):

> *Make your conversational contribution such as is required, at the stage at which it occurs, by the accepted purpose or direction of the talk exchange in which you are engaged.*
>
> Grice ([1975] 1989: 26)

The CP is met by upholding the following categories and maxims in conversation (Grice [1975] 1989: 26–27):

The category of Quantity refers to 'the quantity of information to be provided' and has two maxims:
- 'Make your contribution as informative as is required (for the current purposes of the exchange)'.
- 'Do not make your contribution more informative than is required'.

The category of Quality has one supermaxim 'Try to make your contribution one that is true' and two further submaxims:
- 'Do not say what you believe to be false'.
- 'Do say that for which you lack adequate evidence'.

The category of Relation has just one maxim:
- 'be relevant'.

The category of Manner relates to not *what* is said but *how* it is said and has one super maxim 'be perspicuous' (i.e. be clear and easy to understand!), and Grice lists a further four maxims (although he says that 'one might need others'):
- 'Avoid obscurity of expression'.
- 'Avoid ambiguity'.
- 'Be brief (avoid unnecessary prolixity)'.
- 'Be orderly'.

Even though the CP, categories and associated maxims are phrased as imperatives they are not rules for conversation! Instead, they are a set of common expectations we have when engaged in conversation. See ▶ Sect. 5.3.1 for ways in which they can be broken and possible implicatures that can arise.

The two characters in *I, DB* may not agree about the direction of their conversation but the CP and related maxims are still applicable as general principles for what interactants may expect from a conversation. When one or more of these maxims is not fulfilled, we may be prompted to search for an implicated meaning. This applies to everyday interaction as well as fictional dialogue. However, because fictional dialogue is scripted, any deviation from conversational norms is likely to be interpretatively significant. The playwright or screenwriter uses dialogue, including conversational norms and implicatures, to convey information about characters, or even to make a point to the audience at the discourse-world level, i.e. a rhetorical aim (see ▶ Chapter 1 and Activity 5.2).

Grice (1975) sets out various ways in which the maxims may not be fulfilled. First, a maxim can be **violated** which is an unostentatious non-fulfilment of a maxim. In such cases, the speaker intends to 'mislead' the other participant. For example, a lie would be a violation of the Quality Maxims. In *I, DB* the Assessor breaks the Quality maxims by stating that she has 'a couple of questions' (Turn 1) when, in the extract, she poses many more than two and Daniel refers to the '52-page form' from which they are drawn (Turn 4). If we believe this disregard for the truth is intended to mislead or go unnoticed, then she can be said to violate the maxim of Quality. The Assessor also violates maxims later in Example 5a. When Daniel asks her 'Are you medically qualified?' (Turn 24), the Assessor replies, "I'm a healthcare professional appointed by the Department of Work and Pensions to carry out assessments for Employment Support Allowance" (Turn 25). This response arguably violates the maxim of Relation, in that it does not directly and relevantly answer the question. From these violations, it might be surmised that the Assessor is not being fully transparent with Daniel.

Flouting a maxim is when a speaker 'blatantly' fails to fulfil a maxim, inviting the other participant(s) to work out how the turn is meaningful within the ongoing conversation. In other words, the speaker raises a **conversational implicature**. Turn 25 may also be said to **flout** the maxim of Quantity, by providing a longer answer than the 'yes/no' that is required. Using full titles for herself, her employer and the scheme, the Assessor creates the implicature that (regardless of the unanswered question as to her medical credentials) she holds institutional authority in this interaction and is sufficiently qualified to assess Daniel.

Other ways to deviate from Grice's conversational maxims include **opting out**, whereby a speaker makes it clear that they are not fulfilling the expectations set out by a maxim in question and the CP. Grice's example is '*I cannot say more; my lips are sealed*'. Thomas (1995) also suggests maxims can be **infringed**,[3] whereby a speaker breaks a maxim unintentionally, because her/his linguistic performance is impaired or underdeveloped (we explore this idea further in ▶ Chapter 8).

Activity 5.2: Conversational Implicatures

Daniel states the following in Turn 22:

No, but I can't guarantee there won't be a first [bowel explosion] if we don't get to the point!

To analyse this utterance using Gricean Pragmatics, consider the following:

i. Does Daniel uphold the Cooperative Principle?
   a. yes
   b. no
ii. Which maxim(s) does he break?
   a. Quality
   b. Quantity
   c. Relation
   d. Manner

iii. In which way(s) are they broken?
      a. Violate
      b. Flout
      c. Infringe
      d. Opt out
  iv. What (if any) is the Conversational Implicature that Daniel wishes to raise with his interlocutor?
  v. Utterances between characters may carry alternative meanings at the author-reader level of discourse. What kind of rhetorical aims do you think the scriptwriter might have for the audience?

 Our answers to these questions are provided on the book's webpage.

5.4 Conversation Analysis

So far, we have looked at utterances in isolation, but Conversation Analysis (CA) provides an approach to the interactive aspect of dialogue. CA, which was first established in the 1970s by Harvey Sacks (see Sacks 1992[4]) and Emanuel Schegloff and Gail Jefferson, uses detailed transcriptions of naturally occurring conversations to find and describe patterns in spoken interaction. Many of the concepts and findings from CA research, some of which we outline in this section, can be usefully applied to the stylistic analysis of drama because they not only provide a framework for analysis but also a set of norms (based on the analysis of many conversations) against which fictional dialogue can be compared. CA, therefore, gives us the tools to analyse and describe fictional conversations, and to demonstrate whether they are 'normal' or deviant in some way.

5.4.1 Turn-Taking and Turn Allocation

A basic tenet of CA is that people engaged in spoken conversation take it in turns to talk, with overlaps occurring briefly and in predictable places (see ▶ Sect. 5.4.5). Conversation proceeds in a series of turn-taking sequences where one turn follows another. It is managed by participants, who tend to recognise when a turn is coming to an end and when there is the possibility of a transition to another speaker (Schegloff 2007: 5). This is known as a **Transition-Relevance Place** (TRP, Sacks et al. 1974: 703) and can be signalled grammatically and/or phonetically. For instance, when the Assessor says in Turn 23, "If you could just answer the question, please", the politeness marker 'please' indicates that the conditional will not be elaborated any further and that the turn has ended, creating a TRP for the addressee to embark on his turn. A further option is that on reaching a TRP the speaker continues to speak (see, for instance, Turns 17 and 19 where the Assessor continues to speak beyond potential TRPs).

Participants in conversation can manage turns using **turn allocation**, whereby the speaker selects the next speaker or where the next speaker self-selects, typically at a TRP. Because *I,DB* takes the form of an interview, the Assessor allocates turns to Daniel through the questioning. As such, her institutional power also grants her control over turn-taking and turn allocation (whose turn it is to speak and when). Where power is more-or-less balanced then turn allocation will be less one sided than in our example.

5.4.2 Topic Control

As well as managing turns, interactants manage the **topic** of conversation in structured ways. Speaking topically (Brown and Yule 1983: 84) can be apparent if utterances contain linguistic elements (e.g. reference, deixis) that tie it back to the preceding utterance. **Topic initiation** is when a turn establishes a new topic that does not relate to the previous turn. In conversation, topic can gradually drift over the course of an interaction with conversational participants mutually generating topics during the interaction (Sidnel 2010: 228). According to Button and Casey (1985, cited in Sidnel 2010), topics can be mutually generated by speakers in one of two ways:

(i) a speaker will try to **elicit** a topic from their interlocutor by, for example, asking questions such as 'what's new?', 'how are things?'; or
(ii) a speaker will try to **nominate** a topic by, for example, asking their interlocutor about people, places or events (e.g. 'was it your interview today?')

Topic elicitation and **nomination** can also relate to power, with speakers using questions ('How was your day?'), statements ('It'd be nice to hear about your day') or even commands ('Tell me about your day!') to control the direction of the conversation. With authority invested in her by the government, the Assessor signals from the outset that she has (a couple of!) set questions for Daniel, which he is expected to answer. As such, the Assessor has **topic control** (control over the topics discussed), including the power to elicit topics from her interlocutor through questioning. The Assessor also controls topic by suppressing what Daniel wants to talk about—his heart—and therefore further demonstrates and exerts her institutional power over Daniel.

5.4.3 Adjacency Pairs

Adjacency pairs are turns that can be expected to occur one after the other. For example, a question is usually followed by an answer, a greeting by another greeting (Schegloff and Sacks 1973: 295–296). Adjacency pairs, therefore, consist of two turns, one each from different speakers coming one after the other, and form pair-types (e.g. question–answer). The sorts of utterances that initiate an adjacency pair (an **initiation**) include questions, requests and offers. The sorts of utterances that respond to an initiation and, therefore, complete the pair, include answers to questions, grants/rejections to requests, acceptance/declination to offers. The initiation and **response** should belong to the same pair-type. So, for example, a question is followed by an answer and not by an acceptance. With the question–answer adjacency pair, the speaker asking the question has, according to Sacks, a "reserved right" to talk again following the answer. Exercising this right to ask another question can result in "chaining" where question and answer sequences could go on indefinitely (Sacks, 1992: 264), as they do in *I,DB*.

Usually, a response immediately follows an initiation, but this is not always the case. It is possible for one or more adjacency pairs to be embedded within the initial pair sequence in what is known as an **insertion sequences**. For example, a question can be followed by another question that seeks clarification which is answered before the original question is answered (Schegloff, 1972: 76–79). There are several insertion sequences in *I,DB*, where Daniel delays answering the question for a few turns (e.g. Turns 4–5, Turns 8–11, Turns 16–17). These sequences are where Daniel tries to seek clarification or even resist the questioning and move the interview on to his chosen topic of discussion—his heart and getting back to work. However, the institutional power held by the Assessor and the inflexibility of the assessment system means that, inevitably, Daniel provides a response.

5.4.4 Preferred/dispreferred Responses

The initiating turn of an adjacency pair can often present different response options. For example, an invitation can be accepted or declined. The different alternatives are valued differently and are referred to as **preferred** and **dispreferred** responses. The preferred response is the one that enables the action to be accomplished while the alternative is dispreferred (Schegloff 2007: 59). In *I,DB*, Daniel is expected to provide answers to the Assessor's questions and these would constitute '**preferred responses**' to the question–answer adjacency pair. Looking at the first three adjacency pairs in *I,DB*, which correspond to Turns 1 and 2, 3 and 4, and 7 and 8, we can see that Daniel provides a **preferred response** in Turn 2 to the first question in Turn 1. But to the second question in Turn 3, which initiates another adjacency pair, Daniel responds to the question with a statement, "I filled this in already on your 52-page form". Because it does not answer the Assessor's question, it is a **dispreferred response**. However, it is still **topical**, as signalled by the use of the deictic demonstrative 'this', with which Daniel refers back to the Assessor's question topic. The Assessor seems to recognise the topicality of Daniel's claim by acknowledging it, leading Daniel to eventually complete the adjacency pair in Turn 6, by answering the question ([*Sighs*] 'Yes'). The third adjacency pair in the extract is initiated with the Assessor's question in Turn 7. Again, Daniel provides a dispreferred response, one which does not directly answer the question. Sacks (1992) calls this a **skip-connect**, whereby speakers do not address the topic in the immediately prior utterance, but in an earlier utterance. Daniel perceives his answer in Turn 6 to the second adjacency pair to be sufficient to address this one and so 'skip-connects' back to that turn.

As the line of questioning continues, Daniel's frustration over his lack of topic control becomes evident in other interactive features. In Turns 10, 16, 18 and 22, he provides dispreferred responses that can be read as '**challenge moves**': elements of conversation that hold up the progression of the topic in the conversation (Burton 1980: 150–151). In fact, although he does provide a response to the Assessors' questions in 16, 18 and 22, he challenges the topic as being irrelevant to his heart condition. In Turn 24, Daniel challenges and inverts the interactional (and institutional) roles, by posing a question to the Assessor. Notice he does this in the same way that the Assessor introduces her line of questioning, by asking, "Can I ask you a question? Are you medically qualified?". As well as taking control of turn allocation, Daniel is also attempting to control the topic through a **topic initiator**, which establishes a topic unrelated to the previous turn. In Gricean terms, by flouting the **maxim of Relation**, Daniel raises an implicature that the Assessor is not qualified to judge his eligibility. Thereafter, by taking control of turn allocation through setting the questions himself, Daniel also succeeds in setting the topic. The structure of interaction—from topic control to turn allocation—pivots around power dynamics, as *I,DB* demonstrates.

5.4.5 Overlapping Talk and Interruptions

Sidnel (2010: 52) notes that, contrary to popular belief, overlapping talk tends only to occur at Transition-Relevance Places when one speaker's turn could be coming to an end. At that point, the other speaker might start talking a fraction of a second before the previous turn ends as they sense the other person is finishing. Such **overlaps**, which although frequent are small and barely noticeable, are thought to help the conversation advance, and indicate speakers are taking notice of and responding to what the other is saying (Sidnel 2010: 53). However, speakers can also talk over each other to retain ownership of the conversational turn and control the conversation, but such incidents are marked and noticeable. Different from overlaps, **interruptions** tend not to occur at Transition-Relevance Places and rather than helping the conversation proceed they can stop conversational actions progressing and signal that the speaker is declining to participate. Overlaps and interruptions are absent from *I,DB* and may feature less in dramatic dialogue simply because it is scripted. When they *do* feature, they are part of the design of the author and are potential messages about characters at the author-reader discourse level and, therefore, interpretatively significant (e.g. see Carol Churchill's play *Top Girls*).

5.5 Politeness and Impoliteness (Im/politeness)

▶ Section 5.2 outlined the ways in which language can be used to perform acts and achieve goals. Part of the social, cultural and linguistic knowledge we acquire as we grow up relates to norms and expectations about which language forms to use in certain interactive contexts; for example, asking for favours or giving our opinions. This pragmatic knowledge is important for making sure that our goals are met while being 'polite', or maintaining good relations with those around us. Common understandings of politeness tend to be restricted to the formulaic expressions necessary to make an utterance 'polite' (e.g. *please* and *thank-you*). But the field of Politeness Studies explores a wider range of phenomena which relate to the fact that conversational interactants simultaneously manage:
a) their own goals ('illocutionary goals', Leech 2014: 78);
b) the need to maintain social relations ('social goals', Leech 2014: 78).

To do so, participants are indirect (▶ Sect. 5.2.2), or adopt a politeness strategy (▶ Sect. 5.5.1). Balancing a) and b) is important in negotiating of one's own needs and wants alongside those of the people with whom we interact. Moreover, under typical conditions, attending to social goals will assist in achieving illocutionary goals. In this section, we explore the important notions of politeness and impoliteness—which are often grouped under the term (im)politeness—and how they relate to fictional dialogue. Our discussion incorporates the work of Leech (2014), Brown and Levinson (1987), Bousfield (2008) and Culpeper (2011).

5.5.1 Face

Face is central to many models of politeness (Leech 2014: 24) and impoliteness (Culpeper 2011: 20), although the term is conceived of in various ways and the negotiation of its meaning is ongoing. Face is said to be derived from a Chinese notion which entered English during the eighteenth or nineteenth century via the phrase 'loss of face' (see St. André 2013: 69). Ervin Goffman famously defined face as 'an image of self delineated in terms of approved social attributes' and 'the positive social value' that a person 'claims' for themselves during interaction with others (Goffman 1967: 5). During interactions we simultaneously seek to maintain our own face while not damaging the face of the other person, and this is achieved by making appropriate linguistic choices during the interaction, or **facework**. Brown and Levinson's (1987) seminal work on politeness develops Goffman's concept of face and divides it into two types:
positive face—'the positive consistent self-image or "personality" (crucially including the desire that this self-image be appreciated and approved of) claimed by interactants';

negative face—'the basic claim to territories, personal preserves, rights to nondistraction—i.e., to freedom of action and freedom from imposition'.

Positive face is consistent with Goffman's definition in that it relates to self-image and to positive values. Negative face introduces an additional component relating to freedom, rights and imposition. According to Brown and Levinson, both kinds of face exist simultaneously, in that we all have both the need to be valued and included (positive face), as well as unimpinged and free (negative face). Attending to positive face involves attempts to close social distance and emphasise common ground between interlocutors. Of course, there are contexts where it is more appropriate and respectful to maintain social distance and not impinge on others, which may require more negative facework. In practice, interactants tend to make use of both kinds of strategies.

5.5.2 Face Threatening Acts and Politeness Strategies

Central to Brown and Levinson's (1987) model of politeness is the idea that some speech events can threaten to damage face and are, therefore, potential **Face Threatening Acts** (**FTA**s). These are linguistic acts that can threaten the hearer's positive or negative face. For example, directives and requests can impose on the hearer's freedoms and therefore threaten to damage negative face. If linguistic work (appropriate to the situation) is not done to reduce or diffuse the threat, then face damage will occur. With the correct redressive linguistic action, then, the threat can be mitigated, and face can be saved. The language used will differ from situation to situation and with different interlocutors. So, the language used when issuing a directive to a friend or close relative is likely to be different to the language used with a work colleague or a great aunt.

Brown and Levinson (1987: 60) propose that when there is the potential for a Face Threatening Act, a speaker has five super-strategies to choose from, illustrated in ◘ Fig. 5.1.

The first super-strategy is a choice whereby the speaker (S) decides to perform the FTA directly (on record) **without redressive action** (**1**, also termed 'baldly'). Brown and Levinson describe this as communicating the FTA "[…] in the most direct, clear, unambiguous and concise way possible" (1987: 69). This would be used in situations when the risk of face damage is low (e.g. where directness is necessary or typical, like an emergency). When the risk of damaging face is higher, the FTA can be performed with redressive action, which would involve mitigating the threat using some of the strategies for **positive politeness** (**2**) and/or **negative politeness** (**3**) outlined in Focus 5.2. When the risk is higher still, speakers can perform the FTA **off record** (**4**), which means hinting at the goal of the FTA but not stating it (see Focus 5.2). Indirectness and going off record both rely on implicatures to convey the goal of the FTA. If the risk is too great, then the FTA is not performed at all (**5**).

Fig. 5.1 Five super-strategies for dealing with a potential Face Threatening Act

```
Potential FTA ─ Do the FTA ─ on record ─ 1. without redressive action (baldly)
                                         with redressive action ─ 2. positive politeness
                                                                   3. negative politeness
                           4. off record
              5. Don't do the FTA
```

Because Brown and Levinson divide face into positive and negative, they split linguistic politeness strategies in the same way. Positive politeness strategies are used to protect the interlocutor's positive face (desire to be appreciated and approved of), and negative politeness strategies protect negative face (desire to be free from imposition). When a speaker adopts super-strategies 2, 3 and 4, they employ a linguistic strategy to manage politeness in interaction. In total there are 25 on-record politeness strategies (Focus 5.2), which serve as a useful analytical checklist for ways in which FTAs can be mitigated, depending on context.

Activity 5.3: Linguistic (Im)politeness—Getting the Salt

If we are to believe what we read in Pragmatics textbooks, people at dinner parties are always wanting someone to pass them the salt.[5] Asking someone to pass the salt is potentially a Face Threatening Act, as you may be impinging on them, which is a threat to negative face. Consider these possible locutions for achieving the illocutionary goal of getting the salt:

Salt!
Pass the salt!
I could do with a bit of salt.
Can I get some salt here?
Please could someone pass the salt over?
Is there any salt down at that end of the table?
Gimme the goddamn salt, you melter!
[Say nothing and get up and get salt for oneself]

a. For each locution, try to decide which of the five super-strategies is being used.
b. If redressive language is used, try to identify what kind of strategy it is (see Focus 5.2).

 Our answers are on the book's webpage.

Fictional Dialogue

Focus 5.2: Brown and Levinson's Politeness Strategies (1987: 103–227)

Super-strategy 2. The FTA is performed on record, using positive politeness	Super-strategy 3. The FTA is performed on record, using negative politeness	Super-strategy 4. The FTA is performed off record
Claim common ground:	1. Be conventionally indirect	1. Invite conversational implicatures:
1. Notice, attend to H's (interests, wants, needs, goods)	**Don't presume/assume:**	a. Give hints
2. Exaggerate (interest, approval, sympathy with H)	2. Question, hedge:	b. Give association rules
3. Intensify interest to H;	a. hedge on illocutionary force (hedges encoded in particles, adverbial clause hedges)	c. Presuppose
4. Use in-group identity markers:	b. Hedges address to Grice's maxims	d. Understate
a. address forms,	c. Hedges addressed to politeness strategies	e. Overstate
b. Use of in-group language or dialect,	d. prosodic/kinesic hedges	f. Use tautologies
c. Use of jargon or slang,	**Don't coerce H:**	g. Use contradictions
d. contraction or ellipsis	3. Be pessimistic	h. Be ironic
5. Seek agreement:	4. Minimize the imposition	i. Use metaphors
a. safe topics,	5. Give deference	j. Use rhetorical questions
b. repetition	**Communicate S's want to not impinge on H:**	2. Be vague and ambiguous: violate maxim of manner
6. Avoid disagreement	6. Apologize:	a. Be ambiguous
a. use token or pseudo-agreement,	a. admit the impingement,	b. Be vague
b. white lies	b. indicate reluctance,	c. Over-generalize
c. hedging opinions	c. give overwhelming reasons,	d. Displace H
7. Presuppose/raise/assert common ground:	d. beg forgiveness	e. Be incomplete, use ellipsis
a. gossip, small talk,	7. Impersonalize S and H	
b. point of view operations (personal-centre switch, time switch, places switch, avoidance of adjustment reports to H's point of view),	a. use performatives,	
c. presupposition manipulations (presuppose knowledge of H's wants and attitudes, presuppose H's values are the same as S's values, presuppose familiarity in S-H relationship, presuppose H's knowledge)	b. imperatives,	
8. Joke	c. impersonal verbs,	
Convey that S and H are co-operators	d. passive and circumstantial voices,	
9. Assert or presuppose S's knowledge of and concern for H's wants	e. replace the pronouns 'I' and 'you' by indefinites,	
10. Offer, promise	f. pluralize the 'I' and 'you' pronouns,	
11. Be optimistic	g. use point-of-view distancing	
12. Include both S and H in the activity	8. State the FTA as a general rule	
13. Give (or ask for) reasons	9. Nominalize	
14. Assume/assert reciprocity	**Redress other wants of H's:**	
Fulfil H's wants for some X	10. Go on record as incurring a debt, or as not indebting H	
15. Give gifts to H (goods, sympathy, understanding cooperation)		

S = Speaker, H = Hearer

See Figure 5.1 for Super-strategies 1 and 5, which do not involve the adoption of any linguistic politeness strategies.

Some of the politeness strategies listed in Focus 5.2 are used by the characters in *I,DB*. As discussed above, the Assessor has the **illocutionary goal** of eliciting responses to specific questions from Daniel, which may best be achieved if she can maintain good relations (**social goal**). Her questions may be understood as potentially impinging on Daniel's **negative face**, insofar as they require his time and effort, and could be invasive of his privacy. In avoidance of these potential FTAs, the Assessor employs several politeness strategies, many of which are negative.

In ▶ Sect. 5.2, the Assessor was shown to use **Indirect Speech Acts** (as in 'Could you just answer the question'), which are considered a negative politeness strategy in Brown and Levinson's model; their effect is to distance her from the illocutionary force in an attempt to maintain Daniel's negative face. Some of her strategies fall under the heading 'don't coerce Hearer' (Focus 5.2); this is despite the fact acknowledged in ▶ Sect. 5.3 that the Assessor has institutional power to do just that. Emphasising their social distance, she gives **deference** to her interlocutor by addressing him as 'Mr Blake' (social deixis, Turns 1 and 19). She **minimises the imposition** of the interview, using the adverb 'just', understatement ('a couple of questions), and the commissive 'It won't take up much of your time' (Turn 1). In an attempt to **impersonalise** the FTAs involved in the interview, the Assessor uses nominalisation and pluralises 1st person pronouns. In Turn 1, she **nominalises** 'your eligibility' (rather than hypothesising, 'if you are eligible') which minimises the risk involved in this interview for Daniel's welfare. By **pluralising** the 1st person pronoun, "If we could just keep to these questions' (Turn 17), even though Daniel is responsible for the dispreferred responses (▶ Sect. 5.4.4), she impersonalises the action. These negative politeness strategies serve the Assessor in (appearing to) attend to Daniel's negative face (his freedoms), while simultaneously exercising her power to ask questions and set the agenda.

However, it is important to emphasise that people often use negative and positive politeness strategies in tandem. The Assessor adopts some positive politeness strategies (Focus 5.2); namely, in Turn 5 she acknowledges that Daniel has already answered these questions, expressing **agreement**. With the adverb 'unfortunately' she expresses **sympathy** and aligns her evaluative **point of view** with his, putting them on **common ground**. She gives positive feedback to one of Daniel's responses (Turn 15: Okay, that's great), **exaggerating approval**. Although she uses more standard forms than Daniel, she does share his use of the Tyneside dialect in using the plural 3rd person pronoun 'us' in place of 'me' (Turn 19), an **in-group identity marker**. These strategies serve the Assessor in maintaining Daniel's positive face, his need to be valued and included. Daniel also uses positive and negative politeness strategies, which we encourage you to explore further in Activity 5.4. But first, in ▶ Sect. 5.5.3, we explore an alternative to politeness in interaction: impoliteness.

5.5.3 Impoliteness

Instead of enhancing or supporting face, **impoliteness** is about attacking face (Culpeper 1996: 356). According to Culpeper:

Situated behaviours are viewed negatively—considered 'impolite'—when they conflict with how one expects them to be, how one wants them to be and/or how one thinks they ought to be. [...] they cause or are presumed to cause offence.

(2011: 23)

Like many of the pragmatic features of dialogue discussed in this chapter, impolite behaviour is judged with reference to the situational context and shared norms. Moreover, according to Culpeper, impoliteness is not inherent to the utterance itself, but in its reception. For fictional discourse, this means that impoliteness may be perceived within the text (by other characters) or in the discourse-world (by readers). Culpeper goes on to note that impolite behaviour can offend to different extents, depending on factors such as the perceiver's sensibilities and their understanding of the intentionality or motivations behind the behaviour. Culpeper (2005: 36–37) helpfully notes that impoliteness is *not*:
– 'incidental face-threat' (a by-product of an action);
– unintentional (including failed attempts at politeness);
– banter (mock impoliteness, see Bousfield [2007]);
– An FTA performed without politeness (without mitigation).

As such, impoliteness occurs when a hearer *believes* that a speaker *intends* to do face damage. Like politeness, impoliteness can also be achieved by going on record or off record. **On-record impoliteness** involves explicitly attacking the face of an interlocutor. **Off-record impoliteness** can be achieved by raising an implicature, through sarcasm (also called 'mock politeness') or by withholding politeness where it might be expected (Culpeper 2005; Bousfield 2007). Culpeper (2011) adopts Brown and Levinson's (1987) model, to set out a series of impoliteness strategies which *damage* positive or negative face, summarised in ◘ Table 5.3.

We now examine *I,DB* for features which may be read as impolite. Certain linguistic forms are more likely to be regarded as impolite, even out of context (Leech 2014; Culpeper 2011; Bousfield 2008). For example, the expletives 'fuckin'' (Turn 18) and 'arse' (Turn 30) are usually regarded as impolite regardless of context but may be markedly impolite in the context of a formal meeting. 'Taboo words' are considered a **positive impoliteness strategy** (◘ Table 5.3), so Daniel's usage may damage the Assessor's positive face (her right to be valued). Readers might vary in their interpretations of these expletives as impolite, based on their understanding of the context of use, whether they arise from his frustrations, or are intended to cause face damage and/or humour. The Assessor recognises the profanity 'fucken' as potentially impolite as she responds, 'Mr Blake, if you continue to speak to us like that, that's not going to be very helpful for your assessment' (Turn 19). Her response could be read as an Indirect Speech Act with the illocutionary force of a 'threat', which would constitute **negative impoliteness** (◘ Table 5.3). More generally, the Assessor may be considered as positively impolite in this interaction because she is 'disinterested, unconcerned, unsympathetic' towards the actual medical issue affecting Daniel's ability to work.

One of the reasons *I,DB* is so interesting for an (im)politeness analysis is that the participants have distinct understandings of the interactive context,

Table 5.3 Culpeper's strategies for positive and negative impoliteness

Strategies designed to damage the addressee's positive face	Strategies designed to damage the addressee's negative face
Ignore, snub; fail to acknowledge the other's presence	Frighten—instil belief that action detrimental to the other will occur
Exclude the other from an activity	Condescend, scorn or ridicule—emphasise your relative power
Disassociate from the other—e.g. deny association or common ground	Be contemptuous
Be disinterested, unconcerned, unsympathetic	Do not treat the other seriously
Use inappropriate identity markers—e.g. use title and surname when a close relationship pertains, or a nickname when a distant relationship pertains	Belittle the other (e.g. use diminutives)
Use obscure or secretive language—e.g. mystify the other with jargon, or use a code known to others in the group, but not the target	Invade the other's space—literally (e.g. position yourself closer to the other than the relationship permits) or metaphorically (e.g. ask for or speak about information which is too intimate given the relationship)
Seek disagreement—select a sensitive topic	Explicitly associate the other with a negative aspect—personalise, use the pronouns 'I' and 'you'
Make the other feel uncomfortable—for example, do not avoid silence, joke or use small talk	Put the other's indebtedness on record
Use taboo words—swear, or use abusive or profane language	Violate the structure of conversation—interrupt
Call the other names, insult, use derogatory nominations	Ask challenging/unpalatable questions (e.g. How come you mess everything up?)
Curse and bestow ill wishes	Threaten
	Silence other (e.g. shut up)
	Dismiss other (e.g. go away)

illocutionary goals, the relevant topic and the appropriate strategies for mitigating these conflicting interests. This discussion has identified only a few of the (im)politeness strategies attributed to the characters in *I,DB* and readers are encouraged to explore further in Activity 5.4.

5.5.4 Issues with (Im)politeness

Brown and Levinson's (1987) model of politeness is one of the most enduring and underscores Culpeper's (2011) model of impoliteness. However, both have their limitations and other models have been advanced to address some of the issues.

For instance, the division of 'face' into positive and negative kinds may not always be clear-cut, as a person's self-value is closely related to their right to freedom. Likewise, positive and negative (im)politeness strategies are not always distinctive. For instance, Daniel's use of the expletive 'fucken' (Turn 18) was described as a positive impoliteness strategy because of its potential damage to positive face (▶ Sect. 5.5.3), but in some contexts it might also be considered a positive politeness strategy, insofar as it can be an in-group identity marker, closing social distance (Focus 5.2). This example highlights the difficulty in ascribing functions to forms in any stylistic analysis, including politeness, and the importance of looking at the context and co-text for evidence; in this case, the Assessor's rebuke (Turn 19) provides evidence for an 'impolite' reading. As Leech (2014: 13) observes, politeness is both a 'linguistic phenomenon' relating to the forms used and a 'social/cultural phenomenon', relating to social factors such as social distance between interactants, the setting of the interaction and type of activity. Seeing politeness consisting of two sub-components acknowledges that words/phrases/sentences in and of themselves are neither polite nor impolite; it is the context in which the words are uttered that gives them their im/polite meaning (see also Spencer-Oatey 2002: 532; Locher and Watts 2005: 29).

Furthermore, the distinction between positive and negative (im)politeness strategies is further confounded by the fact that interlocutors tend to blend the two (▶ Sect. 5.5.2). The distinction between negative and positive politeness is not absolute and, in fact, is better thought of as two sides of the same coin in facework. Another issue with Brown and Levinson's model is that it suggests the purpose of *all* politeness is to mitigate potential FTAs. This ignores the possibility that politeness may be serving some other, more constructive aim, an issue addressed by Leech's (2014) alternative model of politeness. By linking particular politeness strategies with personal qualities (e.g. reticence and modesty), Leech's framework has benefits for drawing out the links between politeness and characterisation (▶ Chapter 6). Despite these caveats, the (im)politeness models summarised above are particularly useful in analysis as they offer a list of linguistic strategies to look for (Focus 5.2 and ◘ Table 5.2), bearing in mind the importance of context in their interpretation.

Activity 5.4: Linguistic (Im)politeness—In Context and Discourse

Sections 5.5.2 and 5.5.3 identified some of the (im)politeness strategies attributed to the two characters in *I,DB*, but there are more to explore.

a. Looking at Daniel's contributions, what kinds of politeness strategies can you identify?
b. Could any of these be considered as impoliteness strategies? If so, which ones? By whom and in what context(s)?
c. The film *I, Daniel Blake* is a social commentary on the difficulties faced by working-class people when the benefits system is overly bureaucratic and unsupportive. How do the politeness strategies used in the two characters' dialogue help to convey this message at the author-reader discourse level?

Our answers to these questions can be found on the book's webpage.

5.6 Corpus Approaches to Dialogue and Pragmatics

In this section, we provide a brief overview of how corpus approaches can be used in analysing dialogue.

5.6.1 Corpus Approaches and CA

Corpus approaches can assist in Conversation Analysis (CA) via annotation of spoken corpora. CA relies on (i) detailed manual markup of transcripts for various features which are then (ii) re-scrutinised manually to find patterns. This process lends itself to corpus annotation because if the first part of the process is carried out using machine readable codes, then the second part can be automated. There are obvious benefits, therefore, for creating CA markup in machine readable form using eXtensible Markup Language (XML)—the de facto standard for corpus annotation (introduced in ▶ Chapter 4, see also Hardie 2014). Rühlemann (2017), for example, explains how XML and CA transcription can be integrated allowing for pattern searches and quantification of conversation features (e.g. backchannels, pauses, pitch changes). Rühlemann's data is from the spoken section of the BNC, a corpus that readers of this book will now be familiar with. As Rühlemann points out:

> while CA researchers have been used to searching their data manually, with all the limitations to size and extractability of data, XML transcripts allow for efficient automatic retrieval, extraction, and analysis of very complex and very large data sets.
>
> Rühlemann (2017: 225)

As Rühlemann goes on to explain, XML markup allows for quantification and statistical examination of features in large data sets.

5.6.2 Corpus Approaches and Pragmatics

Pragmatic phenomenon, such as speech acts, implicature and (im)politeness, cannot be identified automatically because there is no one-to-one connection between form and function. Pragmatic meaning is meaning that emerges in the context of interaction. Consequently, corpus studies involving pragmatic phenomenon tend to rely on manual analysis and corpus annotation. For example, Culpeper and Archer (2008) manually analyse a 79,000-word corpus of trial proceedings and play texts for requests and commands and annotate the corpus to show where a request has happened and what type of request it is (direct/indirect). Other corpora that have been annotated for speech acts include SPICE Ireland (see Kirk 2016) and Weisser (2015, 2016, 2018); the latter has developed a corpus annotation tool that semi-automates the task of speech act analysis in corpora. Once a corpus has been annotated for speech acts, then the annotation can be used to carry out further work in other areas of Pragmatics, such as politeness. For example, speech acts that are inherently face threatening (such as directives) can be searched for within the corpus and then any features of politeness identified (see, e.g., Ronan 2022).

An alternative possibility is a form-to-function approach where forms are searched for in a corpus and then assessed for their pragmatic function. For example, Culpeper and Kyto (1999) investigate hedges (discourse/pragmatic markers) in the corpus of Early Modern English Dialogues (a 1.2-million-word corpus containing several different text types including courtroom transcriptions, witness statements and play texts). Hedges can modify pragmatic force (Culpeper and Kyto 1999: 297) and can be used as intensifiers ('very', 'really', 'super'), or to indicate, for example, certainty/uncertainty ('I'm sure'/'I think'). Hedges can be used to mitigate face threatening acts and therefore be involved in politeness. Conversely, they can also accentuate face threats, so can be used in impoliteness.

Similarly, speech acts can be identified in a corpus by searching for Illocutionary Force Indicating Devices (IFIDS), such as performative verbs (e.g. 'order', 'warn') or phrases ('can I get', 'would you mind'). For example, Lutzky and Kehoe (2017) assess apologies in a 630-million-word corpus of blogs by searching for 'sorry' and inflected forms of 'pardon', 'excuse', 'afraid', 'apologise', 'forgive, 'regret' and 'apology' (see also, Harrison and Allton 2013; and Page 2014); Su (2017) looks at requests in a corpus of scripts from the TV sitcom The Big Bang Theory by searching for "conventionalised sequences" such as 'would you like to' and 'I want you to'.

 Corpus KWIC-ie: 'Sorry' in the spoken section of the BNC
Using the spoken section of the BNC, examine how sorry is used in spoken discourse and explore whether there are any patterns of usage.
  How often is 'sorry' used in the speech act of apology?
  Can you see any problems with this approach?

Instructions and discussion can be found on the book's webpage.

A problem with the form-to-function approach is that it depends on formulating a comprehensive search list. If the search list is deficient, then so too are the results. But even with a well-constructed list of search terms, the researcher will not know if they have missed something. Also, the search results will contain lots of examples that are not related to speech acts and therefore require manual analysis to ascertain function.

5.6.3 Using n-grams to Find Pragmatic and Conversational Features

In this section, we test out the potential for n-grams to provide a way in to conversational and pragmatic analysis. N-grams are a consecutive string of words, where n is the number of words in the string. So, a single word is a 1-gram, two words is a 2-gram, a string of 3 is a 3-gram and so on. Many corpus tools will automatically search for n-grams in a corpus and provide a list of the most frequent sets of consecutive word strings. These n-grams can provide a focus for further analysis within the data they occur.

To illustrate the potential of n-gram analysis, we used *AntConc* (Anthony 2022) to calculate the n-grams in character dialogue in Season 1 (S1) of the TV sitcom *The Big Bang Theory* (*TBBT*). *TBBT* has been the subject of several studies including those that incorporate a corpus approach (see, e.g., Bednarek 2012; Su 2017; Van Zyl and Botha 2016). All these studies have been interested in the construction of character (the topic of our next chapter), particularly on the rather unusual character of Sheldon Cooper—an arrogant, extremely socially awkward know-it-all who finds it difficult to relate to other humans. For reasons of space, we focus here on the speech of the main character, Sheldon, and look at the most frequent n-gram in all his turns combined from S1: 'I don't'. This is a 3-gram ('do' and 'n't' are counted as separate words), and it occurred 35 times in Sheldon's speech. This gave us a manageable amount of data to examine in more detail via concordance lines (see ◘ Fig. 5.2) and using the tools we describe in this chapter as frameworks for analysis.

In terms of (im)politeness, the occurrences of 'I don't' show that Sheldon tends to be contrary and therefore tends to seek disagreement (positive face impoliteness). For example, when Penny (another central character) proposes a surprise birthday party for Leonard (Sheldon's roommate, friend and colleague), his response is 'I don't see this as a promising endeavour'. Similarly, when Leonard proposes he might ask someone at work out on a date, Sheldon's response is 'I don't think you have a shot there'. Sheldon is also contemptuous (negative face impoliteness) (e.g. 'I don't want to criticise your rhetorical style, but …'; 'I don't know, but if cats could sing, they'd hate it too' [Penny's singing]; 'unlike you, I don't need validation from lesser minds') and condescending, another negative face impoliteness (e.g. 'I don't know how, but she's cheating' [Penny beats Sheldon at Halo]; 'I don't think I need to tell you what an honour this is [Sheldon asks Penny to be on his Halo team; the honour is Penny's, of course]). Also, Sheldon does not take others seriously (another negative impoliteness strategy). For instance, when a colleague, Lesley, solves an equation he has been struggling with, he says that she got lucky. Leonard reminds Sheldon that he does not believe in luck, to which Sheldon replies, 'I don't have to believe in it for her to be lucky'.

Some of the instances of 'I don't' can also be analysed from a CA perspective whereby they count as dispreferred responses, which can be seen as violations of the structure of conversation— another negative face impoliteness strategy. For example, when Penny asks to talk to him, Sheldon replies 'I don't care for chit-chat',

1	Why can't she get her own TV. No	I don't.	And neither do you. You did not brea
2	I wanted to have a costume meeting.	I don't	care if anybody gets it, I'm going as
3	interest I'm aware of, and you know	I don't	care for chit-chat. Well alright, but I
4	told you you could touch my board?	I don't	come into your house and touch your
5	pithelial cells slough off naturally, but	I don't	condemn those who seek to accelera
6	Ah, because it's in Long Beach, and	I don't	drive. No, of course not, there's no co
7	Leonard a present before the party?	I don't	drive, and the only things available
8	if cats could sing, they'd hate it too.	I don't	guess. As a scientist I reach conclusi
9	he's not that intelligent. She got lucky	I don't	have to believe in it for her to be
10	whiny and annoying. I'd love to, but	I don't	have tangerine chicken. Show me yo
11	ry colleagues. No we don't. So what?	I don't	issue invitations to your mother. And
12	to spell out everything for this girl.	I don't	know what your odds are in the wor
13	me down to pet stores to look at cats.	I don't	know if I can take it. Oh, good lord.
14	tle of Gettysburg. We don't eat here,	I don't	know what's good. Statistically unli
15	30's gangster. No, no, wait, hold on.	I don't,	know what the protocol is here. Do I
16	e cornered, cover me. Okay, that's it,	I don't	know how, but she is cheating. No-o
17	not have teen fetishes, too late, I win.	I don't	know, but if cats could sing, they'd h
18	occasion? What? No you didn't. Okay,	I don't	know where you just came from, but
19	t's worth, I thought it was humorous.	I don't	know what you were worried about.
20	ve explained repeatedly, unlike you,	I don't	need validation from lesser minds.
21	funny here. Sick? What kind of sick?	I don't	need you to guess, I need you to kno
22	itch. Gentlemen. Gentlemen. Actually,	I don't	need a team, I could easily defeat you
23	Dr Emile Farminfarmian. Okay, sure.	I don't	see a problem with that. Good for y
24	care for chit-chat. Well alright, but	I don't	see this as a promising endeavour. I h
25	h, I wish it were that simple. You see,	I don't	spend much time here and so I've n
26	o, don't. Or the one. Dammit, I'll do it.	I don't.	Teams are traditionally named after f
27	irt. I think this is the place. Leonard,	I don't	think I can do this. No. We are com
28	with the limp and the lazy eye? Well,	I don't	think you have a shot there. I have n
29	the fourth member of our Halo team.	I don't	think I need to tell you what an honor
30	had a little misunderstanding. Huh.	I don't	understand the question. Oh. I hadn't
31	to provide one. That's your opinion.	I don't	understand the question. Who? That
32	understand to be your thesis. Why?	I don't	understand. Yes, we shared a uterus
33	w energy, plus your irritability... Oh!	I don't.	usually pick up on those things. Good
34	and its impact vis-a-vis taste. As do I.	I don't	want my job back. I've spent the last
35	s noteworthy. Oh. Okay. You know,	I don't	want to criticise your rhetorical style

◘ **Fig. 5.2** Concordance of 'I don't' in Sheldon's speech In S1 *TBBT*

and when Penny has important news and announces it by saying 'guess what?', Sheldon replies, 'I don't guess'. These then disrupt the 'normal' flow of the conversation and stop Penny reaching her conversational goals.

There are only two instances of 'I don't' that are of limited pragmatic and conversation interest (lines 6 and 23 in ◘ Fig. 5.2), suggesting that n-gram analysis could usefully be expanded out to all seasons of TBBT—for Sheldon at least. Whether n-grams are as useful for other characters in the sitcom remains to be investigated; Sheldon, after all, is a highly unusual character and so much of what he says is loaded pragmatically and goes against the 'norm'. Part of the complexity of Sheldon's character is that he is incapable of 'normal' human interactions and finds it difficult to relate to others, particularly emotionally. A consequence of that is he does not show sympathy or empathy. It is debatable, therefore, whether the impoliteness in the concordances counts as impoliteness in Culpeper's (2005) terms if it is unintentional/accidental and not intended to cause offence. The instances, nonetheless, can be used to establish Sheldon's character (see ▶ Chapter 6 on characterisation).

5.7 Conclusions

This chapter has introduced models for the analysis of interaction, drawing from Pragmatics—Speech Act Theory, the Cooperative Principle and (Im)politeness—as well as Conversation Analysis. These approaches were designed for the analysis of real spoken interaction; yet, insofar as fictional interaction is based on what we know and expect from real conversation, these models are applicable and fruitful in the analysis of fictional dialogue. In fact, the Pragmatics of fictional discourse can be all the more interesting, because of the complexity of the discourse structure. Character dialogue is imbued with pragmatic strategies and interactive patterns that carry meanings between characters, but also carry meanings between the author and reader. *I, DB* provided one interaction that illustrates the interplay of all the models covered in this chapter. It also served to demonstrate how different characters, their competing interactive goals and strategies can allow the author to provide a social critique of institutions, to question their power and bureaucracy, and emphasise the humanity of those who need their support. Although this chapter deals mostly with drama, the frameworks we use are equally applicable to dialogue in prose fiction.

In the corpus section of this chapter, we noted that corpus approaches to dialogue rely on manual intervention. However, corpus searches can provide a focus for analysis. Many previous studies prepare word lists to guide their searches and subsequent analyses. We explored the possibility of using n-grams to find a focus for analysis. The concordances for the n-grams were then analysed using existing pragmatic and conversational frameworks. The main methodological point here is that any such analysis should be systematic and rigorous, thus accounting for every instance in the data.

- **Further Reading**

For book length examinations of impoliteness: Culpeper (2011)
An example of a stylistic analysis using (im)politeness: Bousfield (2007)
For a different approach to politeness: Leech (2014)
For an accessible guide to Pragmatics: Thomas 1995 and its relevance to fictional discourse, see Locher and Jucker (2017)
For more on corpus approaches to Pragmatics, see:
Corpus Pragmatics: The International Journal of Corpus Linguistics and Pragmatics.
There are also a few edited volumes, including:
Corpus Pragmatics: A Handbook (Aijmer & Rühleman 2014).
Corpora: Pragmatics and Discourse (Jucker & Hundt 2009).
Pragmatics and Corpus Linguistics: A Mutualistic Entente (Romero-Trillo 2008).

- **Resources**

AntConc (Anthony 2022): a free to download corpus analysis tool; see Lawrence Anthony's website for more detail: ▶ https://www.laurenceanthony.net/

- **Notes**

1. 'Dialogue' is derived from ancient Greek *dia*, meaning through, and *logos*, meaning speech, and is conversation between two or more people (Wales 2011: 114).
2. Sometimes referred to as the 'pragmatic turn' in Stylistics; see Leech and Short (2007).
3. The term 'infringe' is used by Grice throughout his 1975 and 1978 papers but is used to mean general non-fulfilment of a maxim and not used in the way described by Thomas.
4. This is a posthumous collection of lectures given by Sacks produced by Gail Jefferson and Emmanuel Schegloff.
5. This example is famously used by Searle (1976) but has been repeatedly used since then in the numerous discussions of Searle's ideas.

References

Aijmer, K., & Rühleman, C. (Eds.). (2014). *Corpus Pragmatics: A handbook*. Cambridge: CUP.
Anthony, L. 2022. *AntConc* (Version 4.2.0) [Computer Software]. Tokyo, Japan: Waseda University. Available from ▶ https://www.laurenceanthony.net/software
Austin, J. L. 1962. *How to Do Things with Words*. Oxford: Oxford University Press.
Austin, J. L. 1979. Performative Utterances. In *Philosophical Papers* 3rd ed, eds. J. O. Urmson and G. J. Warnock, 233–252. Oxford University Press.
Bednarek, M. 2012. Constructing Nerdiness: Characterisation in The Big Bang Theory, *Multilingua* 31, 199–229.
Bousfield, D. 2007. "Never a Truer Word Said in Jest": A Pragmastylistic Analysis of Impoliteness as Banter in Henry IV, part I. In *Contemporary Stylistics*, eds. M. Lambrou and P. Stockwell, 209–220. London: Continuum.
Bousfield, D. 2008. *Impoliteness in Interaction*. Philadelphia and Amsterdam: John Benjamins.
Brown, P. and Levinson, S. C. 1987. *Politeness: Some Universals in Language Usage*. Cambridge: Cambridge University Press.
Brown, G. and Yule, G. 1983. *Discourse Analysis*. Cambridge and New York: Cambridge University Press.
Burton, D. 1980. *Dialogue and Discourse: A Socio-linguistic Approach to Modern Drama Dialogue and Naturally Occurring Conversation*. London: Routledge and Kegan Paul.
Button, G. and Casey, N. 1985. Topic Nomination and Topic Pursuit. *Human Studies* 8, 3–55.
Culpeper, J. 1996. Towards an Anatomy of Impoliteness. *Journal of Pragmatics*, 25, 3: 349–367. ▶ https://doi.org/10.1016/0378-2166(95)00014-3
Culpeper, J. 2005. Impoliteness and Entertainment in the Television Quiz Show: 'The Weakest Link'. *Journal of Politeness Research* 1, 1: 35–72.
Culpeper, J. 2011. *Impoliteness: Using Language to Cause Offence*. Cambridge: CUP
Culpeper, J., & Archer, D. 2008. Requests and Directness in Early Modern English Trial Proceedings and Play-Texts, 1640–1760. In *Speech Acts in the History of English*, Eds. A. H. Jucker, & I. Taavitsainen, 45–84). Amsterdam: John Benjamins.
Culpeper, J., Kyto, M. 1999. Modifying Pragmatic Force: Hedges in a Corpus of Early Modern English Dialogues. In: *Historical dialogue analysis*, Eds. A. J. H. Jucker, G. Fritz, F. Lebsanft, 293–312. Amsterdam: John Benjamins.

Goffman, E. 1967. *Interaction Ritual: Essays in Face-to-Face Behavior.* Chicago: Aldine Publishing
Grice, H. P. 1975. Logic and Conversation. In *Syntax and Semantics*, Vol. 3, Speech Acts, eds. P. Cole & J. L. Morgan, 41–58. New York: Academic Press.
Grice, H. P. 1978. Further Notes on Logic and Conversation. In *Pragmatics*, Vol. 9, Syntax and Semantics, ed. P. Cole. New York: Academic Press.
Grice, H. P. [1975] 1989. Logic and Conversation. In *Studies in the Way of Words*, ed. H. P. Grice, 22–40. Cambridge, MA and London: Harvard University Press.
Hardie, A. 2014. Modest XML for Corpora: Not a Standard, But a Suggestion. *ICAME Journal*, 38: 73–103.
Harrison, S., and Allton, D. 2013. Apologies in Email Discussions. In *Pragmatics of Computer-Mediated Communication*, eds. S. C. Herring, D. Stein, & T. Virtanen, 315–337. Berlin: Walter de Gruyter.
Jucker, A., Schreier, D., and Hundt, M. (Eds.). (2009). *Corpora: Pragmatics and discourse.* Amsterdam: Rodopi.
Kirk, J. M. 2016. The Pragmatic Annotation Scheme of the SPICE-Ireland Corpus. *International Journal of Corpus Linguistics* 21, 3: 299–322.
Leech, G. 2014. *The Pragmatics of Politeness.* Oxford: OUP
Leech, G. and Short, M. 2007. *Style in Fiction: A Linguistic Introduction to English Fictional Prose.* 2nd ed. London and New York: Longman.
Locher, M. A. and Jucker, A. H. eds. 2017. *The Pragmatics of Fiction: Literature, Stage and Screen Discourse.* Edinburgh: Edinburgh University Press.
Locher, M. A. and Watts, R. J. 2005. Politeness Theory and Relational Work. *Journal of Politeness Research*, 1, 1: 9–33.
Lutzky, U, and Kehoe, A. 2017. "I Apologise for My Poor Blogging": Searching for Apologies in the Birmingham Blog Corpus. *Corpus Pragmatics* 1, 37–56.
Page, R. 2014. Saying 'Sorry': Corporate Apologies Posted to Twitter. *Journal of Pragmatics*, 62, 30–45.
Romero-Trillo, J. (Ed.). (2008). *Pragmatics and corpus linguistics: A mutualistic entente.* Berlin: Mouton.
Ronan, P. 2022. Directives and Politeness in SPICE-Ireland. *Corpus Pragmatics* 6, 175–199.
Rühlemann, C. 2017. Integrating Corpus-Linguistic and Conversation-Analytic Transcription in XML: The Case of Backchannels and Overlap in Storytelling Interaction. *Corpus Pragmatics* 1, 201–232.
Sacks, H. 1992. *Lectures on Conversation, Vols I and II.* Oxford, UK: Blackwell.
Sacks, H., Schegloff, E. A., and Jefferson, G. 1974. A Simplest Systematics for the Organization of Turn-taking for Conversation. *Language* 50, 4: 696–735.
Schegloff, E. A. 1972. Notes on a Conversational Practice: Formulating Place. In *Studies in Social Interaction*, ed. D. Sudnow, 75–119. New York: Free Press.
Schegloff, E. A. 2007. *Sequence Organization in Interaction: Volume 1.* Cambridge and New York: Cambridge University Press.
Schegloff, E. A. and Sacks, H. 1973. Opening Up Closings. *Semiotica*, 7: 289–327.
Searle, J. R. 1969. *Speech Acts.* Cambridge and New York: Cambridge University Press.
Searle, J. R. 1976. A Classification of Illocutionary Acts. *Language in Society*, 5, 1: 1–23.
Searle, J. R. and Vanderveken, D. 1985. *Foundations of Illocutionary Logic.* Cambridge and New York: Cambridge University Press.
Sidnel, J. 2010. *Conversation Analysis: An Introduction.* London: John Wiley and sons.
Spencer-Oatey, H. 2002. Managing Rapport in Talk: Using Rapport Sensitive Incidents to Explore the Motivational Concerns Underlying the Management of Relations. *Journal of Pragmatics*, 34: 529–545.
St. André, J. 2013. How the Chinese Lost 'Face'. *Journal of Pragmatics*, 55: 68–85.
Su, H. 2017. Local Grammars of Speech Acts: An Exploratory Study. *Journal of Pragmatics* 111, 72–83
Thomas, J. 1995. *Meaning in Interaction: An Introduction to Pragmatics.* London: Routledge
Van Zyl, M. and Botha, Y. 2016. Stylometry and Characterisation in *The Big Bang Theory*, *Literator* 37, 2: a1282.

Wales, K. 2011. *A Dictionary of Stylistics*. Harlow, UK: Pearson Education Ltd.
Weisser, M. 2015. Speech Act Annotation. In *Corpus Pragmatics: A Handbook*, eds. K. Aijmer & C. Rühlemann, 84–113. Cambridge: Cambridge University Press.
Weisser, M. 2016. DART: The Dialogue Annotation and Research Tool. *Corpus Linguistics and Linguistic Theory*, 12, 2: 355–388.
Weisser, M. 2018. *How to Do Corpus Pragmatics on Pragmatically Annotated Data: Speech Acts and Beyond*. Amsterdam: John Benjamins.

Fictional Character

Supplementary Information The online version contains supplementary material available at ▶ https://doi.org/10.1007/978-3-031-10422-0_6.

© The Author(s), under exclusive license to Springer Nature Switzerland AG 2023
J. Lugea and B. Walker, *Stylistics*,
https://doi.org/10.1007/978-3-031-10422-0_6

6.1 Thinking About Characters

In this chapter, we turn our attention to the characters that populate fictional texts. The term **character** may have an unproblematic meaning and use in everyday language, but when it comes to analysing what a fictional character actually *is* (i.e. its status of existence or **ontology**), the issue is more complex. For example, do characters exist only in the text or do they exist in the mind of the reader? What makes us believe in a character, and even like or dislike them? What makes us capable of predicting their behaviour? To address these questions, this chapter outlines different approaches to understanding fictional characters, their ontological status and the processes by which they are created. We introduce Culpeper's (2001) work on characterisation, which treats the process as an interplay between language, cognition and knowledge about the real world and its people. Following Culpeper (2001), we use **character** to mean the people (or beings) that inhabit the fictional world, and **characteristics** for the "qualities […] that combine to form a person's personality" (2001: 2). **Characterisation** is the process of forming an impression of a character and their characteristics. Later in this chapter, we will discuss the factors that combine to form those impressions before going on to demonstrate how the characterisation process works by applying a revised version of Culpeper (2001) model to an extract from a novel. Although Culpeper devised his model mainly for the analysis of characters in drama, the version we present here is adapted for application to prose fiction as well, based on Walker (2012). Before reading on, start thinking about character by completing Activity 6.1.

Activity 6.1: Discussion Point: Sherlock Holmes
The fictitious detective, Sherlock Holmes, originated in the printed stories of Arthur Conan Doyle, which have since been reprinted and translated many times and staged in several theatre, film and TV dramatisations, including a BBC adaptation set in modern times. Fans can buy merchandise, including a board game, and visit his 'home' at 221B Baker Street, London.

Q1. What does this reveal about the ontological status of character, i.e. how/where they exist?

Q2. What does this reveal about the characterisation process, i.e. how characters are created?

 We provide our responses to the questions on the book's webpage.

6.2 Characters: In the Text or in the Mind?

A long-standing debate concerning the ontology of fictional characters is whether they can be considered 'real', existing independently of the text, or whether they are simply 'words', existing only in the text in which they appear (see, e.g., Rimmon-Kenan 2002: 33; see also Eder et al. 2010). Culpeper (2001: 6–8) summarises the two, often competing, standpoints as *humanising* and *de-humanising*, respectively.

6.2.1 Humanising: Characters in the Mind

The humanising stance contends that readers respond and react to fictional characters as though they were real people. Treating fictional characters in this way is something that many of us do from time to time, particularly with characters that are brought to life each week on TV. For example, in 2017, Detective Inspector, Alec Hardy, a character played by David Tennent in the UK TV drama series *Broadchurch*, apparently caused uproar on social media because he made a cup of tea using a microwave oven. *The Daily Mirror*, a popular UK national newspaper, reported that Hardy "thought that it would be OK to make tea in the microwave" (Minn, 2017), therefore ascribing thoughts (unscripted by the writer) to a fictitious character. On Twitter, one viewer tweeted the following:

> Ok, someone please tell Alec Hardy that you DON'T microwave tea. #broadchurch

The tweet appears to suggest that it is possible to have a conversation with Alec Hardy outside the script and therefore outside the fictional world in which he exists.

The example above demonstrates the possibility of characters existing outside the text(s) in which they were created (see also the Sherlock Holmes example in Activity 6.1). We can see further evidence of this in 'fanfiction' where readers re-imagine characters from their favourite texts in plots of their own writing. Established authors also use characters created in other texts for new stories; for example, P. D James uses characters created by Jane Austen in *Pride and Prejudice* for her murder mystery, *Death Comes to Pemberley*.

According to Bortolussi and Dixon (2003: 135), an extreme humanising approach treats characters as having "coherent fully developed and consistent personalities [...] psychological motives and unconscious drives", and such "motives" and "drives" are supposedly "accessible through the inferential procedures of personality theory and psychotherapy". Perhaps the most famous example of this extreme view is A. C. Bradley ([1904] 2007), who famously undertook psychological analyses of some of Shakespeare's characters.

6.2.2 De-humanising: Characters in the Text

The de-humanising approach understands character as a series of linguistic features in the text that combine to create a linguistic sign rather than any living entity. Attention is, therefore, focused solely on the linguistic features that provide information about character in the text, such as the way they are described and presented. The advantage of this approach is that the text is indisputable and gives readers access to the same character information. However, the often-quoted extreme of this view (see, e.g., Culpeper 2002: 33) is that of Weinsheimer concerning Jane Austen's *Emma*:

> Emma Woodhouse is not a woman nor need be described as if **it** were.
> Weinsheimer (1979: 187; emphasis added)

Weinsheimer, therefore, refuses to acknowledge that 'Emma' and 'Woodhouse' are anything more than words in the text and refuses to assign even a gender to those linguistic forms. However, as Chatman notes:

> [t]he equation of characters with 'mere words' is wrong [...] we recall fictional characters vividly, yet not a single word of the text in which they came alive [...]
> Chatman (1978: 118)

Here, Chatman suggests that a view of character which acknowledges only linguistic forms fails to recognise the role of the readers in creating an impression of a character. As Culpeper observes, "[c]haracters remain as words in the text only when those words have no readers or listeners" (Culpeper 2001: 9), suggesting that characterisation requires the text as well as human cognition. Consequently, characterisation is increasingly seen as both a humanising and a de-humanising process where textual features contribute to readers' mental construction of and conclusions about a character. In the next section, we introduce research that combines cognitive and psychological approaches with linguistic frameworks for analysing character and understanding the process by which readers form impressions of characters, i.e. characterisation.

6.2.3 Humanising + De-humanising: Characters in the Text and Mind

A cognitive approach to the study of character recognises the role of both the text *and* the mind. This combination of *text + mind* is sometimes referred to as bottom-up (text) and top-down (mind) processing, where readers form an impression of a character using a combination of textual information and cognition (Culpeper 2001: 11; see also Eder et al. 2010: 5; Schneider 2001). When we infer character traits, scholars argue that we use the same cognitive processes that we use for real people. For example, Culpeper (2001: 87) suggests that our "[...] knowledge of real-life people is our primary source of knowledge used in understanding characters". In ▶ Chapter 8, we expand on the capacity for people to use their own subjective experience to imagine how others' minds work (i.e. mind-modelling). Suffice to note here that the background knowledge we bring to a text is crucial for, firstly, recognising textual information that relates to character (Culpeper 2001: 47) and then utilising that information to develop an understanding of characters. For example, Culpeper suggests (drawing on theories from Social and Cognitive Psychology) that readers use knowledge of social categories, including:

- **personal categories**—knowledge about people's interests, habits, traits and goals;
- **social role categories**—knowledge about people's kinship roles (e.g. father, sister), occupational roles (e.g. teacher, bricklayer) and relational roles (e.g. husband/wife, friend);
- **group membership categories**—knowledge about social group variables such as age, sex, religion, social class, nationality.

Also important are the social schemata associated with the membership of social categories (Culpeper 2001: 75–79) as these provide information typically associated with social categories which can include 'prototypical' members as well as less obvious 'peripheral' members.

Other theories discussed by Culpeper aim to explain the cognitive mechanisms that enable readers to infer character from the information in the text and include:
- attribution theories, which explain how we attribute the behaviour of a person to a person's disposition; and
- foregrounding theory, which helps to explain how a character's behaviour (linguistic and other) can indicate character traits (Culpeper 2001: 115–135).

These theories attempt to explain how we differentiate and extract character information from linguistic (and other) behaviour, and how we then use it. For example, James Gandolfini in the US TV show *The Sopranos* belongs to the social category of 'mafia-boss', which triggers a social schema from which we might infer other potential traits, such as: violent, criminal, tough. However, from the outset of season 1 of *The Sopranos*, Gandolfini begins to have panic attacks, which goes against the typical 'mafia-boss' schema. Gandolfini's outward physical disturbances indicate (via attribution) that the character is suffering from some mental stress and anxiety. While a mafia-boss is prototypically 'tough', Gandolfini's anxiety attacks and his need for therapy challenge our schematic knowledge about the 'mafia-boss' category. Arguably, this 'schema-refreshing' deviation from the norms of this social category (see Culpeper, 1998) is what contributes to the dramatic tension and, indeed, the characterisation in *The Sopranos*.

6.2.4 Summary

The combined approach to characterisation acknowledges the importance of readers' background knowledge and cognitive processes in interaction with the text. The relevant knowledge and cognitive processes are triggered by information relating to character in the text, known as the **textual cues for characterisation** (see also Pfister, 1988; Rimmon-Kenan, 2002), and it is these cues that we will look at next.

6.3 Textual Cues

Textual cues for characterisation are linguistic triggers in the text that can prompt readers to create mental impressions of characters. Culpeper (2001)[1] makes a distinction between **explicit** and **implicit** character cues (cf. Rimmon-Kenan 2002: 59–60: direct definition and indirect presentation). Explicit cues are where authors, narrators or other characters explicitly name a character's characteristics; implicit cues refer to character information that is displayed through a character's appearance, actions and behaviours (including what they say and how they say it) from which a reader might infer character traits. For example, if we are told that a character is anti-social, then this would be an example of an explicit character cue. Prototypically, such cues involve traits being attributed to characters in copular clauses (e.g. she/he was a misanthrope). However, if a character is reclusive, seeks isolation and is uncommunicative when engaged in conversation then, from this behaviour, we might infer that they are anti-social. In this section, we focus on implicit cues for characterisation and present the list proposed, in the main, by Culpeper (2001). The list is not exhaustive but is the most useful for the study of character and characterisation.

6.3.1 Character Names

The names assigned to characters by an author can communicate characteristics about a character (such as gender) and give rise to culturally based associations or connotations. Joseph Kasof's research into people's responses to names concluded that forenames "differ in attractiveness and connote impressions of the names bearer's age, intellectual competence, race, ethnicity, social class, and other attributes" (Kasof 1993: 140; cited in Culpeper 2001). Kasof's findings, therefore, suggest that character names can be cues for characterisation. Character names can also be "meaningful" (Culpeper 2001: 231) in that they encode characteristics of the character (cf. 'telling' and 'interpretive' names, Pfister 1988:194; 'analogous' names, Rimmon-Kenan 2002: 68). For example, Bram Stoker's choice of the name 'Dracula' for his vampire character is meaningful because, according to Wilkinson's *An Account of the Principalities of Wallachia and Moldovia* (which Stoker apparently consulted when writing *Dracula*), "Dracula in the Wallachian language means Devil" (Wilkinson 1820: 19). Therefore, anyone reading *Dracula* for the first time with no prior knowledge of the fictional character of Count Dracula but with some knowledge of Wallachian might suspect from the outset that the Count has a bit of a dark side and is someone not to be crossed.

6.3.2 Actions

According to Rimmon-Kenan (2002: 61–63), the physical actions that characters perform in a text can have a symbolic dimension and imply character traits. Such actions might be one-off or habitual, planned or contemplated. Rimmon-Kenan also suggests that actions that are not performed ('non-actions') can imply character traits. Readers may use actions to create an impression of a character and part of the inferencing might be via a cause-and-effect relation. The example Rimmon-Kenan gives is that if character X kills a dragon, we might infer that X is brave. Thinking back to 'Mr Loveday's Little Outing', we noted in ▶ Chapter 4 that Mr Loveday performed lots of kind actions for his fellow inmates and these actions might lead the reader to infer that he is a caring person.

6.3.3 Visual Features

A character's visual features can trigger impressions of personality types and play a "key role in person perception and characterisation" (Culpeper 2001: 221). Rimmon-Kenan also notes a "relation between external appearance and character-traits" (2002: 65–66). Culpeper (2001) divides these cues into two sub-categories:
(i) Kinesic features—dynamic features, such as gait, posture, body language, gestures, facial expressions.
(ii) Relatively static body features—such as clothes, height and weight. Rimmon-Kenan notes that some appearance features are within a character's control or show choice (e.g. clothes, hairstyle) while others are "beyond a character's control" (2002: 66).

For example, turning once again to 'Mr Loveday's Little Outing', the reader is told by the 3rd person (heterodiegetic) narrator that Lord Moping (who is a long-term resident in an asylum) creates a "shuffling, skipping sound" when he walks, that he moves with a "jogging gait" and that he has "restless, quizzical eyes". From these kinesic features, the reader might infer that Lord Moping walks and moves in a noticeably different manner and suggests an air of agitation and restlessness, perhaps showing that he feels pressed by a sense of great busyness. These three descriptions help to reinforce the impression that he has problems with his mental health and play on the probable standard schema that people who are suffering mental health issues will present outward, visual manifestations of those issues. By way of contrast, the narrator introduces Mr Loveday to the reader with the following description: "an elderly little man with full white hair and an expression of great kindness". These descriptions of visual features begin to paint a picture of a harmless old man, partly using 'elderly' and 'little', and partly through the evaluative description of his facial expression, which assists the reader in the process of characterisation. Further descriptions of Mr. Loveday also provide evaluative accompaniments to the visual features; for example, we are told that Mr Loveday has "gentle, blue-grey eyes". Here the narrator attributes a non-visual quality (gentle) to a physical feature (eyes), suggesting that the character of the person to whom the eyes belong is also gentle (for discussion of this device see Rimmon-Kenan, 2002: 66). Such evaluations guide the reader's perception about a character. With 'Mr Loveday's Little Outing', however, we find at the end of the story that the narrator has been misleading us.

6.3.4 Accent and Dialect

Accent and dialect are strong triggers for social schema. As Culpeper (2001: 206) points out, they can indicate a character's regional background and social class. Accent and dialect can be indicated by spelling, lexis, morphology and syntax. For example, in the following extract from *Wuthering Heights*, Mr Lockwood (Heathcliff's new tenant) is making an unplanned visit to Wuthering Heights (Heathcliff's home) and is confronted by Joseph an elderly servant at the house:

(1) 'What are ye for?' he shouted. 'T' maister's down i' t' fowld. Go round by th' end o' t' laith, if ye went to spake to him.'

'Is there nobody inside to open the door?' I hallooed, responsively.

Wuthering Heights (Brontë 1847)

Brontë attempts to capture Joseph's Yorkshire dialect (associated with area of England where the novel is set) in written form (**eye dialect**), using regional lexis (e.g. 'laith' is a barn), grammatical forms (e.g. the archaic personal pronoun 'ye' and archaic past tense form 'spake' instead of 'speak'), contracted forms—some of which join with the following word (known as proclitics), and non-standard spellings to indicate pronunciation (e.g. 'maister' instead of 'master', 'went' instead of 'want'). Additionally, Joseph's opening question is a dialectal turn of phrase meaning something like 'what do you want?'. Joseph's regional dialect contrasts sharply with the 'standard' English of Mr Lockwood which also serves to highlight the contrast between their social classes and status.

Accent can also be named and described. For example, in Evelyn Waugh's short story, 'Mr Loveday's Little Outing', the third-person narrator describes Mr Loveday as having "a gentler tone, with a slight rural burr". While such descriptions tell the reader about the accent rather than the accent being enacted as we saw in the example above, they nonetheless act as characterisation cues. Note, then, that the options for representing the 'voices' of characters use the Discourse Presentation categories outlined in ▶ Chapter 4, and also contribute to the characterisation process.

6.3.5 Paralinguistic Features

Brown (1990: 112) describes paralinguistic features as "[…] aspects of speech that contribute to the meaning over and above what the verbal element of the message means", suggesting that such features "[…] contribute to the expression of attitude by a speaker". These include non-fluency features, loudness and voice quality and can lead to impressions about emotional states and personality. For instance, graphology can express aspects of a character's paralinguistic performance such as uppercase letters to indicate loudness, italics to indicate vocal emphasis. In the following example Barnes' novel *Talking it Over*, spaces in between individual letters in words can indicate slower than normal speech:

(2) Val: You're pathetic, you know that? You two. *Pa the tic.*

Barnes (1991: 219)

Val's slow delivery of the insult indicates the deliberate intent.

Reporting clauses that accompany direct speech and thought presentation (see ▶ Chapter 4) can provide information about, for example, the tone of voice, the pitch and the speed of delivery. Turning once again to 'Mr Loveday's Little Outing', Lord Moping is said to have a "high peevish voice" and says something "rather petulantly". The adjectives 'high' and 'peevish' and the adverb 'petulantly' are descriptions (and evaluations) from the narrator of Lord Moping's voice, which suggest attitudes such as irritability and impatience and a tone like that of a spoilt child. According to Brown (1990: 119-121), they might also indicate that Lord Moping's speech was also louder and possibly faster than normal. By contrast, Mr. Loveday's voice is described as having a "gentler tone, with a slight rural burr". According to Brown (1990: 119-121), the gentler tone suggests a lower than normal pitch, softer than normal loudness and slower than normal delivery. This information can be linked with schemata concerning the type of voice associated with, perhaps, a carer or nurse, and complements the visual cues to Mr. Loveday's character discussed above. Importantly for the story, it is perhaps not the sort of voice you might associate with a man who takes pleasure in killing young women.

6.3.6 Syntax

As well as indicating dialect, syntax can also indicate states of mind. For example, questions can indicate inquisitiveness, conditionals uncertainty and imperatives power status. However, as we saw in ▶ Chapter 5, such structures do not offer a one-to-one fit. For example, imperatives can be used to issue invitations (e.g. 'have some cake!'). Similarly, it is too simplistic to say that a character who always asks questions is inquisitive since questions can, for example, be used to criticise indirectly (e.g. 'are you sure you want to go out wearing that?'). It is sometimes useful, therefore, to consider speech acts when looking at syntactic patterns. As we will see in ▶ Chapter 8, syntactic choices can also indicate a character's cognitive habits.

6.3.7 Lexis

We have already seen that lexis can indicate dialect. According to Culpeper (2001), lexis can also show formality, education and social class. These might be indicated by lexical richness, colloquial versus standard forms, and (in English) the choice of Latinate over Germanic words, since the former often have more formal or educated connotations than the latter, for historical reasons. Lexis also includes social markers (such as pronouns and honorifics) and "surge features" (Taavitsainen 1999: 219–220). The latter are "outbursts of emotions" where "[t]he speaker's or narrator's mental afflictions or temporary states of mind find linguistic outlets", which include "exclamations, swearing, and pragmatic particles" (Taavitsainen 1999: 219–220). Exclamations may signal emotions such as regret, disdain or surprise, while swearing may signal anger or frustration. Pragmatic particles (also known as pragmatic markers and discourse markers) include such word forms as 'so', 'well', 'why' and 'what' and can express, for example, surprise or indignation. We will see some example of surge features later in ▶ Sect. 6.5.

6.3.8 Conversational Structure

As we saw in ▶ Chapter 5, conversational structure considers, for example, turn-taking and topic control. These and other conversational elements can also be character cues from which we might infer character traits. The extract from *I, Daniel Blake* which we looked at in ▶ Chapter 5 demonstrated that such conversational elements can be an indication of power and status. We showed that by taking control of turn allocation and attempting to control topic, Daniel attempts to challenge the interactional and institutional roles in his interview by posing a question to the person employed by the government to assess him. Daniel, therefore, attempts to gain (discursive) power and demonstrates his frustration with the system, as well as his tenacity in trying to stand up against the system, implicitly contributing towards his characterisation.

6.3.9 Conversational Implicature

Culpeper (2001) includes Grice's Cooperative Principle (Grice 1975) in his framework to explain how implicit meanings can be produced through a character's speech. Characters who violate, flout or infringe Grice's maxims might cause readers to form particular impressions about them. For example, we saw in ▶ Chapter 5 in the extract from *I, Daniel Blake* that Daniel's Assessor violates and flouts the maxims of relation and quantity in order to mislead Daniel and to maintain institutional and discursive power. These breaks in Grice's maxims help to characterise the Assessor as an unfeeling cog in the government machine.

6.3.10 (Im)Politeness

Linguistic (im)politeness can indicate personality traits of a character depending on how they mitigate or otherwise threats to face, and whether they attack their interlocutor's face. In ▶ Chapter 5, we saw how the Assessor in the extract from *I, Daniel Blake* maintained a professional front by being linguistically polite and attending to both the positive and negative faces of Daniel. These helped to show how the Assessor remained cool and detached from the person in front of her. Daniel, on the other hand, showed his frustration with the assessment process and the lack of understanding of his individual needs by swearing which was impolite in the context it occurred.

6.3.11 Context and Contrasts

Context is the company a character keeps and/or the setting the character finds itself in, which might be indicative of character, assuming (as the humanising approach does) that characters have a choice of where and with whom they spend their time. For example, a character who apparently chooses to reside in a house in the middle of nowhere might be viewed as reclusive (see ▶ Sect. 6.5). Additionally, as we saw in 6.3.3. above, setting up characters in contrast to one another (e.g. Lord Moping vs. Mr Loveday) can also be a strategic cue designed by the author to highlight particular characteristics of a character (see also ▶ Sect. 6.6).

6.3.12 Summary

The list of implicit character cues is summarised in ◘ Fig. 6.1 and is numbered for ease of reference. Note that the cues relate to and are delivered at different language levels, which we introduced in ▶ Chapter 1 (graphology, morphology, lexis, syntax, pragmatics). Some cues (xiii, ix and x) are to do with performance and are inferred from what characters say and how they say it. These cues are most relevant to dialogue, which we discussed in ▶ Chapter 5. Other cues (ii and iii) are delivered via descriptions and so characteristics must be inferred from what we are told about a character by the author, narrator or another character. Some cues (iv and v) can be encoded orthographically and graphologically. In the next section, we think about the source of character cues in more detail.

Checklist of implicit character cues:
   i. Character names – including meaningful names
   ii. Actions (and non-actions)
   iii. Visual features – appearance, kinesics (body language, gestures, facial expressions)
   iv. Accent and dialect
   v. Paralinguistic features – including tone and voice pitch
   vi. Lexis – including Germanic vs. Latinate; lexical richness; surge features; social markers
   vii. Syntax
   viii. Conversational structure – including turn-taking, turn length, topic control, interruptions
   ix. Conversational implicature
   x. (Im)Politeness
   xi. Context and contrasts – settings and contextual considerations

◘ Fig. 6.1 Checklist of implicit character cues

6.4 The Source of Character Cues

Culpeper's (2001) characterisation model was developed for drama and so only considered cues attributable to the playwright and to characters. Walker (2012) expands Culpeper's model for application to prose fiction, by considering the role of the narrator in generating character cues. McIntyre (2014) points out that, while all characterisation cues originate from a text's author regardless of the text genre, they can occur at any of the three levels of discourse that we introduced in ▶ Chapter 1:

author → reader
narrator → narratee
character → character.

In this section, we discuss, using examples from plays and prose, the sorts of cues that can typically occur at the three discourse levels. Our discussion begins with the character → character discourse level and works upwards.

6.4.1 The Character → Character Discourse Level

Cues at the character → character discourse level can be both explicit and implicit. Character traits are largely derived from characters' discursive behaviour, particularly in plays. As Short (1989: 149) notes, interactions between characters become "messages *about* the characters" at the author → reader discourse level. Conversational structure, Gricean implicature and (im)politeness are, therefore, important characterisation cues at this discourse level.

Characterisation cues can also be present in descriptions apparently supplied by characters. Culpeper (2001) notes that characters can describe themselves—known as **self-presentation**—and other characters—known as **other-presentation**.[2] For example, in *Pygmalion*, Eliza Doolittle describes herself (six times) as "a good girl" and this self-presentation explicitly states one of her characteristics. Professor Higgins' housekeeper, Mrs Pearce, describes Eliza to Higgins as "quite a common girl, sir. Very common indeed", and this other-presentation makes explicit reference to one of Eliza's characteristics albeit from Mrs Pearce's point of view. Professor Higgins describes Eliza along similar lines saying that she is "so deliciously low—so horribly dirty" and provides both an explicit and an implicit cue, where the description of her appearance implies the poverty Eliza is forced to live in and her social status. However, Higgins describes Eliza in this way in her presence! This is a significant Face Threatening Act which is not mitigated and serves as an implicit cue about Higgins: he is unfeeling and inconsiderate. This example shows that cues can simultaneously operate as both self- and other-presentation and be both explicit and implicit.

Depending on the context, the reader may evaluate the source of the information differently. For example, if we do not trust a character, we are not likely to believe their description of themselves or another character and we may instead consider their motives. This might lead readers not to take such cues at face value or even to discount them.

6.4.2 The Narrator → Narratee Discourse Level

In prose fiction, narrators play a considerable role in how we form impressions of characters. Descriptive commentaries of characters are presented at the narrator → narratee discourse level and can provide both **explicit** and **implicit** character cues. For example, consider this short extract from the opening from *Emma*:

(3) Emma Woodhouse, handsome, clever, and rich, with a comfortable home and happy disposition, seemed to unite some of the best blessings of existence; and had lived nearly twenty-one years in the world with very little to distress or vex her.

Emma (Austen 1816)

In the extract, Emma Woodhouse is described to us by a heterodiegetic third-person narrator as 'handsome'. This is a visual feature and an **implicit** cue to characterisation from which we might begin to build a positive impression of Emma and attribute to her positive qualities (see Culpeper 2001: 224). The next adjective attributed to Emma Woodhouse is 'clever', which is an explicit cue because it directly attributes a positive and desirable personality trait to Emma, rather than the reader inferring it from evidence in the text. The description of 'rich, with a comfortable home' places Emma in a particular social sphere, which might trigger our background knowledge about social categories and roles (at the time *Emma* was written). Emma's 'happy disposition' is another **explicit** cue that directly attributes a personality trait to the character. We also learn Emma's age, which again places her in a particular social grouping from which we might infer further personality traits, or attitudes (e.g. towards men), and we learn that she has lived carefree, which again might help to place her in a particular social position.

Consider now the opening lines from Muriel Spark's short story 'You should have seen the mess' where a homodiegetic first-person narrator (who we discover a little further into the story is a 17-year-old female called Lorna) tells her story (sentences are numbered for reference):

(4) (i) I am now more than glad that I did not pass into the grammar school five years ago, although it was a disappointment at the time. (ii) I was always good at English, but not so good at the other subjects!!! (iii) I am glad that I went to the secondary modern school, because it was only constructed the year before. (iv) Therefore it was much more hygienic than the grammar school.

'You should have seen the mess' (Spark 1972)

As in Example (3), the characterisation in (4) occurs at the narrator → narratee discourse level. However, because Lorna is describing herself, albeit at two different points in time (then and now), it can be seen as **self-presentation**. The characterisation largely involves **implicit** cues. We find out that Lorna did not go to grammar school but a new secondary modern. This not only places the story temporally and geographically (in 1960s Britain), but also places the character in a particular social and educational category (non-grammar school) from which readers might make inferences about Lorna's intellectual and academic capabilities. To make those inferences, however, we need to know that children who passed an exam at 11 years old (known as the 11+) were able to go to grammar school, which focused on more academic studies and preparing students for university, whereas those who failed the exam had to go to secondary modern schools, which were less focused on academic achievement and more on vocational qualifications such as typing. Readers might also make inferences about Lorna's academic acumen and intellectual ability by her performance as a narrator. For example, she demonstrates that her skills of reasoning are skewed when she asserts that *new* equals *hygienic* (and *old* equals *unhygienic*). Also, Lorna claims to be good at English but finishes sentence (ii) with three exclamation marks. This graphological (and grammatical) deviation arguably breaks Grice's maxim of quantity and might be interpreted as Lorna making a joke (or being ironic), in which case the break is ostentatious and therefore a flout at the narrator → narratee level of discourse. However, the start of the story Lorna sets a rather formal tone with the official sounding "pass into grammar school", so it seems more likely (due to the attempt at formality) that she is making a mistake, meaning that the break is an infringement (her performance is impaired, for some reason). This creates an implicature at the author → reader level of discourse about Lorna's personality.

Notice that in Example (3) where the narrator is heterodiegetic, we are likely to take the information at face value. Bortolussi and Dixon (2003) note that where an evaluation is made by the narrator and there is no evidence to suggest otherwise then the reader assumes that the narrator knows best. In extract (4), however, the characterisation made by the narrator is countered by other evidence in the text, and it is likely that we are less trusting of the homodiegetic narrator's judgements.

6.4.3 The Author → Reader Discourse Level

Character cues at the author → reader discourse level include character names and the strategic cues designed by the author such as the juxtaposing of contrasting character. In plays, where prototypically there are two levels of discourse, both explicit and implicit characterisation cues also occur in stage directions. Like narration, stage directions can contain descriptive commentaries of, say, the visual features of characters (including their clothes and mannerisms), and the way they talk (including accent and paralinguistic features). For example, these stage directions from near the start of *The Playboy of the Western World* introduce three of the characters in the cast as they enter for the first time:

(5) She [Margaret Flaherty] goes behind counter. Michael James, fat jovial publican, comes in followed by Philly Cullen, who is thin and mistrusting, and Jimmy Farrell, who is fat and amorous, about forty-five.

J. M. Synge (1911 [1907])

The brief descriptions include explicit cues which describe character traits ('jovial', 'mistrusting' and 'amorous') as well as implicit cues that describe visual features ('fat' and 'thin'), the profession of one of the characters ('publican') and the age of another ('about forty-five').

6.5 Working with Culpeper's Textual Cues on Prose Fiction

In this section, we put Culpeper's checklist of cues into practice in an analysis of the characterisation of Heathcliff in an (edited) extract from the opening pages of Emily Brontë's *Wuthering Heights*. The narrator is Mr Lockwood, a newly arrived tenant on Heathcliff's land (all emphasis added):

(6) 1801. - I have just returned from a visit to <u>my landlord</u> - the <u>solitary</u> neighbour that I shall be troubled with. This is certainly a beautiful country! In all England, I do not believe that I could have fixed on a situation so completely removed from the stir of society. A perfect <u>misanthropist's</u> heaven: and Mr. Heathcliff and I are such a suitable pair to divide the <u>desolation</u> between us. <u>A capital fellow</u>! He little imagined how my heart warmed towards him when I beheld his <u>black eyes withdraw so suspiciously under their brows</u>, as I rode up, and when <u>his fingers sheltered themselves, with a jealous resolution, still further in his waistcoat</u>, as I announced my name.

'Mr. Heathcliff?' I said.

<u>A nod was the answer.</u>

'Mr. Lockwood, your new tenant, sir. I do myself the honour of calling as soon as possible after my arrival, to express the hope that I have not inconvenienced you by my perseverance in soliciting the occupation of Thrushcross Grange: I heard yesterday you had had some thoughts -'

<u>'Thrushcross Grange is my own, sir,' he interrupted, wincing. 'I should not allow any one to inconvenience me, if I could hinder it - walk in!'</u>

<u>The 'walk in' was uttered with closed teeth, and expressed the sentiment, 'Go to the Deuce:' even the gate over which he leant manifested no sympathising movement to the words; and I think that circumstance determined me to accept the invitation: I felt interested in a man who seemed more exaggeratedly reserved than myself.</u>

[...]

The apartment and furniture would have been nothing extraordinary as belonging to a homely, northern farmer, with a stubborn countenance, and stalwart limbs set out to advantage in knee-breeches and gaiters. Such an individual seated in his arm-chair, his mug of ale frothing on the round table before him, is to be seen in any circuit of five or six miles among these hills, if you go at the right time after dinner. But Mr. Heathcliff forms a singular contrast to his abode and style of living. He is <u>a dark-skinned gipsy</u> in aspect, in dress and manners a gentleman: that is, as much a gentleman as many a country squire: rather <u>slovenly</u>, perhaps, yet not looking amiss with his negligence, because he has an <u>erect and handsome figure</u>; and rather <u>morose</u>. Possibly, some <u>people might suspect him of a degree of under-bred pride; I have a sympathetic chord within that tells me it is nothing of the sort: I know, by instinct, his reserve springs from an aversion to showy displays of feeling - to manifestations of mutual kindliness. He'll love and hate equally under cover, and esteem it a species of impertinence to be loved or hated again. No, I'm running on too fast: I bestow my own attributes over-liberally on him.</u>

The first thing to notice about this extract is that information about character is coming from Mr Lockwood, a homodiegetic narrator (i.e. he is also a character in the text-world). The author, Brontë, has, therefore, structured the discourse so that characterisation cues relating to Heathcliff are filtered through the perception and point of view of Mr Lockwood. Lockwood provides readers with lots of detailed **other-presentation** about Heathcliff, his new landlord and neighbour, employing both **implicit** and **explicit** characterisation cues. An interesting paradox throughout this extract is that the narrator's positive attitude towards his neighbour (e.g. "A capital fellow!", "how my heart warmed to him"), runs contrary to inferences that can be drawn from the implicit characterisation cues about Heathcliff in Lockwood's narration.

Implicit cues include references to Heathcliff's social role (landlord) and relationship (neighbour), his physical attributes (black eyes, dark skin, an erect and handsome figure) and his dress (waistcoat, slovenly) and his body language (eyes withdrawing; fingers sheltered deeper into his waistcoat). Mr Lockwood—and the reader—rely on knowledge of social categories to be able to construct impressions of people and characters. Our societal expectation of a landlord, based on their property assets, is that they are of a high socio-economic class. In turn, this activates a schema about dress and behaviour that is fitting of the land-owning class in Victorian England, or what is 'prototypical' of such a social category. However, Mr Lockwood is surprised by the primitive dwellings and by Heathcliff's looks. He likens Heathcliff's abode and lifestyle to that of a homely farmer, imagining a hypothetical figure drinking beer at the table. These interpretative leaps that our narrator makes can be described in terms of attribution theory where—based on social knowledge—certain lifestyle habits are attributable to certain social categories. But, as our narrator observes, "Mr. Heathcliff forms a singular contrast to his abode and style of living. He is a dark-skinned gipsy in aspect, in dress and manners a gentleman". This statement about the central character betrays the narrator's social prejudices, as Mr Lockwood aligns ethnicity with class. In this way, Mr Lockwood's explicit other-presentation of Heathcliff may also give away an implicit self-characterisation cue that the tenant is a bigot. However, as twenty-first-century readers, we can interpret the narrator's prejudices (or lack of authorial judgement) in the context of social advancements over the last two centuries since the novel was written. Social changes aside, the impression that is emerging of Heathcliff through Mr Lockwood's account is rich with contradictions;

Heathcliff seems to defy Lockwood's attempts at social categorisation. In his non-conformance with social schemata, the characterisation of Heathcliff is schema-refreshing and captures the interest of the narrator and, as a result, the reader.

Despite Mr Lockwood's explicit reference to Heathcliff as a 'gentleman' and a 'capital fellow', the many implicit cues with regard to Heathcliff's verbal and physical behaviour would indicate otherwise. Upon Mr Lockwood's arrival, Heathcliff's body parts are described in retreating movements, "wincing", his "black eyes withdraw so suspiciously under their brows", "his fingers sheltered themselves, with a jealous resolution, still further in his waistcoat". The inward direction and mistrustful manner of Heathcliff's movements (expressed by the evaluative adverbials 'suspiciously' and 'with jealous resolution') suggest a social withdrawal from Lockwood's intrusion on his property, at odds with the tenant's cheer. These descriptions of Heathcliff's body language are combined with reports of character actions and narrator (adverbial) evaluations and interpretations, giving character cues that are both implicit and explicit.

Verbally, Heathcliff's paucity of speech reflects his unwelcoming attitude, which Lockwood is observant enough to note, "appeared to demand my speedy entrance, or complete departure". In lieu of an answer to Lockwood's opening question, Heathcliff just nods. His subsequent conversational turn is an interruption, and a forceful assertion, "I should not allow anyone to inconvenience me". Even Lockwood seems to be able to read the real meaning behind Heathcliff's "walk in!" as "Go to the Deuce:". This 'invitation' is issued as a command, is bare and lacks social niceties. Additionally, the narrator's interpretation of the utterance as intending the opposite of what was said is supported by physical clues. Both Heathcliff's clenched teeth (a physical sign of tension and far from a welcoming smile) and his lack of movement in opening the gate support our narrator's suspicion that he is not welcome. Nevertheless, Lockwood is fascinated "in a man who seemed more exaggeratedly reserved than myself", likening Heathcliff's character to his own. As readers, we might disagree with his **explicit self-characterisation** as 'reserved' based on implicit self-characterisation cues: Lockwood's language use is fluent and prolific, and his social visit is enthusiastic and persistent, even in the face of hostility. This verbal and social behaviour is not usually attributable to a reserved person.

Given the discrepancies between the narrator's character judgement and the characterisation cues he presents us with, the reader may begin to question the reliability of Mr Lockwood as narrator and source of character information. In attempting to reconcile Heathcliff's schema-breaking characteristics, Mr Lockwood recognises that "some people might suspect [Heathcliff] of a degree of under-bred pride" and distances himself from this view: "I have a sympathetic chord within that tells me it is nothing of the sort". The last statement is also a self-characterisation cue referring to the narrator's supposed innate understanding of others. Contrary to what other people see in Heathcliff, Lockwood claims to "know, by instinct", that Heathcliff is capable of both love and hate in equal measures, and is simply a deeply private person. Despite Lockwood's use of epistemic certainty in the modal lexical verb 'know', his previous misjudgements might make the reader doubtful. Indeed, after a surge of conjectural explicit other-presentation about Heathcliff, the narrator admits, "No, I'm running on too fast: I bestow my own attributes over-liberally on him". This final line in the extract confirms some earlier hints at Lockwood's over-alignment of Heathcliff's character with his own, which have led to some narratorial misjudgements about the character. It might also urge the reader to align their view of Heathcliff with the popular one that Lockwood dismisses of Heathcliff as having "under-bred pride".

Despite any misgivings the reader may have about the narrator's reliability, it is through this complex prism that we begin to put together one of the most vivid and thorny characters in English literary history. No doubt, the difficulty Lockwood has in categorising and in interacting with Heathcliff contributes to our experience of the character and the lasting impression he has made.

 Activity 6.2: Identify the Character Cues

In the following extracts, identify the character cues using the framework described in the previous sections. Say which discourse level the cues occur at. What impressions of character do the cues create?

(i) These stage directions introduce Eliza Doolittle in Shaw's (1916) *Pygmalion*
THE FLOWER GIRL (She sits down on the plinth of the column, sorting her flowers, on the lady's right. She is not at all an attractive person. She is perhaps eighteen, perhaps twenty, hardly older. She wears a little sailor hat of black straw that has long been exposed to the dust and soot of London and has seldom if ever been brushed. Her hair needs washing rather badly: its mousy color can hardly be natural. She wears a shoddy black coat that reaches nearly to her knees and is shaped to her waist. She has a brown skirt with a coarse apron. Her boots are much the worse for wear. She is no doubt as clean as she can afford to be; but compared to the ladies she is very dirty. Her features are no worse than theirs; but their condition leaves something to be desired; and she needs the services of a dentist).

(ii) A little later in the first scene, Higgins (the note taker) says this to Eliza (the flower girl):
THE NOTE TAKER [Higgins]: (explosively) Woman: cease this detestable boohooing
instantly; or else seek the shelter of some other place of worship.
THE FLOWER GIRL [Eliza]: (with feeble defiance) I've a right to be here if I like, same as you.
THE NOTE TAKER [Higgins]: A woman who utters such depressing and disgusting sounds has no right to be anywhere–no right to live....

(iii) Now identify character cues in this extract from the opening of Charlotte Brontë's (1847) *Jane Eyre*:
... Eliza, John, and Georgiana were now clustered round their mama in the drawing-room: she lay reclined on a sofa by the fireside, and with her darlings about her (for the time neither quarrelling nor crying) looked perfectly happy.

Me, she had dispensed from joining the group; saying, "She regretted to be under the necessity of keeping me at a distance; but that until she heard from Bessie, and could discover by her own observation, that I was endeavouring in good earnest to acquire a more sociable and childlike disposition, a more attractive and sprightly manner — something lighter, franker, more natural, as it were — she really must exclude me from privileges intended only for contented, happy, little children."

 Our answer can be found on the book's webpage.

6.6 Using Corpus Tools to Analyse Characters in a Play

In this section, we show how corpus approaches can be used to analyse character in a play. The corpus approach we will focus on in this section is keywords. Recall from ▶ Chapter 1 that keywords are those words in a text (or corpus) that occur more than you would expect by chance when compared with another text (or corpus). Keyword analysis is, therefore, used to discover the statistically salient words in a text or corpus.

Keywords have been used productively for the analysis of character. Notably, Culpeper (2002) demonstrates how keywords can help to establish lexical and grammatical patterns for the main characters in Shakespeare's *Romeo and Juliet*, some of which indicate of character traits. Other studies that combine keywords with Culpeper's (2001) textual cues to explore the characters include Bednarek's (2010) investigation of the North American TV show *Gilmore Girls*, and McIntyre's (2010) analysis of the film *Reservoir Dogs*.

In our case study, we use keywords to investigate the characters Eliza Doolittle, Professor Higgins and Colonel Pickering in Shaw's play *Pygmalion*. We adopt Culpeper's (2002) methodological approach (which was inspired by Enkvist 1973) whereby we make text-internal comparisons between different characters in the same play. Using *AntConc* (Anthony, 2022) we compare all the words spoken by one character against all the words spoken by the other characters combined (e.g. all Eliza Doolittle's words compared against all the words of all other characters).

6.6.1 Using AntConc to Explore Characters in Shaw's Pygmalion

In this section, we will briefly set out what we did and how we did it and then discuss some of the results to demonstrate how a keyword analysis might proceed.

 Instructions on how to do these comparisons can be found on the book's webpage.

6.6.1.1 Preparing the Play Text for Analysis

Using a plain text version of *Pygmalion* downloaded from the **Project Gutenberg** website, we extracted all the words spoken by Eliza into a new, separate file (ELIZA.txt). We repeated this process for both Higgins and Pickering and created two more text files (HIGGINS.txt and PICKERING.txt). The words of all the other characters were extracted and put into another file (OTHERS.txt). The remaining stage directions were not used for our analysis because these relate to the author → reader discourse level, and our focus was on character cues at the character → character discourse level.

6.6.1.2 Generating Keywords

Using the **Keyword List** function in *AntConc* and our character text files we made three keywords comparisons:

1. ELIZA.txt compared against HIGGINS.txt + PICKERING.txt + OTHERS.txt
2. HIGGINS.txt compared against ELIZA.txt + PICKERING.txt + OTHERS.txt
3. PICKERING.txt compared against ELIZA.txt + HIGGINS.txt + OTHERS.txt

This series of three comparisons allowed us to find out which words are used by Eliza, Higgins and Pickering more often in the play than would be expected by chance alone when compared against the words of all other characters.

6.6.1.3 Analysis of the Keywords

The three comparisons produced three sets of keywords, which are shown in ◘ Table 6.1. These are words that appear (statistically) more in all of the conversational turns of a character than they do in all the turns of all the others combined. The statistical test that calculates the keyness (which we do not have room to describe here; see McIntyre and Walker 2019 for an overview) merely indicates the probability that the difference is 'real'. It is, therefore, up to the analyst to work out whether that statistical keyness equates to linguistic salience and interpretative importance. Keywords, then, can be seen as a list of possibilities for further, more focused analysis of a text or corpus.

The next stage of our keyword analysis is to determine whether the keywords act as cues for characterisation in the play, which can be done using sorted concordance lines to help identify patterns of usage for a keyword. In our discussion below, we will focus on the keywords from the lists that are pronouns and those that relate to surge features. With these and all keywords we need to ask whether their overuse has a bearing on character.

- **Pronouns**

Eliza uses 'I' and 'me' more than the other characters in the play. A noticeable pattern with 'I' in her turns is that of *I + verb* at the end of a turn: *I am, I do, I did, I didn't, I don't, I will*. For example, "I'm a good girl, I am"; "I know what the

Fictional Character

Table 6.1 Keywords for Eliza, Higgins and Pickering sorted by keyness (raw frequencies shown in brackets)

No	Eliza	Higgins	Pickering
1	i (289)	pearce (27)	higgins (27)
2	me (115)	shall (27)	we (25)
3	ah (27)	find (13)	mrs (14)
4	ow (23)	damned (8)	party (5)
5	oo (12)	of (158)	doolittle (11)
6	care (15)	her (103)	eliza (16)
7	ooh (6)	human (9)	really (10)
8	flower (12)	soul (9)	
9	t (122)	other (16)	
10	captain (5)	bother (6)	
11	called (4)	damn (6)	
12	e (4)	life (13)	
13	road (4)	george (10)	
14	tottenham (4)		

like of you are, I do". This emphatic repetition is an implicit cue for the characterisation of Eliza because it is partly indicative of her Cockney accent and sets her aside from the others in the play that speak Standard English. It also shows that Eliza is often in a state of indignation, especially when talking to Professor Higgins, and helps to indicate her determination to stand up for herself. This indignation and determination are also shown in the main syntactic pattern involving 'I' in her speech, which is I + negated verb (e.g. *I didn't/I don't*) or negative adverb (*never*). This pattern shows that she is often denying or contradicting what has been said about her. By doing so, she is reacting to what she hears (usually from Higgins and Pickering) and standing up for herself.

Higgins' keywords include the pronoun *her*. Most of the occurrences happen in the first part of the play when Eliza first comes to the house. The overuse demonstrates that Higgins uses 'her' rather than other (more polite) terms of address such as 'Eliza', 'Miss Doolittle', 'your daughter', or 'the young lady' thus indicating how he views Eliza and how little worth she has to him at the start. Also worth noting are the numerous examples where Higgins is giving orders, such as "take her away"; "wallop her". These syntactic cues show that Higgins talks about Eliza in the third person while she is in fact present in the room, again indicating his lack of acknowledgement of her as a person.

By contrast, Picking uses the pronoun 'we' indicating that he is inclusive in the way he conceptualises his social space and the actions he is involved in. His other keywords show that, rather than use pronouns, he calls people by their names (Eliza) and uses titles. From these implicit cues, we can infer that Pickering is polite.

- **Surge Features**

Eliza's keywords include 'ah', 'ow', 'oo' and 'ooh'. These 'words' indicate the sounds that Eliza makes when she is excited or flustered and can be seen as surge features. They also indicate the sound of her Cockney accent and they become symbolic of Eliza before and after elocution lessons. They are implicit cues because they are regarded as unladylike outbursts that place her in a social category. In Higgins' view, they place her in the gutter.

The keywords 'damned', 'damn' and 'bother' show that Higgins also has regular outbursts where he uses mild expletives. They are nevertheless marked and unusual for the society he keeps and help to characterise him as a rather bad-tempered person.

By contrast, Pickering does not have outbursts and does not swear. The keyword 'really' in his list shows that he sometimes uses this intensifier if pushed (e.g. "I really must interfere"). This is a further indicator of Pickering's politeness and gentlemanlike behaviour.

6.6.2 Summary of Case Study

These brief comments about some of the keywords show how they can be used to highlight characterisation cues in the text. Notice that many of the keywords are very low frequency so it is difficult to use them to make general assertions but grouping some of them can suggest a trait that is more general across the character's discourse.

6.7 Conclusions

In this chapter, we have taken the view that fictional character is a matter of text and cognition. Information in the text interacts with our background knowledge and activates schemas that together create an impression of character. The information in the text that helps to create an impression of character are characterisation cues which can be either explicit or implicit. We saw that making the explicit/implicit distinction can be complex in practice, because the information in an explicit character cue could still require some inferential effort and could still imply or suggest character traits. It should be borne in mind, then, that the explicit/implicit distinction is not an either/or relationship. In the chapter, we presented a checklist of implicit cues for characterisation developed by Culpeper (2001) with the addition of the cue of 'actions' proposed by Rimmon-Kenan (2002). Some cues (conversation structure, conversational implicature and (im)politeness) relate to discursive performance of characters and are most relevant at the character → character discourse level particularly in plays. Other cues, such as actions and visual features, must be supplied via descriptions and are most relevant at the author → reader and narrator → narratee discourse levels, where the narrative level is an innovation based on Walker (2012). Paralinguistic features and accent and dialect can be described or related to the reader orthographically (e.g. via spelling) or graphologically (e.g. via uppercase letters). Textual cues for characterisation, therefore, can be delivered via any of the language levels we introduced in ▶ Chapter 1, and the list and discussion in this chapter are not exhaustive. ▶ Chapter 8 returns to the subject of fictional characters by considering, more specifically, how their minds are constructed and read in narrative discourse.

- **Further Reading**

Bednarek (2010) uses both keyword and key n-gram analysis to distinguish characters by their use of terms of address, discourse markers, greetings, pronouns, and emotive language.

Culpeper (2009) goes on to develop his analysis of characters in *Romeo and Juliet* using *WMatrix*. He assesses the usefulness of keyness comparisons at the grammatical and semantic level.

McIntyre (2010) utilises the semantic functionality of *Wmatrix* to analyse character in *Reservoir Dogs*.

Walker (2010) uses *Wmatrix* to examine characters in Julian Barnes' novel *Talking It Over*.

- **Resources**

AntConc (Anthony 2022): a free to download corpus analysis tool; see Lawrence Anthony's website for more detail: ▶ https://www.laurenceanthony.net/.

- **Notes**

1. The original version of Culpeper's (2001) model implies that information about 'other' characters can only ever be explicit. However, Walker (2012) points out that this division does not account for explicit statements about character that involve descriptions which, according to the framework, are implicit cues. For example, while descriptions of visual features (and possibly paralinguistic features) might be self- or other-presentation (depending on who is being described and by whom), they might, at the same time, also be implicit cues. Therefore, the discussion of characterisation cues in this chapter reflects the fact that self-/other-presentation can be implicit and/or explicit depending on what is being described. Walker (2012) also questions the assumption suggested by Culpeper's framework that implicit and explicit cues always originate from the characters because they may also come from narrators and authors. For example, information about paralinguistic features, which includes non-fluency features, loudness and voice quality, might be indicated to readers via stage directions in a play or via narration.
2. Pfister (1988) makes a similar distinction using the terms self-commentary and outside-commentary.

References

Anthony, L. 2022. *AntConc* (Version 4.2.0) [Computer Software]. Tokyo, Japan: Waseda University. ▶ https://www.laurenceanthony.net/software.
Austen, J. 1816. *Emma*. London: John Murray.
Barnes, J. 1991. *Talking It Over*. London: Jonathan Cape.
Bortolussi, M. and Dixon, P. 2003. *Psychonarratology: Foundations for the Empirical Study of Literary Response*. Cambridge and New York: Cambridge University Press.
Bednarek, M. 2010. *The Language of Fictional Television: Drama and Identity*. London: Continuum.
Bradley, A. C. 2007 [1904]. *Shakespearean Tragedy: Lectures on Hamlet, Othello, King Lear, MacBeth*. 4th Edition. London: Palgrave.
Brontë, C. [Currer Bell]. 1847. *Jane Eyre: An Autobiography*. London: Smith, Elder & Co.
Brontë, E. [Ellis Bell]. 1847. *Wuthering Heights*. London: Thomas Cautley Newby.
Brown, G. 1990. *Listening to Spoken Discourse*. 2nd ed. London: Longman.
Chatman, S. 1978. *Story and Discourse: Narrative Structure in Fiction and Film*. Ithaca: Cornell University Press.
Culpeper, J. 1998. Inferring Character from Texts: Attribution Theory and Foregrounding Theory. *Poetics* 23: 335–361.
Culpeper, J. 2001. *Language and Characterisation: People in Plays and Other Texts*. London. Longman.
Culpeper, J. 2002. Computers, Language and Characterisation: An Analysis of Six Characters in Romeo and Juliet. In *Conversation in Life and in Literature: Papers from the ASLA Symposium, Association Suedoise de Linguistique Appliquee (ASLA)*, 15, eds. U. Melander-Marttala, C. Ostman, and M. Kytö, 11–30. Universitetstryckeriet: Uppsala.
Culpeper, J. 2009. Keyness: Words, Parts-of-speech and Semantic Categories in the Character-talk of Shakespeare's Romeo and Juliet. *International Journal of Corpus Linguistics* 14, 1: 29–59.
Eder, J., Jannidis, F. and Schneider, R. 2010. *Characters in Fictional Worlds: Understanding Imaginary Being in Literature, Film, and other Media*. Berlin: De Gruyter.
Enkvist, N. 1973. *Linguistic Stylistics*. The Hague: Mouton.
Kasof, J. 1993. Sex Bias in the Naming of Stimulus Persons. *Psychological Bulletin*, 113, 1: 140–63.
McIntyre, D. 2010. Dialogue and Characterization in Quentin Tarantino's Reservoir Dogs: A Corpus Stylistic Analysis. In *Language and Style*, eds. D. McIntyre and B. Busse, 162–182. Basingstoke: Palgrave.
McIntyre, D. 2014. Characterisation. In *The Cambridge Handbook of Stylistics*, eds. P. Stockwell and S. Whiteley, 149–164. Cambridge and New York: Cambridge University Press.
McIntyre, D. and Walker, B. 2019. *Corpus Stylistics: Theory and Practice*. Edinburgh: Edinburgh University Press.
Minn, H. 2017. Broadchurch viewers in uproar at David Tennant's character and his shocking tea-making skills. *Daily Mirror* 13/07/2017. Available at: ▶ https://www.mirror.co.uk/tv/tv-news/broadchurch-viewers-uproar-david-tennants-10022861 (Accessed 10/04/2023).
Pfister, M. 1988. *The Theory and Analysis of Drama*. Cambridge and new York: Cambridge University Press.
Rimmon-Kenan, S. 2002. *Narrative Fiction*. London: Methuen.
Schneider, R. 2001. Towards a Cognitive Theory of Literary Character: The Dynamics of Mental-Model Construction. *Style* 35, 4: 607–633.
Shaw, G. B. 1916. *Pygmalion*. Harmondsworth, Middlesex, England: Penguin Books Ltd.
Short, M. 1989. Discourse analysis and the analysis of drama. In *Language, discourse and literature*, eds. R. Carter and P. Simpson 139–168. London: Unwin Hyman.
Spark, M. 1972. You should have seen the Mess. In *The Second Penguin Book of English Short Stories*, ed. C. Dolley, 301–307. London: Penguin Books.
Synge, J. M. 1911 [1907]. *The Playboy of the Western World*. Dublin: Maunsel and Company LTD.
Taavitsainen, I. 1999. Personality and Styles of Affect in The Canterbury Tales. In *Chaucer in Perspective: Middle English Essays in Honour of Norman Blake*, ed. G. Lester, 218–234. Sheffield: Sheffield Academic Press.

Walker, B. 2010. WMatrix, Key Concepts and the Narrators in Julian Barnes's Talking It Over. In *Language and Style*, eds. D. McIntyre and B. Busse, 364–387. Basingstoke: Palgrave.

Walker, B. 2012. *Character and Characterisation in Julian Barnes's* Talking It Over: *A Corpus Stylistic Analysis*. Unpublished PhD thesis: Lancaster University.

Weinsheimer, J. 1979. *Theory of Character*. Poetics Today 1,1-2:185-211

Wilkinson, W. 1820. *An Account of the Principalities of Wallachia and Moldavia*. United Kingdom: Longman, Hurst, Rees, Orme, and Brown.

Metaphorical Language

Supplementary Information The online version contains supplementary material available at ▶ https://doi.org/10.1007/978-3-031-10422-0_7.

© The Author(s), under exclusive license to Springer Nature Switzerland AG 2023
J. Lugea and B. Walker, *Stylistics*,
https://doi.org/10.1007/978-3-031-10422-0_7

Activity 7.1: What is an Elephant?
We start this chapter with an activity. Before reading on, make a list of what you know about elephants. If you are doing this in a group, only share your knowledge once you have completed your list. The reason for doing this activity will become clear later in the chapter.

7.1 Introduction

In this chapter, we dip our toe into **metaphorical language** and consider the analysis of metaphor, metonymy and simile in texts. Traditionally referred to as **figures of speech** or **tropes**, metaphorical language was for a long time viewed simply as deviant and creative language use for artistic and rhetorical purposes (for example, in literary and oratorical genres such as poetry and political speeches). Since the late 1970s, however, this view has been challenged by scholars who argue that metaphorical language is a cognitive as well as a linguistic phenomenon that is prevalent in all forms of communication. Early work on the interface between metaphorical language and cognition include I. A. Richards (1936), who was the first to consider the role of cognition[1] in metaphor comprehension, and Max Black (1955, 1977), who developed some of Richards' ideas (see also, the collection edited by Ortony 1979, 1993). However, it is the work of George Lakoff and Mark Johnson that has been the most influential in establishing a cognitive understanding of metaphor, metonymy and (subsequently) simile. In their view, metaphor and metonymy are cognitive processes that we use to conceptualise our world and metaphorical language is the linguistic realisation of the way we conceptualise things. They also demonstrated how metaphors are not just a property of rhetorical genres but are pervasive in everyday language and can be revealing about how language users conceptualise the world.

Our discussion of metaphorical language in this chapter integrates linguistic and cognitive approaches. We start by introducing some key notions from Cognitive Linguistics which we then use in a practical guide for the analysis and interpretation of metaphor, metonymy and simile. We finish the chapter with an overview of how corpus approaches can assist in the exploration of metaphorical language in texts.

7.2 Literal and Figurative (Non-literal) Language

When we think of literal meaning we tend to think of the entity or action a lexical item denotes in the world. So, for example, the literal meaning for 'drink' would be the action of taking liquid into the mouth and swallowing it. If we accept this position, then figurative or non-literal meaning is where a lexical item is used to refer to something other than the worldly action or entity it denotes.

For instance, if we drink in a view, then we do not mean "take the view into the mouth and swallow it"; instead, we mean that we visually take in the view. Figurative language, then, can be said to be where a lexical item "has been given a referential meaning outside its normal range of meanings" (Leech 2008: 21). But what counts as 'the normal range'? Normal may include figurative usage if it is well established. For example, the use of 'drink' (usually with 'in') to describe visual or aural reception (i.e. drinking in sights/sounds) occurs often enough to warrant a mention in dictionaries. To get round this issue, researchers who have worked extensively on metaphorical language across large amounts of text (see for example Steen et al. 2010) suggest that the most basic and historically earliest meaning of a lexical item should be seen as literal. Other meanings that have developed over time and extended the basic meaning are taken to be non-literal or figurative. This approach provides a practical solution for analysing texts and offers a way to overcome what is a complex issue [see *further reading*].

7.3 Encyclopaedic Knowledge, Concepts and Domains

A central idea within a cognitive linguistic approach to semantics is **Encyclopaedic Knowledge** which, according to Langacker (2008: 32), is "an open-ended body of knowledge" within which "lexical meaning resides". Encyclopaedic Knowledge is a structured, organised system of **concepts** and **conceptual domains**. A concept is a mental representation of an entity, action, process, or emotion. Concepts are derived from bodily experiences including sight, sound, taste, smell and touch and are a "basic unit of knowledge" (Evans 2019: 7, 395). For any concept to be understood, we require knowledge of a range of other interconnected concepts which combine to form a coherent area of connected knowledge, known as a conceptual domain. Domains are networks of concepts, and these are activated by lexical items (Langacker 2008: 47). Lexical items, then, are points of entry to Encyclopaedic Knowledge (hereafter EK) accessing a particular **concept** or **conceptual domain** (Evans 2019: 352).

Langacker (2008: 42) theorises that a linguistic expression "does not have a fully determinate meaning". Instead, meaning depends on which elements of Encyclopaedic Knowledge are activated by a word/phrase, and that depends on co-textual and contextual factors. We therefore interpret a lexical item (word or phrase) using a combination of Encyclopaedic Knowledge, context and co-text. For example, the word 'bank' will activate different conceptual domains within our Encyclopaedic Knowledge (e.g. river, finance) depending on the co-text and context of use. Langacker (1987, 2008) posits the idea of **centrality**, where some knowledge is central to a concept, and some is more peripheral.[2] Central knowledge is more likely to be activated than peripheral knowledge.

Let us now return to Activity 7.1 at the start of this chapter where we asked you to write down what you know about elephants. Our assumption is that central knowledge about elephants is likely to include knowing that elephants are large (the largest) land mammals, have big ears, long trunks and large tusks. It is highly likely, therefore, that your list contained body parts such as 'trunk' and 'tusks' as these things are central to the concept of ELEPHANT (small caps are used when referring to domains and concepts). Each of these body parts are themselves concepts (TUSK, TRUNK) which are part of the domain of ELEPHANT, which will include other interconnected concepts and experiences. The concept TUSK will have its own domain which will include concepts such as IVORY as well as ELEPHANT and possibly other animals such as walrus, boar and narwhal. The theory goes, then, that the linguistic item 'elephant' activates multiple domains (a domain matrix) from which the concept ELEPHANT emerges. The domains that are activated will depend on the context the linguistic item is used and might include shape, sound, smell (if you have first-hand experience), class (elephants are mammals), geography (elephants tend to live in specific land regions on Earth), social practices (elephants live in herds), as well as human practices such as big game hunting and killing elephants for their ivory tusks.

Over the course of this chapter, we will return to ideas of Encyclopaedic Knowledge, domains and centrality introduced above and use them in our explanation of how to analyse and interpret metaphorical language.

7.4 Metaphor: Text and Cognition

Traditionally, metaphor was seen as a linguistic phenomenon, as mere flourishes in style, and the preserve of poets and politicians. Now, however, there is general acknowledgement that rather than being simply a matter of language, metaphors are conceptual in nature, pervasive in all discourse, with many entrenched in our everyday language (e.g. 'I see what you mean'; 'I'm feeling down'). As Cameron and Deignan (2003: 674) note, "(…) metaphor emerges from the dynamics of language and thinking, and is at the same time conceptual and linguistic."

The term 'metaphor' is derived from ancient Greek for *carry across* or *carry over* (where *meta* = *over/across* and *phore* = *carry*) and refers to a situation where a concept (such as an object, action, or emotion) from one domain (the target) is talked about using concepts from another domain (the source).[3] The result is that attributes associated with one domain are 'carried across' (or mapped) to the other. Because similarities between the two domains are implied, metaphor is fundamentally a comparison.

Our discussion of metaphor in this chapter focuses on the analysis of metaphor in fiction and adopts a textual and a cognitive approach. Our starting point for analysis is the linguistic instantiations of metaphor, because these are how metaphors are communicated in texts; indeed, Goatly (1997: 42) stresses the linguistic and textual nature of metaphors. We incorporate cognitive approaches in the analysis to help explain how metaphors make meaning. The analytical approach we set out synthesises the work of several scholars including Lakoff and Johnson (1980), who posited an influential and widely adopted theory of conceptual metaphor (see Focus 7.1), and Leech (1969) and Steen (c, 1999b, 2009) who both set out step-by-step guides for the analysis of metaphor, with Steen incorporating conceptual approaches.[4]

Focus 7.1: Conceptual Metaphor Theory

Conceptual Metaphor Theory (CMT) puts metaphor at the centre of our thought processes and theorises about how we conceptualise and make sense of the world and how our knowledge is structured. According to Lakoff and Johnson (1980), CMT explains how we understand one conceptual domain, known as the **target domain**, by drawing on another conceptual domain, known as the **source domain**. Target domains tend to be concrete, less complex and more familiar (e.g. journeys, containers, plants). Conceptual metaphors are written in small capital letters and phrased as statements in the form: TARGET DOMAIN IS SOURCE DOMAIN. For example, LOVE IS A PLANT, where LOVE is the target, and A PLANT is the source. This form of labelling is a shorthand for saying that we conceptualise love as a plant and that there are correspondences or mappings between the two domains. The theory goes that these mappings are pre-existing in our cognition, and through them we use knowledge of the source domain to talk about and make sense of aspects of the target domain (see Lakoff 1993).

The conceptual understanding proposed by CMT is manifest in the ways in which we express ourselves in language and give rise to linguistic metaphors (i.e. the metaphors we find/use in texts). According to Gibbs (2011), the metaphorical patterns we find in language provide evidence for "enduring metaphorical mappings." (Gibbs 2011: 532). In other words, conceptual metaphors prompt recurrent and systematic linguistic metaphors that use lexical items from the identified domains of meaning. This means that apparently different linguistic metaphors can be related conceptually. For example, the linguistic expressions 'our love blossomed' and 'our love withered and died' draw on the same conceptual metaphor: LOVE IS A PLANT.

7.4.1 Analysing Metaphor

Our aim in this section is to provide a way to analyse linguistic metaphor (as opposed to, say, visual metaphor[5]), drawing on cognitive theories of grammar and semantics. We will use (1) to demonstrate a process for analysing metaphor in texts based on Leech's (1969: 153–156) three stages of analysis and Steen's (1999a, 1999b, 2009) five analytical steps. Our discussion is also augmented by the insights provided by Miller (1993), Semino et al. (2004) and Deignan (2016). The steps discussed below are not meant to reflect the activities our brains go through when processing metaphor, but rather offer a method to analyse linguistic metaphor and explain our interpretations (Steen 1999a: 59). We will start by considering a metaphor concerning love, extracted from the HUM19CUK corpus of nineteenth-century novels:

(1) Love is a thorny plant.
Richelieu: A Tale of France (George Payne, 1825)

The metaphor in example (1) is formed of a copular clause where the main verb is a form of 'be' which 'links' the subject of the clause to a noun phrase complement. These sorts of '*X is Y*' metaphors are known as explicit metaphors for reasons that will become clear below. Before reading on, complete Activity 7.2.

> **Activity 7.2: What Does 'Love is a thorny plant' Mean?**
> Consider the following questions:
>
> a) How did you recognise (1) as a metaphor?
> b) Which lexical items are used literally and which figuratively?
> c) What is being compared with what in the metaphor?
> d) What in your opinion is the meaning conveyed by the metaphor?
> e) How did you arrive at your interpretation?

7.4.1.1 Stage I: Identify the Language that Invites a Figurative (Non-literal) Reading

In the first stage of our analysis, we will address parts (a) and (b) of Activity 7.2.

Part of the reason we recognise (1) as a metaphor is that the statement is incongruent (we return to the notion of incongruity in our discussion of humour in ▶ Chapter 9). This is because it offers a definition that is inconsistent with our knowledge of the world (see Miller 1993: 380). By that we mean love (an emotional state) cannot also be a thorny plant (a physical entity). If the statement were, for example, 'a rose is a thorny plant' then that would be consistent with our knowledge. To resolve the incongruency and make sense of the statement, we must evaluate some part of (1) as figurative. This brings us on to both Leech's (1969: 154) and Steen's (2009) first stage in the analysis of linguistic metaphor, which is to distinguish the non-literal language from the literal. Working out what is literal/non-literal can be a matter of evaluating the metaphorical expression's context and co-text (see ▶ Chapter 1 for more on these terms). With (1), it is apparent from the fictional context that the noun phrase 'love' refers conventionally to an emotional state (or something similar, like romantic love relationships), so it follows that if 'love' is literal then the noun phrase 'a thorny plant' must be non-literal. It also follows that, rather than see the *X is Y* structure as a definition, we must understand it as metaphorical, and a comparison between the two otherwise unrelated concepts (see Leech 1969: 151). This leads us on to our next stage of analysis.

7.4.1.2 Stage II: What is Being Compared with What?

So far, we have established that (1) is incongruent unless seen as a metaphorical comparison where 'love' is literal and 'thorny plant' figurative. The next stage of analysis, which addresses part (c) of Activity 7.2, explicates the comparison that is being made in the metaphor. With our *X is Y* metaphor, both sides of the comparison are overtly present in the metaphorical expression (hence the term 'explicit metaphor'). The literal part of the metaphor, 'love', is being compared to the non-literal part, a 'thorny plant'. The copular verb 'is' expresses a relationship of similarity between the two noun phrases.

Within the cognitive linguistic tradition, metaphor is a comparison between different conceptual domains and any analysis needs to consider the concepts and domains involved in the metaphor. Recall from our discussion of Encyclopaedic

Metaphorical Language

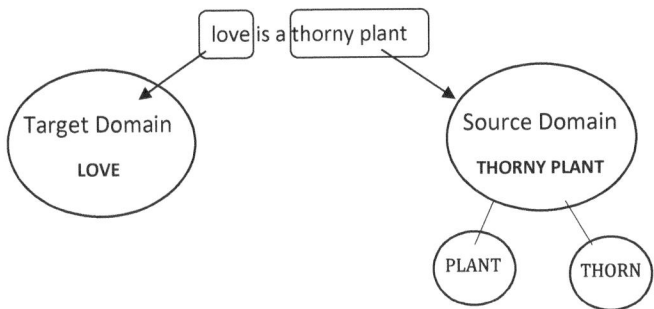

Fig. 7.1 Source and target domains

Knowledge in ▶ Sect. 7.3, lexical items can be seen as access points to conceptual domains. In (1) the two noun phrases, 'love' and 'a thorny plant', activate corresponding domains: LOVE, which is the target domain, and THORNY PLANT, which is the source domain (Focus 7.1). The domain THORNY PLANT involves two concepts PLANT and THORNY, with the latter indicating 'has thorns', which involves the concept THORN. ◘ Figure 7.1 aims to show these interconnected concepts and domains (the sizes of the circles are not important).

The comparison implied by (1) suggests similarities (or 'grounds' for comparison[6]) between LOVE and THORNY PLANT. Following Miller (1993: 377) and Steen (1999a: 68), a useful way to rephrase the relationship of similarity in (1) is:

> some properties of LOVE are similar to some properties of THORNY PLANT

Our next stage of analysis is to explore the similarities implied by the comparison between the two conceptual domains. By doing this, we start to think about the meaning(s) conveyed by the metaphor (◘ Fig. 7.1).

7.4.1.3 Stage III: What Kinds of Mappings Does the Comparison Invite?

This stage of the analysis deals with part (d) in Activity 7.2.

Within a cognitive approach to metaphor, similarities are implied by what are known as cross-domain correspondences (also referred to as correlations) between the source and the target domain (Lakoff and Johnson 2003: 246). For our analysis, we must use our Encyclopaedic Knowledge to posit properties of the source domain, THORNY PLANT, that reasonably correspond to properties of the target domain, LOVE. The source domain suggests the properties that are to be mapped onto the target domain, and the target domain steers inferences about which properties are relevant (Glucksberg and McGlone 1999: 1543–4; see also Black 1962, who talks about a "filtering" process).

As we identified in ◘ Fig. 7.1, our domain of THORNY PLANT has directly associated concepts of PLANT and THORN. Central to the concept of THORN is knowledge that thorns are sharp and have the capacity to cause pain by puncturing and scratching the skin. Indeed, this is their *raison d'être* since their ability to cause injury provides protection for the plant. Therefore, the concept of PAIN might well be part of the domain matrix that is activated by 'thorny plant'. If so, we might infer from (1) that, like thorny plants, love has the capacity to cause pain, but emotional pain rather than physical pain. On this basis, ◘ Fig. 7.2 posits cross-domain mappings that emerge from the comparison between target and source domains which potentially give rise to a set of implications about love.

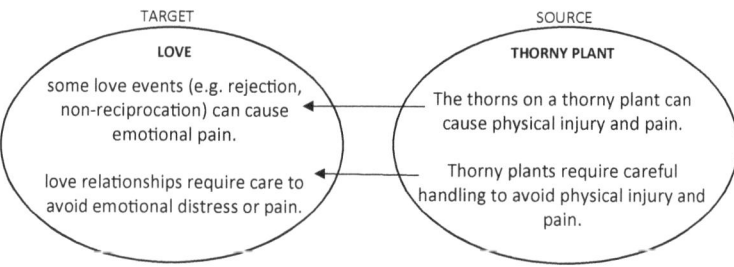

◘ **Fig. 7.2** Conceptual mappings between THORNY PLANT and LOVE

Our proposed mappings suggest that an interpretation for (1) is that love has the capacity to cause pain. While thorns are not themselves pain, they can cause physical pain and similarly love can also cause emotional pain. The emotional sensation caused by, for example, rejection corresponds with the physical pain caused by a thorn puncturing the skin. Note, though, that thorns (and the pain they can cause) are just one aspect of the conceptual domain of THORNY PLANT; there are many other (less painful) attributes that we might have considered such as flowers, leaves and fruit. These may be mapped onto the domain of LOVE to correlate with more positive aspects than rejection, such as a sense of fulfilment.

7.4.1.4 Stage IV: What (if any) Conceptual Metaphors Underpin the Metaphor?

A further stage in an analysis of linguistic metaphor suggested by Steen (1999a: 59) is to consider the conceptual metaphor(s) (see Focus 7.1) that might form the basis for the linguistic metaphor. Lakoff and Johnson (1980) theorise conceptual metaphors are pre-existing mappings that form part of our conceptual system and a mechanism by which we conceptualise aspects of the world. According to this view of metaphor, the metaphors in language are the linguistic instantiations of these existing conceptual mappings (although, Lakoff and Johnson note that this is not always the case and that some metaphors are 'novel'; see Focus 7.2). In our example, we could say that the existing conceptual mappings that are exploited are, in increasing levels of generality, as follows (conceptual metaphors are written in small capital letters as a statement):

> LOVE IS A PLANT.
> LOVE IS A LIVING THING.
> LOVE IS A PHYSICAL ENTITY.
> EMOTION IS A PHYSICAL ENTITY.

A further conceptual metaphor we might consider in (1) relates to thorns and pain where the cause of the pain (the thorn) is conceptualised as the pain itself. Other research has shown linguistic evidence to support such a cross-domain mapping with Kövecses (2008) suggesting the conceptual metaphor PAIN IS A SHARP OBJECT, and Semino (2010) suggesting PAIN IS CAUSE OF PHYSICAL DAMAGE. We might also hypothesise that in (1) emotional pain (anxiety/emotional distress) is conceptualised as physical pain. This conceptualisation of emotional pain is posited by Grady (1997: 166) who proposes the conceptual metaphor DISTRESS IS PHYSICAL INJURY. We can see, then, that there is a possibility that the interpretation of our linguistic metaphor, 'love is a thorny plant', might rely on more than one conceptual metaphor (on this point, see Vervaeke and Kennedy 1996) and result from multiple conceptual mappings.

These conceptual metaphors are, of course, hypotheses about how we conceptualise a particular concept and pre-existing mappings in our cognitive apparatus. This is precisely what an analysis using Conceptual Metaphor Theory entails: hypothesising or searching for the more abstract, superordinate concepts which account for the various linguistic instantiations of the conceptual metaphor. Whether such mappings exist is open to debate (see, for example, the discussions in Deignan 2016; Glucksberg and McClone 1999). One way in which these hypotheses can be investigated is to look at other language data to see whether additional examples can be found that seem to be motivated by a particular conceptual metaphor. For example, the LOVE IS A PLANT conceptual metaphor might be supported by further examples of plant-based metaphors along the lines of 'love blossoming', 'love withering', or 'love bearing fruit'.[7]

For the stylistician, conceptual metaphor analysis (i.e. positing superordinate domains and their mappings) can be useful for making reasoned generalisations on the basis of evidence in the text about the way a text, a narrator, or a character construes aspects of the world (see, for example, Semino and Swindlehurst 1996). Conceptual metaphor can, therefore, be a useful tool for studying point of view and mind style (see ▶ Chapter 8).

7.4.1.5 Summary of the Stages of Metaphor Analysis

The stages of analysis set out above identified the figurative language, identified what is being compared to what conceptually, and then proposed a set of mappings that suggested the grounds for comparison and therefore the similarities implied by the metaphor. These mappings help to reach an interpretation of the meaning of the metaphor, and/or help to explain the how an interpretation was reached (which answers question (e) above). The final stage in an analysis of linguistic metaphor suggested by Steen (1999a: 59) is to consider the conceptual metaphor(s) that might prompt the linguistic metaphor. Notice that each step in our analysis takes us further away from the linguistic instantiation of the metaphor which was our starting point. Care needs to be taken when carrying out the analysis to set out and justify as clearly as possible the mappings because as Steen (2009: 219) notes, "this is the most problematic part" of this analytical process (also on this point, see Semino et al. 2004).

Activity 7.3: Exploring Similarities and Cross-Domain Mappings

Consider the following example and write down possible cross-domain mappings based on your knowledge of 'devouring flames' and 'love'.

> love is a devouring flame
>
> *The Epicurean* (Thomas Moore, 1827)

What, if any, problems do you encounter?

⤓ *We provide our response on the book's webpage.*

7.4.2 Analysis of Non-Explicit Metaphor

So far, we have established the central idea that metaphor is comparison; something is being compared to something else in some way or another. In (1) the 'X is Y' metaphor makes explicit the two things that are being compared. However, not all metaphors have that structure and in this section, we analyse a metaphor that does not set out target and source domain explicitly. The example we will consider is from Tennyson's (1842) poem 'Ulysses':

(2) …. I will drink.
    Life to the lees

 Activity 7.4: What Does 'drink life to the lees' Mean?

Before reading on, consider the following questions:

(i) How did you recognise (2) as a metaphor?
(ii) Which lexical items are used literally and which figuratively?
(iii) What is being compared with what?
(iv) What do you consider to be the meaning conveyed by the metaphor?
(v) How did you arrive at your interpretation?

In the text-world of the poem, Ulysses is not literally drinking life, so the clause, which extends over two lines of the poem, refers unconventionally to something else. Activity 7.4 asks you to think about what that 'something else' is. Our thoughts are that Ulysses utilises an established phrase ('drink to the lees') to express an attitude towards life and old age. Drinking, say, wine to the lees involves consuming every drop of wine in the glass and not stopping until you reach the yeasty sediment at the bottom (also known as dregs). Ulysses expresses a similar sentiment to life by stating his desire to continue doing the various activities he did when he was younger and not ceasing such activities because he is now old. Using conventional metaphors (see Focus 7.2), we might express this sentiment as 'living life to the full' or 'getting the most out of life'. As stylisticians, we are interested in explaining our responses to texts, so let us now consider how we might analyse (2) using the series of steps we introduced above.

7.4.2.1 Stage I: Identify the Features that Invite a Figurative (Non-literal) Reading

The first stage of our analysis is to work out which lexical items are used figuratively (non-literally) by considering whether the referent is unconventional and incongruous in the context of the text. ◘ Figure 7.3 sets out a series of questions that aim to help us do this. Each question relates to the basic meaning of the lexical item.

		Yes	No
i	Does 'life' refer to (say) the period of existence between birth and death?	☐	☐
ii	Does 'drink' refer to the act of drinking (i.e. imbibing liquid) ?	☐	☐
iii	Does 'lees' refer to yeasty sediment that accumulates in alcoholic drinks such as beer and wine during fermentation; also known as dregs?	☐	☐
iv	Does 'to the lees' refer to drinking a fermented beverage (e.g. beer) to the yeasty sediment at the bottom of the container it is in?	☐	☐

◘ **Fig. 7.3** Determining metaphorical language in 'drink life to the lees'

If we consider the option that 'drink' and 'lees' refer conventionally to the physical action of drinking and yeasty sediment, respectively, then it follows that 'life' is being used metaphorically and must refer unconventionally to a liquid that is produced via fermentation. This interpretation would be reasonable if the poem was about, for example, someone who liked beer so much they referred to it as 'life'. This would make a comparison between beer and life from which we might infer that, for the speaker in the poem, beer is life. However, the poem is not about beer; it is about growing old and reaching the final years of life. As we mentioned in ▶ Sect. 7.3, context and co-text are important for interpreting the meaning of lexical items. It seems reasonable, therefore, to assume that in the context of the poem, the answer to question (i) is 'yes'; 'life' does refer conventionally to a concept that we might describe as (something like) that period between birth and death.

If the word 'life' is being used conventionally then it follows that the remaining questions (ii, iii and iv) must be answered with 'no' because life is not a liquid and so cannot be drunk. Consequently, 'drink' cannot refer to imbibing liquid, and lees cannot be yeasty sediment because life is not a beverage that is produced via a process of fermentation. The words 'drink' and 'lees' are therefore incongruous in the context in which they occur, and we can conclude that they are being used figuratively.

7.4.2.2 Stage II: What is Being Compared with What?

Our next stage is to spell out what is being compared to what in (2). This task is less straightforward than it was with example (1) because in (2) the two elements of the metaphor are not stated explicitly so we must "construct" them (see Leech 1969: 154) through a series of steps.

We have established that the lexical item 'life' is used literally, and this is an access point to the conceptual domain LIFE. Similarly, the non-literal lexical items 'drink' and 'lees' are access point to the source domains DRINK and LEES.

The metaphorical comparison involves a combination of these elements but also the structures they are part of. So, it is the complete idea of 'drinking to the lees' that forms the source domain, while the target domain is some literal action involving life. Following Steen (2009: 203–4), the comparison can be expressed like this:

> Ulysees DRINKING X TO THE LEES is similar to Ulysees Y-ING LIFE TO THE Z.
> (where 'Y-ing life' means doing *something* with life).

We have used small capitals above to indicate that the source and target domains are two parallel conceptual structures (Miller 1993: 384), and it is these structures that form the basis of the metaphorical comparison. This comparison, along with the source and target, are set out in ◘ Fig. 7.4 (following Leech 1969: 153). As ◘ Fig. 7.4 shows, though, the structures at this stage of the analysis are incomplete with missing elements indicated by X, Y and Z.

Source	I [Ulysses]	will	drink	X	to the	lees
Target	I [Ulysses]	will	Y	life	to the	Z

◘ Fig. 7.4 Source and target in 'I will drink life to the lees'

To help work out what similarities are being implied by the metaphor, we now construct the analogy that is being drawn by the comparison by proposing fillers for the X, Y and Z slots (Leech 1969: 153; see also Leech 2008 and Short 1996). As Miller (1993) stresses, though, this is an interpretation and is not meant to suggest that there is one word that will fit each slot:

> The claim is not that the author had particular words in mind, but that he had a general concept ... that we are trying to appreciate and make explicit.
> Miller (1993: 384–5).

Consider first the X 'slot' in the source. From our Encyclopaedic Knowledge, we know that the canonical action of drinking normally requires an animate subject and a physical, liquid object, fit for consumption (e.g. water). The prepositional phrase 'to the lees' potentially activates conceptual knowledge that focuses the choice of liquid to those produced via a process of fermentation (e.g. beer) because, strictly speaking, only those types of drink contain lees.

Metaphorical Language

*Before reading on about the Y and Z slots, try the **Corpus KWIC-ie:** What do we typically 'do' with life?*

> **Corpus KWIC-ie: What do we typically 'do' with life?**
> Use the BNC to investigate which verbs frequently co-occur with 'life'? Are there any instances of 'life' as the direct object of 'drink'?
>
> Is 'life' typically a Direct Object, or does it more readily take another grammatical role?
>
> ⬇ *Instructions and answers are on the book's webpage.*

Turning now to the Y and Z slots in ◘ Fig. 7.4, the Y slot is for verbs that conventionally have 'life' as their subject, and the Z slot is for nouns that conventionally might be part of a prepositional phrase that follows 'life'. Plausible candidates for the Y slot are 'live' or 'enjoy', while the Z slot could reasonably be filled by 'end' or 'finish'.

◘ Figure 7.5 sets out target and source again with the empty slots filled and presents what Steen (1999a: 68) calls the "nonliteral analogy". The analogy helps to show that conceptually the metaphor is comparing LIFE with a DRINK and the LIVING OF LIFE with DRINKING A DRINK. So, following Leech (1969), we can say that:

Life is like a drink with lees in *some way or other*
Living life is like drinking a drink with lees in *some way or another*.
Lees are like the end of life in *some way or another*

Source	I	will	drink	liquid	to	the	lees
Metaphorical expression	I	will	drink	life	to	the	lees
Target	I	will	live	life	to	the	end

◘ **Fig. 7.5** Source and target analysis of 'drink', 'life' and 'lees'

7.4.2.3 Stage III: What Kinds of Mappings Does the Comparison Invite?

There are several different concepts and mappings involved in this metaphor, which conceptualises 'living life' as drinking a liquid. We now propose correlations or mappings between the conceptual domains that are activated by the metaphor which Stage II helped us to spell out. Some of the possible mappings are summarised in ◘ Fig. 7.6. These mappings are our suggestions and readers may have others in mind. The key is to explain how they are derived with reference to the conceptual analogy that is being drawn by the metaphor. For example, an alternative to 'live' might be 'enjoy' on the basis that a central part of our knowledge of drinking is that it is enjoyable (whether the drink is, for example, water, tea, coffee, soda, or beer). So, arguably, drinking life maps onto enjoying life.

7.4.2.4 Stage IV: What (if Any) Conceptual Metaphors Underpin the Metaphor?

Our final stage is to consider the possible conceptual metaphor(s) that may give rise to the linguistic metaphor in (2). One possibility is LIFE IS A FLUID IN A CONTAINER since the metaphor relies on the idea that a full container correlates with the whole period of a life, an empty container correlates with death/end of life and emptying the container correlates with progression through life. We can hypothesise that 'drinking life' conceptualises 'living' as a single physical, bodily action, which could be summarised as: LIVING IS CONSUMING LIQUID. Alternatively (or additionally), we could also say that ADVANCING FROM BIRTH AND DEATH IS LIQUID EMPTYING FROM A CONTAINER. A useful notion to help explain this is 'correlated experience' (Kövecses 2000: 70–1) which for our example would mean the event of drinking a liquid is accompanied by the event of the glass emptying until the glass contains no more liquid.

The metaphor in (2) also seems to suggest some sort of conceptual mapping between time (if life is viewed as a period of time) and physical matter (like a liquid), where more liquid is more time. Coupled with the idea of liquid being in a container, then time becomes finite. We might also hypothesise that a more superordinate category exists along the lines of ABSTRACT CONCEPT IS PHYSICAL ENTITY, or ABSTRACT CONCEPT IS PHYSICAL ACTION ON PHYSICAL ENTITY. These hypotheses could be explored by looking at more data, perhaps using corpora, as we discuss in ▶ Sect. 7.7.

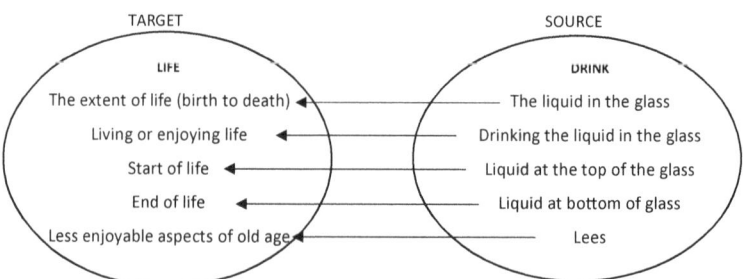

Fig. 7.6 Conceptual mappings between DRINK and LIFE

◎ **Focus 7.2: Conventional, Creative, and Dead Metaphors**

Conventional metaphors are those which are judged to be commonplace and result from an established way in which we (or a defined cultural group) conceptualise things. Such usage might be so well established that we no longer recognise the language as metaphoric. Conventional metaphoric usage can be recorded in dictionaries, or 'lexicalised' (Ritchie 2013: 12). For example, 'heart' has numerous recorded metaphorical uses (e.g. 'a change of heart'; 'lose heart'), where 'heart' means some sort of emotional response. Also, the names of new inventions/phenomena are often metaphorical extensions of existing words. For instance, Information Technology reuses numerous existing words metaphorically (e.g. 'web', 'mouse' and 'virus').

Some metaphors are so conventional they are said to be 'dead', such as 'leg' to mean leg of a table (etc.) and 'wing' to include those on a plane. Black (1977: 439) suggests that dead metaphors are examples of catachresis (a rhetorical figure meaning using a word in the wrong sense) which have led to polysemy. Charteris-Black (2014: 171-2) prefers the term 'entrenched' to 'dead' as it recognises the conceptual basis for metaphor and that some conceptual mappings are deeply rooted in our cognition.

In contrast to conventional metaphors, novel (or creative) metaphors are unusual comparisons that are not the linguistic instantiations of existing conceptual mappings and do not encode linguistically the ways in which we normally conceptualise the world (see Lakoff and Johnson 2003 [1980]: 54). Instead, they convey new, creative ways of conceptualising ideas or feelings. According to Steen et al. (2010), they are created deliberately by the text producer (rather than just 'happening' because they are part of our conceptual system) and the reader/hearer might have to exert extra cognitive effort to decipher and interpret them.

7.5 Metonymy

From the Greek for 'change of name', metonymy is another trope where, according to Wales (2011: 268), the name of a referent is replaced either by:

(i) the name of an attribute of the referent (e.g. in 'we were helped by many willing hands', 'hands' replaces people) or
(ii) the name of entity related to referent in some way (e.g. 'the law' can replace 'the police').

Metonymy therefore exploits contiguity between the two entities (Jacobson 1956: 69) meaning that they are closely connected in some way. For Lakoff and Johnson (1980: 40), who offer a conceptual explanation of metonymy, the contiguity is down to the two entities belonging the same conceptual domain. So, whereas metaphor concerns mapping across two different conceptual domains (source domain and target domain), metonymy is a single mapping within one domain be-

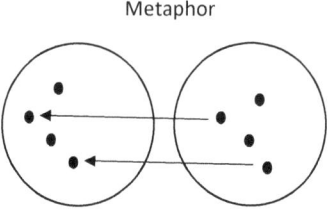

■ Fig. 7.7 Metonymic and metaphorical mappings

tween two concepts (see ■ Fig. 7.7). So, to take the 'the law' = 'the police' example above, if we assume there exists some sort of LAW AND ORDER conceptual domain, the concept LAW (a governing set of rules) maps onto the closely connected concept POLICE within the same domain.

7.5.1 Analysing Metonymy

Consider now the following old joke made famous (in the UK at least) by Donald McGill[8]:

(3) Male: Do you like Kipling?
    Female: I don't know … I've never kippled.

The joke relies partly on the common practice of referring to the published works of an author using just the family name of the author. In this way, the text linguistically encodes a metonymical relationship between two entities (author and author's works). According to Lakoff and Johnson (1980: 36), one entity—in our case 'Kipling'—*stands for* another—in our case 'the published works of Rudyard Kipling'. In this relationship, the concept KIPLING is the source of the metonymy, and the target is the concept THE WORKS OF RUDYARD KIPLING. There is just one conceptual domain in play, which we will gloss as RUDYARD KIPLING THE AUTHOR, and this must be activated by the lexical item 'Kipling' for the metonymy to be successful. According to Leech (1969: 148–9), the literal (or conventional) meaning of the word 'Kipling' (the family name of the author) is **replaced** by the non-literal meaning which in this case is 'the works of Kipling'. The metonymic relationship in (3) is shown in ■ Fig. 7.8.

For the metonymy to be successful, the domain RUDYARD KIPLING THE AUTHOR must be accessed, and the family name of the author must be mapped onto the works of the author. The hearer/reader must work out this relationship to understand the metonymy and the utterance. In example (3), the male speaker makes a metonymic connection between author and published work and assumes that Rudyard Kipling is well known enough for the hearer to understand that 'Kipling' refers to the written works of Kipling. There is also an assumption at the author-reader level of discourse that the reader will also realise that 'Kipling' references 'the works

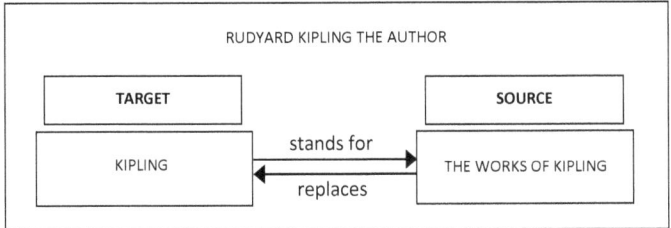

● **Fig. 7.8** Metonymic relationship between 'Kipling' and 'the works of Kipling'

of Rudyard Kipling'. The joke, then, is that the female hearer does not recognise Kipling as a metonymy and apparently understands 'kippling' to be the -ing form (the present participle) of the verb 'kipple'. Using her knowledge of English grammar, she replies by forming a regular past participle of 'kipple' by adding 'ed'. At the author-reader level of discourse, the reader is left cogitating the possible meanings of 'to kipple' (see ▶ Chapter 9 for more about incongruity and humour).

7.5.2 Conceptual Metonymies

In a similar way to conceptual metaphors, linguistic metonyms can be grouped under a single conceptual metonymic category that highlight the conceptual relationship. For example, the relationship between writer and written works (as in 'Kippling') can be summarised as PRODUCER FOR PRODUCT. Like conceptual metaphors, conceptual metonymies are written in small capitals with the source coming first and the target second. The 'FOR' is short for 'stands for'. Numerous metonymic relationships have been identified (see, for example, Littlemore 2015); ● Table 7.1 lists just a handful of them.

● **Table 7.1** Examples of conceptual metonymies

Metonymy	Example
PART FOR WHOLE	For example, body parts can refer to people (e.g. bums on seats)
WHOLE FOR PART	For example, 'Town' can refer to people in the town, or the name of a country can refer to some group within the country, such as sports teams
PRODUCER FOR PRODUCT	For example, Hoover, Budweiser and Jacuzzi can be used to refer to their products
PLACE FOR EVENT	For example, Selma, Tiananmen Square and Vietnam can refer to events that happened (e.g. protests, wars) in that location
PLACE FOR INSTITUTION	For example, Downing Street, The Whitehouse and The Kremlin can all refer to the government administration that officially resides there

Activity 7.5: Metonymy—What Stands for What?

Look at the following two extracts from the HUM19CUK corpus, find the metonymy and work out *what* **stands for** *what*.

> (i) "…But I never thought anything of it at the time; but now all the town is talking about it …"
>
> *Wives and Daughters: An Every-day Story* (Elizabeth Gaskell, 1864)

> (ii) "With a mixture of pleasure and fear she hid it [a copy of the scriptures] from all eyes, and was like one who had received a divine guest under her roof, and felt fearful of betraying its divinity to the world."
>
> *The Mummy!* (Jane Loudon, 1827)

We provide our analysis on the book's webpage.

7.5.3 Metonymy and Point of View

Lakoff and Johnson (1980) note that metonymy can structure our attitudes. Metonymies in a text can also betray a writer's, narrator's or character's attitude or world view, and this can be important for stylisticians. For example, in the following extract from *Heart of Darkness* the homodiegetic narrator refers to porters—who are natives of the (probably African) country in which most of the action occurs—by their body parts:

> (4) Day after day, with the stamp and shuffle of sixty pair of bare feet behind me, each pair under a 60-lb. load
>
> *Heart of Darkness* (Joseph Conrad, 1900)

In (4) pairs of feet **stand for** people in a PART FOR WHOLE metonymy. Littlemore (2015: 24) suggests that such metonymies are reductive and depersonalising and, in some circumstances, can have a dehumanising effect. This appears to be the effect in Conrad's novel, which was famously criticised by Achebe (1988) for its racist, colonial attitudes (see also Mastropierro and Conklin 2019).

Activity 7.6: Wouldn't You Just Die Without Mahler?

Consider this short extract from the play *Educating Rita* by Willy Russell.
i. Identify the metonymy and say what type it is.
ii. Say whether 'die' is used literally or non-literally. Give reasons for you answer.

Context: *Set in the UK, Rita is a so-called 'mature student' taking an Open University degree in English Literature. She is looking for a flat to rent. The scene begins with Rita outside a house ringing the doorbell. Classical music can be heard coming from inside. The door is answered by a young woman; the music is now much louder.*

RITA: Erm... I've come about the advert. You know, for sharing the flat.
TRISHA: Wouldn't you just die without Mahler? <long pause> Oh! What am I doing? Come in, come in.

 We give our analysis on the book's webpage.

⊚ Focus 7.3: Synecdoche

Derived from Greek 'understanding one thing with another', **synecdoche** is seen by some scholars as a specific type of metonymy (see, for example, Leech 1969, Wales 2011) whereby the name of the referent is replaced by a part of the referent. For example, body parts are often used to mean people, as in 'a helping pair of hands'. Several discussions of metonymy (including Lakoff and Johnson 1980: 35–6; Littlemore 2015: 23; Knowles and Moon 2006: 48) acknowledge the term (and the phenomenon it refers to) but choose not to use it, preferring instead to use the term 'metonymy' and to specify the type (PART FOR WHOLE). This approach renders the term synecdoche superfluous and avoids (perhaps unnecessary) problems differentiating between synecdoche and metonymy. For further discussion on metonymy and synecdoche, see Steen (2007: 209–10).

7.6 Simile

Like metaphors, similes are a comparison between two concepts from different domains that rely on cross-domain mappings. Consequently, Goatly (1997: 225) suggests that they require similar cognitive activities to those for understanding metaphor (on this point, see also Miller 1993: 375). Similes make the comparison between target and source domains explicit by one of any number of different lexical signals, the prototypical ones being 'as' or 'like' (X is like a Y). Other lexical signals are possible including the following:
- forms of 'resemble' and 'seem',
- 'similar (to)',
- 'the same way',
- 'impression of/that',
- 'unlike',
- 'more/less ... than',
- and comparative inflection plus 'than' (e.g. lovelier than).

For comprehensive inventories of lexical signals of similes, see Goatly (1997: 173–174), Ho (2011: 161) and Steen et al. (2010: 40–1). Leech (1969: 156) notes that some lexical signals can provide information about the manner of comparison being made. For example, 'more/less ... than' presents a 'relationship of inequality' rather than 'equality' (Leech 1969: 156).

7.6.1 Analysing Simile

Consider now the simile in (5) which is taken from the 1980s UK sitcom *Blackadder II*. The simile is uttered by Blackadder, the eponymous hero of the sitcom, in the episode titled 'Beer', and presents relationships of both inequality and equality. In the story, which is set in sixteenth-century Elizabethan England, Blackadder is being visited by his puritanical aunt and uncle, Lord and Lady Whiteadder. Blackadder, who is hoping to inherit money from his relatives, describes them in the following way:

> (5) **Blackadder:** They have one great redeeming feature: their wallets. More capacious than an elephant's scrotum and just as difficult to get your hands on.
> *Blackadder II*, 'Beer' (Curtis and Elton, 1986)

Before reading on, consider what you understand by the simile by completing Activity 7.7.

> **Activity 7.7: What Does Blackadder's Simile Tell Us About His Relatives?**
> Based on Blackadder's simile, answer the following questions about Lord and Lady Whiteadder:
> – Are their wallets small or big?
> – Is getting your hands on their wallets easy or difficult?
> – Are they poor or rich?
>
> Consider how you reached your conclusions and what knowledge you needed to draw upon. Was there any knowledge you did not have? For example, have you ever seen an elephant's scrotum (or managed to get your hands on one)? If not, what inferences did you make about this part of an elephant's anatomy, and how did you make them?

Our understanding of the simile is that Lord and Lady Whiteadder are very wealthy but are reluctant to share their wealth. Let us now analyse the simile to explicate the motivation for this understanding.

7.6.1.1 Target and Source Domains

The simile signals explicitly that a comparison is being between Lord and Lady Whiteadder's wallet and an elephant's scrotum as well as the grounds for the comparison: capaciousness and difficulty of obtainment. The linguistic forms 'more … than …' and 'just as …' also tell us about the manner of comparison. The simile therefore makes explicit the target domain (WALLET) and source domain (ELEPHANT'S SCROTUM) and indicates the cross-domain similarities (and therefore mappings) between these two disparate concepts. This is fortunate because had

Blackadder said, 'their wallets are like an elephant's scrotum', we would have no doubt been left wondering what sorts of similarities he was implying. We still, nonetheless, need to ask what the comparison means and what it tells us about Lord and Lady Whiteadder. To make sense of the similarities and interpret the comparisons, we need to draw on our Encyclopaedic Knowledge of the concepts that the simile activates: WALLET and ELEPHANT SCROTUM.

Lord and Lady Whiteadder's wallets are not just capacious, they are more capacious than an elephant's scrotum. So, just how big are their wallets? While the answer might seem obvious, it is worth considering how we reach an understanding about the relationship of inequality presented in the simile, especially when (we assume) most of us have never even seen an elephant's scrotum, let alone got our hands on one. Thinking back to Activity 7.1, it is likely that our central knowledge of elephants includes that they are very large (the biggest) land mammals with some very large body parts (e.g. ears, tusks). We might reasonably assume, therefore, that elephant scrotums are also big. Therefore, anything that is bigger (and more capacious) would be very big indeed! So, while the explicit comparison made by the simile signals cross-domain mappings in relation to size, our Encyclopaedic Knowledge helps us to elaborate on the conceptual nature of the source domain and incorporate it into the implied meaning (see Steen 2009: 207).

Let us turn now to the level of difficulty in getting the wallets, which is established in the simile by the relationship of equality ('just as'). The question we might ask is: 'just how difficult is it to get your hands on Lord and Lady Whiteadder's wallets?' The answer is that it is very difficult. Why? Because, even without first-hand experience, we assume that getting your hands on an elephant's scrotum would be very awkward business indeed, not least because bull elephants can be aggressive, territorial creatures.[9]

7.6.1.2 Literal and Figurative Language

So far, we have side-stepped the issue of whether the lexical items involved in the simile are used literally or figuratively. Recall that when we analysed metaphors, separating figurative from literal language was an important initial step. With similes, it is normal for the lexical items to be used literally, to refer directly to their referents and the concepts they activate (Steen 2009: 207). So, in our simile, 'elephant's scrotum' is used literally and refers directly to that object. It is, nonetheless, involved in the metaphoric comparison. By contrast, however, 'wallet' is used metonymically, which means it refers indirectly to some closely related concept within the same conceptual domain. This adds a level of complexity to the simile and its meaning. A central feature of the concept WALLET is that they are containers for money, and we need to understand that WALLET maps onto its contents (i.e. MONEY) in a CONTAINER FOR CONTENTS metonymy. In many English language communities, this is an established metonymic relationship that is likely to be part of Encyclopaedic Knowledge and therefore recognised. So too is 'large wallet' to mean 'large quantity of money' in a SIZE OF CONTAINER FOR QUANTITY OF CONTENTS relationship, and that the owner of a large wallet is rich in an OBJECT FOR (SOCIAL) CATEGORY relationship (if we see 'rich' as a social category).

So, if Lord and Lady Whiteadder have big wallets (which we have established they have), then they are wealthy. And, if it is difficult to get hold of their wallets (which we have established it is), then it is extremely difficult to obtain money from them and/or they are reluctant to share their wealth.

Notice also that the simile uses the well-established idiomatic phrase 'get your hands on', which is figurative (meaning to obtain or acquire). Conceptually, the idiom relies on the notion that physically holding something in your hand is equal to possession. Conceptually, similar idiomatic expressions would include, for example, 'out of reach' and 'within my grasp'. Humour is created by ambiguity (see ▶ Chapter 9 for more on ambiguity) whereby both the literal and non-literal readings of 'get your hands on' are simultaneously activated within the two conceptual domains involved in the comparison. In the domain of MONEY or WEALTH, the figurative meaning is most likely (i.e. gain possession—although possession could involve physically touching the coinage). In the domain of elephants, the figurative meaning does not make sense, so the literal reading comes to the fore.

7.6.1.3 Simile Summary

The simile in (5) is a complex of metonymic and metaphoric mappings both within and between domains and employs both literal and figurative language. The comparison set up by the simile involves the concepts WALLET and ELEPHANT'S SCROTUM but these need to be appreciated in broader domains of meaning (something like WEALTH/MONEY and ELEPHANT respectively) to explicate the meaning of the simile. The comparison triggers cross-domain mappings relating size (rather than, say, contents or colour) whereby the size of an elephant's scrotum is explicitly offered as an object for comparison. Elaborating on the conceptual nature of the source domain via our Encyclopaedic Knowledge enabled us to describe the similarities, and therefore mappings, in more detail and explain the implied meaning of the simile.

   **Activity 7.8: As Busy as Bees**

Consider the following example of simile from HUM19CUK:

> Mrs Halifax, Jem Watkins, and his Jenny, were as busy as bees all morning.
> *John Halifax, Gentleman* (Dinah Maria Mulock Craik, 1857)

i. How active were the people mentioned in the simile?
ii. How did you reach this conclusion?
iii. State the source, target and domain mappings.
iv. What knowledge do you need to establish the mappings?

 We provide our answers on the book's webpage.

7.7 Metaphorical Language and Corpora

In this section, we discuss some of the possibilities for exploring metaphorical language using corpora and corpus tools. Metaphor research using corpus approaches is problematic simply because, as we have discovered in this chapter, identifying metaphor relies on identifying figurative use of lexical items, and this is something computers cannot do. Nor can computers work out conceptual mappings or grounds for comparison. Additionally, these mappings (e.g. HAPPY IS UP; SAD IS DOWN) can be manifested in any number of linguistic forms (such as 'her mood lifted'; 'her spirits sank') so knowing what forms to search for in a corpus is tricky. There are nevertheless important ways in which corpus approaches can assist in the analysis of metaphor not least by providing supporting evidence for intuitions concerning the salience of different metaphors in different texts (on this point, see Gibbs 2017; Stefanowitsch 2006).

7.7.1 Concordance Lines and Metaphor

To use corpora and corpus tools to explore metaphors, we first need to establish what linguistic forms we should look for in the corpus or text. For example, if we were interested in metaphors relating to the target domain LOVE, then a starting point would be to carry out a corpus search for occurrences of the lexical item 'love' and possibly other associated forms such as 'loves', 'loved' and 'loving'. Similarly, we might also search for lexical items that relate to source domains. For example, source domains used to talk about love might include HEAT or FLORA, so searching for lexical items that connect to these domains (e.g. 'flame', 'blossom') could reveal metaphors in the data. However, in both cases, we first need to establish which lexical items to search for in the first place.

A method proposed by Deignan (2005: 93) that can help to define a list of search terms for investigating target and source domains is to create a list of synonyms provided by a thesaurus. For example, if we are investigating the target domain LOVE, we would investigate near synonyms for 'love', such as 'attachment', 'endearment', 'devotion' and 'affection'. With this approach, concordances for every synonym are generated and examined for metaphorical usage. Similarly, if we were interested in the source domain of HEAT, we would create a list of possible search terms from the semantic field of 'heat' and then search for each of these terms in a corpus. In this way, the target domains that the source domains map onto can then be identified using concordance lines.

Another method is to conduct a pilot analysis of a small subset of a text or corpus and use those results as a starting point for the analysis of the main body of data. For example, Koller's (2004) analysis of war metaphors in business texts was informed by a pilot analysis of a small corpus which suggested a list of lexical expressions from the semantic field of war (for more on this method, see also Cameron and Deignan 2003; Charteris-Black 2004).

Once you have chosen your search term(s), concordance lines make a useful starting point for the subsequent investigation of metaphor. Recall that concordance lines list every instance of a search term in a text or corpus along with some of the surrounding co-text. Concordances are usually shown in what is known as **KWIC** (**K**ey **W**ord **I**n **C**ontext) format, where **K**ey **W**ord means the search term, and **C**ontext is the surrounding co-text. ◘ Figure 7.9 shows a small sample (20 occurrences out of 184) of sorted concordance lines for the word 'love' from the HUM19CUK corpus where 'love' is followed immediately to the right by 'is'. These concordance lines therefore help to identify explicit metaphors like the one we analysed earlier in this chapter in example (1).

Using concordances typically involves the rigorous and systematic manual examination of each concordance line. By that we mean that every concordance line should be evaluated in some way or another and the evaluation process should be the same for each concordance, perhaps informed by some external framework for analysis. Depending on the data used, this can be a time-consuming undertaking. For example, say we were investigating the target domain of LOVE via the word 'love' in the HUM19CUK corpus, this would involve examining 9995 concordances, each containing one occurrence of 'love'. Sorting concordances and exporting them to a spreadsheet (e.g. Excel) can be useful for organising, categorising and quantifying the data. ◘ Figure 7.9 shows concordances for 'love' (the search term) sorted by the first three words that occur to the right of the search term. The sorted results help to highlight patterns in the data which can provide a focus for analysis. For example, in concordances 6 and 8 in ◘ Fig. 7.9, the subject complements 'fire' and 'flame' are access points to similar source domains and mappings and evidence for a conceptual metaphor of LOVE IS FIRE (see Charteris-Black 2017) or more generally EMOTIONS ARE NATURAL FORCES (see Kövecses 2000; Omori 2008

1	The youngness of people in	love	is a caution!" And I should like to
2	Ah! how much easier to part where	love	is a certainty; and now this was the
3	you call love woke up. Your man's	love	is a child's love for butterflies. You
4	so at his own imaginings. So his	love	is a crystal Goddess, set upon an obelisk;
5	with the power to begin with; but	love	is a delicate essence, as volatile as it
6	take the thing quite differently; with us	love	is a devouring flame! a fire that absorbs
7	Caroline?" "Love a crime! No, Shirley;	love	is a divine virtue. But why drag that
8	love, my dear," said Lyndall. "A man's	love	is a fire of olivewood. It leaps
9	been all that he ought to have been.	Love	is a great purifier, and love for a
10	of things than ye young persons think for	Love	is a mere bauble, and no human being
11	murmurs.' 'Now in my opinion,' said I, '	love	is a mystical sympathy, which unfolds
12	, and see in the world only his Julia!	Love	is a passion in which soul and body
13	, I think I could preach a better myself.	Love	is a passion that has been much talked
14	no longer young are liable to forget that	love	is a plant of early growth, and that
15	to Eustace, I cannot be divine." "But	love	is a potent and untameable passion,
16	you can't demonstrate to me that his	love	is a reality." "But I KNOW it is!"
17	to be coaxed back in the old direction.	Love	is a sacred stream which withdraws itself
18	love in that way; it is not pretty.	Love	is a serious thing." "My dear mamma,
19	yours commonplace, then?' 'Desperately.	Love	is a very old and common thing, and
20	of her has gone from me. The word	"love"	is a weariness to me. If only our

◘ **Fig. 7.9** Extract of a sorted concordance of 'love' from HUM19CUK

7.7.2 Semantic Tags and Metaphor

Wmatrix (Rayson 2009) can annotate a corpus or text for semantic categories, which means that rather than searching for individual lexical items, semantic groupings can be explored. For example, ◘ Fig. 7.10 shows a concordance produced by *Wmatrix* for the semantic domain 'aircraft and flying' from a corpus of Jane Austen's novels. Fifty-five words received this tag in the whole corpus. ◘ Figure 7.10 shows just the first twenty occurrences in the order they appear in the corpus. We can see from the figure that most are forms of 'fly'. While none are to do with aviation, the concordances show that there is a mixture of both literal and metaphorical uses. For example, line 3 refers to flying a kite, lines 1 and 6 involve conventional metaphors relating to time flying (e.g.), and in lines 17 and 18 cognitive activity is the target domain. Once again, each concordance needs to be inspected and assessed for metaphorical usage and what domain is being targeted (◘ Fig. 7.10).

1	he in-betweens, that the evening	flew	away at a very unusual rate; and
2	asted power and freedom, all are	flown	. Lord of the earth and sea, he b
3	temper. I shall never forget his	flying	Henry 's kite for him that very wi
4	is poor mother! Well, time does	fly	indeed! --and my memory is very b
5	proportionate depression. It soon	flies	over the present failure, and beg
6	-half my time. I never knew days	fly	so fast. A week tomorrow! --And
7	very kind neighbour!' And then	fly	off, through half a sentence, to
8	rother, Mr. Suckling, sometimes	flies	about. You will hardly believe me
9	, she bounded higher than ever,	flew	farther down the middle, and was
10	pain and with contrition; but no	flight	of generosity run mad, opposing a
11	eeably than those which have just	flown	away. At present, nothing goes s
12	he noise of a child than he could	fly	; if, indeed, he should ever get
13	tward door, temptingly open on a	flight	of steps which led immediately to
14	re of day behind. A considerable	flight	of steps landed them in the wilder
15	on his encouragement, to such a	flight	of audacious independence, it was
16	e would now have answered for her	gliding	about with quiet, light elegance
17	g down her mind from its heavenly	flight	by saying, But what is it that you
18	ke her cousins! And her thoughts	flew	to those absent cousins with most
19	up every dearer plan in order to	fly	with her. He stopt. And what, s
20	could no more walk than you could	fly	! It has not been so dirty the who

◘ Fig. 7.10 Wmatrix concordance for semantic category M5: Flying and aircraft

Wmatrix can also be used to look at a list of all the word types that are in a domain. For example, ◘ Table 7.2 shows the ten most frequent word types (out of 186) assigned to the 'Anatomy and physiology' semantic category in the Jane Austen corpus. In total, 3038 words (tokens) in the corpus are in this category of which 464 are 'heart'. Once again, concordances for every instance of these word types in the corpus can be examined for metaphorical or, indeed, metonymical usage. In this way, *Wmatrix* automatically provides a list of search terms within a particular semantic domain that might be of interest.

Table 7.2 The ten most frequent 'Anatomy and physiology' word types in the Jane Austen Corpus

Rank	Word-type	Freq
1	heart	464
2	eyes	285
3	body	262
4	head	196
5	hand	183
6	face	134
7	eye	117
8	hands	87
9	consciousness	82
10	tears	69

7.8 Taking Stock of Metaphorical Language

In this chapter, we have explored metaphorical language by looking at three tropes: metaphor, metonymy and simile. With metaphorical language, writers invite us to share in a new or different understanding of something. We started by introducing Encyclopaedic Knowledge, concepts and domains, which are key ideas relating to metaphorical language, before moving on to describe a method for the analysis of metaphor, metonymy and simile which incorporates both text and cognition. Along the way, we introduced Conceptual Metaphor Theory (CMT) which suggests that metaphors are fundamental to the way we experience things and the way we conceptualise the world. That being the case, the theory accounts in part for how we understand metaphor in a text. The analytical tools we introduced help to uncover and understand textual metaphor by exploring both linguistic and cognitive interpretative processes. Understanding and interpreting linguistic metaphor is partly a matter of comparison in the text, understanding in the brain and thinking about two things simultaneously. Processing metaphor relies on our knowledge of language, the world and our experiences, and can offer us new ways of conceiving of things.

- **Further Reading**

An 'old school' guide to analysing metaphorical language, including a three-stage framework for the analysis of metaphor: Leech, G. N. (1969) *A Linguistic Guide to English Poetry*. London: Longman.

Steen has described his five-stage framework for metaphor analysis in a number of publications. This is one of the latest and follows up on some of the critiques made on earlier versions:

Steen, G. (2009). From linguistic form to conceptual structure in five steps: analyzing metaphor in poetry. In *Cognitive poetics: Goals, gains and gaps*, eds. G. Brône and J. Vandaele, 197–226. Berlin: Mouton de Gruyter.

Using numerous examples, this book attempts to show how CMT can be applied to poetry: Lakoff, G. and Turner, M. (1989) *More than cool reason: a field guide to poetic metaphor*. Chicago: University of Chicago Press.

An accessible overview of several approaches to/theories about metaphor: Ritchie, D.L. (2013) *Metaphor*. Edinburgh: Edinburgh University Press.

For an overview of metaphor, an examination of Steen's analytical framework and a critique of Conceptual Metaphor Theory: Deignan, A. H. (2016) From Linguistic to Conceptual Metaphors. In: Semino, E and Demjen, Z, (eds.) *The Routledge Handbook of Metaphor and Language. Routledge Handbooks in Linguistics*. London: Routledge.

- **Resources**

Wmatrix (Rayson 2009): for more details, see the *Wmatrix* website:
▶ https://ucrel.lancs.ac.uk/wmatrix/
HUM19CUK: corpus of nineteenth century novels.

- **Notes**

1. West (2013) argues that Richards was a 'protocognitivist' who laid the foundation for cognitive stylistics.
2. A connected but different idea to centrality is that of prototypicality, which is to do with category membership. For example, a chair can be seen both as an object and as a category with a variety of members. Within the category of 'chair', all members will have (a) central characteristic(s) (e.g. a place to park your backside), but some members will be more prototypical than others (e.g. an armchair might be seen as more prototypical than an office chair).
3. The long-standing terms for the components of a metaphor introduced by I. A. Richards ([1936] 1965: 95–7) are tenor and **vehicle**, where tenor is what is being talked about (i.e. the topic of the metaphor) and vehicle is the expression used to talk about the tenor. Richards' terms have, in the main, been supplanted by the terminology introduced by Lakoff and Johnson (1980), with **target domain** corresponding with tenor and **source domain** corresponding with vehicle.
4. We have simplified Steen's steps, which utilise propositional calculus, so that readers do not first need to learn propositional calculus before they can analyse metaphor in texts. A consequence of this is that we have one less step than Steen.
5. See, for example, *Multimodal Metaphor* edited by: Charles J. Forceville and Eduardo Urios-Aparisi (2009).
6. The term proposed by Richards (1936 [1965]) for the implied similarities is the **ground** of the metaphor.
7. We made these up, but they seem reasonable, which might be further evidence to support the conceptual basis of the metaphor.

8. Donald McGill designed risqué seaside postcards (an example of a sauce domain) and this joke appeared on one of them.
9. The potential elephant in the room with this simile is that elephants do not have scrotums. However, even if you knew this, it is likely that the simile still makes sense. Indeed, the difficulty of getting your hands on one increases infinitely.

References

Black, M. 1977. More about Metaphor *Dialectica* 31, 3/4: 431–457.
Black, M. 1962. *Models and Metaphors*. Ithaca, N.Y.: Cornell University Press.
Black, M. 1955. Metaphor *Proceedings of the Aristotelian Society, New Series, Vol. 55* (1954–1955), 273–294 Oxford University Press.
Cameron, L. and Deignan, A. 2003. Combining Large and Small Corpora to Investigate Tuning Devices Around Metaphor in Spoken Discourse. *Metaphor and Symbol* 18, 3: 149–160.
Charteris-Black, J. 2017. All-Consuming Passions: Fire Metaphors. *Fiction. E-rea: Revue Électronique d'Études sur le Monde Anglophone*, 15. ▶ https://doi.org/10.4000/erea.5992.
Charteris-Black, J. 2014. *Analysing Political Speeches: Rhetoric, Discourse and Metaphor*. Basingstoke: Palgrave Macmillan.
Charteris-Black, J. 2004. *Corpus Approaches to Critical Metaphor Analysis*. Basingstoke Palgrave Macmillan.
Deignan, A. H. 2016. From Linguistic to Conceptual Metaphors. In *The Routledge Handbook of Metaphor and Language*, eds. E. Semino and Z. Demjen, 102–116. London: Routledge.
Evans, V. 2019. *Cognitive Linguistics: A Complete Guide*. Edinburgh: Edinburgh University Press.
Gibbs, R. W. Jr. 2017. *Metaphor Wars: Conceptual Metaphors in Human Life*. Cambridge: Cambridge University Press.
Gibbs, R. W. Jr. 2011. Evaluating Conceptual Metaphor Theory, *Discourse Processes* 48, 8: 529–562.
Grady, J. 1997. *Foundations of Meaning: Primary Metaphors and Primary Scenes*. Unpublished Doctoral Dissertation, University of California, Berkeley.
Goatly, A. 1997. *The Language of Metaphors*. Oxford: Blackwell.
Glucksberg, S. and McClone, M. 1999. When love is not a journey: What metaphors mean. *Journal of Pragmatics* 31: 1541–1558.
Ho, Y. 2011. *Corpus Stylistics in Principles and Practice: A Stylistic Exploration of John Fowles' The Magus*. London: Continuum
Jacobson, R. 1956. Two Aspects of Language and Two Types of Aphasic Disturbances. In *Fundamentals of Language* R. Jacobson and M. Halle, 55–76. The Hague, NL: Mouton and Co.
Koller, V. 2004. Metaphor and Gender in Business media Discourse. *A Critical Cognitive Study*. Basingstoke: Palgrave Macmillan.
Kövecses, Z. 2008. The conceptual structure of happiness and pain. In *Reconstructing Pain and Joy: Linguistic, Literary and Cultural Perspectives*, eds. C. Lascaratou, A. Despotopoulou and E. Ifantidou, 17-33. Cambridge: Cambridge Scholars Publishing.
Kövecses, Z. 2000. *Metaphor and Emotion: Language, Culture, and Body in Human Feeling*. Cambridge: Cambridge University Press.
Lakoff, G. and Johnson, M. 1980. *Metaphors We Live By*. Chicago: University of Chicago Press.
Lakoff, G. 1993. The Contemporary Theory of Metaphor. In *Metaphor and Thought*. 2nd ed, ed. A. Ortony, 202–251. Cambridge: Cambridge University Press.
Lakoff, G. and Johnson, M. 2003. *Metaphors We Live By*. 2nd ed. Chicago: University of Chicago Press.
Leech, G. 1969. *A Linguistic Guide to English Poetry*. Harlow, England: Pearson Education.
Leech, G. 2008. *Language in Literature: Style and Foregrounding*. London and New York: Routledge.
Langacker, R. W. 1987. *Foundations of Cognitive Grammar*, Vol. 1: Theoretical Prerequisites. Stanford: Stanford University Press.

Langacker, R. W. 2008. *Cognitive Grammar: A Basic Introduction*. Oxford: Oxford University Press.

Littlemore, J. 2015. *Metonymy: Hidden Shortcuts in Language, Thought and Communication*. Cambridge: Cambridge University Press.

Mastropierro, L., & Conklin, K. (2019). Racism and Dehumanisation in Heart of Darkness and its Italian Translations: A Reader Response Analysis. *Language and Literature* 28, 4: 309–325. ▶ https://doi.org/10.1177/0963947019884450.

Miller, G. 1993. Images and Models, Similes and Metaphors. In *Metaphor and Thought*. 2nd ed, ed. A. Ortony, 357–400. Cambridge, England: Cambridge University Press.

Ortony, A., ed. 1993. *Metaphor and Thought*. 2nd ed. Cambridge: Cambridge University Press.

Ortony, A., ed. 1979. *Metaphor and Thought*. Cambridge, England: Cambridge University Press.

Omori, A. 2008. Emotion as a Huge Mass of Moving Water, *Metaphor and Symbol* 23, 2: 130–146.

Rayson, P. 2009. *Wmatrix: A Web-Based Corpus Processing Environment*. Computing Department, Lancaster University. ▶ http://ucrel.lancs.ac.uk/wmatrix/

Richards, I. A. 1936. *The Philosophy of Rhetoric*. Oxford: Oxford University Press.

Ritchie, D.L. 2013. *Metaphor*. Edinburgh: Edinburgh University Press.

Semino, E. 1997. *Language and World Creation in Poems and Other Texts*. London and New York: Longman.

Short M 1996. *Exploring the Language of Poems, Plays and Prose*. Harlow: Longman.

Semino, E. 1997. Language and World Creation in Poems and Other Texts. London and New York: Longman.

Semino, E. 2010. Descriptions of Pain, Metaphor and Embodied Simulation. *Metaphor and Symbol* 25: 205–226.

Semino, E., Heywood, J., Short, M. 2004. Methodological Problems in the Analysis of Metaphors in a Corpus of Conversations about Cancer. *Journal of Pragmatics* 36, 7: 1271–1294.

Stefanowitsch, A. 2006. Words and their Metaphors: A Corpus-based Approach. In *Corpora in Cognitive Linguistics: Corpus-based Approaches to Syntax and Lexis*, eds. S. Gries and A. Stefanowitsch, 63–104. Berlin: Mouton de Gruyter.

Steen, G. 1999a. From Linguistic to Conceptual Metaphor in Five Steps. In *Metaphor in Cognitive Linguistics: Selected Papers from the 5th International Cognitive Linguistics Conference, Amsterdam, 1997*, eds. R. W. Gibbs, and G. J. Steen, John Benjamins Publishing: Amsterdam, NL.

Steen, G. 1999b. Analyzing Metaphor in Literature: With Examples from William Wordsworth's "I Wandered Lonely as a Cloud". *Poetics Today* 20, 3: 499–522.

Steen, G. 2007. Finding Metaphor in Grammar and Usage: A Methodological Analysis of Theory and Research. Amsterdam and Philadelphia: John Benjamins.

Steen, G. 2009. From linguistic form to conceptual structure in five steps: analyzing metaphor in poetry. In *Cognitive poetics: Goals, gains and gaps*, eds. G. Brône and J. Vandaele, 197-226. Berlin: Mouton de Gruyter.

Steen, G. J., Dorst, A. G., Herrmann, J. B., Kaal, A. A., & Krennmayr, T. 2010. Metaphor in Usage. *Cognitive Linguistics* 21, 4: 765–796.

Wales, K. 2011. *A Dictionary of Stylistics*. Harlow, UK: Pearson Education Ltd.

Mind Style

Supplementary Information The online version contains supplementary material available at ▶ https://doi.org/10.1007/978-3-031-10422-0_8.

© The Author(s), under exclusive license to Springer Nature Switzerland AG 2023
J. Lugea and B. Walker, *Stylistics*,
https://doi.org/10.1007/978-3-031-10422-0_8

8.1 Introduction

Most readers of fiction will be familiar with the experience of 'getting inside the head' of a character, one of the key sources of pleasure in reading. As Zunshine attests, "our enjoyment of fiction is predicated—at least in part—upon our *awareness* of our 'trying-on' mental states *potentially available* to us but at a given moment *differing* from our own" (2006: 17, emphasis in original). Sometimes fiction gives us intimate access to the *inner* workings of a character's mind. We feel as they do; we think as they do. By seeing the world through the filtering vision of another person, we gain a fresh perspective: a 'mind style'.

All of the textual phenomena that we have looked at so far, such as dialogue, character and metaphor, contribute to the creation of literary-linguistic style. As with any kind of style in language, mind style is the result of patterned linguistic choices. When those features are interpreted by readers as contributing towards a 'style of thinking' in a character or narrator, they can be called a mind style. But what kind of language choices should we look out for? Mind style is an *effect*, the effect of understanding the text-world through the mind of another, not a *model*; it does not tell us how to analyse the language that leads to its creation. The ways in which fictional minds have been explored in the history of Stylistics mirrors the conceptual development of the field: from formalist beginnings to discursive, pragmatic and cognitive approaches, to corpus methods. Likewise, this chapter begins by outlining the lexico-grammatical features traditionally associated with mind style (► Sect. 8.2), followed by the pragmatic dimension (► Sect. 8.3), and then the more cognitive approaches which—given their dealings with mental processes—are well suited to investigating fictional minds (► Sect. 8.4). Throughout, we draw on previous research, which tends to focus on 'deviant' mind styles (► Sect. 8.3). The chapter culminates by employing a novel combination of corpus techniques and Cognitive Grammar (► Sect. 8.7) to elaborate on a classic mind style analysis (Leech and Short 1981/2007).

First, it is worth noting how mind style relates to some of the models we have covered so far in this book. ► Chapter 6 illustrated how textual cues work together with socio-cognitive categories to create fictional characters; while the focus there was on characters as whole beings, mind style is particularly about characters' cognitive functioning (the overlap between fictional characters and their minds is discussed in Sects. 8.3 and 8.4.3). ► Chapter 2 explored how participants in discourse co-create a text-world, using textual cues and contextual knowledge to create a mental representation of the discourse. Those mental representations may also include understandings of the mental functioning of enactors in the text-world. As outlined in ► Chapter 3, fiction also invites the reader to adopt a perspective—a view of that text-world. Mind style and viewpoint are complementary but distinct concepts, as Semino and Swindlehurst (2002: 143) observe:

> Clearly, we can perceive a character's mind style only if we are presented with his or her point of view. The reverse however, is not always true. The access to a character's point of view does not necessarily imply access to his or her mind style […] At a basic level, then point of view and mind style are clearly distinct. Point of view

concerns the angle or perspective from which the fictional world is presented and mind style the way in which the fictional world is perceived and conceptualized by the mind whose point of view is adopted.

The narrative modes which allow for mind style to be presented are homodiegetic narratives or heterodiegetic narratives that give access to character thoughts, e.g. through Free Indirect Thought (Rundquist 2020; Lugea, 2022). The mind style concept originates with Fowler, who proposed that it corresponds with ideological point of view (▶ Chapter 3, ▶ Sect. 2.4); that is, "the system of beliefs, values and categories by reference to which a person or a society comprehends the world" (1986/1996: 134). However, researchers investigating mind style since have tended to relate it more to an individual, psychological viewpoint, preserving ideological viewpoint for more socially shared world views (Semino and Swindlehurst 2002; Semino 2007), meaning political ideologies, such as 'socialism', or religious ones, such as 'Taoism'. We endorse this view that mind style is a reflection of an individual, idiosyncratic perspective, although the division between personal and social world views is admittedly difficult to delineate in theory and in practice (McIntyre 2005; Semino 2007; Nuttall 2018).

Indeed, when he first introduced the term 'mind style', Fowler described it as "any distinctive linguistic presentation of an *individual* mental self" (1977: 103, our emphasis). He went on to describe how mind style arises out of "consistent linguistic choices which build up a continuous, pervasive, representation of the world" (1986: 9), highlighting the cumulative effect of patterns in language in forging a particular way of thinking in an enactor. In other words, the linguistic choices the author makes accumulate over the course of a text to forge a particular world view. For this reason, mind style is ripe for corpus investigation, allowing the analyst to identify and quantify the cumulative features that contribute to mind style (▶ Sect. 8.7).

8.2 Mind Style: Lexico-Grammatical Features

In M.A.K. Halliday's Systemic Functional Linguistics (Halliday 1994; Halliday and Matthiessen 2014), he identifies three purposes—or **metafunctions**—of language: the organisation of words and grammar into discourse (the **textual metafunction**), encoding interactional relationships (the **interpersonal metafunction**) and representing experience (the **ideational metafunction**). These three metafunctions are said to work together in creating meaning in language use, and this broad understanding of language in general underscores much research in Stylistics (Simpson 1993; Nørgaard 2003; Canning 2014; Simpson and Canning 2014). Fowler proposed that mind style draws mainly on the **ideational function** of language; in other words, if we want to find out how mind style is created, we need to look at the features that contribute towards the representation of experience. Helpfully, Halliday's systemic functional approach to language identifies key areas where the ideational metafunction is carried out; one of these is is **transitivity** (▶ Sect. 2.3.2).

8.2.1 Transitivity

When you select and conjugate a verb, you make **transitivity** choices, encoding the event as a process and assigning participant roles to those involved (Sect. 2.3.2, ◘ Table 2.2). Most verbal processes have a subject, a participant responsible for the verb (e.g. 'I think'). However, when the **passive voice** is used, this participant can be removed or, at least, postponed (e.g. 'It is thought [by experts])', which is a way of removing agency and responsibility for an action particularly favoured by the media and in political discourse (Simpson et al. 2018). Some verbs are **intransitive**, meaning they do not affect a second participant (e.g. 'I ran'). On the other hand, when a verb is used transitively it has an effect on another participant (e.g. 'I hit *him*'), and depending on the kind of process used, there are different terms for this affected participant (for a useful overview of Halliday's transitivity model, see Simpson 1993: 86–117, or Simpson and Canning 2014). Already, you can see the myriad of options available in transitivity, and the choices that a speaker (or writer) makes are indicative of their particular experience of the world. Thus, the transitivity model is a useful tool for analysing mind style (see ► Sect. 8.5 for an application of Langacker's 'action chains' as a Cognitive Grammar alternative).

In a now classic study, Halliday (1971, reprinted in Weber 1996 and Burke 2017) investigated the transitivity processes used to represent the mental experience of Lok, a Neanderthal character in William Golding's novel *The Inheritors*. Using past tense and third-person deixis, the narrative is from the perspective of a heterodiegetic narrator (► Chapter 3). Despite the external perspective, the narrator adopts the psychological viewpoint of the focalising character, Lok:

> (1) The bushes twitched again. Lok steadied by the tree and gazed. A head and a chest faced him, half-hidden. There were white bone things behind the leaves and hair. The man had white bone things above his eyes and under the mouth so that his face was longer than a face should be. The man turned sideways in the bushes and looked at Lok along his shoulder. A stick rose upright and there was a lump of bone in the middle. Lok peered at the stick and the lump of bone and the small eyes in the bone things over the face. Suddenly Lok understood that the man was holding the stick out to him but neither he nor Lok could reach across the river. He would have laughed if it were not for the echo of the screaming in his head. The stick began to grow shorter at both ends. Then it shot out to full length again.
> The dead tree by Lok's ear acquired a voice.
> "Clop!"
> His ears twitched and he turned to the tree. By his face there had grown a twig: a twig that smelt of other, and of goose, and of the bitter berries that Lok's stomach told him he must not eat. This twig had a white bone at the end.

If you are reading this passage for the first time out of context, it might not be clear that the more advanced *Homo sapiens* character draws an arrow and shoots it at Lok the Neanderthal, hitting the tree beside him. Certainly, there are some unusual linguistic choices which make the passage difficult to process and that reflect an observably 'different' world view, characterised by Lok's naivety towards the more advanced species attacking him. Halliday's (1971) ground-breaking transitivity analysis of this text revealed a peculiar grammar that consists of a distinct lack of human subjects and direct objects, suggesting the character does not fully comprehend cause and effect. One way this is achieved is through avoiding the use of transitive verbs where they would otherwise be natural. For example, rather than observing the man raising the stick, where 'raised' is a transitive verb with the man as agent and the stick as object, Lok simply observes 'the stick rose upright'. In Lok's conceptualisation of events, non-animate objects are responsible for actions, as in the material processes "the bushes twitched" and "a stick rose upright and [...] grew shorter at both ends", and in the existential process "there had grown a twig". In failing to identify the *Homo sapiens* as the actor in the material process or himself as the goal, Lok reveals his incomprehension of the situation. Through the relational process with the dead tree "acquiring a voice", Lok misattributes the sound "clop" to the inanimate tree, not fully understanding the flight and impact of the arrow on the tree beside him. Furthermore, Lok perceives his own body parts as responsible for material processes ("his ears twitched") and verbal processes ("Lok's stomach told him"), where instead we might expect him to be the agent of behavioural or mental processes (e.g. 'Lok heard' or 'Lok thought'). This suggests the Neanderthal has an instinctive physiological response to sensual stimuli, rather than a rationalised one. Halliday concluded that the transitivity patterns (only briefly summarised here) reflect the novel's underlying theme, the "limitations of understanding, whether cultural or biological, of Lok and his people, and their consequent inability to survive when confronted with beings at a higher stage of development" (1971: 345).

Halliday's (1971) analysis of the language attributed to Lok in *The Inheritors* demonstrated the link between transitivity patterns and a distinctive representation of a mental self, and paved the way for Fowler's (1977; 1986/1996) development of the term mind style.

☐ **Corpus KWIC-le: How is 'Gazed' Typically Used?**
What sort of constructions is 'gazed' typically used in? Based on your own language knowledge, you will probably have intuitions about what sorts of subject that tend to accompany the verb, and what (if anything) tends to follows the verb. These intuitions can be tested using a corpus and collocation.

⬇ *Use the Instructions on the book's webpage to calculate the left and right collocates (i.e. words that frequently occur to the left and right) of 'gazed' in the BNC.*

8.2.2 Underlexicalisation

Just like grammatical structures, the specific words chosen by—or attributed to—people are clues as to the ideational content of their minds. Fowler (1986/1996) built on Halliday's transitivity analysis of Lok by examining the lexical choices and how they relate to the character's mind style. As you might have observed in the passage above, Lok lacks the vocabulary to describe the unfamiliar experiences that arise as a result of encountering the new human species. He refers to an unknown *arrow* as a 'stick' or a 'twig that smelt of other' with 'a white bone at the end'. Fowler (1986/1996) called this phenomenon **underlexicalisation**, referring to a character's lack of lexicon to describe a concept unfamiliar to them. Instead, a more general word is used or the concept is paraphrased. In the examples listed above, a 'twig' and a 'stick' account for the basic physical properties of an arrow, but not its use as a weapon. The crucial arrowhead is also described by recourse to its physical properties, "a white bone", neglecting its purpose. The unfamiliar, repellent smell—perhaps a poison—is simply described as "other", with no conceivable referent. In the same passage, Lok describes the man he encounters as having "white bone things above his eyes and under the mouth so that his face was longer than a face should be", reflecting the distinctive features of the new human species. However, this form of underlexicalisation is not expressed through a simpler, alternative word, but through **circumlocution**, paraphrasing at length because he lacks both the conceptual and linguistic basis to process the *Homo sapiens*' features.

Leech and Short (1981/2007) also identify underlexicalisation in their analysis of Benjy's mind style in the opening passage of *The Sound and the Fury*. Benjy, who has a learning disability, is watching some people on the grass through a fence: "They took the flag out and they were hitting. Then they put the flag back and they went to the table, and he hit and the other hit". Lacking the noun to describe the game of golf before him, Benjy circumlocutes the concrete event by instead describing the actions involved. These examples demonstrate how lexis and grammar are interconnected; the lexical choices (or lack of) combine with the morpho-syntactic choices in transitivity to create the characters' mind styles. Leech and Short note that, like Lok, "Benjy appears to have an imperfect understanding of cause and effect. But unlike Lok, he does not avoid the use of transitive verbs. Rather, he uses them freely as if they were intransitive" (1981/2007: 165). Leech and Short are referring to the fact that the verb 'hit' usually has an object, but Benjy does not perceive the object (or the purpose) of the people's actions. Going beyond transitivity, Leech and Short comment on 33-year-old Benjy's childlike sentence structure, which "shows a tendency common in the writing of young children to string sentences or paratactic and coordinated main clauses together instead of resorting to subordination or sentence division" (1981/2007: 165). Even in the brief example quoted above, you can see Benjy's frequent use of the coordinating conjunction 'and', his short, simple sentences, abruptly divided and begun again with the simple additive adverb 'then' (see Bockting [1995] on the mind styles of Faulkner's other characters).

But what is the literary effect of these lexical and morpho-syntactic patterns? In reading the passages cited above, you may have found it difficult to imagine the text-world, given the lack of lexical specificity and explicit correlation between cause and effect. When reading the novels in their entirety, processing is made slightly easier by the authors' use of some clues; for example, in the scene where Benjy watches people 'hitting' on the grass, Faulkner includes the Free Direct Speech "Here, caddie" which, although Benjy may not be able to attribute to a speaker or interpret, the reader can use to help process Benjy's limited account of the game of golf.

Some literary critics and readers would say that the difficulty in processing literary language is part of the enjoyment. Presentation of events through an unusual mental filter can contribute to the 'defamiliarising' experience that the Russian Formalists proposed is central to literary reading (▶ Chapter 1.1). The two mind styles we have discussed so far lack understanding and consequently present a rather limited view of the text-world. However, in lacking the conceptual and linguistic abilities to describe what they see, the characters force the reader to think about supposedly everyday things—such as the human face and a game of golf—completely anew. Leech and Short observe that, "[w]ith its childlike vision, such language borders on poetry in recapturing a pristine awareness of things" (1981/2007: 166).

In dedicating an entire chapter of *Style in Fiction* to the topic, Leech and Short (1981/2007: 150–167) galvanised mind style as a significant object of enquiry in stylistic analysis. They note that mind style can be found in very 'local' linguistic structures, meaning that one can encounter mind style at the clause or sentence level. However—like Fowler—they recognise the cumulative effect of linguistic choices in contributing towards an emergent mind style; as such, mind style is forged over the course of a text and, if you want to analyse it in a full-length novel or play, a corpus approach lends itself well (e.g. McIntyre and Archer 2010; Semino 2007; Semino 2011; Mahlberg et al 2016; Lugea 2022). We elaborate on Leech and Short's qualitative analysis of Benjy's mind style in ▶ Sect. 8.5, using a corpus-cognitive approach.

Leech and Short proposed that mind style can be a property at any level of discourse (see ▶ Chapter 1). In other words, mind style can be attributed to a particular character in a play (McIntyre 2005; McIntyre and Archer 2010), to the narrator of a given novel or to an author over several works, or perhaps even studied across a fictional genre. Scholars have investigated the mind styles of a 'proto-human' (Semino 2011) and even vampires (Nuttall 2015; 2018). Recently, stylisticians have considered mind style as potentially observable in non-fictional texts (Gregoriou 2007a; Emmott and Alexander 2016). Despite this broad understanding in principle, research on mind styles has—in practice—tended to focus on the workings of fictional characters' minds. It also shows a bias towards prose fiction, although some work explores mind style in poetry (Semino 2011), drama (McIntyre 2010; Lugea 2016b) and even film (Montoro 2010).

8.3 Different Mind Styles

Leech and Short's (1981/2007) seminal chapter on mind style had a section on 'normal mind styles' and another on 'more unusual mind styles'. Although they proposed a continuum "from mind styles which can easily strike a reader as natural and uncontrived [...], to those which clearly impose an unorthodox conception of the fictional world" (1981/2007: 151), you may have noticed that the mind styles exemplified so far pertain to characters with highly idiosyncratic mental functioning: Lok, a Neanderthal, and Benjy, a man with learning difficulties. Indeed, most of the research on mind style has tended to focus on 'deviant' or unusual mind styles. This trend is based on the simple fact that 'marked' linguistic choices are more readily identifiable by their very nature, yielding studies in unusual cognitive patterns as a consequence. As Short observes, when it comes to language "the more normal the choices become, the less force the mind-style concept tends to have" (1994: 2505). Therefore, while almost all texts have some discernible style, the presence of a perceiving mind becomes all the more marked—and interesting—the more idiosyncratic that style. The term mind style is used by Semino, a key figure in the development of the concept:

> to capture those aspects of world views that are primarily personal and cognitive in origin, and which are peculiar to a particular individual, or common to people who have the same cognitive characteristics (for example as a result of *a* similar mental illness or of a shared stage of cognitive development [...]).
>
> Semino (2002: 97, our emphasis)

This definition of the concept reflects the considerable academic interest in mind styles that are constitutive of a recognisable cognitive impairment or condition. Mind style studies have explored characters with autism (Semino 2007, 2014a, 2014b), schizophrenia (Bockting 1995; Semino and Swindlehurst 1996), paranoia (Bockting 1995; Montoro 2011), depression (Demjén 2015) and dementia (Lugea 2016b, 2022; Harrison 2017), some of which are detailed in the remainder of this chapter. However, like Nuttall (2018: 20), we believe that restricting mind style study to "just those minds we are able to define or diagnose in psychological terms risks losing some of the critical value and attractiveness" of the concept.

More broadly, mind style studies have also explored the capacity for texts to represent cognition not just as related to mental illnesses or impairments, but also to criminal behaviours (Gregoriou 2007a, 2007b; Dutta Flanders 2017) and marked personality traits (McIntyre 2005; McIntyre and Archer 2010) and even drunkenness (Rundquist 2020). Furthermore, scholars have studied the particular mind styles used in literary genres such as gothic and horror (Fowler 1996; Zupan 2008), speculative fiction (Hoover 2016; Nuttall 2015, 2018),), absurdism (Lugea 2016b) and satire (Hoover 2016); these analyses have provided grounds to relate the concept not just with individual ways of thinking, but with wider aesthetic effects in literature (Halliday 1971; Hoover 2016).

Mind style is most obvious and remarkable when it deviates from conceptual and linguistic norms, and psychological conditions provide an identifiable break from these norms. 'Trying on' the minds of characters living with a particular condition may be schema-refreshing, allowing us to see things anew and providing the defamiliarising experience fundamental to literary reading (▶ Chapter 1). It may even facilitate empathetic engagement with the lived experience of that condition in a way that would otherwise never be possible. Rundquist observes the power of narrative fiction, in particular, to "access thoughts and other facets of consciousness that do not take linguistic form at all, and it can represent these phenomena with language" (2014: 172). As such, fiction has the power to provide readers with simulations of psychological experiences which otherwise remain inaccessible—and often—unverbalised. In other words, 'trying on minds' is not simply an aesthetic exercise but a significant way in which literature conveys meaning, probes humanity and stretches the limits of readers' experience.

8.4 Mind Style in Interaction

Early studies in mind style focused on lexico-grammatical features (▶ Sect. 8.1). But the 'pragmatic turn' (Leech and Short 1981/2007: 284), which influenced stylistic scholarship in general in the last two decades of the twentieth century, has also had an effect on how and where we search for mind style. Because Pragmatics allows us to understand how meaning is created in interaction (▶ Chapter 5), it can shed a light on how characters' interactive tendencies can be indicative of their cognitive functioning.

A good example of how pragmatic patterns can be indicative of mind style, is Semino's (2007; 2014a; 2014b) research on fictional characters with Autism Spectrum Disorders (ASDs). ASDs refer to a range of conditions which affect a person's ability to communicate and interact and can result in repetitive behaviour. Theory of Mind is the human ability to understand and predict other's behaviour, based on inferences or 'mentalising'; that is, imagining how they might be thinking. It is an ability we acquire as children and use to understand the thoughts, motivations and actions of people around us. A body of research in Psychology suggests that people with ASDs develop Theory of Mind later, or perhaps not to a full extent (Berenguer et al. 2020). Difficulties with Theory of Mind partly explain the psychological reasons behind the communicative behaviours of people with ASDs and why their interactions may not cohere with widely held pragmatic norms, such as those introduced in ▶ Chapter 5.

One of the characters with an ASD explored by Semino (2007) is Christopher, a boy with Asperger's syndrome in *The Curious Incident of the Dog in the Night-Time* (Haddon 2003). The following scene occurs early in the novel and so serves to establish Christopher as a character with a particular mind style; here, he is upset after having found his neighbour's dog dead, impaled with a fork:

> (2) Then the police arrived. I like the police. They have uniforms and numbers and you know what they are meant to be doing. There was a policewoman and a policeman. The policewoman had a little hole in her tights on her left ankle and a red scratch in the middle of the hole. The policeman had a big orange leaf stuck to the bottom of his shoe which was poking out from one side. The policewoman put her arms round Mrs Shears and led her back towards the house.
> I lifted my head off the grass.
> The policeman squatted down beside me and said, "Would you like to tell me what's going on here, young man?"
> I sat up and said, "The dog is dead."
> "I'd got that far," he said.
> I said, "I think someone killed the dog."
> "How old are you?" he asked.
> I replied, "I am 15 years and 3 months and 2 days."
>
> Haddon (2003: 7)

In lexico-syntactic terms, Christopher's language use is simple and literal, perhaps more so than might be expected of a fifteen-year-old, for example, in the two simple one-clause sentences that open the extract: "Then the police arrived. I like the police". Note, also, how Christopher repeats definite references (e.g. 'the police') from one clause to the next, instead of replacing the nouns with a pronoun (e.g. 'them') to refer anaphorically back to the noun (e.g. 'The police arrived. I like *them*'). The effect of the lexical repetition is to lend the prose referential precision, privileging accuracy over variety, as well as a monotonous quality that may be associated with repetitive behaviours in ASDs.

8.4.1 Cooperative Principle

In addition to Christopher's marked lexico-syntactic choices, Semino demonstrated how his interactive behaviour is indicative of his mind style. Drawing on Pragmatics, she observed Christopher's unorthodox use of Grice's Cooperative Principle (▶ Sect. 6.3) which suggests that interlocutors' conversational contributions adhere to norms of Quantity, Quality, Manner and Relation (relevance). In addition to repeating nouns where pronouns would suffice, Christopher's narrative in this extract provides the reader with details that are irrelevant to the narrative progression, such as the footwear of the police officers, infringing the maxim of Relation. In interaction with the other characters, his conversational contributions provide too much or not enough information (infringing Quantity) or irrelevant information (infringing Relation). For example, when asked by the policeman to explain what is going on, his response is "the dog is dead", which is not 'as informative as is required' (Grice 1989: 26) to fulfil the maxim of Quantity, as the dead dog is already apparent to the characters. On the other hand, when asked his age, his answer is over-informative, again breaking the maxim of Quantity and, arguably, Relevance. Semino proposes that Christopher has no intention of deceiving his interlocutors, meaning these are infringements of the maxims and indications of the difficulty Christopher has in filtering irrelevant details from his environment when interacting with others. Semino links Christopher's inability to infer what other people know—and therefore how much information to give them—to the lack of Theory of Mind in some ASDs.

Moreover, the character's ability to observe and recall details (such as his age to the day) is remarkable and can also be read as a characteristic of high-functioning autism or Asperger's syndrome. Notice that a maxim Christopher does not break is Quality; in fact, so careful is he to be accurate and truthful, that he sometimes says what is obvious ('the dog is dead") or over-precise ("I am 15 years and 3 months and 2 days"), leading to the infringement of the other maxims, and even the referential repetition observed earlier. It could be argued that Christopher upholds the maxim of Quality at the expense of the remaining maxims.

8.4.2 Politeness

Adherence to the maxim of Quality may also explain Semino's findings that autistic characters' "relentless approach to sincerity affects their ability to manage other characters' faces in interaction" (2014a: 149). Participants in interaction can

Mind Style

make use of politeness strategies to manage their own needs and wants with respect to others' needs and wants (Sect.5.5), but people with autism may not be able to conceptualise the latter. Consequently, they may not make use of politeness strategies in the same way. Semino cites another example involving Christopher, wherein he reports a conversation he had with his teacher, Siobhan:

> (3) I also said that I cared about dogs because they were faithful and honest, and some dogs were cleverer and more interesting than some people. Steve, for example, who comes to school on Thursdays, needs help to eat his food and could not even fetch a stick. Siobhan asked me not to say this to Steve's mother.
>
> Haddon (2003: 6)

When he says "I cared about dogs because they were faithful and honest", Christopher *explicitly* emphasises how he values honesty, then he goes on to *implicitly* indicate how this value contributes towards his mind style: comparing a human's behaviour to a dog's is a Face Threatening Act towards the human concerned. Christopher reports how he makes this potential FTA in conversation with his teacher and he does not personally recognise the potential FTA; instead, readers are left to infer it and to 'mentalise' that the teacher also inferred it, which would explain why she asked him not to repeat it. As well as demonstrating the value of concepts from Pragmatics in the analysis of mind styles in narrative and interaction, this example serves to highlight the significant cognitive work required on the part of readers to construct mind styles, based not only on textual clues, but also on our understanding of how real minds work and our ability to **mentalise**, that is, infer the mental states of others (and characters). In the next section, we consider how cognitive approaches to mind style not only reveal how character minds are constructed in text (▶ Sect. 8.5.1, ▶ Sect. 8.5.2), but also how readers' cognition is involved in constructing fictional mind styles (▶ Sect. 8.5.3/8.6).

Keen readers might have noticed how the pragmatic cues to Christopher's autistic mind style could also be considered as implicit characterisation cues under Culpeper's model of characterisation (▶ Chapter 6). As mentioned in ▶ Sect. 8.0, characterisation encompasses all the features that make up a character, including physical and explicit cues, whereas mind style is the result of more implicit features which suggest a particular way of thinking. We recognise the distinction is not absolute and the boundary is explored further in ▶ Sect. 8.5.3/8.6.

8.5 Cognitive Approaches to Mind Style

While Pragmatics helps to account for how meaning is made in context, cognitive approaches provide insight on the role of cognition in interpreting texts and in understanding the fictional minds depicted therein. As Semino attests, "if mind style is to do with the linguistic construction of a particular conceptualisation of a textual world, it is best approached by combining the linguistic patterns with theories of cognition" (2002: 98). This section demonstrates how Schema Theory (▶ Sect. 8.5.1) and Conceptual Metaphor Theory (▶ Sect. 8.5.2) have been used to explore the mental functioning of characters. We also incorporate insights from Cognitive Psychology and Poetics to discuss how readers *perceive* the fictional mind constructed in language (▶ Sect. 8.4.3).

8.5.1 Schema Theory

Schema Theory holds that prior knowledge is 'schematic', meaning it is stored in pre-packaged 'schemata', or bundles of knowledge about a particular concept (▶ Sect. 1.3.2). It can be used to consider a) what characters know or expect, but also b) what readers know or expect about how minds work; in fact, mind style is the intersection of both—and most interesting when they differ (▶ Sect. 8.3). As outlined in ▶ Sect. 1.3.2, texts can reinforce, add to, or challenge our existing schemata, with the most thought-provoking literature being that which 'makes you think' or challenges your own world view. In relation to mind style, the idiosyncratic ways of conceiving the fictional world (as exemplified in Lok, Benjy, Christopher, etc.) challenge the reader's schematic knowledge, providing both difficulty and pleasure in reading.

In ▶ Sect. 8.2.2, it was described how the first scholars working on mind style observed how characters' knowledge or lack thereof influenced lexicalisation patterns, leading to 'underlexicalisation'. Schema Theory helps to explain how these characters lack not only the lexical means to describe their experiences, but also the schematic knowledge necessary to process it. Therefore, Lok did not have the requisite cognitive schemata to describe the *Homo sapiens*' 'bow and arrow', nor understand how the bow fires an arrow, nor the purpose of the arrow. This underlying lack of cognitive schemata is the reason for the underlexicalisation and the strange transitivity choices attributed to the focalising character.

Schema Theory was applied to fictional mind style by Semino (2002) in her account of Alekos in *Captain Corelli's Mandolin*. A minor character, he is a shepherd living in isolation with his goats on a mountain on a small Greek island during the World War II. A soldier parachutes onto the mountainside, something entirely alien for the shepherd, who lacks the schemata for parachutes, radio communication and modern weaponry. The result of this conceptual gap is the now-familiar phenomenon of underlexicalisation: Alekos describes the soldier as an 'angel', his parachute a 'mushroom' and his grenades 'pinecones'. However, Semino points out that underlexicalisation only goes so far in accounting for these misnomers, as Alekos *actually believes* the soldier is an angel. She notes that, "he appears to have a tendency to conceive of new aspects of experience in terms of his knowledge of nature and of religion" (2002: 105), pointing out that his lexical choices for unknown entities result in metaphors (see ▶ Chapter 7). Indeed, in each of these examples, Alekos draws on the source domains NATURE and RELIGION to describe the wartime target domain, contributing to a pattern of metaphorical choices which Semino identifies as a "cognitive habit that characterises his mind style" (2002: 103). One of the significant effects of Aleko's mind style is to provide an "endearingly naïve view of the world" (2002: 105) in a novel heavy with the realities of war.

8.5.2 Conceptual Metaphor Theory

We can now add metaphors to the armoury of linguistic features that can contribute towards fictional mind style. In ▶ Sect. 7.2.3, Conceptual Metaphor Theory was introduced as part of our cognitive organisation of experience, in everyday and fictional discourses. According to Conceptual Metaphor Theory, speakers draw from a source domain in order to describe something in the target domain. In their analysis of the novel *One Flew Over the Cuckoo's Nest*, Semino and Swindlehurst (1996) relate the narrator's conventional and creative use of metaphors to his particular mind style. Bromden is a schizophrenic patient in a mental hospital; his narration is replete with metaphors drawing from the source domain MACHINERY. These span from conventional metaphorical expressions such as, "I'm running out of steam" and "I don't want to throw a spanner in the works", to more marked metaphors that refer to society as "the Combine [harvester]" and the mental hospital patients as "machines with flaws inside that can't be repaired". The prominence of mechanical metaphors in Bromden's narration can be explained by his professional experience as an electrician and a harrowing personal experience in a WWII air raid which led to his mental breakdown. Machinery is a source domain that is both familiar and relevant to Bromden and, as such, a conceptual and linguistic resource to process the target domains which are more difficult for him to understand and verbalise: society in general and emotions pertaining to himself and others.

Semino and Swindlehurst propose that Bromden's use of metaphor is indicative of his mental illness and mind style. Critics read *One Flew Over the Cuckoo's Nest* as a powerful critique of institutions and of socio-political oppression of individuals. The MACHINERY metaphors that Bromden employs contribute to this interpretation, emphasising the de-personified automation of institutional power. Notice, however, that if mind style is defined as a 'personal world view' and distinguished from an 'ideological point of view', as Semino suggests, this argument is difficult to make. We suggest that, as is often the case, the issue can be clarified by considering the discourse structure of fiction. At the text-world level, Bromden's MACHINERY metaphors contribute towards his personal world view (i.e. mind style), but on the discourse-world level, they can be interpreted as contributing to the author's ideological world view which is critical of institutional power and control over individuals.

8.6 Reading Fictional Minds

Mind style research is firmly rooted in Stylistics and is therefore text-driven and focussed on stylistic features which lead to its emergence. So far, this book has emphasised the active role of the reader in processing textual cues to construct fictional character (▶ Chapter 6) as well as an understanding of their mind (this chapter). In ▶ Sect. 8.3, we suggested that experiencing the text-world from the psychological perspective of a character that is somehow 'different' from ourselves might facilitate understanding or even empathy towards others. Parallel to stylistic research on mind style, is a body of research into fictional minds emanating from the neighbouring disciplines of Cognitive Literary Studies, Narratology and Cognitive Poetics. True to the cognitive doctrine, this work focuses more on the readers' *experience* of fictional minds; this includes their ongoing cognitive processing of characters' fictional mental functioning, as well as reader engagement with, and maybe even empathy towards, those fictional characters.

Often using empirical reader-response methods, research in these fields has explored the ways and the extent to which readers engage with fictional characters; for instance, do we identify with or relate to them? Do we feel with or for them? Are we moved to imagine or hypothesise about them beyond the text? Can fictional characters move us to re-calibrate our understanding and approach to real people? Strong claims have been made about the impact of reading on our capacity for empathy, even our social attitudes and real-world behaviours (e.g. Mar et al. 2009). The work of Keen (2006; 2007; 2013) is the most cautious and comprehensive in exploring **narrative empathy**, which arises when a reader shares a character's perspective and feeling. Some stylisticians have suggested that fictional mind styles can invite narrative empathy (Nuttall 2018; Lugea 2022), but research is ongoing in attempting to pinpoint the stylistic features which might facilitate empathy in readers (Fernández-Quintanilla 2020), acknowledging, of course, that a lot of what contributes towards a reader's response comes from top-down processing (▶ Chapter 6).

On a more theoretical level, research in the fields listed above has explored the fictional minds in ways that intersect with characterisation (▶ Chapter 6) and mind style (this chapter). The narratologist Palmer (2002; 2003; 2004) advances a rather essentialist view on fictional minds: "novel reading *is* mind-reading" (2007: 217, our emphasis). In other words, Palmer attributes everything we do when reading novels as contributing towards the construction of fictional mind(s). He criticises the distinction that scholars make between characterisation, on the one hand, and consciousness presentation, on the other, arguing that narrative fiction generally links "the thought of characters to the social and physical context" (2004: 69). Palmer's criticisms challenge traditional boundaries between areas of narratology that are essentially dealing with the same phenomenon—the fictional representation of experience. However, in blurring these traditional distinctions he also dismisses the linguistic criteria used to distinguish between various strategies such as, for example, the categories of speech and thought presentation (▶ Chapter 4). We maintain that, for reasons outlined in ▶ Chapter 1, mind style—like any kind of style in language—can only reliably and rigorously be studied with reference to the textual features that contribute towards its cognitive construction (see also Rundquist 2014, 2020).

As discussed in ▶ Sect. 8.4, Theory of Mind is a term used in Philosophy, Psychology and Neuroscience to describe the human awareness that others have their own mind and the ability to mentalise, based on behavioural and contextual information. For example, if I notice a person stub their toe and curse profusely, my capacity for Theory of Mind would allow me to infer that they are experiencing pain and perhaps frustration. While this concept can be used to explain how Christopher's interactive practices reveal a lack of intersubjective understanding, Theory of Mind can also be applied to the experience of reading literature. Cognitive literary scholars have adopted the terms 'mind-reading' (Kidd and Castano 2013), 'mind attribution' (Zunshine, 2006; Palmer, 2007; Nuttall, 2015) or 'mind-modelling' (Stockwell, 2009; Stockwell and Mahlberg, 2015) from Psychology and Philosophy, where they are used to refer to the human capacity to infer the mental states of others. Applied to reading fiction, these terms describe how readers interpret textual cues to construct and develop mental representations of fictional characters. Stockwell and Mahlberg define **mind-modelling** as readers' creation of "a working model of the characteristics, outlook, beliefs, motivations and consequent behaviour of others" (2015: 132; see also Stockwell, 2009). Their definition points to the wider scope of 'mind-modelling' than that of mind style. While mind style is limited to the textual patterns that contribute towards a character's particular way of thinking, 'mind-modelling' and related terms involve readers' processing of transient mental states, as well as non-cognitive characteristics. In fact, mind-modelling is more closely aligned with characterisation (Culpeper, 2001) which pertains to readers' construction of whole characters, not just their mental functioning. Cognitive poetic studies in mind-modelling have applied Culpeper's model (Stockwell and Mahlberg 2015), used Text World Theory (Stockwell 2009) or Cognitive Grammar (Nuttall, 2015, 2017; Harrison 2017). We use CG's action chains to elaborate a mind style analysis in ▶ Sect. 8.7.

8.7 Mind Style: Text, Corpus and Cognition

In the introduction to this chapter, we proposed that corpus techniques are particularly suited to investigating mind style because they reveal quantitative patterns that may accumulate in creating a particular 'way of thinking'. Despite this, corpus approaches to mind style are adopted in just a few studies (Hoover 1999; Semino 2007; McIntyre and Archer 2010; Lugea, 2022).

We now demonstrate how corpora can be used to explore mind style by elaborating on an earlier example from the research. In ▶ Sect. 8.1.2, we referred to Leech and Short's seminal mind style analysis of Benjy from Faulkner's *The Sound and the Fury*, a narrator who has learning difficulties and is unable to speak. According to Leech and Short (1981/2007: 164), his narration suggests that he has "a very simple and extremely restricted mind style, with little ability to use abstract terms or terms related to the thing described." Based on the first 28 sentences of his narration, Leech and Short (1981/2007: 164–6) make a number of observations about Benjy's language use, which we summarise in ◨ Table 8.1.

Corpus methods allow us to continue Leech and Short's analysis by looking at Benjy's whole narration. Note that they observe certain features are over- or under-used. The only way to make that claim empirically is to contrast Benjy's narration with other, comparable narrations, performing a keyword analysis.

Using *AntConc* (Anthony 2022), we used keywords to investigate the whole of Benjy's narration in light of Leech and Short's analysis. We first extracted Benjy's narration from the rest of the novel, which is also narrated by other characters, and loaded the file into *AntConc*. We then compared the words in Benjy's narration against a comparable reference corpus; that is, a larger corpus that

◘ **Table 8.1** Leech and Short's 1981/2007: 164–6) qualitative analysis of Benjy's mind style

i) underlexicalisation and lexical repetition (especially verbs);

ii) mono-syllabic words;

iii) short average sentence length;

iv) concrete words (rather than abstract);

v) transitive verbs without objects;

vi) over-use of simple past tense;

vii) a general lack of: adjectives; prepositional phrases; definite/indefinite articles; pronouns; co-ordination and subordination; and adverbials (except those to do with space)

is similar in as many ways as possible except for the controlled variable: it is not Benjy narrating. We used a purpose-built reference corpus, the **1920s sampler**—a 800,000-word corpus of 1920s US prose fiction containing 80 10,000-word extracts from 80 novels by 80 different writers. The comparison produced 204 **positive keywords** (words statistically over-represented in Benjy's narration) and 44 **negative keywords** (words statistically under-used). ◘ Table 8.2 shows (for reasons of space) the top 40 positive and negative keywords in Benjy's narration ordered by statistical significance (Log Likelihood/LL) along with their raw frequency.

The preponderance of names in the positive keyword list is commonplace and not usually interpretatively important because a narrative inevitably uses its characters' names more frequently than other narratives. However, Benjy's under-use of personal pronouns 'his', 'her' and 'their' (negative keywords) indicates that he repeats the names of other characters rather than replacing them with pronouns. Taken together, these positive and negative keywords correlate with Leech and Short's observations that Benjy uses lexical repetition, concrete rather than abstract words, and under-uses pronouns (◘ Table 8.1, points i, iv and vii).

There is additional corpus evidence to support their claim that Benjy prefers concrete words over abstract ones (◘ Table 8.1, iv) if we examine the statistically over-used verbs that appear in Benjy's positive keyword list (◘ Table 8.2): 'said', 'came'/'come', 'go'/'going'/'went'. These verbs are broadly descriptive of the actions, lacking detail on the way the act is performed. The past tense reporting verb 'said' is the most statistically over-used keyword, suggesting that Benjy reports directly what other characters say, without interpreting their manner or intention. For example, Benjy presents a question asked by Caddy like this: "'Is mother very sick?" Caddy said'. In this case, it is left to the reader to interpret the Direct Speech as a question, as Benjy opts for the reporting verb 'said' over 'asked'. The fact that 'said' is so significantly over-used contributes to the lexical repetition, especially of verbs described by Leech and Short (◘ Table 8.1, i).

The lemmas 'come' and 'go' are very prevalent in Benjy's narration, which may also contribute to Leech and Short's reading of concreteness and repetitiveness. These verbs encode the direction of movement in relation to the speaker and emphasise Benjy's spatial awareness of his surroundings, perhaps at the

◘ Table 8.2 Benjy's positive and negative keywords

	Positive keywords			Negative keywords		
Rank	Word	Freq	LL	Word	Freq	LL
1	said	907	1996.94	of	127	402.87
2	caddy	288	1132.33	a	162	240.99
3	dilsey	192	793.29	had	29	190.78
4	luster	152	625.29	as	21	142.9
5	quentin	141	599.83	his	74	122.74
6	versh	130	597.82	an	1	117.78
7	p	145	592.09	the	862	84.91
8	jason	120	528.52	would	8	76.39
9	you	721	442.66	which	1	74.19
10	dont	114	440.22	from	22	58.37
11	hush	107	420.35	their	4	53.64
12	aint	97	386.82	man	10	50.83
13	mother	132	280.07	men	1	47.61
14	went	160	271.82	that	154	47.37
15	cant	57	259.28	but	54	47.14
16	benjy	66	223.82	for	69	44.95
17	going	130	219.05	don	4	39.69
18	frony	43	195.66	not	53	33.35
19	i	651	188.29	might	1	30.36
20	roskus	40	186.43	was	193	29.81
21	we	215	164.77	her	133	28.85
22	here	130	144.57	very	1	28.78
23	father	86	136.27	its	1	27.05
24	t	277	130.09	by	23	26.44
25	maury	35	128.12	or	11	25.98
26	fence	34	123.62	only	5	25.6
27	come	121	118.44	such	1	23.92
28	get	110	115.41	with	99	22
29	got	97	114.63	left	2	21.74
30	hear	59	114.01	life	1	21.58
31	branch	27	113.28	himself	2	21.3
32	crying	30	108.3	these	1	20.96
33	wont	28	107.65	so	32	20.85

(continued)

Table 8.2 (continued)

	Positive keywords			Negative keywords		
Rank	Word	Freq	LL	Word	Freq	LL
34	up	169	100.99	who	13	20.23
35	me	184	97.76	made	5	19.78
36	came	99	92.65	woman	2	19.69
37	cry	35	89.47	been	23	18.53
38	hill	27	86.14	though	1	17.88
39	mammy	17	85.91	once	1	17.57
40	tonight	29	85.28	well	11	17.27

expense of other levels of understanding. Clicking on the keyword 'went' displays the concordance lines, which can be organised alphabetically by the word immediately to the right. Unsurprisingly, this reveals that many are the spatial prepositions (e.g. 'along', 'away', 'back', 'down'), further specifying the direction of movement. However, some of these concordances are marked; for example, the many instances of 'went away' do not include any attempt from the narrator to interpret how, where or why. Moreover, aside from the prepositions to the right of 'went', there are several instances of 'went black', some of which are found in the following scene at the end of Benjy's narration:

> (4) "Hush." Dilsey said. "You go to sleep."
> The room <u>went black</u>, except the door. Then the door <u>went black</u>. Caddy said, "Hush, Maury," putting her hand on me. So I stayed hushed. We could hear us. We could hear the dark.
> It went away, and Father looked at us. He looked at Quentin and Jason, then he came and kissed Caddy and put his hand on my head.
> "Is Mother very sick." Caddy said.
> "No." Father said. "Are you going to take good care of Maury."
> "Yes." Caddy said.
> Father went to the door and looked at us again. Then the dark came back, and he stood black in the door, and then the door turned black again.
> Caddy held me and I could hear us all, and the darkness, and something I could smell. And then I could see the windows, where the trees were buzzing. Then the dark began to go in smooth, bright shapes, like it always does, even when Caddy says that I have been asleep.

We now consider how Benjy (called Maury in extract 4) repeatedly depicts events using a marked verbal pattern. As stylisticians are increasingly using Langacker's Cognitive Grammar (CG) to describe event construal, rather than Halliday's transitivity model, we apply the CG model to extract (4).

Langacker's CG treats the clause as an **action chain**, a "series of forceful interactions, each involving the transmission of energy [...] from one participant to the next" (2008: 355–6), much like billiard balls "moving through space and impacting one another through forceful physical contact" (2008: 355). The participants have 'archetypal roles' in the canonical clause. An **agent** "is an individual who wilfully initiates and carries out an action, typically a physical action affecting other entities. It is thus an 'energy source' and the initial participant in an action chain" (Langacker 2008: 356, emphasis in the original). The **patient** is "something that undergoes an internal change of state... Typically inanimate and nonvolitional, a patient usually changes as the result of being affected by outside forces. It is then an 'energy sink' and the final participant in an action chain" (Langacker 2008: 356). With CG's emphasis on the participants and the dynamic relations between them in action chains, verbal processes are not categorised as they would be in Hallidayan transitivity analysis (◘ Table 2.2). Nuttall remarks that in CG "[i]t is not the *type* of process that matters most [...] but the way in which its participants are attended to" (2019: 165). In the extract above, Benjy represents some events using the canonical action chain e.g. *Father looked at us*. ◘ Figure 8.1 represents Benjy's use of the 'canonical' (typical) clause structure, where the **agent** is the energy source and a **patient** is the energy sink.

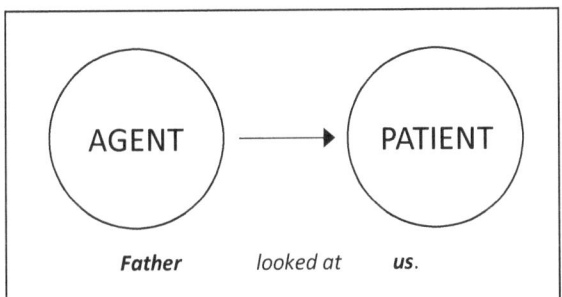

◘ **Fig. 8.1** Benjy's use of the canonical action chain

Central to CG is the concept of of **construal**, which describes 'our ability to conceive and portray the same situation in alternate ways' (Langacker 2008: 43). Much like the emphasis on 'choice' in SFL—even if it is 'unconscious' choice (Simpson and Canning 2014: 287)—the speaker or writer has alternative options for construing events in action chains. Repeatedly, Benjy prefers to construe the scene with constructions like 'the room/door went dark'. It takes some inferencing work on the part of the reader to identify the true 'energy source' behind the darkness. Understanding the scene as one in which Benjy is being put to bed by senior members of the family, Dilsey and Father, the reader might discern from Benjy's reports of their speech ("Hush". Dilsey said. "You go to sleep") and actions ('Father went to the door') that these characters turned out the light, causing the room to turn black, and closed the door to the lit hallway, causing the

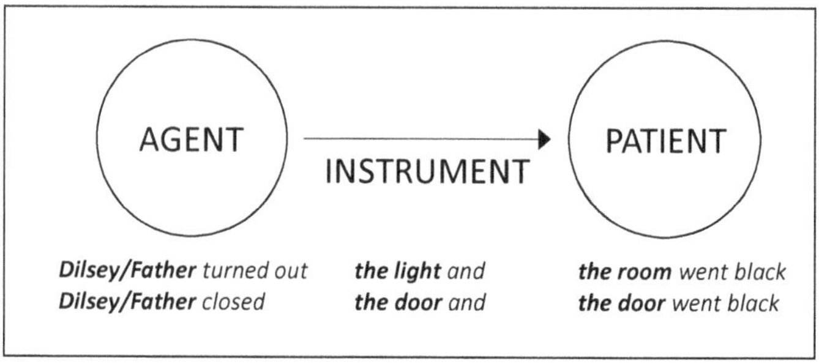

Chapter 8 · Mind Style

Fig. 8.2 A canonical construal of events described in extract 4

door to turn black. Canonical construal of these events would be expressed by the action chain in ◘ Fig. 8.2.

◘ Figure 8.2 illustrates Langacker's assertion that an 'inanimate' patient usually 'changes as the result of being affected by outside forces'. However, throughout this extract, Benjy casts what would typically be the patient (such as the room, the door, the trees), in the atypical role of *agent* in a patientless action chain: "the dark came back", "the trees were buzzing". In the latter example, the reader can only surmise the energy source for buzzing trees—perhaps 'the wind blew through the trees'? The non-canonical action chains that Benjy uses are represented in ◘ Fig. 8.3.

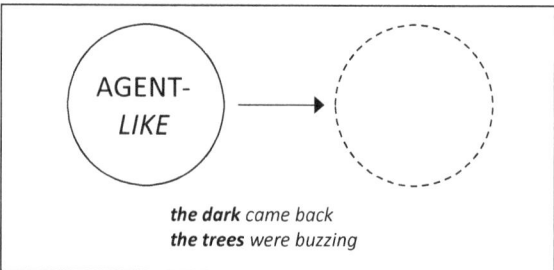

Fig. 8.3 Benjy [Maury]'s non-canonical construal of events in extract 4

The effect of structures like those in ◘ Fig. 8.3 is one where agency is atypically attributed to the end-state (the darkness/blackness), at the expense of an understanding of the true agency or energy source behind the event, as depicted in ◘ Figs. 8.1 and 8.2. In relation to Benjy's mind style, this could be taken as supplementary evidence for Leech and Short's suggestion that Benjy has 'an imperfect understanding of cause and effect'. Their analysis was based on the observation that Benjy tends to use 'transitive verbs without objects' (Table 1, v), like 'hitting' (► Sect. 8.12). This action chain analysis goes further by demonstrating how Benjy construes events by attributing agency to the patient, whose salience as the energy sink takes precedence for Benjy. He seems to be unconscious of the energy source and subsequent chain of events which lead to the the patient's salience.

However, non-canonical action chains like those in ◘ Fig. 8.3 only account for some of the verbs in extract (4). The clauses which use a change-of-state verb ("the room went black", "the door turned black") are not considered as action chains at all in CG; instead, they are viewed as static, atemporal relations between participants. Nuttall (2019: 164) points out how this tallies with Text World Theory's distinction between propositions which contribute to world-building and those which are function-advancing (▶ Chapter 2). As such, clauses such as 'the room went dark' are not action chains, but static descriptions of the participants, objects and entities which contribute to the construction of the text-world and do not advance the action. Analysed in this way, Benjy's narration might be viewed as one which construes and constructs the world around him by describing participants (agents and patients), incognisant of their roles as energy sources or sinks. Moreover, he seems unaware of the action chains which lead to these patients becoming salient enough for him to construe them as agents.

Presented repeatedly with static descriptions of participants and action chains that do not depict the transfer of energy canonically (e.g. ◘ Figure 8.3), the experience of reading Benjy's narration is certainly 'difficult' as critics have noted (Longley 1973; Ross and Polk 1996: 4). But if the reader can surpass the difficulty, the challenge of decoding Benjy's non-canonical action chains, or inferring what the action chains might be behind his opaque static descriptions ('the room went dark'), might be the reader's reward in itself.

8.8 Summing up

The last section demonstrated how corpus techniques can identify keywords in a particular text, forming a sound basis for developing a qualitative CG analysis of the character's mind style. The keyword analysis carried out in ▶ Sect. 8.7 is similar to that used in ▶ Chapter 6 for understanding characterisation in *Pygmalion*. The main difference is that the comparison is not text internal (comparing character's speech from the same play), but against an external comparator (corpus of 1920s fiction). This means that the analysis in ▶ Sect. 8.5 shows how Benjy is a different narrator compared with narrators generally (if our 1920s corpus represents a general picture of how narrators perform). Culpeper (2001, 2009), citing Enkvist (1973), suggests that some keywords can be seen as marking style but it would be prudent to note that they may not all, nor always, be indicative of mind style. They are, after all, just words that happen to be more frequent in one text when compared to another. However, using the corpus technique to identify the kinds of words that Benjy over-/under-uses and combining these insights with existing and original qualitative analysis gives rise to a literary interpretation that is empirical, objectively identified by the corpus and supported by evidence in the text, as well as that advanced by earlier studies (see McIntyre and Archer 2010, for another example of testing qualitative mind style research with corpus methods).

The results of the keyword analysis provided quantitative evidence to support Leech and Short's (1981/2007) qualitative analysis of Benjy's mind style. The concordance lines also highlighted an extract (4) worthy of further qualitative analysis, to which we applied the CG action chain framework to further understand Benjy's mind style. Doing so allowed us to elaborate on Leech and Short's findings, with the revelation that Benjy focuses on the patient—the end-result of events—describing the world around him without outlining the action chains underlying events. Thus, the action chain analysis provided supplementary evidence, using a Cognitive Grammar approach, that Benjy has a limited understanding of cause and effect. This analysis encapsulates the fusion of textual, corpus and cognitive approaches espoused in this book.

Activity 8.1: Whose Mind Style?

Read the following excerpt from a novel and answer the questions below.

> The News was boring but sometimes I watched it properly, all of it. I thought that the Americans were fighting gorillas in Vietnam; that was what it sounded like. But it didn't make any other kind of sense.
>
> The Israelis were always fighting the Arabs and the Americans were fighting the gorillas. It was nice that the gorillas had a country of their own, not like the zoo, and the Americans were killing them for it.
>
> There were Americans getting killed as well. They were surrounded and the war was nearly over. They had helicopters. Mekong Delta. Demilitarised zone. Tet Offensive.
>
> The gorillas in the zoo didn't look like they'd be hard to beat in a war. They were nice and old-looking, brainy-looking and their hair was dirty. Their arms were brilliant; I'd have loved arms like that.
>
> I was up for the gorillas even though two of my aunties and uncles lived in America.
>
> Doyle (1993: 225).

a. Describe the gender, age and any other features you can discern about this narrator.
b. What lexical choices lead you to these conclusions?
c. What grammatical choices lead you to these conclusions?
d. Are there any other features that contribute towards your impression of this narrator's mind style?
e. As a reader, what schematic knowledge helped you process this text?
f. Does this text 'refresh' any existing schemata you may have held? Or does it have a 'defamiliarising' effect? If so, how?

An answer to this task is provided in the 'Mind Style' video on the book's webpage.

- **Further Reading**

Semino, E. (2007) 'Mind Style 25 years on'. *Style* 41:2, 153–203.

Leech, G. and Short, M. (1981/2007). Mind style. *Style in Fiction: A Linguistic Introduction to English Fictional Prose*, pp. 150–167.

- **Resources**

AntConc (Anthony 2022): ▶ https://www.laurenceanthony.net

References

Anthony, L. 2022. *AntConc* (Version 4.2.0) [Computer Software]. Tokyo, Japan: Waseda University. ▶ https://www.laurenceanthony.net/software

Archer, D. and Bousfield, D. 2010. 'See Better, Lear'? See Lear Better! A Corpus-Based Pragma-Stylistic Investigation of Shakespeare's *King Lear*. In *Language and Style*, eds. D. McIntyre, and B. Busse, 183–203. Basingstoke: Palgrave.

Bockting, I. 1995. *Character and Personality in the Novels of William Faulkner*. Lanham, New York and London: University of America Press.

Burke, M., ed. 2017. *Stylistics. Vol 1. Critical Concepts in Linguistics*. London and New York: Routledge.

Canning, P. 2014. Functionalist Stylistics. In *The Routledge Handbook of Stylistics*, ed. M. Burke, 45–67. London and New York: Routledge.

Culpeper, J. 2001. *Language and Characterisation: People in Plays and Other Texts*. London: Longman.

Culpeper, J. 2009. Keyness: Words, Parts-of-speech and Semantic Categories in the Character-talk of Shakespeare's Romeo and Juliet. *International Journal of Corpus Linguistics* 14, 1: 29–59.

Doyle, R. 1993. *Paddy Clarke Ha Ha Ha*. London: Minerva.

Dutta Flanders, R. 2015. *The Language of Suspense in Crime Fiction: A Linguistic Stylistic Approach*. Houndsmills, Basingstoke: Palgrave.

Emmott, C. and Alexander, M. 2016. Defamiliarization and Foregrounding: Representing Experiences of Change of State and Perception in Neurological Illness Autobiographies. In *The Bloomsbury Companion to Stylistics*, ed. V. Sotirova, 289–307. London and New York: Bloomsbury.

Enkvist, N. 1973. *Linguistic Stylistics*. The Hague: Mouton.

Fowler, R. 1977. *Linguistics and the Novel*. London: Methuen.

Fowler, R. 1986/1996. *Linguistic* Criticism. 2nd ed. Oxford: Oxford University Press.

Gregoriou, C. 2007a. The Stylistics of True Crime: Mapping the Minds of Serial Killers. In *Contemporary Stylistics*, eds. M. Lambrou and P. Stockwell, 19–31. London and New York: Continuum.

Grice, P. 1989. *Studies in the Way of Words*. Cambridge, MA, and London: Harvard University Press.

Haddon, M. 2003. *The Curious Incident of the Dog in the Night-Time*. London: Jonathan Cape.

Halliday, M.A.K. 1971. Linguistic Function and Literary Style: An Inquiry into the Language of William Golding's The Inheritors. In *Literary Style: A Symposium*, ed. S. Chapman, 330–365. London and New York: Oxford University Press.

Halliday, M.A.K. 1994. *An Introduction to Functional Grammar*. 2nd ed. London: Arnold.

Halliday, M.A.K. and Matthiessen, C. 2014. *Halliday's Introduction to Functional Grammar*. 4th ed. London and New York: Routledge.

Harrison, C. 2017. Finding Elizabeth: Construing episodic memory in Elizabeth is Missing by Emma Healey. *Journal of Literary Semantics* 46, 2: 131–151.

Hoover, D. L. 1999. *Language and Style in "The Inheritors"*. Lanham: University Press of America.

Hoover, D. L. 2016. Mind style. In *The Bloomsbury Companion to Stylistics*, ed. V. Sotirova, 325–40. London and New York: Bloomsbury.

Keen, S. 2006. A Theory of Narrative Empathy. *Narrative* 14, 3: 207–236.

Keen, S. 2007. *Empathy and the Novel*. Oxford: Oxford University Press.

Keen, S. 2013. Narrative Empathy. In *The Living Handbook of Narratology*, eds. P. Hühn, J.C. Meister, J. Pier, and W. Schmid. Hamburg: Hamburg University. ▶ http://www.lhn.uni-hamburg.de/article/narrative-empathy (view date: 6th April 2023)

Langacker, R. W. 2008. *Cognitive Grammar: A Basic Introduction*. Oxford: Oxford University Press.

Leech, G. and Short, M. 1981/2007. *Style in Fiction: A Linguistic Introduction to English Fictional Prose*. 2nd ed. Harlow: Longman.

Longley, J.L. 1973. Who Never had a Sister: A Reading of The Sound and the Fury. *Mosaic* 7, 1: 35–53.

Lugea, J. 2016b. Code-switching in the Text-world of a Multilingual Play: The Senile Mind Style in You and Me. In *World Building: Discourse in the Mind*, eds. J. Gavins and E. Lahey, 221–40. London and New York: Bloomsbury.#

Lugea, J. 2022. Dementia Mind Styles in Contemporary Narrative Fiction. *Language and Literature* 31, 2: 168–195.

Mahlberg, M., Stockwell, P., de Joode, J., Smith, C. and O'Donnell, M. Brook. 2016. CLiC Dickens– Novel Uses of Concordances for the Integration of Corpus Stylistics and Cognitive Poetics. *Corpora* 11, 3: 433–463.

Mar, R.A., Oatley, K. and Peterson, J.B. 2009. Exploring the Link between Reading Fiction and Empathy: Ruling out Individual Differences and Examining Outcomes. *Communications* 34, 4: 407–428. ▶ https://doi.org/10.1515/COMM.2009.025.

McIntyre, D. 2005. Logic, Reality and Mind Style in Alan Bennett's The Lady in the Van. *Journal of Literary Semantics* 34: 21–40.

McIntyre, D. and Archer, D. 2010. A Corpus-based Approach to Mind Style. *Journal of Literary Semantics* 39: 167–82.

Montoro, R. 2011. Multimodal Realisation of Mind Style in Enduring Love. In *Telecinematic Discourse: Approaches to the Language of Films and Television Series*, eds. R. Piazza, M. Bednarek, R. Rossi, 69–84. Amsterdam and Philedelphia: John Benjamins.

Nørgaard, N. 2003. *Systemic Functional Linguistics and Literary Analysis*. A Hallidayan Approach to Joyce. A Joycean Approach to Halliday. Odense: University Press of Southern Denmark.

Nuttall, L. 2015. Attributing Minds to Vampires in Richard Matheson's I Am Legend. *Language and Literature* 24, 1: 23–39.

Nuttall, L. 2018. *Mind Style and Cognitive Grammar: Language and World View in Speculative Fiction*. London and New York: Bloomsbury.

Nuttall, L. 2019. Transitivity, Agency, Mind Style: What's the Lowest Common Denominator?. *Language and Literature* 28, 2: 159–179.

Palmer, A. 2002. The Construction of Fictional Minds. *Narrative* 10, 1: 28–46.

Palmer, A. 2003. The Mind Beyond the Skin. In *Narrative Theory and the Cognitive Sciences*, ed. D. Herman, 322–348. Chicago IL: CSLI Publications.

Palmer, A. 2004. *Fictional Minds*. Lincoln, NE: University of Nebraska Press.

Palmer, A. 2007. Universal Minds. *Semiotica* 165: 205–225.

Ross, S.M. and Polk, N. 1996. *Reading Faulkner: The Sound and the Fury*. Jackson: University Press of Mississipi.

Rundquist, E. 2014. How is Mrs Ramsay thinking? The Semantic Effects of Consciousness Presentation Categories within Free Indirect Style. *Language and Literature* 23, 2: 159–174.

Rundquist, E. 2020. The Cognitive Grammar of Drunkenness: Consciousness Representation in Under the Volcano. *Language and Literature* 29, 1: 39–56.

Semino, E. 1997. *Language and World Creation in Poems and Other Texts*. London and New York: Longman.

Semino, E. 2002. A Cognitive Stylistic Approach to Mind Style in Narrative Fiction. In *Cognitive Stylistics: Language and Cognition in Text Analysis*, eds. E. Semino and J. Culpeper, 95–122. Amsterdam and Philadelphia: John Benjamins.

Semino, E. 2007. Mind Style 25 years on. *Style* 41, 2: 153–203.

Semino, E. 2010. Descriptions of Pain, Metaphor and Embodied Simulation. *Metaphor and Symbol* 25: 205–226.

Semino, E. 2014a. Pragmatic Failure, Mind Style and Characterisation in Fiction about Autism. *Language and Literature* 23, 2: 141–158.

Semino, E. 2014b. Language, Mind and Autism in Mark Haddon's The Curious Incident of the Dog in the Night-Time. In *Linguistics and Literary Studies*, eds. M. Fludernik and D. Jacob, 279–303. Berlin: De Gruyter.

Short, M. 1988. Speech Presentation, the Novel and the Press. In *The Taming of the Text*, ed. W. van Peer. London: Routledge.

Short, M. 1994. Mind Style. In *Encyclopaedia of Language and Linguistics*, ed. Roger E. Asher, 2504–5. Oxford: Pergamon Gregoriou, C. 2007b. *Deviance in Contemporary Crime Fiction*. Houndsmills, Basingstoke: Palgrave Macmillan.

Simpson, P. 1993. *Language, Ideology and Point of View*. London and New York: Routledge.

Simpson, P. and Canning, P. 2014. Action and Event. In *The Cambridge Handbook of Stylistics*, eds. P. Stockwell and S. Whiteley, 281–299. Cambridge: Cambridge University Press.

Simpson, P., Mayr, A. and Statham, S. 2018. *Language and Power: A Resource Book for Students*. 2nd ed. London and New York: Routledge.

Stockwell, P. 2009. *Texture: A Cognitive Aesthetics of Reading*. Edinburgh: Edinburgh University Press.

Stockwell, P. and Mahlberg, M. 2015. Mind-modelling with Corpus Stylistics in David Copperfield. *Language and Literature* 24, 2: 129–147.

Weber, J. J., ed. 1996. The Stylistics Reader: From Roman Jakobson to the Present. London: Arnold.

Zunshine, L. 2006. *Why we read Fiction: Theory of Mind and the Novel*. Columbus, OH: Ohio State University press.

Zupan, S. 2008. Mind style, modality and Poe's 'The Fall of the House of Usher'. In *The State of Stylistics.*, ed. G. Watson, 451–71. Amsterdam and New York: Rodopi.

9

Humour

Supplementary Information The online version contains supplementary material available at ▶ https://doi.org/10.1007/978-3-031-10422-0_9.

© The Author(s), under exclusive license to Springer Nature Switzerland AG 2023
J. Lugea and B. Walker, *Stylistics*,
https://doi.org/10.1007/978-3-031-10422-0_9

9.1 Introduction

In this, the penultimate chapter of the book, we explore humour in fiction. Like **mind style** (the topic of the previous chapter), humour is an *effect* created by the language choices of the text producer and experienced by the text receiver. Unlike mind style, however, humour is found in a great range of discourse types including spontaneous spoken interactions, political discourses, news, advertising and, of course, fictional texts, bringing it squarely into the scope of Stylistics. Humour is not only pervasive, but also inherently creative because it involves 'language play', deviation and therefore foregrounding at the different language levels we introduced in ▶ Chapter 1. While humour does not feature in other introductions to Stylistics, our view is that the stylistician's toolkit is incomplete without the means to examine the textual and discursive features that give rise to this textual effect. In this chapter, therefore, we will introduce approaches from (Cognitive) Psychology, Linguistics and Pragmatics for analysing humour, and revisit frameworks already covered in this book that also provide insights into the creation of humour in texts.

9.1.1 Verbal Humour

This chapter focuses on **verbal humour**, which is humour that derives specifically from language choices (Attardo 1994). Verbal humour is distinct from **visual humour**, which is expressed through the visual mode[1] (e.g. slapstick or caricature), and **referential humour**, which relates to *what* is expressed (i.e. meanings) rather than *how* it is expressed (i.e. language choices) (see Attardo 1994: 95). Because verbal humour concerns language choices, it is, as we noted above, particularly relevant for Stylistics and there is a growing body of stylistic research that focuses on humour. For instance, Dore (2015), Dynel (2016) and Marszalek (2016, 2019) all explore humour in films and TV series and consider the role of humour in characterisation,[2] while Marszalek (2013, 2016, 2020) uses **Text World Theory** to account for the development of humour across longer stretches of text. This latter type of humour, which Marszalek refers to as 'humorous worlds', depends on familiarity with the world of the text for the humorous effect, as opposed to 'local humour' which remains funny beyond the text-world. We will return to Marszalek's notion of 'humorous worlds' when we come to examine examples of humour from a variety of fictional genres later in this chapter.

9.1.2 Chapter Structure

Our discussion of verbal humour centres on two key components: **ambiguity** and **incongruity**. We begin, in ▶ Sect. 9.2, by looking at the semantic ambiguity involved in puns, and we illustrate the use of puns in fiction by analysing the opening paragraph of a short story. In ▶ Sect. 9.3, we introduce the General Theory of Verbal Humour (Attardo and Raskin 1991; Attardo 1997) and demonstrate its relevance for stylistic analysis by returning to the short story introduced in ▶ Sect. 9.2. In ▶ Sect. 9.4, we explore how other forms of incongruity already covered in this book can bring about humour in fictional texts. Specifically, we examine humorous examples of metaphor and simile, as well as impoliteness strategies and how they relate to the General Theory of Verbal Humour. In ▶ Sect. 9.5, we move on to the topic of **irony**, which is an important literary device, and examine its relation to humour. Finally, in ▶ Sect. 9.6, we discuss how researchers can use corpora to explore humour and irony in texts.

9.2 Verbal Humour: Ambiguity

Verbal humour often arises from language users being creative with the various possibilities for ambiguity in language and meaning. From a cognitive perspective, ambiguity occurs when two or more different concepts can be accessed from the same linguistic form. When more than one sense, meaning or concept can be accessed from one lexical item, a **pun** is created (Attardo 1994). Punning relies on the ambiguity that arises from **polysemy** where one word has many different but related meanings, and **homonymy** where different words happen to share the same form (**homographs**) or the same sound (**homophones**) but have different, unrelated meanings. For example:

- The word 'bank' has several different but (according to the OED online) related meanings so is polysemous.
- The words 'lead' (pronounced /lɛd/) meaning a type soft metal and 'lead' (pronounced /liːd/) meaning to be at the front are homographs because they have the same written form but have different, unrelated meanings.
- The words 'bite', 'bight' and 'byte' are homophones because they are pronounced in a similar way (/baɪt/) but have different, unrelated meanings.

It is worth noting that the difference between polysemy and homonymy is often not a clear-cut, two-way distinction. For example, the word 'bit' can be seen as polysemic because it has multiple related meanings including small amount, the past participle of 'bite', and the metal mouthpiece of a bridle. These meanings, according to the OED online, have shared origins in Old English and so are related. However, when 'bit' is used to mean a unit of information in computing (from a blend of 'binary' and 'digit'), it could be seen as a homonym because it shares the same form (homograph) and pronunciation (homophone) but has a different unrelated meaning. When analysing puns, it is therefore necessary to consider all the possibilities for ambiguity rather than a binary categorisation. It is also important to examine which language levels are involved in creating ambiguity (e.g. semantic, graphological, phonological; see ▶ Chapter 1, Focus 1.1). Homophonic puns work best when delivered orally, as in performed dramatic dialogue or spoken poetry, because they rely on an ambiguity that is present at the level of spoken language. Homographic puns, however, work best in written discourse because they rely on ambiguity that is present at the graphological level of language.

Activity 9.1: Punning in Plays

Look at the following examples of puns from two plays and answer the questions below.
a. Context: In Shakespeare's *Romeo and Juliet*, Mercutio has been stabbed by Tybalt and is dying.
   Mercutio: Ask for me tomorrow, and you shall find me a grave man.
b. Context: In Wilde's *The Importance of Being Earnest*, Jack has been pretending his name is Ernest to win over his love interest, Gwendolen. By the end of the play, however, the truth about Jack's real name comes out. This is the final line of the play:
   Jack: I have finally learned the vital Importance of Being Earnest.

i. For each example, identify the lexeme where an ambiguity is exploited.
ii. Is the ambiguity at the semantic level (i.e. polysemic pun), the graphological level (i.e. homographic pun), or at the phonological level (i.e. homophonic pun)?
iii. Both examples are scripted dialogue, written to be performed. How does that affect the meaning, delivery, and interpretation of the puns? Consider the discourse structure of plays (see ▶ Chapter 1).

 Answers are on the book's webpage.

9.2.1 An Example of Punning from Prose Fiction

The following extract from the opening of a short story provides an example of punning:

> (1) You had to get out of them occasionally, those Illinois towns with the funny names: Paris, Oblong, Normal. Once, when the Dow Jones dipped two hundred points, the Paris paper boasted a banner headline NORMAL MAN MARRIES OBLONG WOMAN. They knew what was important. They did! But you had to get out once in a while, even if it was just across the border to Terre Haute, for a movie.
> 'You're Ugly Too' (Moore 1991: 67)

The pun is contained in the newspaper headline that the narrator reports to the narratee/reader. The headline exploits the ambiguity of the words 'normal' and 'oblong' which can mean 'typical' and 'rectangular', respectively, or refer to towns in Illinois. The words, then, can either be understood as adjectives or as proper nouns and humour is created by this semantic ambiguity. That 'oblong' and 'normal' can also refer to the names of town is established in the opening sentence of the story and this crucial bit of information allows readers unfamiliar with Illinois town names to share the joke and contemplate the situation where a normal [typical] man does indeed marry an oblong [rectangular] woman.

As well as the wordplay that is reliant on the semantic ambiguity of 'oblong' and 'normal', there are other 'strands' of humour in this extract that are significant to the short story's development of a humorous world. For example, the newspaper headline, which is foregrounded by **graphological** deviation (uppercase letters in contrast to the lowercase narrative), contains Free Direct Writing (see ▶ Chapter 4) which distances the narrator from the presented discourse both representationally and attitudinally. This helps to contrast the serious downturn of the Dow Jones against the newspaper's absurd pun, and contributes towards **bathos**, which is a poetic effect achieved when a text descends from a serious tone or topic to a ludicrous or absurd one.³ By doing so, the narrator distances herself from the local people, creating humour though the resultant social contrast.

Throughout the short story from which Example (1) is drawn, the narrator frequently uses verbal humour, including irony and sarcasm. However, the use of humour does not mean she is happy; the full story depicts her as having difficulties relating to people and fitting in socially. Therefore, as well as creating humour, the narrator's disparagement towards the townsfolk of Illinois highlights the character's self-alienation thus contributing to her characterisation and (somewhat ironically!) the story's sadness. Humorous discourse, then, can serve much more complex stylistic purposes than simply inviting laughter.

In the next section, we will draw on Example (1) again to illustrate how humour is more than simply 'ambiguity', as it is based on juxtaposing incongruous elements. Using Example (1), we develop the idea of incongruity to consider how such incongruous elements might be conceived of as **scripts**. In Sects. 9.4 and 9.5, we go on to consider how scripts can be opposed to convey irony and sarcasm, two other kinds of humour.

9.3 Verbal Humour: Incongruity

In this section, we move on to the second strand in our discussion of humour—incongruity.

9.3.1 Incongruity and Resolution Theories

Since Aristotle's fourth-century BC *Poetics*, verbal humour is understood as relying on the unexpected occurrences of words and a recipient who "understands the point" (1412b). Today, it is widely accepted across a range of disciplines that humour is the result of an 'incongruity' between two juxtaposed or mismatched elements. In the 1970s, cognitive psychologists advanced 'incongruity-resolution' theories (Shultz 1972; Suls 1972, 1983), according to which a joke sets up an expectation, which is then thwarted by the punch line (**incongruity**), requiring the listener to re-evaluate initial information provided (**resolution**). Stylistic research has applied incongruity-resolution models to humorous texts in a range of genres, including narrative (e.g. Hidalgo Downing 2000a; Marszalek 2013), drama (McIntyre and Culpeper 2010) and satirical magazines (Simpson 2003). Although the incongruity-resolution models account for a wide range of humorous discourse, they lack precision with regards to what 'incongruity' means in linguistic terms, as well as the conceptual means for resolving verbal humour. The General Theory of Verbal Humour, which we outline below, aims to address these shortfalls.

9.3.2 The General Theory of Verbal Humour (GTVH)

The General Theory of Verbal Humor (GTVH) is based on incongruity-resolution theories but aims to offer a more comprehensive way of understanding how humour is created in discourse. Based on Raskin's earlier (1985) Semantic Script Theory of Humor (SSTH), it was devised by Attardo and Raskin (1991) and later modified (Attardo 1997, 2001; Attardo et al. 2002). The GTVH draws on Cognitive Psychology, Semantics and Pragmatics to provide a framework for the analysis of humour across discourse types, including literary texts (see Attardo 2001, 2002).

9.3.2.1 The GTVH's Three Phases

Like the theories that preceded it, GTVH maintains that verbal humour processing entails incongruity and resolution but, importantly, proposes an initial **set-up** phase:
1. Set-up
2. Incongruity (or script opposition)
3. Resolution

We will explain these three phases using the puns on 'oblong' and 'normal' from Example (1).

First, the groundwork is laid in the **set-up** phase, which is not in itself humorous but draws on accessible information to provide the context for the later phases. In Example (1), the narrator named the Illinois towns for the reader in the opening sentence, creating the set-up for the pun.

After the set-up comes the incongruity and resolution phases. The GTVH therefore tallies with incongruity-resolution theories by recognising these two stages as essential in processing humour. However, the GTVH incorporates Raskin's (1985) proposal that the second phase, **incongruity**, is more clearly defined as a pair of opposing scripts. The psychological concept of a script shares much in common with the concept of a schema, a package of knowledge which we introduced in ▶ Chapter 1 (▶ Sect. 1.3.2). In relation to humour specifically, Attardo (1997: 402) defines scripts as, "collections of semantic information pertaining to a given subject" and emphasises their embeddedness in cultural and societal knowledge, which produces expectations and influences choices. Script opposition means that for a text to be a joke, it needs to fulfil two conditions:
i. that the text has to be compatible with two different scripts and
ii. that these two scripts are opposite "in a special sense" (Raskin 1985: 109).

Raskin goes on to explain that script opposition does not necessarily entail **antonymy** (i.e. lexico-semantic opposites, such as 'tall' and 'short'), but that it can refer to an actual situation being contrasted with a non-actual situation, or a normal state of affairs being contrasted with an abnormal or implausible state of affairs. Looking again at Example (1), there are two compatible scripts in the headline, "NORMAL MAN MARRIES OBLONG WOMAN". One script is 'real' in which a man from Normal marries a woman from Oblong, while the other script is much more implausible and absurd, in which a normal [typical] man marries an oblong-shaped woman. According to GTVH, the pun in Example (1) can be read as humorous because the lexical ambiguity in the puns 'oblong' and 'normal' leads to an incongruous opposition of the real and the unreal scripts.

The third phase of GTVH, the **resolution**, involves the recipient's recognition of two compatible—but opposing—scripts. The reader of the headline 'NORMAL MAN MARRIES OBLONG WOMAN' will only be able to reach a resolution of the incongruity if s/he has access to the required contextual information about Illinois placenames, as provided in the set-up. However, an interesting proviso Attardo adds is that if "the resolution does not have to be complete and does not have be to be realistic or plausible—it is a playful resolution" (1994: 144; see also Attardo 2015). Resolution, then, does not necessarily entail 'solving' the incongruity, but finding some way in which the opposed scripts might be considered coherent or appropriate (Oring 2003). This proviso may explain how some **absurd** or apparently meaningless texts can be humorous. Readers of the pun in Example (1) achieve its resolution simply by being able to recognise the dual meanings and their coherence with both scripts. It is not clear whether the newspaper journalists intended the pun or whether the adjectives aptly describe the bride and groom, but such a degree of resolution is not necessary for the pun to be humorous.

9.3.2.2 Script Opposition and Irony

The order in which scripts are presented or processed may be significant for the humorous effect. According to Attardo (1997), usually jokes first present a script that is a neutral, typical state of affairs and, second, a script that is 'marked' or surprising. He proposes that, in the process of decoding a joke, the first neutral script is rejected in favour of a second marked script. However, considering the puns in the headline "NORMAL MAN MARRIES OBLONG WOMAN", we suggest that readers would process the adjectives as carrying their everyday, descriptive meanings first. That is, the reader might first be surprised by the marked, unreal script of an oblong-shaped woman. Langacker's notion of centrality (see ▶ Sect. 7.3) supports our presumption that more central, everyday meanings should be the most accessible. Second, readers will use the information provided in the set-up to create the real, unmarked script in which the groom is from Normal and the bride is from Oblong. Therefore, this joke seems to defy Attardo's typical ordering of opposed scripts by inviting a marked reading first and an unmarked reading second.

Giora (1995) proposes that movement from a marked meaning to an unmarked meaning is a key feature of **irony**, a rhetorical device which shares much in common with humour, though it may not always be funny. As such, the order of script opposition in the punning headline might invite an ironic reading. Example (1) is drawn from a short story which has an overall ironic or sardonic tone. In addition to the ordering of scripts, some other discursive features which contribute to an ironic reading are visible in Example (1). When the narrator remarks "Once, when the Dow Jones dipped two hundred points", the narrator establishes a plausible item for headline news: a national economic downturn. The expectation established by this clause is not fulfilled, and instead the narrator relays what actually happened, with the reporting clause "the Paris paper boasted…" and a direct presentation of their chosen headline. The incongruity between the narration and the reported headline is emphasised graphologically by the uppercase letters, as well as by the use of the reporting verb 'boasted' which is at odds with the content of the headline (we return to 'boasted' later in the chapter, in ▶ Sect. 9.6). As such, the simple puns in the headline are embedded inside another ironic joke, one made by the narrator, in which the script of what *might* be expected to be headline news is contrasted with the script of what *actually* made the headline news.

In Example (1), the narrator invites the reader to share in a disdainful viewpoint towards the provincial townsfolk, creating a scornful humour from the incongruity between our shared expectations and their behaviour. In the sections that follow, we introduce additional concepts from the GTVH that consider participant roles in humorous discourse, and advance pragmatic accounts of **sarcasm** and **irony** that can help explain how Example (1) can be read in such ways (see Johnson and Arp 2015 for an alternative exploration of humour in this story).

9.3.2.3 The GTVH's Knowledge Resources

The GTVH identifies six Knowledge Resources (KRs), which are key phenomena activated in the set-up, incongruity and resolution, and that can be considered in the analysis of verbal humour. According to Attardo and Raskin (1991), the KRs are: **script opposition**, which we have already discussed; **logical mechanism**, which are the mechanisms that help to create and resolve the joke; the **situation** of the joke; the **target** of the joke; **narrative strategy**, which is how the text is organised; and the **language** used in the joke. Each of these KRs is glossed in ◘ Table 9.1. In the table, we have organised the KRs differently to Attardo and Raskin (1991) to illustrate how these six concepts can be used to consider the way jokes operate at the level of text, discourse and cognition.

Below, we demonstrate how the six KRs can be applied to a humorous text, using Example (2), which comprises of an (unattested) interaction between the heavyweight boxing legend, Muhammad Ali, and a female flight attendant:

(2) **Flight Attendant:** Buckle your seatbelt, Mr Ali. We are about to take off.
    Muhammad Ali: Superman don't need no seatbelt!
    Flight Attendant: Superman don't need no airplane neither.
                                    (example drawn from Veale 2009: 282)

Ali compares himself to Superman metaphorically, suggesting both are too heroic to require a seatbelt on an airplane. If you read Ali's contribution as humor-

Humour

Table 9.1 The Knowledge Resources (KRs) used in verbal humour, according to the GTVH (Attardo and Raskin 1991; Attardo 1997)

	Six Knowledge Resources (KRs)	Definition	Description
Text	1. Language	The choices on the levels of language which contribute towards verbal humour	According to Simpson and Bousfield, "a large part of the stylistic analysis of humor […] involves identifying an incongruity in a text and pinpointing *where* in the language system it occurs" (2017: 159, our emphasis). The language **KR** emphasises the importance of analytic precision about how an ambiguity is expressed textually, and on which linguistic level
Discourse	2. Narrative strategy	The narrative organisation of a humorous text	Although Attardo (2001: 23) recognises that not all jokes are narratives, he suggests that most can be paraphrased in a narrative form. The narrative strategy refers to the form a joke can take, such as a simple narrative or a dialogue. Sub-genres of jokes—such as 'knock-knock jokes—often follow formulaic narrative strategies. Satire often imitates the narrative strategy of a non-humorous discourse type (e.g. news)
	3. Target	The people, groups or institutions whom a joke makes fun of, commonly known as the 'butt' of the joke	Although not all jokes have a target, humorous discourse has long been associated with an expression of social superiority or aggression (e.g. by the philosopher Thomas Hobbes; Billig 2005). Sociological or sociolinguistic approaches to humour often emphasise the use of humour in forming out-groups (targets) and, consequently, in-groups (hence the term 'in-joke'). Aggression towards a target can be found in jokes based on cultural stereotypes and in certain forms of humour (e.g. sarcasm and satire)
Cognition	4. Situation	Refers to the objects, participant, instruments and activities involved in the joke's setting	Some jokes will be reliant on a much more elaborate situation than others. Attardo (1994: 225) suggests that the set-up phase is largely responsible for creating the situation, although he later notes a lack of research on the situation KR (2001: 24), which may be a consequence of its vague definition. We propose the situation be considered as the text-world in which the joke occurs (see ▶ Sect. 9.3.2.3)
	5. Script opposition	The incongruous opposition of two scripts	Raskin (1985) proposed that incongruity is a pair of opposing scripts where an actual situation is contrasted with a non-actual situation, or a normal state of affairs is contrasted with an abnormal or implausible state of affairs. See overview in ▶ Sect. 9.3.2.1
	6. Logical mechanism	The rule or logic we use to identify opposing scripts and (partly) resolve the incongruity	There are many ways in which jokes can ask us to perform logical gymnastics. Attardo et al. (2002) advance a list of 27; these include rhetorical figures and simple ways of opposing scripts, such as juxtaposition, exaggeration or (false) analogy, as well as more complex operations such as role reversal, faulty reasoning, and figure/ground reversal

ous, it is because he draws an analogy (one of the logical mechanisms of humour) between two scripts: himself and Superman (script opposition). However, here we focus on the humour in the Flight Attendant's retort.

The first two turns provide the set-up phase for the Flight Attendant's joke. Ali's turn provides a fictional **situation** and **script opposition** (Ali is Superman). As Attardo (2001) admits, the existing definition of the **situation** KR is vague and we propose that Text World Theory offers a solution: a joke's situation can be understood as the text-world in which it occurs. The quick-witted flight attendant does not directly challenge the situation presented by Ali, choosing instead to maintain the text-world enactor and location to advance a new, related pair of opposing scripts (superman and airplane). Her own joke is based on the same text-world but re-focuses attention from the seatbelt to the wider context of the airplane; this is the **logical mechanism** by which her joke works.[4] Attardo recognises that the logical mechanism can depend on a 'local' logic, meaning "a distorted, playful logic, that does not necessarily hold outside the *world* of the joke" (Attardo 2001: 25, our emphasis). As discussed in ▶ Sect. 9.1, Marszalek (2013, 2016, 2019, 2020) deems the text-world in which a joke occurs as important for a humorous reading. Although Attardo (2001: 57–59) suggests that the text-world might be significant in interpreting humorous discourse, he does not integrate the framework into the GTVH. We propose that the **situation** KR might helpfully be understood as 'the text-world', entailing the co-text and context within which a joke and its logical mechanisms occur. The flight attendant's joke would not be logical outside of the situation that Ali has provided, that is, the ongoing text-world of the conversation. The flight attendant creates a new script opposition between the incompatible 'superman' and 'airplane', negating Ali's metaphor by highlighting the 'false analogy' which, according to Attardo et al. (2002), is another logical mechanism. The **language** Knowledge Resource also plays a part in the humour with the Flight Attendant's use of multiple negation ("do<u>n't</u> need <u>no</u> airplane <u>neither</u>"). This mirrors Ali's African American Vernacular English and creates morpho-syntactic parallelism between the turns, using the linguistic similarities to emphasise the conceptual contrast and therefore challenge Ali's characterisation of himself as superhuman (**target** KR). All of this is carried out during a conversation (**narrative strategy** KR), which may have been invented for humorous intent.

9.3.2.4 GTVH Summary

The GTVH is not without its drawbacks some of which we have already discussed, such as the difficulty in defining the situation KR (for which we proposed using the text-world framework). In addition, script opposition and incongruity account for a wide range of humorous texts, yet their scope may be *too* broad because incongruity also characterises non-humorous experiences, such as unwelcome surprises. Moreover, as Simpson (2003: 40–42; 2006: 428) notes, the incongruous script opposition supposedly fundamental to humour is comparable to the schema-refreshing deviation supposedly fundamental to literary texts

(▶ Sect. 1.3.2). Therefore, while incongruity is important in humour, it is not a defining feature. Similarly, many of the logical mechanisms proposed by Attardo et al. (2002)—such as parallelism, false analogy and figure/ground reversal—also contribute towards foregrounding which may or may not be humorous. As such, there are no criteria to discern why some foregrounded features contribute to humour while others do not. Despite these caveats, the GTVH provides the most comprehensive framework for a stylistic analysis of humour in texts covering, as we have demonstrated, the textual, discursive and cognitive strategies involved. In the next section, we will continue our exploration of humour by returning to two topics already introduced in this book that involve incongruity and can create foregrounding: metaphorical language and impoliteness. Our aim is to re-examine these features through the lens of humour and the GTVH.

 Activity 9.2: Apply the GTVH to a Joke
(a) *Two guys walk into a bar. The third one ducks.*
i. Identify the set-up, incongruity and resolution phases for joke (a).
ii. Identify any of the six Knowledge Resources relevant for processing joke (a). **Note:** not all six may be significant e.g. not all jokes have a 'target'; the 'situation' may be minimal).

 Answers are on the book's webpage.

9.4 Verbal Humour: Metaphor and Impoliteness

The GTVH identifies incongruity as an important component of humour. As we noted above, however, it is not a defining feature. In this section, we will briefly examine metaphorical language and impoliteness, both of which also involve incongruity, to consider their potential for humour creation.

9.4.1 Metaphorical Language and Humour

▶ Chapter 7 outlined how metaphors work in terms of comparing a target domain (X) to a source domain (Y), inviting comparison across common ground (Z). While everyday metaphors use conventional mappings between target and source domains (e.g. LIFE IS A JOURNEY), literary metaphors often invite more unexpected and surprising mappings (e.g. LIFE IS A DRINK). Therefore, literary metaphors, like humorous discourse, operate by opposing incongruous scripts. Yet not all literary metaphors are funny and not all humour is metaphorical. So, how are metaphors and humour distinct? Based on his observations on a small corpus of humorous metaphors, Attardo (2015: 95) proposes the following answer:

Humor always involves non-fully resolved incongruities. Metaphors, conversely, fully resolve the incongruity of the mapping between domains. The proposed explanation for humorous metaphors (*stricto sensu*) is that they are metaphors in which the incongruity of the mapping of different domains is not fully resolved by the interpretation (finding appropriateness/resolution) of the metaphor...

Following this definition, we can see that while humorous metaphors take the form of a metaphor, the mapping between two domains is not fully resolvable, creating the potential for humour. Dore (2015) adopts Attardo's definition when she considers the humorous use of metaphors by the characters in the television show *Friends* and how they contribute to characterisation. The following extract is from the first episode, where it is important that writers establish characters. With her friend Ross in the room, Rachel is trying to explain to her father on the phone why she jilted her groom at the alter:

(3) **Rachel:** C'mon Daddy, listen to me! It's like, it's like, it's like all my life, everyone has always told me 'You're a shoe! You're a shoe! You're a shoe! You're a shoe!' And today I just stopped and I said, 'What if I don't wanna be a shoe? What if I wanna be a- purse, y'know? Or a- or a hat!' ... No, I'm not saying I want you to buy me a hat I'm saying I am a ha- It's a metaphor, Daddy!
Ross: You can see where you have trouble.

Friends, Episode 1 (Dore 2015: 203)

Describing one's identity as a fashion accessory is an unconventional metaphor. The target and source domains are incongruous, as evidenced by (i) Rachel's difficulty with articulating the metaphor, (ii) her father's misinterpretation of it as a literal request to buy her a new hat and (iii) Ross pointing out the 'trouble' with it. According to Dore (2015), this incongruity lends the metaphor its humour.

It is also worth noting here that, aside from the humour, metaphor use by characters can contribute towards our understandings of their personality (▶ Chapter 6) and how their minds operate (▶ Chapter 8). In this example, the fact that Rachel draws on the source domain of fashion to describe herself invites a comparison along the grounds of material, consumerist and ornamental objects. Her metaphor use here can be read as an implicit cue contributing to an emerging characterisation of Rachel as superficial and materialistic. Her father's interpretation of her metaphorical language as a literal request for a new hat helps to advance this characterisation as well as contributing to establishing a **humorous world**.

Without claiming his account is complete, Attardo (2015) goes on to describe other ways metaphors can be humorous. One alternative strategy is a metaphor's exploitation of an inherently (referentially) funny source domain to describe the target domain. For example, the following exchange from BBC's pseudo-historical comedy *Blackadder* (1989) ends with a humorous simile:

(4) **Private Baldrick:** I have a plan, sir.
Captain Blackadder: Really, Baldrick? A cunning and subtle one?
Private Baldrick: Yes, sir.

> **Captain Blackadder:** As cunning as a fox who has just been promoted to Professor of Cunning at Oxford University?
> *Blackadder Goes Forth*, 'Goodbyee' (Curtis and Elton 1989)

Captain Blackadder uses the conventional, idiomatic simile 'cunning as a fox' but post-modifies the head noun 'fox' with an elaborate relative clause that exaggerates the animal's level of cunning to absurd extremes. The source and the target domains can be fully resolved, as 'cunning' applies equally well to both the 'plan' (the target domain) and the characteristics of this very particular kind of fox (the source domain). The source domain is where the real joke lies: a script for the animal 'fox' is opposed to a script wherein a fox is promoted to professorship (for his expertise in cunning) at a prestigious university. The logical mechanism through which the joke works is exaggeration. Attardo (2015) points to other research (Veale and Hao 2007a, b) which has found through Google searches that a significant proportion (20%) of similes which use a "as X as NP" structure like the *Blackadder* example, is ironic. In ▶ Sect. 9.4, we elaborate a definition of irony that might further explain how this exaggerated simile could be read as ironic.

9.4.2 Impoliteness and Humour

In ▶ Chapter 5 (▶ Sect. 5.5.3), we introduced impoliteness, and defined it as a perceived intentional linguistic attack to an interlocutor's face. Although there has been a significant body of research on impoliteness in literary and telecinematic discourse (see McIntyre and Bousfield 2017 for a useful summary and case study), surprisingly little of it has addressed the contribution of impolite interaction towards humour. Simpson and Bousfield (2017) identify some crossovers. Impoliteness involves an incongruity—one between verbal behaviour and social expectations—and so has the potential to be humorous. Impoliteness also shares other functions with humour in terms of its capacity to be socially transgressive, to exert power and superiority, and to relieve tension (Simpson and Bousfield 2017). In the following exchange, also from *Blackadder*, the eponymous hero uses both on record and off record impoliteness towards a Young Crone for humorous effect:

> (5) **Young Crone**: Two things, my Lord, must ye know of the Wise Woman. First… she is a *woman*! And second… she is…
> **Blackadder**: Wise?
> **Young Crone**: *[normal]* You *do* know her, then?
> **Blackadder**: No, just a wild stab in the dark - which, incidentally, is what *you'll* be getting if you don't start being a bit more helpful!
> *Blackadder II*, 'Bells' (Curtis and Elton 1989)

Blackadder guesses the second attribute of the 'Wise Woman' easily, based on her name, which the Young Crone does not seem to comprehend and mistakes for Blackadder's familiarity with her. In asking, "You *do* know her, then?" the Young Crone contributes the first 'joke' to the exchange, comically oblivious to what is evident. Blackadder's retort, 'just a wild stab in the dark' provides a second joke, using an idiom to overstate the difficulty of arriving at this conclusion, providing an example of sarcasm (described further below), an **off-record** form of impoliteness. Then, by switching attention from the figurative to a literal meaning of this idiom and using it to threaten the Young Crone, Blackadder also expresses **on-record** impoliteness. Blackadder's impolite and sarcastic verbal behaviour towards the Young Crone may not invite laughter at the level of character interaction, but is humorous for the viewing audiences at the discourse-world level.

While **sarcasm** is the expression of mock politeness to create social disharmony, **banter** is the expression of mock impoliteness to create social harmony (Leech 1983/2014; Bousfield 2007; Toddington 2008). When, in Example (3), Ross points out that Rachel's use of metaphor is flawed, 'You can see where you have trouble', he lightly engages in what might be viewed as banter, typical of interactions between the characters in *Friends*. Although there is not the space to develop the analysis here fully, we hope to have demonstrated how models covered thus far in the book have the potential to be developed through the lens of humour.

9.5 Irony

Irony is a phenomenon found in all kinds of discourses, from social media interactions to political satire, but is particularly prevalent in literary discourse and fictional dialogue, where meaning is often implied. As with humour, irony depends on participants sharing expectations and appreciating their disruption.

9.5.1 Referential Irony

Like humour, irony can arise through non-verbal means. **Situational irony** occurs when a series of events give rise to an ironic situation (Attardo 2000). **Dramatic irony** is the effect achieved when discourse participants (e.g. a writer and the reader) know more than the fictional characters depicted (Booth 1974). In Text World Theory terms, situational irony occurs at the level of the text-world, while dramatic irony occurs when discourse-world participants know more than text-world enactors. Both situational and dramatic irony are found in the referential content, meaning they are based on events and referents in the discourse rather than the particular verbalisation. In contrast, irony that is expressed through language is known as **verbal irony**.

9.5.2 Verbal Irony

9.5.2.1 Irony and Implicature

Since classical times, there have been two broad definitions of verbal irony. In Quintillian's narrow definition, irony invites us to understand the *opposite* of what was said. In Cicero's broader definition, irony asks us to look for meaning *other* than the literal one (Müller 2018). Quintillian's narrow definition remains popular and pervasive, including amongst literary critics (e.g. Colebrook 2004). If we are to believe that verbal irony is only expressed by saying the opposite of what you mean, a linguistic definition of irony might be that it flouts the Gricean maxim of Quality to raise an implicature (see ▶ Chapter 5). Yet ironic utterances are not always untrue. Simpson (2011) observes that saying "I just love sunny weather" when it is pouring rain outside is ironic, but not necessarily false nor 'opposite to what is meant'. If we assume that the speaker *does* love sunny weather, then the utterance can be interpreted as flouting the maxim of Relation, not Quality, because the speaker is saying something that is deliberately irrelevant to the discourse context (a rainy day) in order to invite the interlocutor to examine the context and arrive at the conversational implicature: that the speaker does not appreciate the day's weather. So Quintillian's narrow definition of irony can, from a linguistic standpoint, be rejected in favour of Cicero's broader definition, which recognises that ironic utterances involve the deliberate flouting of *some* conversational strategy, in order to raise an **implicature**. Simpson (2011) categorises this broader definition as **oppositional irony**, which is "situated in the space between what you say and what you mean" (Simpson and Bousfield 2017: 161) and can be usefully analysed using Gricean Pragmatics.

Let us now reconsider Example (5), which we flagged as having a potential ironic reading, in the light of Simpson's notion of oppositional irony. Looking back at Example (5), we suggested that Blackadder's retort, "No, just a wild stab in the dark!", might be read as ironic. Blackadder's utterance is metaphorical and therefore flouts the maxim of Quality. The implied meaning is that he made a wild guess and had no idea whether his guess was right or wrong. While it is true that he did guess the Wise Woman's main attribute is that she is wise, we can assume that it was not a wild guess and that he knew he was correct. This is because her 'wisdom' is easily discernible from her name. Blackadder's retort is therefore not untrue nor is it completely true; rather it is a deliberate *over*statement or exaggeration of the truth and therefore an example of **hyperbole**. According to Carston and Wearing (2015), overstatement and understatement are common strategies in expressing irony, and further demonstrates how irony is not necessarily the exact *opposite* of what is true but can involve stretching or bending the truth.

9.5.2.2 Irony and Cognitive Linguistics

Irony poses an interesting phenomenon for cognitive linguists precisely because its meaning depends on activating the unsaid, shared expectations language users hold (Gibbs and Colston 2007; Müller 2018). Linguists have approached irony cognitively using Relevance Theory or Pretence Theory (Clark and Gerrig 1984). Another cognitive approach is advanced by Sperber and Wilson, who—like Nash—emphasise irony's basis on pre-existing assumptions. Their model of **echoic irony** (Sperber and Wilson 1981; Wilson and Sperber 1992) is based on their claim that all instances of verbal irony are echoic, in that they *mention* a real or imagined previous *use* of language. They provide the following example (1981: 306, emphasis in original):

A. I'm tired. (**use**)
B. *You're* tired! What do you think *I* am? (**mention**)

Sperber and Wilson propose that B's utterance can be interpreted as ironic because it echoes back (mention) a previous utterance (use). As they explain, "ironical utterances are cases of mention [and] the propositions mentioned are ones that have been, or might have been, actually entertained by someone" (Sperber and Wilson 1981: 309). The use/mention distinction is clear in the **adjacency pair** above, but less so in ironic utterances that do not explicitly echo a prior utterance. For instance, stating 'I just love sunny weather' on a grey, wet day is not an echo of any real nor imaginable previous utterance, yet Sperber and Wilson would argue that the utterance *is* an ironic mention because it is an echo of hopes or expectations for sunny weather which would constitute the 'use' (1981: 310). Critics of the use-mention distinction invalidate the claim that it applies to all instances of irony and point out the lack of supporting empirical evidence (Attardo 2000; Simpson 2003, 2011). Thinking again about Blackadder's hyperbolic utterance in Example (5), this does not lend much support to the use-mention distinction, as it is difficult to conceive of an anterior utterance to which it might refer back and, in any case, the exercise seems somewhat futile and artificial. However, the understanding of irony as echoic mention has some value, especially when considering discourse forms such as **satire** and **parody,** which draw on an earlier discourse (use) to create a new parody or satirical text (mention).

9.5.2.3 Simpson's (2011) Conceptual Paradox

Simpson provides an over-arching definition of irony that attempts to account for several different categories, verbal and referential, oppositional and echoic:

> the perception of a conceptual paradox, planned or un-planned between two dimensions of the same discursive event.
>
> Simpson (2011: 39)

This definition has the advantage of (i) capturing the incongruity necessary for ironic humour; (ii) highlighting a paradox in irony without limiting it to truth conditions; and (iii) emphasising the fact that the paradox must be *perceived*. Simpson's (2011) definition of irony applies well to Example (5), as the implicature generated from Blackadder's hyperbolic utterance points to the paradox between (i) the Young Crone's expectation that the Wise Woman's attributes are not discernible from her name, and (ii) the obvious reality that they are. Simpson's definition emphasises the importance of *perceiving* the paradox inherent in ironic utterances and in Example (5) we can see that the issue of who perceives what is key to its humour.

We can also note an additional dimension to Blackadder's retort that his irony serves to highlight the stupidity of his interlocuter, the Young Crone. Earlier, we described **sarcasm** as off-record impoliteness, but it can also be characterised as an *aggressive* form of ironic humour, i.e. one which has a target—one of Attardo's (2000) KRs. In sum, Blackadder's retort can be characterised as ironic, but the added element of aggression towards a target renders it sarcastic. Additionally, the audience can enjoy perceiving the paradox Blackadder highlights and therefore shares in the ridiculing of the target of his sarcastic comment. And because the audience knows more than the Young Crone, this adds a certain dramatic irony to the humorous experience.

Activity 9.3: Irony and Sarcasm

Looking again at Example (1), analyse the narrator's exclamation referring to the provincial Illinois newspaper, using concepts outlined in ▶ Sect. 9.4.2:

"They knew what was important! They did!".

i. In what ways can Grice's Cooperative Principle be applied? Does this utterance break any maxims? If so, in which ways?
ii. Sperber and Wilson (1981) propose that irony is always 'echoic'. Does this utterance refer back to any real or imagined discourse?
iii. How can Simpson's (2011) definition of irony be applied to this utterance?
iv. Would you agree that this utterance is ironic and/or sarcastic? Give reasons for your answer, based on your answers for parts i–iii and with specific reference to textual features of the utterance.

 Answers are on the book's webpage.

9.6 Corpus Approaches to Humour

Until recently, corpus approaches to humour have been rare (Partington 2017). This is partly because, as we pointed out at the start of this chapter, humour is an effect achieved through ambiguity in meaning, making it not readily identifiable by corpus software. Nonetheless, there are ways to explore humour via corpus methods. In this section, we point readers to some such studies and provide an example of how a corpus might be used to support a humorous or ironic reading.

Some scholars have simply searched for the term they are interested in; Partington (2006), for example, searches for 'laughter' in the metadata of a corpus of transcribed speech and the results bring up humorous interactive exchanges for his subsequent analysis. A large reference corpus can provide insights for the researcher who wants to better understand a term through its usage and meta-language; the BNC is used in this way by Simpson (2011) investigating 'irony', and by Sinkeviciute (2013) investigating 'teasing'. But 'real' instances of such humorous exchanges cannot be found through a single search term. Veale observes that "to process irony a computer needs the ability to retrieve either the appropriate utterance or the appropriate norm" (2013: 329). If a researcher does not have a specific utterance to examine in the corpus, and the corpus does not recognise the expectation which irony (or humour) thwarts, then we might be left in a double bind!

One way around the difficulty is for the researcher to create their own corpus which matches their particular research aims. For example, the transcripts of hundreds of scenes from TV sitcoms form the corpora created by Dynel (2011) and Feyaerts et al. (2015), compiled according to the kinds of humorous interactions under investigation. A stylistic enquiry into humour in a text may focus on a specific feature or group of features, as Hidalgo Downing (2003) does when she carries out a corpus investigation of negation and its contribution to the black humour in the novel *Catch 22*. Her research demonstrates that by establishing a hypothesis about *how* humour might be textually manifest in the data, the researcher can indirectly access the phenomenon in a corpus. Alternatively, the results of a corpus analysis can be used to direct the researcher towards features of interest for a more qualitative analysis (to find a 'way in'). For example, Partington (2008) investigates PG Woodhouse's humorous prose by creating a corpus of some of his novels and comparing the data to reference corpora to find keywords; the results can signal to the researcher what in the data merits further qualitative analysis. One finding was that Woodhouse frequently uses a striking mix of formalisms *and* informalisms very closely in the same segment of text, such as, "As regards his getting blotto" (2008: 191). The corpus analysis showed Partington what was characteristic of Woodhouse's style, then those characteristics could be related to humorous effects, including **register humour** (see ▶ Sect. 9.1.2).

9.6.1 Using a Corpus to Investigate 'Boasted'

Earlier in this chapter (▶ Sect. 9.2.1), we argued that the narrator of Example (1) takes an ironic stance towards the provincial townsfolk of Illinois. We cited the marked/unmarked order of script opposition in the newspaper headline as evidence and invited readers to apply the theories of irony outlined in ▶ Sect. 9.4.2 to a different utterance in the same extract (Activity 9.3). A site of verbal humour more generally in the extract was identified in the narrator's opposition of (a) the script of what *might* be expected to be headline news with; (b) the script of what *actually* made the headline news: "Once, when the Dow Jones dipped two hundred points, the Paris paper boasted a banner headline NORMAL MAN MARRIES OBLONG WOMAN". Now, we suggest that one feature of this sentence which adds to both the humour and the irony is the incongruity between the phrase "boasted" and the joke-bearing headline it introduces. We hypothesise that the noun phrase which usually complements 'boasted' is complimentary or positive (i.e. something actually worth boasting about). The only way to substantiate this claim is to support it with quantitative, empirical data of real language use, as found in a corpus.

9.6.1.1 Sorted Concordances

Example (1) is drawn from a contemporary American short story, so a comparable reference corpus is the one-billion-word Corpus of Contemporary American English (COCA), which can be accessed through an online interface. In order to filter out instances of 'boasted' as a reporting verb, we used the search term 'boasted a' to focus on its use as a relational verb introducing a noun phrase, which we hypothesised would contain positive, impressive things. The COCA online interface produced 267 hits, two of which were irrelevant, bringing our total to 265. Calculating the **collocates** of 'boasted' is one way to indicate which words are found next to 'boasted a' most frequently, but with so many different possibilities for the sorts of things that can be boasted, this line of investigation was unrevealing. Instead, we downloaded the **concordances** to an Excel spreadsheet, which could then be re-ordered alphabetically according to the word immediately to the right of 'boasted a'. We then assessed the noun phrases that followed 'boasted a' to see whether they were complimentary or positive things. We found that the first 23 results were numerals, as in "boasted a 99.6% safety rating". We also found that numbers appeared frequently elsewhere in the data, either in noun form ("million", "multitude") or later in the noun phrase (e.g. "population of 300,000"). This indicates that the phrase 'boasted a' connotes a 'sizeable' relation. We also examined the adjective involved in the noun phrases, and many of these (see ◘ Table 9.2) were adjectives of extent ('boasted a full/panoramic/vast') or of positive affect, such as 'keen', 'perfect', 'real', special', 'state-of-the-art' and 'tremendous'. Using sorted concordances of this corpus search, we were able to support our intuition that 'boasted a' has positive **semantic prosody** (Louw 1993) in everyday usage.

Now we have empirical evidence to support our hypothesis that the joke-bearing absurd headline that completes 'boasted a' in Example (1) seems incongruous. Previous research on semantic prosody has indicated that a 'collocational clash' can be used to create irony or humour (Louw 1993; Partington 1995; Bednarek 2008); certainly, surprising lexical combinations conform to the mechanisms of verbal humour and irony outlined in this chapter: incongruity and thwarting expectations. By drawing together these various pieces of evidence—applying the GTVH and theories of irony, as well as supporting our intuitions about language use through corpus research—a stronger and more robust argument for our humorous and ironic reading of Example (1) can be made. This is the stuff of Stylistics.

◘ **Table 9.2** Adjectives involved in the noun phrases following 'boasted a'

160 degree, 230 pound, 24 story, Alaskan, beautiful, better, brilliant, British, built-in, carved, cerebral, coffin-handled, combined, comparative, complete, daily, decorated, delicious, droid, dusty, effective, feature-length, Ferrari-like, fine, first-class, frescolike, front, full, full-time, German, good-sized, growing, hard, healthy, high, higher, historical, huge, joyful, keen, large, live, lively, local, long, low-post, lustrous, magnificent, major, manly, new, now-empty, once-in-a-lifetime, one-room, online, palatial, panoramic, perfect, plump, posh, prime, prominent, promising, pronounced, psychiatric, ready, real, rear-engine, resurgent, secluded, see-through, separate, sharp, shorter, significant, single, sizeable, small, sophisticated, spare, special, spot-on, state-of-the-art, stellar, strategic, strong, substantial, tall, thick, triple-A, vibrant, vast, wall-length, wall-sized, weighty, well-shot, wide, wooden, working

9.7 Conclusions

Given that this chapter constitutes the first review of the vast field of humour studies for Stylistics scholars, there has been a lot of ground to cover. This chapter began by outlining some fundamental characteristics of humorous discourse: ambiguity, incongruities and their resolution. ▶ Section 9.3 introduced the General Theory of Verbal Humour, suggesting ways it can be adapted. First, we demonstrated that when decoding a joke's opposing scripts, it *is* possible to move from a marked to an unmarked meaning, an alternative form of script opposition which may create irony. Second, we emphasised the GTVH's value for Stylistics by organising its Knowledge Resources (KRs) in terms of their contribution to a joke's construction at the level of text, discourse and cognition, the mainstays of stylistic enquiry. Third, we suggested that the situation KR could be better defined by approaching it as the text-world of a joke, thereby including the co-text and context relevant in processing humorous discourse. With such modifications, we have integrated the GTVH within a Stylistics research paradigm. In ▶ Sect. 9.4, we continued our exploration of incongruity in relation to humour and revisited metaphorical language and impoliteness. We re-examined them using the GTVH to help understand how some incongruity is humorous while some is not. ▶ Section 9.5 explored various cognitive and Pragmatics approaches to irony, an effect which, like humour, is based on a perceptual paradox. ▶ Section 9.6 outlined some of the possible approaches to humour using corpus methods and illustrated how a corpus can be used to test the researcher's intuitions about normal language usage to make valid, empirically sound claims about incongruous or unexpected language use.

This chapter has made humour's relevance to Stylistics clear. Bringing together other strands from this book, this chapter demonstrated the role humour has in forging narrative voices, creating characters, understanding their relationships and involving discourse participants in intersubjective positioning towards humourists and their targets. We believe there are some topics that not only merit further research, but that stylisticians are best equipped to answer. For example: what is the relationship between humour and absurdity? Why might Free Indirect Style lend itself to irony? And, more ambitiously, if literature and humour rely on such similar verbal and logical mechanisms, along which lines can they be distinguished? We hope this chapter inspires future scholarship across these symbiotic fields and provides a toolkit to account for humorous or ironic readings of texts.

- **Further Reading**

Goatly, A. 2012. *Meaning and Humour*. Cambridge: Cambridge University Press. This book provides a useful introduction to humour. There is also a useful overview of how non-literal figures of speech (such as metaphor, metonymy, simile, hyperbole and irony) relate to humour on pages 166–193.

For readers interested in humour in spoken discourse:

Dynel, M. 2009. Beyond a Joke: Types of Conversational Humour. *Language and Linguistics Compass* 3, 1: 1284–1299. ▶ https://onlinelibrary.wiley.com/doi/pdf/10.1111/j.1749-818X.2009.00152.x.

Readers interested in an in-depth account of parody and satirical discourse: Simpson, P. 2003. *On the Discourse of Satire: Towards a Stylistic Model of Satirical Humour*. Amsterdam and Philadelphia: John Benjamins.
For a discussion of how hyperbole relates to irony and metaphor, see Carston and Wearing (2015).
Readers interested in humour in extended texts and the use of Text World Theory in the analysis of humour can consult Marszalek's work (2013, 2016, 2019, 2020).

- **Resources**

Corpus of Contemporary American English (COCA): ▶ https://www.english-corpora.org/.

- **Notes**

1. Note, though, that humour can of course be multimodal.
2. For other stylistic research in telecinematic discourse see, for example, Piazza et al. (2011), Bednarek (2011, 2018), and Hoffman and Kirner-Ludwig (2020).
3. The juxtaposition of two different styles for a humorous effect is also said to contribute towards **register humour** (Attardo 1994; Partington 2006, 2008).
4. According to Veale (2001), the logical mechanism at work in the flight attendant's joke is a 'figure/ground reversal', which works by shifting attention from the 'seatbelt' (the figure) to the wider context of the 'airplane' (the ground). Veale (2009) argues that figure and ground reversal is key to verbal humour. Veale's use of the terms figure/ground is based on their use in cognitive linguistics, drawing on Gestalt Psychology. The 'ground' is the element that is conceived of as forming the background, whereas the 'figure' is what is conceived of in the foreground, the focus of attention (see Stockwell 2002: 15–25).

References

Attardo, S. 1994. *Linguistic Theories of Humor*. Berlin, New York: Mouton de Gruyter.
Attardo, S. 1997. The Semantic Foundations of Cognitive Theories of Humor. *Humor: The International Journal of Humor Research* 10, 4: 395–420.
Attardo, S. 2000. Irony as Relevant Inappropriateness. *Journal of Pragmatics* 32: 793–826.
Attardo, S. 2001. *Humorous Texts: A Semantic and Pragmatic Analysis*. Berlin and New York: Mouton de Gruyter.
Attardo, S. 2002. Cognitive Stylistics of Humorous Texts. In *Cognitive Stylistics: Language and Cognition in Text Analysis*, eds. E. Semino and J. Culpeper, 231–250. Amsterdam and Philadelphia: John Benjamins.
Attardo, S. 2015. Humorous Metaphors. In *Cognitive Linguistics and Humor Research*, eds. G. Brône, K. Feyaerts and T. Veale, 91-110. Berlin and New York: Mouton de Gruyter.
Attardo, S. and Raskin, V. 1991. Script Theory Revis(it)ed: Joke Similarity and Joke Representation Model. *Humor: International Journal of Humor Research* 4, 3/4: 293–347.
Attardo, S., Hempelmann, C. F. and DiMaio, S. 2002. Script Oppositions and Logical Mechanisms: Modeling Incongruities and their Resolutions, *Humor* 15, 1: 3–46.
Bednarek, M. 2008. Semantic Preference and Semantic Prosody Re-Examined. *Corpus Linguistics and Linguistic Theory* 4, 2: 119–139.

Bednarek, M. 2011. *The Language of Fictional Television: Drama and Identity*. London and New York: Continuum.

Bednarek, M. 2018. *Language and Television Series: A Linguistic Approach to TV Dialogue*. Cambridge: Cambridge University Press.

Billig, M. 2005. *Laughter and Ridicule: Towards a Social Critique of Humour*. London: Sage.

Booth, W. C. 1974. *A Rhetoric of Irony*. Chicago and London: University of Chicago Press.

Bousfield, D. 2007. "Never a Truer Word Said in Jest": A Pragmastylistic Analysis of Impoliteness as Banter in Henry IV, part I. In *Contemporary Stylistics*, eds. M. Lambrou and P. Stockwell, 209–220. London: Continuum.

Carston, R. and Wearing, C. 2015. Hyperbolic Lnguage and its Rrelation to Metaphor and Irony. *Journal of Pragmatics* 79: 79–92.

Clark, H. H. and Gerrig, R. J. 1984. On the Pretense Theory of Irony. *Journal of Experimental Psychology* 113, 1: 121–126.

Colebrook, C. 2004. *Irony*. London: Routledge.

Curtis, R. and Elton, B. 1989. *Blackadder Goes Forth*. BBC.

Dore, M. 2015. Metaphor, Humour and Characterization in the TV Comedy Programme Friends. In *Cognitive Linguistics and Humor Research* eds. G. Brône, K. Feyaerts, and T. Veale, 191–214. Berlin and New York: Mouton de Gruyter.

Dynel, M. 2011. "I'll Be There for You!" On Participation-Based Sitcom Humour. In *The Pragmatics of Humour Across Discourse Domains*, ed. M. Dynel, 33–50. Amsterdam and Philadelphia: John Benjamins Publishing.

Dynel, M. 2016. Conceptualising Conversational Humour as (im)politeness: The Case of Film Talk. *Journal of Politeness Research* 12, 1: 117–146.

Feyaerts, K., Brône, G. and Ceukelaire, R. 2015. The Art of Teasing: A Corpus Study of Teasing Sequences in American Sitcoms between 1990 and 1999. In *Cognitive Linguistics and Humor Research*, eds. G. Brône, K. Feyaerts and T. Veale, 215–242. Berlin: De Gruyter Mouton.

Gibbs, R. W. Jr. and Colston, H. L. (Eds.). 2007. *Irony in Language and Thought: A Cognitive Science Reader*. London and New York: Lawrence Erlbaum.

Giora, R. 1995. On Irony and Negation. *Discourse Processes* 19: 239–264.

Hidalgo Downing, L. 2000a. Negation, Text Worlds and Discourse: The Pragmatics of Fiction. Advances in *Discourse Processes series. Vol. 66* Stamford, CT: Ablex Publishing.

Hidalgo Downing, L. 2000b. Negation in Discourse: A Text World Approach to Joseph Heller's Catch-22. *Language and Literature* 9, 3: 215–239.

Hidalgo Downing, L. 2003. Negation as a Stylistic Feature in Joseph Heller's Catch-22: A Corpus Study. *Style* 37, 3: 318–341.

Hoffman, C. and Kirner-Ludwig, M. (Eds.). 2020. *Telecinematic Stylistics. Advances in Stylistics series*. London and New York: Bloomsbury.

Johnson, G. and Arp, T.R. 2015. Chapter 7: humor and irony. *Perrine's Literature: Structure, Sound & Sense*. 12th edition. Stamford, CT: Cengage Learning.

Leech, G. 1983/2014. *Principles of Pragmatics. Longman Linguistics Library*. Abingdon and New York: Routledge.

Louw, W.E. 1993. Irony in the Text or Insincerity in the Writer? The Diagnostic Potential of Semantic Prosodies. In *Text and Technology*, eds. M. Baker, G. Francis, and E. Tognini-Bonelli. Amsterdam and Philadelphia: John Benjamins.

Marszalek, A. 2013. It's Not Funny out of Context: A Cognitive Stylistic Approach to Humorous Narratives. In *Developments in Linguistic Humour Theory*, ed. M. Dynel, 393–421. Amsterdam and Philadelphia: John Benjamins.

Marszalek, A. 2016. The Humorous Worlds of Film Comedy. In *World-building: Discourse in the Mind*, eds. J. Gavins and E. Lahey, 203–219. London: Bloomsbury.

Marszalek, A. 2019. Constructing inferiority through comic characterization: Self-deprecating humour and cringe comedy in High Fidelity and Bridget Jones's Diary. In *Experiencing Fictional Worlds. Linguistic Approaches to Literature series, 32*, eds. B. Neurohr and L. Stewart-Shaw, 119–134. Amsterdam and Philadelphia: John Benjamins.

Marszalek, A. 2020. *Style and Emotion in Comic Novels and Short Stories*. London and New York: Bloomsbury.
McIntyre, D. and Bousfield, D. 2017. (Im)Politeness in Fictional Texts. In *The Palgrave Handbook of Linguistic (Im)politeness*, eds. J. Culpeper, M. Haugh, and D. Z. Kádár, 759–783. Basingstoke: Palgrave.
McIntyre, D. and Culpeper, J. 2010. Activity Types, Incongruity and Humour in Dramatic Discourse. In *Language and Style*, eds. D. McIntyre and B. Busse, 204–222. Basingstoke: Palgrave Macmillan.
Moore, L. 1991. *Like Life*. New York: Plume.
Müller, W. G. 2018. Irony in Jane Austen: A Cognitive-Narratalogical Approach. In *How to Do Things with Narrative: Cognitive and Diachronic Perspectives*, eds. J. Alber and G. Olsen, 43–64. Berlin: Mouton DeGruyter.
Oring, E. 2003. *Engaging Humor*. Urbana and Chicago: University of Illinois Press.
Partington, A. 1995. Kicking the Habit: The Exploitation of Collocation in Literature and Humour. In *Linguistic Approaches to Literature*, ed. J. Payne, 25–44. University of Birmingham, UK: English Language Research.
Partington, A. 2006. *The Linguistics of Laughter: A Corpus-Assisted Study of Laughter-Talk*. London: Routledge.
Partington, A. 2008. From Wodehouse to the White House: A Corpus-Assisted Study of Play Fantasy and Dramatic Incongruity in Comic Writing and Laughter-Talk. *Lodz Papers in Pragmatics* 4, 2: 189–213. ► https://doi.org/10.2478/v10016-008-0013-3.
Partington, A. 2017. Corpus-assisted Studies of Laughter and Humor-talk. In *The Routledge Handbook of Language and Humor*, ed. S Attardo, 322–339. London and New York: Routledge.
Piazza, R., Bednarek, M. and Rossi, F. (Eds.). 2011. *Telecinematic Discourse: Approaches to the Language of Films and Television*. Amsterdam and Philadelphia: John Benjamins.
Raskin, V. 1985. *Semantic Mechanisms of Humour*. Dordrecht: D. Reidel.
Shultz, T. R. 1972. The Role of Incongruity and Resolution in Children's Appreciation of Cartoon Humor. *Journal of Experimental Child Psychology* 13, 3: 456–477.
Simpson, P. 2003. *On the Discourse of Satire: Towards a Stylistic Model of Satirical Humour*. Amsterdam and Philadelphia: John Benjamins.
Simpson, P. 2006. Humor: Stylistic Approaches. In *Encyclopedia of Language and Linguistics*, ed. K Brown, 426–429. Amsterdam and London: Elsevier.
Simpson, P. 2011. 'That's Not Ironic, That's Just Stupid!': Towards an Eclectic Account of the Discourse of Irony. In *The Pragmatics of Humour Across Discourse Domains*, ed. M. Dynel, 33–350. Amsterdam and Philadelphia: John Benjamins Publishing.
Simpson, P. and Bousfield, D. 2017. Humor and Stylistics. In *The Routledge Handbook of Language and Humor*, ed. S Attardo, 158–173. London and New York: Routledge.
Sinkeviciute, V. 2013. Decoding Encoded (Im)politeness: "Cause on My Teasing You Can Depend". In *Developments in Linguistic Humour Theory*, ed. M. Dynel, 263–287. Amsterdam and Philadelphia: John Benjamins.
Sperber, D. and Wilson, D. 1981. Irony and the Use-Mention Distinction. In *Radical Pragmatics*, ed. Peter Cole, 295–318. New York: Academic Press.
Stockwell, P. 2002. *Cognitive Poetics: An Introduction*. London and New York: Routledge.
Suls, J. 1972. A Two-Stage Model for the Appreciation of Jokes and Cartoons: An Information Processing Analysis. In *The Psychology of Humor*, eds. J. Goldstein and P. McGhee, 81–100. New York: Academic Press.
Suls, J. 1983. Cognitive Processes in Humor Appreciation. In *Handbook of Humor Research, vol. 1*, eds. P McGhee and J Goldstein, 39–57. New York: Springer Verlag.
Toddington, R. 2008. (Im)politeness in Dramatic Dialogue: Understanding Face-attack in Shakespeare's Othello. In *The State of Stylistics*, ed. W. Greg, 427–450. New York: Rodopi.
Veale, T. 2009. Hiding in Plain Sight: Figure-ground Reversals in Humour. In *Cognitive Poetics: Goals, Gains and Gaps*, eds. G. Brôle and J Vandaele, 279–288. Berlin and New York: Mouton de Gruyter.

Veale, T. and Hao, Y. 2007a. Learning to Understand Figurative Language: From Similes to Metaphors to Irony. In *Proceedings of CogSci, The 29th Annual Meeting of the Cognitive Science Society*, 683–688. Mashville, USA.

Veale, T. and Hao, Y. 2007b. A Context-Sensitive Framework for Lexical Ontologies. *The Knowledge Engineering Review* 23, 1: 101–115.

Wilson, D. and Sperber, D. 1992. On Verbal Irony. *Lingua* 87: 53–76.

How to 'Do' Stylistics

Supplementary Information The online version contains supplementary material available at ▶ https://doi.org/10.1007/978-3-031-10422-0_10.

© The Author(s), under exclusive license to Springer Nature Switzerland AG 2023
J. Lugea and B. Walker, *Stylistics*,
https://doi.org/10.1007/978-3-031-10422-0_10

10.1 Introduction

In this book, we have introduced readers to some of the analytical models and frameworks useful for stylistic analysis. While we do not claim to have captured all available analytical models, the preceding chapters nonetheless equip readers with a 'toolkit' to undertake stylistic research (see ◘ Table 10.1 for a summary). The 'toolkit' metaphor is common in discussions about Stylistics (Wales 2014) because it captures two important features:

1. the 'work' of Stylistics is practical and hands-on, dissecting a text to explain how the textual features lead to poetic effects;
2. there are a range of methods and analytical models that suit different research aims and questions.

The stylistic toolkit provides you with the tools you need to examine a text, and the tools you choose to use will depend on your text and what your aims are.

Throughout this book, we have demonstrated how to use the various analytical models and frameworks and offered readers the chance to practice doing analyses via activities. In this chapter, we move on from individual isolated analyses to consider the stylistic method more broadly, with a view to doing a Stylistics project using the toolkit we have introduced. Afterall, there is no point in having a toolkit if you do not know how to use it. We should point out, though, that this chapter is not intended as a prescriptive rulebook for stylistic research because when it comes to its theories and methods, Stylistics is eclectic (Jeffries 2000; Sotirova 2016). Stylistics adopts numerous analytical frameworks from other sub-disciplines of Linguistics as well as other fields of research and, consequently, there is not one way to 'do' Stylistics.

However, having taught Stylistics in various settings, we recognise that students inevitably come to this 'interdiscipline' (Leech 2008) of Stylistics from different academic backgrounds and thus doing a Stylistics project can be a novel and challenging experience. Literature students, for example, may be new to the theories and methods of language analysis, while those well grounded in Linguistics may not be used to dealing with literary genres. We also recognise that Stylistics is often a subject taught to learners of English as a second language, to support their understanding of the workings of both the literature and language in Anglophone cultures. This chapter aims to support all kinds of scholars to design (▶ Sect. 10.1), carry out (▶ Sect. 10.2) and write up (▶ Sect. 10.3) their own stylistic research.

We start our discussion of how to do Stylistics by outlining how to go about choosing data and analytical frameworks in a principled way, based on research aims.

10.2 Research Design

A good rule of thumb for starting a Stylistics project is to choose text(s) that you find interesting, particularly because of the way language is used. This way, you might be more likely to, first, have observations to make about the textual features and, second, have an interpretation of the textual function i.e. the purpose of those features. As a reader, you form impressions of texts you have read and these impressions can form the basis of a hypothesis (for useful advice on forming research hypotheses, see McIntyre and Walker 2019). In stylistic research, it is not sufficient to base claims on your impressions of a text because these are subjective opinions and are not **falsifiable**.

Falsification is an idea proposed by Karl Popper (1959) as the basis of scientific method whereby it must be possible to test a theory or hypothesis and conceivably prove it wrong. Indeed, Popper proposed that science should aim to disprove theories rather than strive to support them. According to Jeffries and McIntyre (2010: 24), falsification is a basic 'requirement' of stylistic research because it entails a research procedure that is clear enough for other researchers to follow, understand, replicate and possibly contradict the findings. In scientific enquiry, which Stylistics aims to practise, there is nothing shameful in being proven wrong; conversely, it means your aims and methods were clear enough to be replicated by other scholars. This honesty and openness should characterise stylistic research.

Activity 10.1: Falsifiable or Not?

Look at the following statements and say whether they are falsifiable. Explain your reasons. If you think they are falsifiable, suggest how you would test them.

1. All Dan Brown's novels are complete and utter guff!
2. Dan Brown's novels consist mostly of simple sentences that are shorter than normal.
3. Dan Brown's novels contain a lot of adverbs; more than in other novels.
4. Dan Brown's The Da Vinci Code contains a lot of direct speech which brings the reader closer to the characters and makes the book super exciting.

 Our answers are on the book's webpage.

10.2.1 Selecting Texts and Analytical Frameworks: A Good 'Fit'

What sort of text do you want to analyse? Fiction or non-fiction? Poetry, drama, prose? News report, speech, advertisement? Whatever text you choose, it is paramount that the model or framework you use for its analysis is suitable and can aptly describe the data. ◘ Table 10.1 provides a list of models detailed in this book and the kinds of texts they 'prototypically' apply to. To summarise, **foregrounding** and **deviation** are, prototypically, the distinguishing features of literary genres, particularly poetry, because this genre is where such devices are prevalent and key to meaning making. In other genres, such as prose fiction, deviation and foregrounding still occur but, by and large, it is sparser and less central to the communication of the message between author and reader. Therefore, a project that focuses on deviation and foregrounding in a novel may produce few

Table 10.1 The stylistic toolkit provided in this textbook

Chapter	Content	Models and key concepts	Prototypically applies to:
1. Style: Text, Cognition and Corpora	Fundamental features and structures of literary texts and readers' understanding	Deviation, parallelism and foregrounding	All kinds of literary, fictional and rhetorical discourse, especially poetry
		Discourse structure	All kinds of discourse
		Schema Theory	All kinds of discourse
2. Worlds	How fictional texts differ from reality in patterned ways and how they create a text-world	Fictional worlds	All fiction
		Text World Theory, transitivity, deixis and reference	All kinds of discourse
3. Point of View	How viewpoint is created in a narrative text	Different kinds of narrator	Narrative prose, or any text with a narrator
		Textual indicators of viewpoint	
4. The Presentation of Speech, Writing and Thought	The ways speech, thought and writing can be (re)presented to blend others' discourse in the text	Speech, Writing and Thought Presentation	Narrative prose or any text where there is an intervening presence that presents other people's discourse
5. Fictional Dialogue	The dialogue and interaction of characters	Conversation Analysis, Speech Act Theory, Gricean Pragmatics and (im)politeness	Drama, or any text that involves scripted or spoken interaction
6. Fictional Character	How characters are textually constructed using what we know about language, cognition and people	Characterisation	Drama and prose fiction
7. Metaphorical Language	The non-literal and figurative language found in fictional texts	Conceptual Metaphor Theory (CMT)	All kinds of discourse
8. Mind Style	How textual patterns accumulate to create a particular 'way of thinking' in a fictional mind	An effect, studied by applying previous models e.g. CMT, transitivity, etc.	Any fictional text where a narrator/character's 'mind' is discernible, and the text is long enough for patterns to emerge
9. Humour	How humour and related effects (e.g. irony and satire) are achieved in discourse	An effect, studied by applying the General Theory of Verbal Humour and other models	All kinds of discourse conveying humour

results and is likely to take an enormous amount of time to obtain them. Of course, some novels will buck this trend. **Text World Theory** can be used to analyse both literary and non-literary texts, whereas **fictional worlds** (as its name suggests) applies only to fiction. Narrative prose has a complex discourse structure which weaves different 'voices' throughout, meaning that **viewpoint** and **discourse presentation** (the presentation of others' speech, writing and thought) are most pertinent to this genre. **Characters** are usually developed in drama and narrative prose, while **dialogue** is the substance of drama, but can be fruitfully analysed in sections of prose as well. **Figurative language** is likely to be extremely prevalent in poetry and essential to the communication of the author's message. However, as we established in ▶ Chapter 7, metaphorical language is everywhere and so, potentially, any text could be usefully analysed for figurative meanings. **Mind style** is traditionally studied in prose fiction while **humour** can arise in any text type with some, such as comedy dramas, being obvious locations for this textual effect.

Applying a model to a different discourse type than the one it was intended for can result in a poor 'fit', where the terms and categories simply do not apply to the data. For example, it may be difficult to analyse viewpoint in a text that lacks any sort of narration of story. For instance, poetry and plays are not always clearly narrated and can lack obvious viewpoint features. Therefore, a project that aims to look at viewpoint in a poem or play might falter at the first hurdle. However, this is a general picture and, as we noted above, Stylistics is eclectic; it is also constantly developing. The ground-breaking work in Stylistics is that which successfully adopts—and, crucially, adapts—models for application to new or non-prototypical texts to help explicate those texts. In each chapter in this textbook, we have, where possible, pointed to research that has applied the models to non-prototypical text types. For example, in ▶ Chapter 3 we noted McIntyre's (2006) work on viewpoint in plays, which investigates stage directions, the use of a dramatic chorus and narrative voiceover. By looking at this sort of innovative work, scholars can investigate the possibilities for themselves, discover how it can be done well, and perhaps try adapting and expanding models for application to alternative text types.

When it comes to selecting models for analysis, a common question from students is, 'how many?'. There is no right answer to this and it is, perhaps, not the correct question to ask. The selection of analytical frameworks and models depends primarily on your research aims and these should guide how you approach your analysis of your chosen text. Practical constraints are also extremely important since limits on time and space dictate how many models you can practically apply to your data. For instance, in your written work, the analytical frameworks and their inherent concepts must be defined before being applied to the data and this will inevitably limit the number of models you are able to use. The number of analytical models used also depends on what you aim to analyse. For example, if you want to explore the construction of characters in a text, Culpeper's (2001) model for analysing characterisation, which encompasses many different frameworks within it, can be used. On the other hand, if you want to explore something quite nebulous—like the 'atmosphere' of a novel, or the 'mind style' of a character—you must consider: (i) how those things are conveyed linguistically in your chosen text; (ii) how you are going to test for their existence (remember falsification!); and (iii) which models best describe those features. A combination of several models may, therefore, be useful for accounting for the phenomenon you want to describe, so long as they are the right 'tools' for the job.

10.2.2 Research Questions

Once you have an idea of the text(s) and applicable model(s) for stylistic analysis, you should consider more carefully what it is that you want to explore. Devising one or more research questions helps to guide methodological decision-making and focus the analysis. It is important that a research question is answerable within the constraints of your project. McIntyre and Walker (2019) make a distinction between 'global' (or 'over-arching') research questions, on the one hand, and 'local' ones, on the other. For example, let's say you are interested in *The Turn of the Screw*, a novella by Henry James. The narrator is a children's governess who recounts spooky events in the family home where she works. The story is interesting because the reader is left unsure if the governess is a reliable source of information, or, if she herself is psychologically disturbed. The viewpoint markers might be an indication of how reliable her narration is. The following method can be used to devise a global research question for your project:

A. **I am studying…** [insert the text(s) and/or model(s)]
   e.g. Henry James' novella *The Turn of the Screw*
B. **in order to find out…** [use questions adverbs **who, what, where, when, why** and - especially useful for Stylistics – **how**]
   e.g. how the governess' viewpoint is constructed
C. **in order to understand…**
   e.g. whether the narrator is (a) reliably recounting a ghost story, or (b) psychologically disturbed.
D. Use A-C to formulate a Research Question:
   RQ. How does Henry James' use of viewpoint markers contribute to the reliability (or otherwise) of the governess' narration in *The Turn of the Screw*?

You may then need pose local questions which, once addressed, will help answer the global question. For instance, the research question "How does Henry James' use of viewpoint markers contribute to the reliability of the governess' narrative in *The Turn of the Screw*? can only be answered by first addressing the following issues:
i. Which viewpoint markers are attributable to the governess?
ii. Do the viewpoint markers contribute to her reliability as a narrator?

These questions are the local research questions and are important because they will inform other methodological decisions, such as which models and data to select.

10.2.3 Data Selection

After choosing your text(s), it is important to consider, more precisely, what constitutes your data. By that we mean deciding whether you are going to analyse the whole text or part(s) of it. Again, this decision is dictated by practical considerations such as time and space, as well as your research questions and the particular approach adopted.

Stylistics utilises both **qualitative** and **quantitative** analytical approaches but, fundamentally, it is a qualitative approach to text analysis whereby a model or framework is applied to data to examine it in detail. Such detailed analysis tends to involve a small amount of data (such as a short poem), especially in the context of a small research project or essay. A qualitative approach to a large amount of data such as a full-length novel or a play can necessitate **data selection**, which should be done in a principled and planned way. Stylistic analysis which does not engage in principled data selection is open to criticism for '**cherry picking**', that is, selecting extracts that simply prove the point the researcher wanted to make in the first place (see more about this below). Here is a guide for choosing an extract from a long text:

i. limit your selection based on formal features, e.g. the direct speech of characters (see, for example, ▶ Sect. 2.4) or, in a text where the narratorial mode varies, you might analyse just one particular mode;
ii. choose an extract that is representative of the whole text in some way;
iii. choose an extract that occurs in a place of importance, e.g. the first depictions of a character can be important for characterisation, the opening scene of a novel can be important for world-building;
iv. choose an extract that has inspired other readers, critics or researchers to make claims which you can explore further through stylistic analysis;
v. replicate the data selection method used in other research;
vi. use corpus approaches to find a 'way in' (see Sects. 2.4.2 and 8.5).

A procedure for data selection can be demonstrated by considering how a researcher could address the research question about *The Turn of the Screw*, formulated above. The question directs the research to the governess' narrative viewpoint, so the lengthy prelude at the start of the novella, which is told from the viewpoint of a different character, can be discounted (as in i. above—limit your selection). The remainder of the novella is from the viewpoint of the governess, making it potential data. It may be possible to investigate the whole of the remainder of the novella, listing and categorising the features as you go, to present results in summary form in the written work. If time does not allow such detail, an extract could be selected using any of the remaining options (ii–vi, above). Whatever option is used, it is good practice to outline the chosen data selection method in written work.

As we mentioned above, Stylistics also utilises quantitative analytical techniques, whereby language features in a text or the results of qualitative analysis are quantified to allow comparisons to be made with other texts or some sort of 'norm'. This important method was demonstrated in ▶ Chapter 4 where we carried out a speech, writing and thought presentation analysis of a short story (Mr Loveday's Little Outing) and tallied up the results of that analysis. This allowed us to (i) present our results neatly and succinctly in the form of a table, and (ii) compare the discourse presentation patterns in the story against those established in previous research. In ▶ Chapter 2, we also showed how the quantitative analysis of modal verbs helps to highlight unusual chapters in a single novel. Such analyses and quantification can be assisted (or made possible!) by using corpus tools. Whether or not to use corpus tools and approaches may be another decision you need to make when designing your project.

10.2.4 Using Corpus Approaches

There are two main ways in which corpora can be used for stylistic research. Firstly, large, ready-made corpora can act as a reference point to provide empirical evidence for language intuitions you might have about language choices in a text, such as whether you think they are odd or carry certain connotations. We saw how this works in ▶ Chapter 9 where we looked at how the lexical item 'boasted' is used 'normally' and compared that to the way it is used in the text under analysis. Secondly, corpus tools can be used directly on the text(s) under investigation to analyse it in various ways. For example, corpus tools can produce concordances, and calculate keywords, and collocates—all of which would be impossible to do manually. Essentially, corpus tools are excellent at quantifying the formal components of texts, and this can be useful for making **quantitative**, linguistic comparisons between groups of texts, individual texts or parts of texts. As we have seen in this book, comparison can help to investigate numerous stylistic concerns, such as text-worlds, characterisation and point of view. Essentially, quantitative comparison can help to identify differences in author, narrator and character style. With corpus approaches, the results supplied by corpus tools provide a quantitative 'way in' to the text being analysed and a focus for further detailed, often qualitative, analysis. ◘ Figure 10.1 sets out these two ways in which corpus approaches can be used for Stylistics.

Corpus tools are less useful, however, for analysing linguistic/pragmatic functions, such as implicature and (im)politeness. Here, human intervention is required meaning that the analysis becomes manual and therefore restricted by, for example, time constraints. As we saw in ▶ Chapter 4, though, corpus annotation can help to record manual analysis thus making it easier to track and quantify, lending the analysis systematicity and rigour.

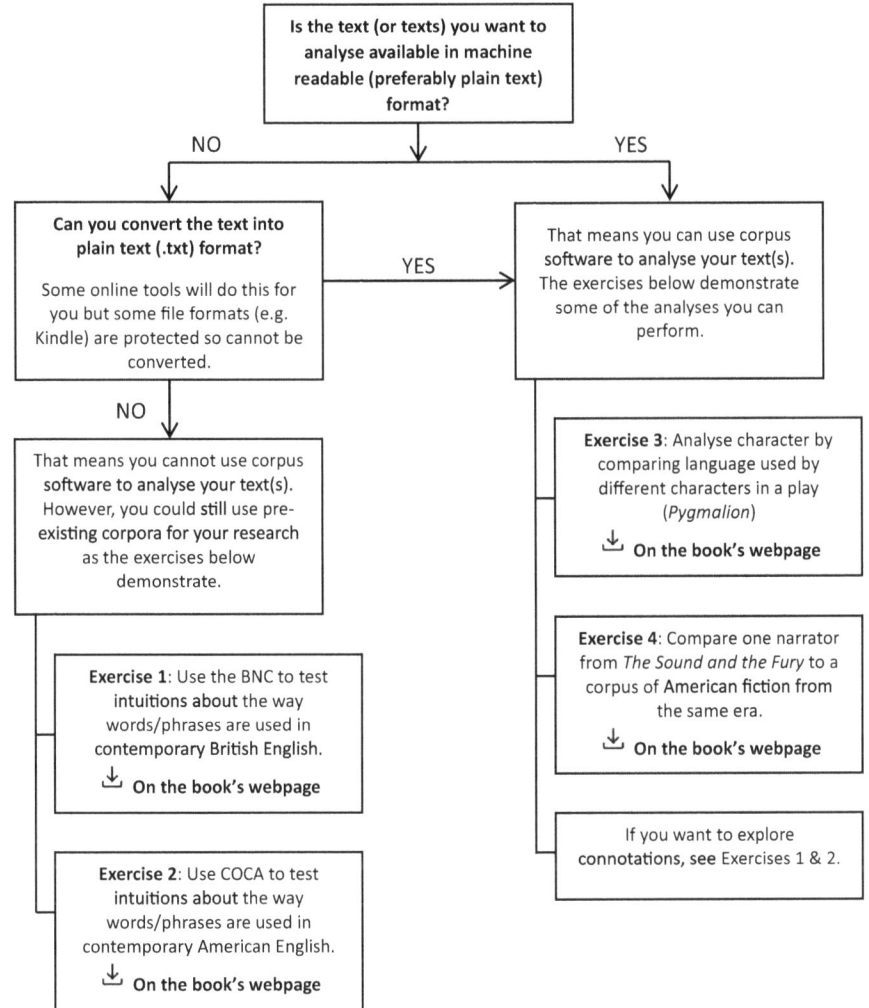

● Fig. 10.1   How can I use corpus methods in my stylistic research?

10.3 The Aims of Stylistic Analysis

Whether you want to analyse a literary or non-literary text, a single poem or a corpus of song lyrics, the basic aim of stylistic analysis is the same: to explain how texts 'work'; how their language produces poetic effects. The process of doing this can be broken into three stages (● Fig. 10.2):
i. *identify* the marked ways in which language is used in a text,
ii. *describe* how they deviate from norms of use, and
iii. *interpret* how these foregrounded features convey meaning and effects.

Fig. 10.2 The stages of stylistic analysis

In practice, the researcher may pass through these stages many times when examining a text. In the sub-sections below, we outline what is involved during each stage and provide some of the theory underpinning the practice.

10.3.1 Identify Language Features

Marked features of language in a text can be *identified* simply by noting what strikes you, the reader, as odd or unusual. A corpus might also indicate how or where a text contains marked features worthy of further analysis (see our case study in ► Chapter 2). Whether by eye or with a corpus, it is not enough to simply engage in **'feature-spotting'** (Giovanelli and Mason 2018: 5); the next step is to consider which frameworks can account for those features. Beginning a stylistic enquiry in this way is called a bottom-up or **inductive** approach.

It is also perfectly reasonable, however, to be motivated to carry out an analysis because of the *effect* a text has on you, even if you cannot pin down any specific language features responsible. In this case, the researcher could consider what the effect is (are you struck by a particular character? their viewpoint? the strange world of a text?) and then examine how this effect is brought about by language choices, which may be manifest across a wide range of features. Alternatively, literary critics or lay-readers may have made claims about text(s) which can then be investigated through a stylistic enquiry. Whether the starting **hypothesis** is based on your own reading or that of another reader, when the approach moves from an hypothesis to an investigation of the text, it is called a top-down or **deductive** approach. Often, a combination of both approaches is used because analysts might have hypotheses about text meaning, as well as a sense of which textual features are marked. The next two stages of analysis make the connections between textual features and textual meaning as explicit as possible.

10.3.2 Describe Language Features

The second stage is to *describe* the marked textual features by applying one or more relevant analytical models. The application of frameworks to texts is fundamental to stylistic analysis because it lends the procedure systematicity. A useful rule of thumb for 'doing' Stylistics is easily remembered as the 'three-Rs', whereby stylistic analysis should be *rigorous*, *retrievable* and *replicable* (Simpson 2004: 4):

- *Rigour* is achieved by applying an analytical model, which provides the analyst with a framework to structure their description and interpretation of a text and its effects.
- *Retrievable* research uses terminology with meanings that are agreed amongst scholars, enabling the findings to be traced, or retrieved, by other scholars.
- *Replicability* is achieved when other researchers can potentially replicate the study to verify or falsify the results (because of the transparent and retrievable nature of a stylistic analysis).

The stylistic method should be explicit and transparent enough for scholars to understand one another's analyses and interpretations and be able to develop the method or findings in their own research. Importantly, the analytical frameworks lend systematicity to stylistic research, but they may not be perfect and often it is only through applying them to new texts or text types that areas for improvement in the models can be identified. Therefore, the process of analysis can lead scholars to suggest modifications to the model. This openness to change helps to sustain and develop the discipline.

10.3.3 Interpretation

Most stylisticians would agree that it is not enough simply to describe textual features, but that a necessary next step is to provide an evaluation or interpretation of their effects (on evaluative Stylistics, see Leech 2008). Consequently, after applying the model(s), the third stage of a stylistic analysis is to *interpret* the findings. This can involve thinking about why the author might have made such textual choices and/or what the choices do for our understanding of the text. At this stage of the process, the analyst tries to understand the link between textual **form** and artistic/poetic/stylistic **function**. If a deductive (top-down) approach was adopted, the analyst demonstrates how the textual features support or reject the hypothesis advanced at the outset. Note, though, that a hypothesis can never be proven true because it is impossible to know if it would apply in every instance. If an inductive approach was adopted, the analyst suggests how foregrounded features *might* contribute to particular effects. Note our caution here: stylistic analysis aims for objectivity, yet the act of interpretation is—to a certain extent—subjective.

10.3.3.1 Fishing for Objectivity

The 'relative objectivity' of Stylistics has endured criticism over the decades (e.g. see the debate develop in Mackay 1996, 1999; Short et al. 1998; Short and van Peer 1999; and levelled in Jeffries 2000). For example, Fish (1973/1996, 1979) advanced a searing critique of Stylistics, which is now as well known as it is well contested (Shen 1988; Toolan 1990/1996, 2014a; Simpson 1993; O'Halloran 2007). Fish claimed that linguistic forms "can be assigned any semantic or psychological value one may wish them to carry" (1973/1996: 99). His main critique was that even if linguistic frameworks are applied to the text(s), the interpretations are 'arbitrary'. He supported this view by pointing to the fact that a form's meaning can change depending on the context. Fish also criticised stylistic enquiry for being 'circular', meaning that the interpretation may derive from pre-existing notions about the text (interpretation → analysis → interpretation). This relates to the trap of 'cherry picking', whereby data is selected simply to prove an existing interpretation. In Fish's view, these dangers mean the application of an analytical model to texts is pointless. With these criticisms, Fish dismissed the stylistic method and any inherent claims to systematicity or objectivity.

10.3.3.2 Interpretive Positivism

Rather than dismiss them, we believe that Fish's criticisms can be taken as advice on 'how **not** to do Stylistics'; indeed, they nicely describe 'bad stylistics' (Eve 2020). The trap of associating form too directly with function is called **interpretive positivism** and can be avoided, as Simpson (1993: 103–109) suggests, simply with a "modicum of caution". Therefore, stylisticians acknowledge that their interpretations may be challenged, but their methods leave no doubt as to how they were derived and therefore facilitate scholarly debate. Because of the reliance on textual (as opposed to extratextual) features, the interpretations that arise from stylistic analysis are more conventional and, usually, more widely acceptable amongst speakers of that language (Shen 1988). Research has shown that differences in textual interpretations are often over specifics, while higher-order interpretations are widely consistent amongst readers (Short et al. 2011). Therefore, interpretations derived from stylistic analysis can lay claim to a degree of objectivity.

10.3.3.3 Aiming for Objectivity

Interpretations about what language *means* are never wholly objective nor definitive (Toolan 1990/1996, 2014a). Even in the hard sciences, many disciplines struggle to pin down absolute objective facts (Jeffries 2000), so to impose such a remit on Stylistics is to demand the impossible. Yet acknowledging the impossibility of wholesale objectivity does not mean that stylistic analysis should not at least *aim* to provide clear and systematic interpretations of texts. McIntyre and Walker (2019: 127) state the case compellingly:

> The only alternative to this objective approach is to make subjective assertions and to argue through force of rhetoric. The problem with this is that subjective assertions are unfalsifiable. They are not open to being proved wrong so we can never know whether a subjective assertion is accurate or not. The alternative to the objective approach, then, is no alternative at all.

As stated in ▶ Sect. 10.1, leaving your methods, analyses and interpretations clear enough to be falsifiable, to be at least up for debate, is the path to objectivity in Stylistics. These disciplinary debates have practical implications for the Stylistics scholar; always try to provide evidence for your interpretations based on:

- features in the co-text; evidence for interpreting a particular feature in a certain way may be found in the text around the feature; evidence for a particular reading can accumulate i.e. 'coherence of foregrounding' (Leech 2008: 64)
- corpus evidence, which can provide evidence of how words/phrases are typically used, though concordances and collocations;
- other sources—readers, including academic ones (literary critics or stylisticians) and non-academic ones (the reading public)—whose interpretations may be relevant to your research.

The next section outlines how the latter two sources of evidence, as well as the rise in cognitivism, provide additional means for advancing interpretations in stylistic analysis.

10.3.4 Supporting Interpretations: Corpora, Cognition and 'Real' Readers

O'Halloran rightfully suggests that Fish's criticisms "should force stylisticians to try to think about how the discipline can be made *more* rigorous and systematic" (2007: 242, our emphasis). O'Halloran's (2007) study, for example, uses a corpus to identify keywords in Joyce's story *Eveline* which are then analysed qualitatively. When a corpus is used in this way (like several examples in this book), it can provide a principled basis for identifying and describing foregrounded features, reduce the potential for arbitrariness and circularity, and produce "interpretations that have been constrained in a principled way" (O'Halloran 2007: 242). As mentioned above, consulting corpora for the common usage of a form can support interpretations about its marked use in a text.

10.3.4.1 Acknowledging and Managing Subjectivity

While objectivity is the aim of the stylistic method, textual interpretation involves some degree of subjectivity and, therefore, it is perfectly acceptable in Stylistics to acknowledge your subjectivity. Such an approach may seem alien to scholars with a background in literary criticism where opaque and unique readings are valued, yet the critic's subjectivity is rarely examined and often obscured. In practice, this approach means you may well include first-person reference in your written work to refer to your methodological decision-making (▶ Sect. 10.1) or to recognise that some aspects of your interpretation may be personal (although refer to the cognitive stylistic models below which provide frameworks for considering reader's subjectivity).

Recognising our subjectivity as analysts not only dispels the criticism levelled at Stylistics for feigned objectivity, but also fits with changing emphases in the discipline. Stylistics has expanded from the formalist, text-centred approach of the early days to increasingly appreciate the context of discourse and, consequently, our role in it as analysts. Over the decades, stylisticians have interrogated the processes of interpretation, often through **empirical** means (that is, by gathering evidence). For example, Short and Van Peer carried out a reading experiment on themselves, finding that interpretation "crucially hinges on expectancies created by linguistic and [cognitive] means" (1989/2017: 168). Their study, which predates the cognitive and empirical turns in the discipline, demonstrates that interpretation depends on cognitive processes and can be investigated empirically. Cognitive Stylistics inherently acknowledges the role of individual, mental processes in reading and interpreting texts. Gavins states:

> Cognitive approaches to literary analysis […] attempt to explain the conceptual processes which may underlie existing consensual responses. […] [I]n the past, formal and functional stylistics may have sacrificed a proper account of these common reading patterns through a focus on the text at the expense of context, the influence of which can itself only be fully understood as a cognitive phenomenon.
>
> Gavins (2012: 360)

Therefore, Gavins contends that understanding the context of the reading experience demands a cognitive approach. Several frameworks outlined in this textbook provide scholars with a robust means for discussing the role of reader cognition in interpretation. Schema Theory provides a mechanism for explaining how readers elaborate on textual cues using memories and experiences, personal and socially shared (▶ Chapter 1; see also Semino 1997). Stockwell (2010) emphasises the affective dimension of schematic experience, whereby deeply personal and individual aspects of experience, such as physical sensations or emotions, can be relived when schemas are activated; this position, informed by the concept of **embodiment** in the cognitive sciences, views reading and interpretation as part of a holistic experience engaging the mind, body and text. In Text World Theory (▶ Chapter 2), the reader is implicitly recognised as a discourse participant involved in shaping the text-world. Text-world analyses, then, often reference the role of the reader, be that the analyst (e.g. Gavins 2016) or 'real' readers (e.g. Whiteley 2016).

10.3.4.2 Reader Response

If Stylistics scholars want to make claims about the effects of textual styles, investigating real readers' responses seems like an obvious route, yet is one that was not widely explored in Stylistics' history. However, reader response research is now on the rise, as evidenced by two special issues in the field's main journal *Language and Literature* dedicated the subject (Swann and Allington 2009; Whiteley and Canning 2017) and an edited volume (Bell et al. 2022). Scholars have gathered reader responses online (Gavins 2013; Lugea 2013; Whiteley 2016; Nuttall 2018), from reading group discussions (Bell et al. 2018; Canning 2017; Peplow et al. 2016; Whiteley 2011), or by using questionnaires (van Peer 2001; Bell et al. 2019) or from experimental methods. Some of these methods are easier to deploy than others and each has their merits. The issue of real readers' responses may have been neglected for so long due to the methodological challenges of accessing readers' 'black box' (Keen 2011: 295), the hidden cognitive processes involved in reading. As Hall (2008) observes, when the researcher tries to capture readers' natural processes and responses, the experiment can invalidate the experience. Despite the methodological challenges it presents, the rise of reader response research demonstrates Stylistics' dedication to understanding interpretation empirically. It goes hand in glove with the rise in Cognitive Stylistics, which focuses on the reader's experience of a text.

It is our contention that by combining cognitive and corpus approaches, the stylistician can both (a) reduce the danger of arbitrary and circular analyses, and (b) account for individual interpretations by considering the role of personal cognitive experience and processes.

10.4 Writing a Stylistics Paper

In this section, we discuss the process of writing a Stylistics paper and suggest a structure for the work. The advice applies to written work in Stylistics regardless of length, from essays to articles, dissertations and theses; consequently, we refer to the written work using the broad term 'paper'.

> Essentially, stylistics is work. You have to have some training in what you're doing, and you have to go through the actual difficult process of sketching the analysis with a pencil or keyboard, or running a concordance or database search [...] before you can then do the hard intellectual work of adapting this material for literary analysis. A stylistic analysis is not simply something that you can have an opinion about – there is a basic level at which you simply have to do it right. Of course, there is a lot more ideology, argument and interpretation built on top of that.
>
> Stockwell and Whiteley (2014: 609)

10.4.1 Preparation

The real 'work' of Stylistics takes place before writing begins (Stockwell and Whiteley 2014). You should use your research ideas to formulate a global research question, or a hypothesis. When considering how the global research question can be answered, you may also devise several local research questions, which can help to make practical methodological decisions. Even before you have fully devised a methodology, it is advisable to experiment by trying out a pilot analysis on a small amount of text. This allows you to test the feasibility of your methods, whether there is a good 'fit' between your analytical approach and the text, and how much data you might need to meet your research aims, within the constraints of the project.

10.4.2 Structure

For linguists, the term **genre** refers to texts that occur in a typical setting and which adhere to particular conventions in form and content. Bitchener (2010) approaches Applied Linguistics dissertations as a genre, providing invaluable sug-

Fig. 10.3 Typical structure of a Stylistics paper

Structure (with bullet points for each section):

- **Introduction**
  - Introduce the text(s) you analyse
  - Introduce the approach you take including the analytical models with references
  - Set out your hypotheses or research question(s)/aim(s)
  - Provide context for the research (i.e. why bother?)

- **Literature Review**
  - Provide an overview of relevant academic scholarship
  - Describe your chosen model(s), define terms and reference sources
  - Weigh up and evaluate sources
  - Summarise primary text(s) for analysis and any relevant secondary scholarship

- **Methodology**
  - Justification of research design and data selection
  - Depending on complexity of your chosen methods, this may be a section in its own right, or subsumed into Literature Review

- **Analysis**
  - Also called discussion and/or findings
  - Forms the bulk of a stylistics paper
  - Application of models to data
  - Identify, describe, interpret
  - May bring in concepts from other sources to analyse data

- **Conclusion**
  - Summarise findings in relation to original research question/aim(s)
  - Consider significance of findings for our understanding of the text and of theory/model(s).
  - Identify limitations of study and areas for future research

- **Appendices**
  - Supplementary materials
  - Data too long to be included in the paper can be included here.
  - Research instruments (e.g. questionnaires)

gestions for form and content, to which we direct scholars who are writing up longer projects. He addresses the fact that established academics tend to assume students will absorb genre-based knowledge from reading in the field. While there may be some truth in that, given the interdisciplinarity of Stylistics, we deem it useful to lay bare some of the tacit norms of Stylistics writing, a genre in its own right. ◘ Figure 10.3 provides a sample structure of a Stylistics paper of any length. The section names are not obligatory and many Stylistics publications follow this structure without using the same section titles. The suggested sections are not equal in terms of length and significance, as described below. Readers interested in a clear and illustrative example of a Stylistics publication that uses the structure we describe below should seek out Mandala (2007).

The **introduction** and **conclusion** serve as bookends—shorter sections (e.g. a paragraph of an essay) that help orient the reader. It is best to leave writing these until last, when the content of the paper is fully defined, so that they can be more concise and persuasive. In the introduction, briefly state what you are going to do, which model(s) you will use, which text(s) you will analyse and what you will demonstrate through this. The introduction outlines research aims, which may include research questions and/or hypotheses to be addressed in the paper. You may also provide a brief context for the research, outlining why it is necessary and what it contributes. Do not worry about spoilers—you want your reader to know what is coming up.

The **literature review** is not a summary of the literary text(s) analysed, but instead refers to an overview of the *academic* scholarship relevant to your study. Of course, it may also be helpful to briefly describe the text(s) for analysis so that your reader has the necessary level of familiarity to be able to understand your subsequent analysis. This step is often overlooked by literature students, because literary scholarship is usually organised according to literary era and familiarity can be assumed. Understandings of your chosen texts within literary criticism can be outlined, forming a springboard for your stylistic analysis. The literature review should form a substantial share of your written work; it is where you demonstrate the breadth of your academic reading, through citations, as well the depth of your understanding, by describing the content. For Stylistics, this is invariably where the writer describes the chosen analytical models, citing who devised them and relevant research that has employed them. By defining the model(s)' categories and terminology in this section, the writer makes some headway towards **retrievable** research, which operates using clearly defined terms. Moreover, clarifying definitions early means the analysis section can be dedicated to applying the frameworks to the text(s). The literature review is an ideal opportunity to demonstrate a critical approach towards your reading. Being critical does not necessarily entail a negative attitude, but rather a capacity to compare and evaluate sources, always with a strong sense of your own research aims, drawing explicit links between others' scholarship and your own. For example, why is one model more appropriate for answering your research question than another? Why might a certain combination of models in tandem help to address your aims? How have other scholars approached this text and why is your approach necessary? In sum, the literature review provides the theoretical context for your study. It can be written prior to analysis, but findings may provide insights that need to be read/written in to the literature review.

The existence and length of a **methodology** section depends on the approach adopted. At the very least, a Stylistics methodology involves selecting model(s), text(s) and data from the text, so the researcher should explain the principles behind these choices (see Sects. 10.2.1 and 10.2.2). For some scholars, only a few statements are necessary, meaning these remarks can be subsumed into another section (e.g. the literature review) rather than meriting a section in their own right. If your methodology is more involved, your description should be too. Any use of corpus methods will inevitably demand an explanation of the design and purpose of the corpus, the tools used and approach adopted (e.g. keywords). The point of this section is to lay bare all the decision-making in the research design, providing justification and rationale for your choices, with reference to how they meet the research aim/questions. This way, the research meets the criterion of **replicability**, whereby scholars can replicate your methods in future research to compare results. It makes sense to design (and perhaps write some of) your methodology before embarking on a full-scale analysis. However, you may find that once you begin the analysis, there are adjustments to be made to your methods (e.g. selecting different data or another model to explain some relevant textual phenomenon you encounter), so a final version of the methodology might not be penned until after the analysis.

> **Focus 10.1: Traps to avoid in stylistic research**
> – **cherry picking**: selecting data that confirms a pre-held interpretation (see ▶ Sect. 10.2.3)
> – **feature-spotting**: labelling features in a text without further describing and interpreting their function (see ▶ Sect. 10.2; Giovanelli and Mason 2018: 5)
> – **interpretative positivism**: the practice of using linguistic descriptions to confirm ready-made interpretations (▶ Sect. 10.2.3, Simpson 1993: 103).

The **analysis**, sometimes called 'discussion and/or findings', should form the bulk of your written work in Stylistics. This is where the selected models are applied to the selected data, identifying marked features, describing them using the model's categories (and sometimes with reference to concepts from other sources) and interpreting their significance for textual meaning. As well as demanding detailed explanation, this is the real 'work' which lends the discipline its **rigour**. As suggested above, it is often useful to experiment with some stylistic analysis before writing your paper. In the preparatory analytical work, you may find that some patterns emerge. For example, you might find that for a certain character *other-characterisation* is generally negative while *self-characterisation* is generally positive. You can then use the patterns that emerge to structure the analysis section by paragraph or sub-section. In this way, the practical 'working-out' behind your analysis is re-organised into a more coherent narrative of your findings. Where a project deals with a lot of data such as when a framework is applied to the full extent of a longer text, the results can be summarised in a table or figure with a written explanation. For example, see our text-world analysis of a chapter from a novel that we presented in ▶ Chapter 2 (▶ Sect. 2.4.3). Similarly, where an analysis has provided quantitative data (e.g. frequencies of certain features), tables or graphs may help to present your findings alongside discussion. The overall organisation of a text and its context (i.e. discourse structure) can usefully be illustrated through diagrams. The main aim of the analysis section is to draw out any patterns that you found when applying the models to the text in preparatory work, so that the reader can better understand how it achieves stylistic effects (i.e. its style). Often, textual effects arise from an accumulation of features, so your argument can be based on cumulative evidence.

The **conclusion** should return to the research question(s) or hypothesis posed at the outset, considering if/how they were addressed by the methods and analysis. Researchers often consider what the findings mean for understandings of the text, but also what applying the models to the text(s) tells us about the theory and analytical apparatus. You might consider how the study could be replicated in a different context to explore certain aspects further. It is perfectly acceptable to acknowledge the limitations of the research and suggest how it can be developed in the future. This encourages **replicability** and a healthy sustainability in the discipline.

Any supplementary material can be included in an **appendix** where readers can peruse it should they want to investigate it further. If your data is too lengthy to be included in the body of your written work, it can be stored in an appendix and referred to (e.g. Appendix A). More experimental Stylistics, such as reader response research, might also include sample questionnaires or other research instruments in appendices.

10.5 Summary

The aim of stylistic analysis is to explain how texts 'work' and how their language leads to particular stylistic (poetic) effects. In this chapter, we have brought together the stylistic toolkit we introduced in preceding chapters and discussed how to apply it to a text. Our aim was to explain to readers how they can go about doing a Stylistics project. We introduced the idea of falsification and explained that any work in Stylistics should be falsifiable, meaning it centres on clear hypotheses or research questions that are testable. We then provided guidance for choosing a text and the tools to analyse it. A key point here is that your data and tools for analysis should be a good fit; there is no point using Conversation Analysis on a text that has no dialogue. This point, however, does not preclude innovation in stylistic analysis and the application of tools in new and original ways. We went on to discuss how to formulate research questions, which are an important step in any Stylistics project. Research questions help to guide your project from the outset but can develop and change as the project progresses. Data selection can be crucial in a Stylistics project, especially when choosing an extract from a text too lengthy to be practically analysed. Thinking about which data to use and avoiding 'cherry picking' is important for any research and something that needs to be clearly described and explained in the project write-up. One way in which data can be selected is using corpus tools as these can provide a quantitative 'way in' to longer texts and provide a focus for analysis. Corpora and corpus tools can also help to support intuitions about language use in a text, which can be invaluable for bolstering any claims you are making about a text. Additionally, corpus approaches can be invaluable for recording detailed qualitative analysis via tagging/annotation, which can make further quantitative analysis possible. A large section of this chapter was devoted to discussing the process of stylistic analysis which can be distilled down to three steps: identify, describe and interpret. Each of these steps requires a further wholly essential trinity: rigour, retrievability and replicability. In combination, these help the stylistician aim for objectivity, manage subjectivity and avoid entanglement in the 'Fish net'. We argue that the combination of cognitive and corpus approaches both reduces the potential for arbitrariness and circularity in analysis and increases awareness of individual interpretations and personal cognitive experiences and processes. The final section of this chapter was devoted to the writing and layout of a Stylistics paper. Stylistics papers aim for clarity and openness and should guide the reader through the data selection, the tools for analysis, the analytical method, the results, the eventual interpretation and conclusion. A paper in Stylistics, like the discipline itself, should provide an understanding or interpretation of a text, and explain how that interpretation was arrived at, with reference to textual and—where relevant—contextual features.

- **Further Reading**

McIntyre, D. and Walker, B. 2019. Testing Hypotheses and Answering Research Questions. In *Corpus Stylistics: Theory and Practice*, eds. D. McIntyre and B. Walker, 111–142. Edinburgh: Edinburgh University Press.

Bitchener, J. 2010. *Writing an Applied Linguistics Thesis or Dissertation: A Guide to Presenting Empirical Research*. Houndmills, Basingstoke: Palgrave Macmillan.

Leech, G. and Short, M. 2007. A Method of Analysis and Some Examples. In *Style in Fiction: A Linguistic Introduction to English Fictional Prose*, eds. Leech and Short, 2nd edition, 60–94. London: Longman.

Jeffries, L. and McIntyre, D. 2010. Methods and Issues in Stylistic Analysis. In *Stylistics*, eds. L. Jeffries and D. McIntyre, 170–190. Cambridge: Cambridge University Press.

This book has focused on text, the verbal code, because that holds primacy in Stylistics. Nonetheless, scholars who want to consider other semiotic modes (i.e. still images, digital, audio-visual or performance elements) will find the means to do so by referring to the burgeoning body of work in:
- telecinematic Stylistics (Piazza et al. 2011; Bednarek 2011, 2018; Toolan 2014b; Hoffman and Kirner-Ludwig 2020);
- multimodal Stylistics (Nørgaard 2010, 2011, 2014, 2018);
- the Stylistics of contemporary media (Ringrow and Pihlaja 2020);
- digital and experimental literature (Gibbons 2012; Bray et al. 2012; Bell et al. 2014);
- comics (Forceville et al. 2014); and
- music (West 2019).

While Stylistics embraces discourses beyond the written mode, they too must be approached with the same rigour, using suitable analytical frameworks. Relevant frameworks may be drawn from disciplines which routinely analyse non-textual modes, such as Semiotics, Multimodal Discourse Analysis and Film Studies.

References

Bednarek, M. 2011. *The Language of Fictional Television: Drama and Identity*. London and New York: Continuum.
Bednarek, M. 2018. *Language and Television Series: A Linguistic Approach to TV Dialogue*. Cambridge: Cambridge University Press.

Bell, A., Ensslin, A. and Rusted, H. K. 2014. *Analyzing Digital Fiction*. Abingdon and New York: Routledge.
Bell, A., Ensslin, A., van der Bom, I., Smith, J. 2018. Immersion in Digital Fiction. *International Journal of Literary Linguistics* 7, 1: 1–22.
Bell, A., Ensslin, A., van der Bom, I., Smith, J. 2019. A Reader Response Method Not Just for 'You'. *Language and Literature* 28, 3: 241–262.
Bell, A., Browse, S., Gibbons, A., and Peplow, D. (Eds.). 2022. *Style and Reader Response: Minds, Media, Methods*. Amsterdam and Philadelphia: John Benjamins.
Bitchener, J. 2010. *Writing an Applied Linguistics Thesis or Dissertation: A Guide to Presenting Empirical Research*. Houndmills, Basingstoke: Palgrave Macmillan.
Bray, J., Gibbons, A. and McHale, B. (Eds.). 2012. *The Routledge Companion to Experimental Literature*. London and New York: Routledge.
Canning, P. 2017. Text World Theory and Real World Readers: From Literature to Life in a Belfast Prison. *Language and Literature* 26, 2: 172–187.
Culpeper, J. 2001. *Language and Characterisation: People in Plays and Other Texts*. London: Longman.
Eve, M. P. 2020. Distance and Depth. Stanford University Press Blog. ▶ https://doi.org/eprints.bbk.ac.uk/30723/1/Distance%20and%20Depth%20-%20Stanford%20University%20Press%20Blog.pdf (Last accessed 22nd June 2020).
Fish, S. 1973/1996. What is Stylistics and Why are they Saying such Terrible Things About it? In *The Stylistics Reader: From Roman Jakobson to the Present*, ed. J.J. Weber, 94–116. London and New York: Arnold.
Fish, S. 1979. What is Stylistics and Why are they Saying such Terrible Things About it? Part II *boundary* 2, 8:1, The Problems of Reading in Contemporary American Criticism: Symposium (Autumn, 1979), 129–146.
Forceville, C., E. El Refaie, G. Meesters. 2014. Stylistics and Comics. In *The Routledge Handbook of Stylistics*, ed. M. Burke, 485–499. Abingdon and New York: Routledge.
Gavins, J. 2012. Leda and the Stylisticians. *Language and Literature* 21, 4: 345–362.
Gavins, J. 2013. *Reading the Absurd*. Edinburgh: Edinburgh University Press.
Gavins, J. 2016. Text-Worlds. In *The Bloomsbury Companion to Stylistics*, ed. V. Sotirova, 444–457. London and New York: Bloomsbury.
Gibbons, A. 2012. *Multimodality, Cognition and Experimental Literature*. London and New York: Bloomsbury.
Giovanelli, M. and Mason, J. 2018. *The Language of Literature: An Introduction to Stylistics*. Cambridge: Cambridge University Press.
Hall, G. 2008. Empirical Research into the Processing of Free Indirect Discourse and the Imperative of Ecological Validity. In *Directions in Empirical Literary Studies: in honour of Willie van Peer*, eds. S. Zyngier, M. Bortolussi, A. Chesnokova and J. Auracher, 21–34. Amsterdam and Philadelphia: John Benjamins.
Hoffman, C. and Kirner-Ludwig, M. (Eds.). 2020. *Telecinematic Stylistics. Advances in Stylistics series*. London and New York: Bloomsbury.
Jeffries, L. 2000. Don't Throw out the Baby with the Bathwater: In Defence of Theoretical Eclecticism in Stylistics. *PALA Occasional Papers*. ▶ https://www.pala.ac.uk/resources.html. Also at: ▶ https://www.researchgate.net/profile/Lesley_Jeffries/publication/237632531_Don't_throw_out_the_baby_with_the_bathwater_in_defence_of_theoretical_eclecticism_in_Stylistics/links/5703d-6dc08ae74a08e245861.pdf
Jeffries, L. and McIntyre, D. 2010. *Stylistics. Cambridge Studies in Linguistics*. Cambridge: Cambridge University Press.
Keen, S. 2011. Readers' Temperaments and Fictional Character. *New Literary History* 42, 2: 295–314.
Leech, G. 2008. *Language in Literature: Style and Foregrounding*. London and New York: Routledge.
Lugea, J. 2013. Embedded Dialogue and Dreams: The Worlds and Accessibility Relations of Inception. *Language and Literature* 22, 2: 133–153.
Mackay, R. 1996. Mything the Point: A Critique of Objective Stylistics. *Language and Communication* 16, 1: 81–93.

Mackay, R. 1999. There Goes the Other Foot—A Reply to Short et al. *Language and Literature* 8, 1: 59–66.

Mandala, S. 2007. Solidarity and the Scoobies: An Analysis of the -y Suffix in the Television Series *Buffy the Vampire Slayer. Language and Literature* 16, 1: 53–73.

McIntyre, D. 2006. *Point of View in Plays: A Cognitive Stylistic Approach to Viewpoint in Drama and other Text-Types.* Amsterdam and Philadelphia: John Benjamins.

McIntyre, D. and Walker, B. 2019. *Corpus Stylistics: Theory and Practice.* Edinburgh: Edinburgh University Press.

Nørgaard, N. 2010. Multimodality: Extending the Stylistic Tool-Kit. In *Language and Style*, eds. D. McIntyre and B. Busse, 433–448. Houndmills Basingstoke: Palgrave Macmillan.

Nørgaard, N. 2011. Multimodal Stylistics: The Happy Marriage of Stylistics and Semiotics. In *Semiotics: Theory and Applications*, ed. S.C. Hamel, 255–260. New York: Nova, pp255–260. Available at: ▶ http://www.nslbooks.com/arts/semiotics-theory-an-applications.pdf#page=271

Nørgaard, N. 2014. Multimodality and Stylistics. In *The Routledge Handbook of Stylistics*, ed. M. Burke, 471–484. Routledge: Abingdon and New York.

Nørgaard, N. 2018. *Multimodal Stylistics of the Novel: More than Words.* Abingdon and New York: Routledge.

Nuttall, L. 2018. *Mind Style and Cognitive Grammar: Language and World View in Speculative Fiction.* London and New York: Bloomsbury.

O'Halloran, K. 2007. The Subconscious in James Joyce's 'Eveline': A Corpus Stylistic Analysis that Chews on the 'Fish Hook'. *Language and Literature* 1, 3: 227–244.

Peplow, D., Swann, J., Trimarco, P., Whiteley, S. 2016. *The Discourse of Reading Groups: Integrating Cognitive and Sociocultural Perspectives.* London: Routledge.

Piazza, R., Bednarek, M. and Rossi, F. (Eds.). 2011. *Telecinematic Discourse: Approaches to the Language of Films and Television.* Amsterdam and Philadelphia: John Benjamins.

Popper, K. R. 1959. *The Logic of Scientific Discovery.* London: Hutchinson & Co. Ltd.

Ringrow, H. and Pihlaja, S. (Eds.). 2020. *Contemporary Media Stylistics.* London and New York: Bloomsbury.

Semino, E. 1997. Language and World Creation in Poems and Other Texts. London and New York: Longman.

Shen, D. 1988. Stylistics, Objectivity and Convention. *Poetics* 17, 3: 221–228.

Short, M. and Van Peer, W. 1989/2017. Accident! Stylisticians Evaluate: Aims and Methods of Stylistic Analysis. In *Stylistics* Vol 1: Theory, Method and History, ed. M Burke, 134–171. Abingdon and New York: Routledge.

Short, M. and Van Peer, W. 1999. A Reply to Mackay. *Language and Literature* 8, 3: 269–275.

Short, M., Freeman, D. C., van Peer, W. and Simpson, P. 1998. Stylistics, Criticism and Mythrepresentation Again: Squaring the Circle with Ray Mackay's Subjective Solution for all Problems. *Language and Literature* 7, 1: 39–50.

Short M, McIntyre D, Jeffries L and Bousfield D. 2011. Processes of Interpretation: Using Meta-Analysis to Inform Pedagogic Practice. In *Teaching Stylistics*, ed. L. Jeffries L and D McIntyre, 69–94. Basingstoke: Palgrave.

Simpson, P. 1993. *Language, Ideology and Point of View.* London and New York: Routledge.

Simpson, P. 2004. *Stylistics: A Resource Book for Students.* London and New York: Routledge.

Sotirova, V. 2016. Introduction: The Discipline of Stylistics. In *The Bloomsbury Companion to Stylistics*, ed V Sotirova, 3–18. London and New York: Bloomsbury.

Stockwell, P. 2010. The Eleventh Checksheet of the Apocalypse. In *Language and Style*, eds. D. McIntyre and B. Busse, 419–432. Basingstoke: Palgrave Macmillan.

Stockwell, P. and Whiteley, S. 2014. Coda: The Practice of Stylistics. In *The Cambridge Handbook of Stylistics*, eds. P. Stockwell and S. Whiteley, 607–615. Cambridge: Cambridge University Press.

Swann, J. and Allington, D. 2009. Literary Reading as Social Practice. *Language and Literature*, 18, 3: 217–344.

Toolan, M. 1990/1996. Stylistics and its Discontents: Or, Getting off the Fish 'Hook'. In *The Stylistics Reader: From Roman Jakobson to the Present,* ed. J.J. Weber, 117–135. London and New York: Arnold.

References

Toolan, M. 2014a. The Theory and Philosophy of Stylistics. In *The Cambridge Handbook of Stylistics*, eds. P. Stockwell and S. Whiteley, 13–31. Cambridge: Cambridge University Press.

Toolan, M. 2014b. Stylistics and Film. In *The Routledge Handbook of Stylistics*, ed. M. Burke, 455–470. London and New York: Routledge.

van Peer, W. 2001. Justice in Perspective. In *New Perspectives on Narrative Perspective*, eds. W. van Peer, and S. Chatman, 325–338. New York: State University of New York Press.

Wales, K. 2014. The Stylistic Tool-Kit: Methods and Sub-disciplines. In *The Cambridge Handbook of Stylistics*, P. Stockwell and S. Whiteley, 32–45. Cambridge: Cambridge University Press.

West, D. (Ed.) 2019. *Language and Literature*, Special Issue: Song Lyrics, 28: 1.

Whiteley, S. 2011. Text World Theory, Real Readers and Emotional Responses to *The Remains of the Day*. *Language and Literature* 20, 1: 23–41.

Whiteley, S. 2016. Building Resonant Worlds: Experiencing the Text-worlds of *The Unconsoled*. In *World Building: Discourse in the Mind*, eds. J. Gavins and E. Lahey, 165–182. London and New York: Bloomsbury.

Whiteley, S. and Canning, P. (Eds.). 2017. Special issue: Stylistic Approaches to Reader Response Research. *Language and Literature*. 26, 2: 71–187.

Supplementary Information

© The Editor(s) (if applicable) and The Author(s), under exclusive licence to Springer Nature Switzerland AG 2023
J. Lugea and B. Walker, *Stylistics*, https://doi.org/10.1007/978-3-031-10422-0

References

Abse, D., (Ed.). 2015. *Favourite Love Poems*. London: Pavillion Books.
Aijmer, K., & Rühleman, C. (Eds.). (2014). *Corpus Pragmatics: A handbook*. Cambridge: CUP.
Alber, J. 2016. Absurd Catalogues: The Functions of Lists in Postmodernist Fiction Author(s). *Style* 50 3: 342–358.
Anand, H. R. 1947 [1935]. *Untouchable: A Novel*. London: Hutchinson International Authors.
Anthony, L. 2022. *AntConc* (Version 4.2.0) [Computer Software]. Tokyo, Japan: Waseda University. Available from ▶ https://www.laurenceanthony.net/software
Archer, D. and Bousfield, D. 2010. 'See Better, Lear'? See Lear Better! A Corpus-Based Pragma-Stylistic Investigation of Shakespeare's *King Lear*. In *Language and Style*, eds. D. McIntyre, and B. Busse, 183–203. Basingstoke: Palgrave.
Attardo, S. 1994. *Linguistic Theories of Humor*. Berlin, New York: Mouton de Gruyter.
Attardo, S. 1997. The Semantic Foundations of Cognitive Theories of Humor. *Humor: The International Journal of Humor Research* 10, 4: 395–420.
Attardo, S. 2000. Irony as Relevant Inappropriateness. *Journal of Pragmatics* 32: 793–826.
Attardo, S. 2001. *Humorous Texts: A Semantic and Pragmatic Analysis*. Berlin and New York: Mouton de Gruyter.
Attardo, S. 2002. Cognitive Stylistics of Humorous Texts. In *Cognitive Stylistics: Language and Cognition in Text Analysis*, eds. E. Semino and J. Culpeper, 231–250. Amsterdam and Philadelphia: John Benjamins.
Attardo, S. 2015. Humorous Metaphors. In *Cognitive Linguistics and Humor Research*, eds. G. Brône, K. Feyaerts and T. Veale, 91-110. Berlin and New York: Mouton de Gruyter.
Attardo, S. and V Raskin 1991. Script Theory revis(it)ed: Joke Similarity and Joke Representation Model. *Humor: International Journal of Humor Research* 4, 3/4: 293–347.
Attardo, S., Hempelmann, C. F. and DiMaio, S. 2002. Script Oppositions and Logical Mechanisms: Modeling Incongruities and their Resolutions, *Humor* 15, 1: 3–46.
Austen, J. 1816. *Emma*. London: John Murray.
Austin, J. L. 1979. Performative Utterances. In *Philosophical Papers* 3rd ed, eds. J. O. Urmson and G. J. Warnock, 233–252. Oxford University Press.
Bal, M. 1997. *Narratology*. 2nd ed. Toronto: University of Toronto Press.
Bartlett, F. C. 1932. *Remembering*. Cambridge: Cambridge University Press.
Beckett, S. 1955. *Molloy*. Trans. by P. Bowles. New York: Grove Press.
Bednarek, M. 2018. *Language and Television Series: A Linguistic Approach to TV Dialogue*. Cambridge: Cambridge University Press.
Bednarek, M. 2011. *The Language of Fictional Television: Drama and Identity*. London and New York: Continuum.
Bednarek, M. 2012. Constructing Nerdiness: Characterisation in The Big Bang Theory, *Multilingua* 31, 199–229.
Bednarek, M. 2008. Semantic Preference and Semantic Prosody Re-Examined. *Corpus Linguistics and Linguistic Theory* 4, 2: 119–139.
Beecher Stowe, H. 1852. *Uncle Tom's Cabin*. Boston: John P. Jewett.
Bell, A. and Ensslin, A. 2011. "I Know what it was. You know what it was": Second-Person Narration in Hypertext Fiction. *Narrative* 19, 3: 311–329. Also available at: ▶ https://s3.amazonaws.com/academia.edu.documents/46441189/Bell_and_Ensslin_2011_Narrative.pdf?AWSAccessKeyId=AKIAIWOWYYGZ2Y53UL3A&Expires=1548344587&Signature=JAZdGQtD396L5DQMuGTl7nVC%2B%2FI%3D&response-content-disposition=inline%3B%20filename%3DI_know_what_it_was._You_know_what_it_was.pdf (Last accessed: 24th January 2019).
Bell, A., Ensslin, A., van der Bom, I., Smith, J. 2019. A Reader Response Method not Just for 'You'. *Language and Literature* 28, 3: 241–262.
Bell, A., Ensslin, A. and Rusted, H. K. 2014. *Analyzing Digital Fiction*. Abingdon and New York: Routledge.

References

Bell, A., Browse, S., Gibbons, A., and Peplow, D. (Eds.). 2022. *Style and Reader Response: Minds, Media, Methods*. Amsterdam and Philadelphia: John Benjamins.
Bell, A., Ensslin, A., van der Bom, I., Smith, J. 2018. Immersion in Digital Fiction. *International Journal of Literary Linguistics* 7, 1: 1–22.
Bernlef, J. 1988. *Out of Mind*. Trans. by A. Dixon. London and Boston: Faber and Faber.
Berenguer, C., Rosello, B., Baixauli, I., García, R. and Miranda, A. 2020. Theory of Mind Profiles in Children With Autism Spectrum Disorder: Adaptive/Social Skills and Pragmatic Competence. *Frontiers in Psychology*. 11: 567401. ▶ https://doi.org/10.3389/fpsyg.2020.567401
Biber, D., Johansson, S., Leech, G., Conrad, S., and Finegan, E. 1999. *The Longman Grammar of Spoken and Written English*. London: Longman.
Bitchener, J. 2010. *Writing an Applied Linguistics Thesis or Dissertation: A Guide to Presenting Empirical Research*. Houndmills, Basingstoke: Palgrave Macmillan.
Billig, M. 2005 *Laughter and Ridicule: Towards a Social Critique of Humour*. London: Sage.
Black, M. 1955. Metaphor *Proceedings of the Aristotelian Society, New Series, Vol. 55* (1954–1955), 273-294 Oxford University Press
Black, M. 1962. *Models and Metaphors*. Ithaca, N.Y.: Cornell University Press
Black, M. 1977. More about Metaphor *Dialectica* 31, 3/4: 431–457
Bockting, I. 1995. *Character and Personality in the Novels of William Faulkner*. Lanham, New York and London: University of America Press.
Booth, W. C. 1974. *A Rhetoric of Irony*. Chicago and London: University of Chicago Press.
Booth, W. C. 1961. *The Rhetoric of Fiction*. Chicago and London: University of Chicago Press.
Bortolussi, M. and Dixon, P. 2002. *Psychonarratology: Foundations for the Empirical Study of Literary Response*.
Bortolussi, M. and Dixon, P. 2003. *Psychonarratology: Foundations for the Empirical Study of Literary Response*. Cambridge and New York: Cambridge University Press.
Bousfield, D. 2007. "Never a Truer Word Said in Jest": A Pragmastylistic Analysis of Impoliteness as Banter in Henry IV, part I. In *Contemporary Stylistics*, eds. M. Lambrou and P. Stockwell, 209–220. London: Continuum.
Bradley, A. C. 2007 [1904]. *Shakespearean Tragedy: Lectures on Hamlet, Othello, King Lear, MacBeth. 4th Edition*. London: Palgrave.
Bray, J. 2007a. The Effects of Free Indirect Discourse: Empathy Revisited. In *Contemporary Stylistics*, eds. M. Lambrou and P. Stockwell, 56–67. London: Continuum.
Bray, J. 2007b. The "Dual Voice" of Free Indirect Discourse: A Reading Experiment, *Language and Literature* 16, 1: 37–52.
Bray, J., Gibbons, A. and McHale, B. eds. 2012. *The Routledge Companion to Experimental Literature*. London and New York: Routledge.
Brock, E. 1977. *Song of the Battery Hen: Selected Poems, 1959–75*. London: Secker and Warburg.
Brontë, C. [Currer Bell]. 1847. *Jane Eyre: An Autobiography*. London: Smith, Elder & Co.
Brontë, E. [Ellis Bell]. 1847. *Wuthering Heights*. London: Thomas Cautley Newby.
Brown, G. 1990. *Listening to Spoken Discourse*. 2nd ed. London: Longman.
Bühler, K. 2011 [1934]. *Theory of Language: The Representational Function of Language*. Trans. by D. F. Goodwin. Amsterdam: John Benjamins.
Burke, M., ed. 2017. *Stylistics. Vol 1. Critical Concepts in Linguistics*. London and New York: Routledge.
Burke, M. 2014. Rhetoric and Poetics: The Classical Heritage of Stylistics. In *The Routledge Handbook of Stylistics*, ed. M. Burke, 11–30. London and New York: Routledge.
Burrows, J. F. 1986. Modal Verbs and Moral Principles: An Aspect of Jane Austen's Style. *Literary and Linguistic Computing* 1,1: 9–23.
Burrows, J. F. 1987. *Computation into Criticism. A Study of Jane Austen's Novels and an Experiment in Method*. Oxford: Clarendon.
Busse, B. 2010. *Speech, Writing and Thought Presentation in a Corpus of Nineteenth-Century English Narrative Fiction*. Bern: University of Bern.
Caldwell, L. 2013. *All the Beggars Riding*. London: Faber and Faber.
Cameron, L. and Deignan, A. 2003. Combining Large and Small Corpora to Investigate Tuning Devices Around Metaphor in Spoken Discourse. *Metaphor and Symbol* 18, 3: 149–160.

Canning, P. 2014. Functionalist Stylistics. In *The Routledge Handbook of Stylistics*, ed. M. Burke, 45–67. London and New York: Routledge.

Canning, P. 2017. Text World Theory and Real World Readers: From Literature to Life in a Belfast Prison. *Language and Literature* 26, 2: 172–187.

Canning, P., Ho, Y. and Bartl, S. 2021. Worlds of Evidence: Visualising Patterns in Witness Statements in the Aftermath of the Hillsborough Football Stadium Disaster. *English Text Construction* 14, 1: 25–67

Carston, R. and Wearing, C. 2015. Hyperbolic Lnguage and its Rrelation to Metaphor and Irony. *Journal of Pragmatics* 79: 79–92.

Carter, R. and Simpson, P. 1989. Introduction. In *Language, Discourse and Literature: An Introductory Reader in Discourse Stylistics*, eds. R. Carter and P. Simpson, 1–21. London and New York: Routledge.

Charteris-Black, J. 2004. *Corpus Approaches to Critical Metaphor Analysis*. Basingstoke Palgrave Macmillan.

Charteris-Black, J. 2014. *Analysing Political Speeches: Rhetoric, Discourse and Metaphor*. Basingstoke: Palgrave Macmillan.

Charteris-Black, J. 2017. All-Consuming Passions: Fire Metaphors. Fiction. *E-rea: Revue Électronique d'Études sur le Monde Anglophone*, 15. ▶ https://doi.org/10.4000/erea.5992

Chatman, S. 1978. *Story and Discourse: Narrative Structure in Fiction and Film*. Ithaca: Cornell University Press.

Chatman, S. 1986. Characters and Narrators: Filter, Center, Slant, and Interest Focus. *Poetics Today* 7, 2: 189–204.

Chatman, S. 1990. *Coming to Terms: The Rhetoric of Narrative in Fiction and in Film*. Ithaca, NY: Cornell University Press

Clark, H. H. and Gerrig, R. J. 1984. On the Pretense Theory of Irony. *Journal of Experimental Psychology* 113, 1: 121–126.

Coates, J. 1983. *The Semantics of Modal Auxiliaries*. London: Croom Helm.

Cohn, D. H. 1978. *Transparent Minds: Narrative Modes for Presenting Consciousness in Fiction*. Princeton University Press

Colebrook, C. 2004. *Irony*. London: Routledge.

Cook, G. 1994. *Discourse and Literature*. Oxford: Oxford University Press.

Cruikshank, T. and Lahey, E. 2010. Building the Stages of Drama: Towards a Text World Theory Account of Dramatic Play-Texts. *Journal of Literary Semantics* 39, 1: 67–91.

Crystal, D. 2008. *Dictionary of Linguistics and Phonetics*. John Wiley & Sons, Incorporated

Culpeper, J. 1998. Inferring Character from Texts: Attribution Theory and Foregrounding Theory. *Poetics* 23: 335–361.

Culpeper, J. 2001. *Language and Characterisation: People in Plays and Other Texts*. London: Longman.

Culpeper, J. 2002. Computers, Language and Characterisation: An Analysis of Six Characters in Romeo and Juliet. In *Conversation in Life and in Literature: Papers from the ASLA Symposium, Association Suedoise de Linguistique Appliquee (ASLA)*, 15, eds. U. Melander-Marttala, C. Ostman, and M. Kytö, 11–30. Universitetstryckeriet: Uppsala.

Culpeper, J. 2005. Impoliteness and Entertainment in the Television Quiz Show: 'The Weakest Link'. *Journal of Politeness Research* 1, 1: 35–72.

Culpeper, J. 2009. Keyness: Words, Parts-of-speech and Semantic Categories in the Character-Talk of Shakespeare's Romeo and Juliet. *International Journal of Corpus Linguistics* 14, 1: 29–59.

Culpeper, J. 2011. *Impoliteness: Using Language to Cause Offence*. Cambridge: CUP

Culpeper, J., & Archer, D. 2008. Requests and Directness in Early Modern English Trial Proceedings and Play-Texts, 1640–1760. In *Speech Acts in the History of English*, Eds. A. H. Jucker, & I. Taavitsainen, 45–84). Amsterdam: John Benjamins.

Culpeper, J., Kyto, M. 1999. Modifying Pragmatic Force: Hedges in a Corpus of Early Modern English Dialogues. In: *Historical dialogue analysis*, Eds. A. J. H. Jucker, G. Fritz, F. Lebsanft, 293–312. Amsterdam: John Benjamins.

Curtis, R. and Elton, B. 1989. *Blackadder Goes Forth*. BBC.

Dancygier, B. (ed.). 2017. *The Cambridge Handbook of Cognitive Linguistics*. Cambridge: Cambridge University Press.

References

Dancygier, B. and Vandelanotte, L. 2017. Viewpoint Phenomena in Multimodal Communication. *Cognitive Linguistics* 28, 371–380.
De Beaugrande, R. A. 1980. *Text, Discourse and Process. Advances in Discourse Processes, Vol. IV*, edited by RO Freedle. Norwood, NJ: Ablex Publishing.
DelConte, M. 2003. Why You Can't Speak: Second-Person Narration, Voice, and a New Model for Understanding Narrative. *Style* 37, 2: 204–219.
Deignan, A. 2005. *Metaphor and Corpus Linguistics*. Amsterdam and Philadelphia: John Benjamins Publishing,
Deignan, A. H. 2016. From Linguistic to Conceptual Metaphors. In *The Routledge Handbook of Metaphor and Language*, eds. E. Semino and Z. Demjen, 102–116. London: Routledge.
Demjén, Z. 2015. *Sylvia Plath and the Language of Affective States: Written Discourse and the Experience of Depression*. London: Bloomsbury.
D'hoker, E. and Martens, G. (Eds.). 2008. *Narrative Unreliability in the Twentieth-Century First-Person Novel*. Berlin: Walter De Gruyter.
Dore, M. 2015. Metaphor, Humour and Characterization in the TV Comedy Programme Friends. In *Cognitive Linguistics and Humor Research* eds. G. Brône, K. Feyaerts, and T. Veale, 191–214. Berlin and New York: Mouton de Gruyter.
Douthwaite, J. 2000. *Towards a Linguistic Theory of Foregrounding*. Alessandria: Edizioni dell'Orso.
Doyle, R. 1993. *Paddy Clarke Ha Ha Ha*. London: Minerva.
Duchan, J. F., Bruder, G. A. and Hewitt, I. E. eds. 1995. *Deixis in Narrative: A Cognitive Science Perspective*. Hillsdale: Lawrence Erlbaum Associates.
Dutta Flanders, R. 2015. *The Language of Suspense in Crime Fiction: A Linguistic Stylistic Approach*. Houndsmills, Basingstoke: Palgrave.
Dynel, M. 2011. "I'll be there for you!" On Participation-Based Sitcom Humour. In *The Pragmatics of Humour Across Discourse Domains*, ed. M. Dynel, 33–50. Amsterdam and Philadelphia: John Benjamins Publishing.
Dynel, M. 2016. Conceptualising Conversational Humour as (im)politeness: The Case of Film Talk. *Journal of Politeness Research* 12, 1: 117–146.
Eder, J., Jannidis, F. and Schneider, R. 2010. *Characters in Fictional Worlds: Understanding Imaginary Being in Literature, Film, and other Media*. Berlin: De Gruyter.
Ehlich, K. 1982. Anaphora and Deixis: Same, Similar, or Different? In *Speech, Place and Action: Studies in Deixis and Related Topics*, eds. R. J. Jarvella and W. Klein, 315–338. New York: John Wiley & Sons.
Emmott, C. and Alexander, M. 2016. Defamiliarization and Foregrounding: Representing Experiences of Change of State and Perception in Neurological Illness Autobiographies. In *The Bloomsbury Companion to Stylistics*, ed. V. Sotirova, 289–307. London and New York: Bloomsbury.
Enkvist, N. 1973. *Linguistic Stylistics*. The Hague: Mouton.
Evans, V. 2019. *Cognitive Linguistics: A Complete Guide*. Edinburgh: Edinburgh University Press.
Evans, V. and Green, M. 2006. *Cognitive Linguistics: An Introduction*. Edinburgh: Edinburgh University Press.
Eve, M. P. 2020. Distance and Depth. Stanford University Press Blog. ▶ https://doi.org/eprints.bbk. ac.uk/30723/1/Distance%20and%20Depth%20Stanford%20University%20Press%20Blog.pdf (Last accessed 22nd June 2020).
Eysenck, M. W. and Keane, M. 2002. *Cognitive Psychology: A Student's Handbook*. London: Routledge.
Fahnestock, J. 2016. Rhetorical Stylistics. *Language and Literature* 14, 3: 215–230.
Feyaerts, K., Brône, G. and Ceukelaire, R. 2015. The Art of Teasing: A Corpus Study of Teasing Sequences in American Sitcoms between 1990 and 1999. In *Cognitive Linguistics and Humor Research*, eds. G. Brône, K. Feyaerts and T. Veale, 215–242. Berlin: De Gruyter Mouton.
Firth, J. R. 1957. *Papers in Linguistics, 1934–1951*. Oxford: Oxford University Press.
Fischer-Starke, B. 2010. *Corpus Linguistics in Literary Analysis*. London: Continuum
Fish, S. 1973/1996. What is Stylistics and Why are they Saying such Terrible Things About it? In *The Stylistics Reader: From Roman Jakobson to the Present*, ed. J.J. Weber, 94–116. London and New York: Arnold.
Fish, S. 1979. What is Stylistics and Why are they Saying such Terrible Things About it? Part II *boundary 2*, 8:1, The Problems of Reading in Contemporary American Criticism: Symposium (Autumn, 1979), 129–146.

Fitzgerald, F. S. 1925/2004. *The Great Gatsby*. New York and London: Scribner.
Fludernik, M. 1993a. Second Person Fiction: Narrative You as Addressee and/or Protagonist. *AAA: Arbeiten aus Anglistik und Amerikanistik* 18, 2: 217–247. Also available at: ▶ https://d-nb.info/1123430284/34 (Last accessed: 24th January 2019).
Fludernik, M. 1993b. *The Fictions of Language and the Languages of Fiction: The Linguistic Representation of Speech and Consciousness*. London: Routledge.
Forceville, C. and Urios-Aparisi E., (Eds.). 2009. *Multimodal Metaphor*. Berlin: Mouton de Gruyter.
Forceville, C., E. El Refaie, G. Meesters. 2014. Stylistics and Comics. In *The Routledge Handbook of Stylistics*, ed. M. Burke, 485–499. Abingdon and New York: Routledge.
Fowler, R. 1977. *Linguistics and the Novel*. London: Methuen.
Fowler, R. 1986/1996. *Linguistic* Criticism. 2nd ed. Oxford: Oxford University Press.
Garside, R. 1987. The CLAWS Word-Tagging System. In *The Computational Analysis of English: A Corpus-based Approach*, eds. R. Garside, G. Leech, and G. Sampson, 30–41. London: Longman.
Garside, R. 1996. The Robust Tagging of Unrestricted Text: The BNC Experience. In *Using Corpora for Language Research: Studies in the Honour of Geoffrey Leech*, eds. J. Thomas and M. Short, 167–180. London: Longman.
Garside, R. and Smith, N. 1997. A Hybrid Grammatical Tagger: CLAWS4. In *Corpus Annotation: Linguistic Information from Computer Text Corpora*, eds. R. Garside, G. Leech, and A. McEnery, 102–121. London: Longman.
Gavins, J. 2000. Absurd Tricks with Bicycles Frames in the Text World of The Third Policeman. *Nottingham Linguistic Circular* 15: 17–33.
Gavins, J. 2001. The Absurd Worlds of Billy Pilgrim. In *Poetics, Linguistics and History: Discourses of War and Conflict*, eds. I. Biermann and A. Combrink, 402–416. Potchefstroom: Potchefstroom University Press.
Gavins, J. 2005. (Re)thinking Modality: A Text-World Perspective. *Journal of Literary Semantics* 34, 2: 79–93.
Gavins, J. 2007. *Text World Theory: An Introduction*. Edinburgh: Edinburgh University Press.
Gavins, J. 2012. Leda and the Stylisticians. *Language and Literature* 21, 4: 345–362.
Gavins, J. 2013. *Reading the Absurd*. Edinburgh: Edinburgh University Press.
Gavins, J. 2016a. Text-Worlds. In *The Bloomsbury Companion to Stylistics*, ed. V. Sotirova, 444–457. London and New York: Bloomsbury.
Gavins, J. 2016b. Stylistic Interanimation and Apophatic Poetics in Jacob Polley's 'Hide and Seek'. In *World-building: Discourse in the Mind. Advances in Stylistics*, eds. J. Gavins and E. Lahey, 277–92. London and New York: Bloomsbury.
Gavins, J. and Lahey, E., (Eds.). 2016. *World-building: Discourse in the Mind. Advances in Stylistics*. London and New York: Bloomsbury.
Gavins, J. and Steen, G., (Eds.) 2003. *Cognitive Poetics in Practice*. London and New York: Routledge.
Genette, G. 1980. *Narrative Discourse: An Essay in Method*. Trans. J. E. Lewin. Ithaca, NY: Cornell University Press.
Genette, G. 1988. *Narrative Discourse Revisited*. Trans. J. E. Lewin. Ithaca, NY: Cornell University Press.
Gibbs, R. W. Jr. 2011. Evaluating Conceptual Metaphor Theory, *Discourse Processes* 48, 8: 529–562.
Gibbs, R. W. Jr. 2017. *Metaphor Wars: Conceptual Metaphors in Human Life*. Cambridge: Cambridge University Press.
Gibbs, R. W. Jr. and Colston, H. L., (Eds.). 2007. *Irony in Language and Thought: A Cognitive Science Reader*. London and New York: Lawrence Erlbaum.
Gibbons, A. 2012. *Multimodality, Cognition and Experimental Literature*. London and New York: Bloomsbury.
Giora, R. 1995. On Irony and Negation. *Discourse Processes* 19: 239–264.
Giovanelli, M. and Harrison, C. 2018. *Cognitive Grammar in Stylistics*. London and New York: Bloomsbury.
Giovanelli, M. and Mason, J. 2018. *The Language of Literature: An Introduction to Stylistics*. Cambridge: Cambridge University Press.
Glucksberg, S. and McClone, M. 1999. When Love is not a Journey: What Metaphors Mean. *Journal of Pragmatics* 31: 1541–1558
Goatly, A. 1997. *The Language of Metaphors*. Oxford: Blackwell

References

Goatly, A. 2012. *Meaning and Humour*. Cambridge: Cambridge University Press.
Gómez-Jiménez, E. 2015. An Introduction to Graphology: Definition, Theoretical Background and Levels of Analysis. *Miscelánea: A Journal of English and American Studies* 51: 71–85.
Grady, J. 1997. *Foundations of Meaning: Primary Metaphors and Primary Scenes*. Unpublished Doctoral Dissertation, University of California, Berkeley
Gregoriou, C. 2007a. The Stylistics of True Crime: Mapping the Minds of Serial Killers. In *Contemporary Stylistics*, eds. M. Lambrou and P. Stockwell, 19–31. London and New York: Continuum.
Gregoriou, C. 2007b. *Deviance in Contemporary Crime Fiction*. Houndsmills, Basingstoke: Palgrave Macmillan.
Grice, P. 1989. *Studies in the Way of Words*. Cambridge, MA, and London: Harvard University Press.
Haddon, M. 2003. *The Curious Incident of the Dog in the Night-Time*. London: Jonathan Cape.
Hall, G. 2015. *Literature in Language Education*. 2nd ed. New York: Palgrave Macmillan.
Hall, G. 2008. Empirical Research into the Processing of Free Indirect Discourse and the Imperative of Ecological Validity. In *Directions in Empirical Literary Studies: in honour of Willie van Peer*, eds. S. Zyngier, M. Bortolussi, A. Chesnokova and J. Auracher, 21–34. Amsterdam and Philadelphia: John Benjamins.
Halliday, M. A. K. 1994. *An Introduction to Functional Grammar*. 2nd ed. London: Arnold.
Halliday, M. A. K. 1971. Linguistic Function and Literary Style: An Inquiry into the Language of William Golding's The Inheritors. In *Literary Style: A Symposium*, ed. S. Chapman, 330–365. London and New York: Oxford University Press.
Halliday, M.A.K. and Matthiessen, C. M. I. M. 2014. *Halliday's Introduction to Functional Grammar*. 4th ed. London and New York: Routledge.
Hardy, T. 1984. *The Life and Work of Thomas Hardy*. In Millgate, M., ed. Houndmills, Basingstoke: Macmillan.
Harrison, C. 2017. *Cognitive Grammar in Contemporary Fiction*. Amsterdam: John Benjamins.
Harrison, C. 2017a. *Cognitive Grammar in Contemporary Fiction. Linguistic Approaches to Literature 26*. Amsterdam and Philadelphia: John Benjamins.
Harrison, C. 2017b. Finding Elizabeth: Construing Episodic Memory in Elizabeth is Missing by Emma Healey. *Journal of Literary Semantics* 46, 2: 131–151.
Harrison, C., Nuttall, L., Stockwell, P. and Yuan, W., (Eds.). 2014. *Cognitive Grammar in Literature*. Amsterdam and Philadelphia: John Benjamins.
Harrison, S., and Allton, D. 2013. Apologies in Email Discussions. In *Pragmatics of Computer-Mediated Communication*, eds. S. C. Herring, D. Stein, & T. Virtanen, 315–337. Berlin: Walter de Gruyter.
Haspelmath, M. 2006. Against Markedness (and what to replace it with). *Journal of Linguistics* 42, 1: 25–70.
Hemingway, E. 1926. Chapter III. In *In our Time*. London: Jonathan Cape.
Hemingway, E. 1926/1962. The Sun Also Rises. In *Three Novels of Ernest Hemingway*, 3–247. New York: Charles Schribner's Sons.
Hidalgo Downing, L. 2000a. Negation, Text Worlds and Discourse: The Pragmatics of Fiction. Advances in *Discourse Processes series. Vol. 66* Stamford, CT: Ablex Publishing.
Hidalgo Downing, L. 2000a. Negation in Discourse: A Text World Approach to Joseph Heller's Catch-22. *Language and Literature* 9, 3: 215–239.
Hidalgo Downing, L. 2003. Negation as a Stylistic Feature in Joseph Heller's Catch-22: A Corpus Study. *Style* 37, 3: 318–341.
Ho, Y. 2011. *Corpus Stylistics in Principles and Practice: A Stylistic Exploration of John Fowles' The Magus*. London: Continuum
Ho, Y., Lugea, J., McIntyre, D., Wang, J. and Xu, Z. 2018. Projecting (un)certainty: A Text-World Analysis of Three Statements from the Meredith Kercher Murder Case. *English Text Construction* 11, 2: 285–316.
Ho, Y., Lugea, J., McIntyre, D., Wang, J. and Xu, Z. 2019.Text-World Annotation and Visualization for Crime Narrative Reconstruction. *Digital Scholarship in the Humanities* 34, 2: 310–334.
Hockett, C. 1977. Jokes. In *The View from Language: Selected Essays*. Athens: University of Georgia Press, 257–298.
Hoffman, C. and Kirner-Ludwig, M., (Eds.). 2020. *Telecinematic Stylistics. Advances in Stylistics series*. London and New York: Bloomsbury.

Hoover, D. L. 2016. Mind Style. In *The Bloomsbury Companion to Stylistics*, ed. V. Sotirova, 325–340. London and New York: Bloomsbury.

Hoover, D. L. 1999. *Language and Style in "The Inheritors"*. Lanham: University Press of America.

Hori, M. 2004. *Investigating Dickens' Style: A Collocational Analysis.* Basingstoke: Palgrave Macmillan

Hunston, S. 2007. Semantic Prosody Revisited. *International Journal of Corpus Linguistics* 12, 2: 249–268.

Hutcheon, L. 1994. *Irony's Edge: The Theory and Politics of Irony*. London: Routledge.

Ikeo, R. 2007. Unambiguous Free Indirect Discourse? A Comparison Between "Straightforward" Free Indirect Speech and Thought Presentation and Cases Ambiguous with Narration. *Language and Literature* 16, 4: 367–387.

Ikeo, R. 2009. An Elaboration of Faithfulness Claims in Direct Writing. *Journal of Pragmatics* 41: 999–1016.

Ikeo, R. 2012. Misleading Speech Report in the Media with a Special Reference to an Australian Defamation Case. *Journal of Pragmatics* 44: 1183–1205.

Ikeo, R. 2016. An Analysis of Viewpoints by the use of Frequent Multi-Word Sequences in DH Lawrence's Lady Chatterley's Lover. *Language and Literature* 25, 2: 159–184.

Jackson, S. 1948/2019. The Lottery. *The New Yorker*, 26th June 1948. ▶ https://www.newyorker.com/magazine/1948/06/26/the-lottery (Last accessed 21st February 2019).

Jacobs, A. M. 2015. Towards a Neurocognitive Poetics Model of Literary Reading. In *Towards a Cognitive Neuroscience of Natural Language Use*, ed. R Willems, 135–159. Cambridge: Cambridge University Press.

Jacobs, A. M. and Lüdtke, J. 2017. Immersion into Narrative and Poetic Worlds: A Neurocognitive Poetics Perspective. In *Narrative Absorption*, eds. F. Hakemulder, M. M. Kuijpers, E. S. Tan, K. Bálint and M. M. Doicaru, 69–96. Amsterdam and Philadelphia: John Benjamins.

Jakobson, R. 1960. Closing Statement: Linguistics and Poetics. In *Style in Language*, ed. T.A. Sebeok, 350–377. Cambridge, MA: MIT Press. ▶ https://monoskop.org/images/8/84/Jakobson_Roman_1960_Closing_statement_Linguistics_and_Poetics.pdf (Last accessed 19/09/2017).

Jacobson, R. 1956. Two Aspects of Language and Two Types of Aphasic Disturbances. In *Fundamentals of Language* R. Jacobson and M. Halle, 55–76. The Hague, NL: Mouton and Co.

Jeffries, L. 2000. Don't Throw Out the Baby with the Bathwater: In Defence of Theoretical Eclecticism in Stylistics. *PALA Occasional Papers*. ▶ https://www.pala.ac.uk/resources.html. Also at: ▶ https://www.researchgate.net/profile/Lesley_Jeffries/publication/237632531_Don't_throw_out_the_baby_with_the_bathwater_in_defence_of_theoretical_eclecticism_in_Stylistics/links/5703d6dc08ae74a08e245861.pdf

Jeffries, L. 2009. *Critical Stylistics: The Power of English*. Houndmills, Basingstoke: Palgrave Macmillan.

Jeffries, L. and McIntyre, D. 2010. *Stylistics. Cambridge Studies in Linguistics*. Cambridge: Cambridge University Press.

Jesperson, O. 1924. *The Philosophy of Grammar*. London: Allen & Unwin.

Johnson, G. and Arp, T.R. 2015. Chapter 7: Humor and Irony. *Perrine's Literature: Structure, Sound & Sense*. 12th edition. Stamford, CT: Cengage Learning.

Jucker, A. H. 2006. 'But 'tis believed that …': Speech and Thought Presentation in Early English Newspapers. In *News Discourse in Early Modern Britain. Selected Papers of CHINED 2004*, ed. N. Brownlees, 105–125. Bern: Peter Lang.

Jucker, A., Schreier, D., and Hundt, M. (Eds.). (2009). *Corpora: Pragmatics and discourse*. Amsterdam: Rodopi.

Keats, J. 1820. *Lamia and Other Poems*. London: Taylor and Hessey.

Keen, S. 2006. A Theory of Narrative Empathy. *Narrative* 14, 3: 207–236.

Keen, S. 2007. *Empathy and the Novel*. Oxford: Oxford University Press.

Keen, S. 2011. Readers' Temperaments and Fictional Character. *New Literary History* 42, 2: 295–314.

Keen, S. 2013. Narrative Empathy. In *The Living Handbook of Narratology*, eds. P. Hühn, J.C. Meister, J. Pier, and W. Schmid. Hamburg: Hamburg University. ▶ http://www.lhn.uni-hamburg.de/article/narrative-empathy(view date: 6th April 2023)

Lutzky, U, and Kehoe, A. 2017. "I Apologise for my Poor Blogging": Searching for Apologies in the Birmingham Blog Corpus. *Corpus Pragmatics* 1, 37–56

Kasof, J. 1993. Sex Bias in the Naming of Stimulus Persons. *Psychological Bulletin*, 113, 1: 140–63.

References

Kirk, J. M. 2016. The Pragmatic Annotation Scheme of the SPICE-Ireland Corpus. *International Journal of Corpus Linguistics* 21, 3: 299–322.
Kilroy, C. 2009. *All Names Have Been Changed*. London: Faber and Faber.
Koller, V. 2004. *Metaphor and Gender in Business Media Discourse. A Critical Cognitive Study*. Basingstoke: Palgrave Macmillan.
Kövecses, Z. 2000. *Metaphor and Emotion: Language, Culture, and Body in Human Feeling*. Cambridge: Cambridge University Press.
Kövecses, Z. 2002. *Metaphor: A practical Introduction*. Oxford: Oxford University Press.
Kövecses, Z. 2008. The Conceptual Structure of Happiness and Pain. In *Reconstructing Pain and Joy: Linguistic, Literary and Cultural Perspectives*, eds. C. Lascaratou, A. Despotopoulou and E. Ifantidou, 17–33. Cambridge: Cambridge Scholars Publishing.
Krapp, G. P. 1925. *The English Language in America. Vol. 1*. New York: Frederick Ungar.
Kumon-Nakamura, S., Glucksberg, S. and Brown, M. 2007. How About Another Piece of Pie: The Allusional Pretense Theory of Discourse Irony. In *Irony in Language and Thought: A Cognitive Science Reader*, eds. R. Gibbs and C. Herbert, 57–96. London and New York: Lawrence Erlbaum.
Lakoff, G. 1993. The Contemporary Theory of Metaphor. In *Metaphor and Thought*. 2nd ed, ed. A. Ortony, 202–251. Cambridge: Cambridge University Press.
Lakoff, G. and Johnson, M. 1980. *Metaphors We Live By*. Chicago: University of Chicago Press.
Lakoff, G. and Johnson, M. 2003. *Metaphors We Live By*. 2nd ed. Chicago: University of Chicago Press.
Langacker, R. W. 1987. Foundations of Cognitive Grammar, Vol. 1: Theoretical Prerequisites. Stanford: Stanford University Press.
Langacker, R. W. 2008. *Cognitive Grammar: A Basic Introduction*. Oxford: Oxford University Press.
Langacker, R. W. 2014. Foreword. In *Cognitive Grammar in Literature*, eds. C, Harrison, L, Nuttall, P. Stockwell and W. Yuan, xiii–xiv. Amsterdam and Philadelphia: John Benjamins.
Leech, G. 1969. *A Linguistic Guide to English Poetry*. Harlow, England: Pearson Education.
Leech, G. 1985. Stylistics. In *Discourse and Literature: New Approaches to the Analysis of Literary Genres*, ed. T. A. van Dijk, 39–58. Amsterdam and Philadelphia: John Benjamins.
Leech, G. 2008. *Language in Literature: Style and Foregrounding*. London and New York: Routledge.
Leech, G. 2014. *The Pragmatics of Politeness*. Oxford: OUP
Leech, G., Garside, R. and Bryant, M. 1994. CLAWS4: The Tagging of the British National Corpus. In *Proceedings of the 15th International Conference on Computational Linguistics (COLING 94)*, Kyoto, Japan, 622–628.
Leech, G. and Short, M. 1981/2007. *Style in Fiction: A Linguistic Introduction to English Fictional Prose*. 2nd ed. Harlow: Longman.
Levin, S. R. 1965. Internal and External Deviation in Poetry. *Word* 21, 2: 225–237.
Levinson, S. C. 1983. *Pragmatics*. Cambridge and New York: Cambridge University Press.
Levinson, S. C. 2006. Deixis. *Pragmatics*. Cambridge and New York: Cambridge University Press, 54–96.
Lewis, D. 1973. Possible worlds. In *Counterfactuals*. D. Lewis, 84–91. Cambridge, MA: Harvard University Press.
Lewis, D. 1986. *On the Plurality of Worlds*. Oxford: Basil Blackwell.
Lindsay, A. D. Trans. 1964. *Plato's Republic*. London and New York: Dent.
Littlemore, J. 2015. *Metonymy: Hidden Shortcuts in Language, Thought and Communication* Cambridge: Cambridge University Press.
Leech, G. 1983/2014. *Principles of Pragmatics. Longman Linguistics Library*. Abingdon and New York: Routledge.
Levinson, S. C. 1983. *Pragmatics*. Cambridge Textbooks in Linguistics. Cambridge: Cambridge University Press
Longley, J.L. 1973. Who Never had a Sister: A Reading of The Sound and the Fury. *Mosaic* 7, 1: 35–53.
Louw, W. E. 1989. Subroutines in the Integration of Language and Literature. In *Literature and the Learner: Methodological Approaches*, ed. R. Carter. London: Pergamon.
Louw, W.E. 1993. Irony in the Text or Insincerity in the Writer? The Diagnostic Potential of Semantic Prosodies. In *Text and Technology*, eds. M. Baker, G. Francis, and E. Tognini-Bonelli. Amsterdam and Philadelphia: John Benjamins.

Louw, B. 2008. Consolidating Empirical Method in Data-Assisted Stylistics: Towards a Corpus-Atested Glossary of Literary Terms. In *Directions in Empirical Literary Studies* eds. S. Zyngier, M. Bortlussi, A. Chesnokova, and J. Auracher, 243–264. Amsterdam and Philadelphia: John Benjamins.

Lubbock, P. 1921. *The Craft of Fiction*. New York: Scribner.

Lugea, J. 2022. Dementia Mind Styles in Contemporary Narrative Fiction. *Language and Literature* 31, 2: 168–195.

Lugea, J. 2020. The Pragma-Stylistics of Internet Memes. In *Contemporary Media Stylistics*, eds. S. Pihlaja and H. Ringrow, 81–106. London and New York: Bloomsbury.

Lugea, J. 2016a. *World-building in Spanish and English Spoken Narratives. Advances in Stylistics series*. London and New York: Bloomsbury. ▶ https://www.bloomsbury.com/us/world-building-in-spanish-and-english-spoken-narratives-9781474282482/

Lugea, J. 2016b. Code-Switching in the Text-World of a Multilingual Play: The Senile Mind Style in You and Me. In *World Building: Discourse in the Mind*, eds. J. Gavins and E. Lahey, 221–40. London and New York: Bloomsbury.#

Lugea, J. 2016c. A Text-World Account of Temporal World-Building Strategies in Spanish and English Spoken Narratives. In *Analysing Discourse Strategies in Social and Cognitive Interaction: Multimodal and Cross-linguistic Perspectives*, eds. M. Romano and D. Porto Requejo, 245–272. Amsterdam and Philadelphia: John Benjamins.

Lugea, J. 2013. Embedded Dialogue and Dreams: The Worlds and Accessibility Relations of Inception. *Language and Literature* 22, 2: 133–153.

Lugea, J. 2020. The pragma-stylistics of 'image macro' internet memes. In *Contemporary Media Stylistics*, eds. H. Ringrow and S. Pihlaja, 81–106. London and New York: Bloomsbury Academic.

Luhn, H. P. 1960. Key Word-in-context Index for Technical Literature (kwic index) *American Documentation* 11, 4: 288–295.

Lyons, J. 1977. *Semantics, Vol. 1 & 2*. Cambridge: Cambridge University Press.

Mackay, R. 1996. Mything the Point: A Critique of Objective Stylistics. *Language and Communication* 16, 1: 81–93.

Mackay, R. 1999. There goes the other Foot—A Reply to Short et al. *Language and Literature* 8, 1: 59–66.

Mahlberg M. 2007. Clusters, Key Clusters and Local Textual Functions in Dickens. *Corpora* 2, 1: 1–31.

Mahlberg, M., Stockwell, P., de Joode, J., Smith, C. and O'Donnell, M. Brook. 2016. CLiC Dickens—Novel uses of Concordances for the Integration of Corpus Stylistics and Cognitive Poetics. *Corpora* 11, 3: 433–463.

Mandala, S. 2007. Solidarity and the Scoobies: An Analysis of the -y suffix in the Television Series *Buffy the Vampire Slayer*. *Language and Literature* 16, 1: 53–73.

Mar, R.A., Oatley, K. and Peterson, J.B. 2009. Exploring the Link between Reading Fiction and Empathy: Ruling out Individual Differences and Examining Outcomes. *Communications* 34, 4: 407–428. ▶ https://doi.org/10.1515/COMM.2009.025.

Margolin, U. 1983. Characterization in Narrative: Some Theoretical Prolegomena. *Neophilologus* 67: 1–14.

Margolin, U. 1990. Individuals in Narrative Worlds: An Ontological Perspective. *Poetics Today* 11, 4: 843–871.

Marszalek, A. 2013. It's Not Funny Out of Context: A Cognitive Stylistic Approach to Humorous Narratives. In *Developments in Linguistic Humour Theory*, ed. M. Dynel, 393–421. Amsterdam and Philadelphia: John Benjamins.

Marszalek, A. 2016. The Humorous Worlds of Film Comedy. In *World-building: Discourse in the Mind*, eds. J. Gavins and E. Lahey, 203–219. London: Bloomsbury.

Marszalek, A. 2019. Constructing Inferiority Through Comic Characterization: Self-Deprecating Humour and Cringe Comedy in High Fidelity and Bridget Jones's Diary. In *Experiencing Fictional Worlds. Linguistic Approaches to Literature series, 32*, eds. B. Neurohr and L. Stewart-Shaw, 119–134. Amsterdam and Philadelphia: John Benjamins.

Marszalek, A. 2020. *Style and Emotion in Comic Novels and Short Stories*. London and New York: Bloomsbury.

Mastropierro, L. 2017. Corpus Stylistics in Heart of Darkness and its Italian Translations. London and New York: Bloomsbury.

References

Mastropierro, L., and Conklin, K. 2019. Racism and dehumanisation in Heart of Darkness and its Italian Translations: A Reader Response Analysis. *Language and Literature* 28, 4: 309–325.

Matlock, T. 2017. Metaphor, Simulation and Fictive Motion. In *The Cambridge Handbook of Cognitive Linguistics*, ed. B. Dancygier, 477–490. Cambridge: Cambridge University Press.

McEnery, T. and Wilson, A. 2001. *Corpus Linguistics*. 2nd ed. Edinburgh: Edinburgh University Press.

McHale, B. 1978. Free Indirect Discourse A survey of recent accounts. *PTL A Journal for Descriptive Poetics and Theory of Literature* 3: 248–287.

McHale, B. 1987. *Postmodernist Fiction*. New York and London: Methuen.

McIntyre, D. 2004. Point of View and Drama: A Socio-Pragmatic Analysis of Dennis Potter's Brimstone and Treacle. *Language and Literature* 13, 2: 139–160.

McIntyre, D. 2005. Logic, Reality and Mind Style in Alan Bennett's The Lady in the Van. *Journal of Literary Semantics* 34: 21–40.

McIntyre, D. 2006. *Point of View in Plays: A Cognitive Stylistic Approach to Viewpoint in Drama and other Text-Types*. Amsterdam and Philadelphia: John Benjamins.

McIntyre, D. 2010. Dialogue and Characterization in Quentin Tarantino's Reservoir Dogs: A Corpus Stylistic Analysis. In *Language and Style*, eds. D. McIntyre and B. Busse, 162–182. Basingstoke: Palgrave.

McIntyre, D. and Archer, D. 2010. A Corpus-Based Approach to Mind Style. *Journal of Literary Semantics* 39: 167–182.

McIntyre, D. and Bousfield, D. 2017. (Im)politeness in Fictional Texts. In *The Palgrave Handbook of Linguistic (Im)politeness*, eds. J. Culpeper, M. Haugh, and D. Z. Kádár, 759–783. Basingstoke: Palgrave.

McIntyre, D., Bellard-Thomson, C., Heywood, J., McEnery, A., Semino, E. and Short, M. 2004. Investigating the Presentation of Speech, Writing and Thought in Spoken British English: A Corpus-based Approach. *ICAME Journal* 28: 49–76.

McIntyre, D. and Culpeper, J. 2010. Activity Types, Incongruity and Humour in Dramatic Discourse. In *Language and Style*, eds. D. McIntyre and B. Busse, 204–222. Basingstoke: Palgrave Macmillan.

McIntyre, D. and Walker, B. 2011. Discourse Presentation in Early Modern English writing: A Preliminary Corpus-Based Investigation. *International Journal of Corpus Linguistics* 16, 1: 101–130.

McIntyre, D. and Walker, B. 2019. *Corpus Stylistics: Theory and Practice*. Edinburgh: Edinburgh University Press.

Miall, D. S. 2006. Experimental approaches to reader responses to literature. In *New Directions in Aesthetics, Creativity, and the Arts* eds. P. Locher, C. Martindale, and L. Dorfman, 175–188. Amityville, NY: Baywood Press.

Miall, D. S. and Kuikan, D. 1999. What is Literariness? Three Components of Literary Reading. *Discourse Processes* 28: 121–138.

Mildorf, J. 2012. Second-Person Narration in Literary and Conversational Storytelling. *Storyworlds: A Journal of Narrative Studies* 4: 75–98.

Miller, G. 1993. Images and Models, Similes and Metaphors. In *Metaphor and Thought*. 2nd ed, ed. A. Ortony, 357–400. Cambridge, England: Cambridge University Press.

Mills, S. 1995. *Feminist Stylistics*. London: Routledge.

Minn, H. 2017. Broadchurch viewers in uproar at David Tennant's character and his shocking tea-making skills. *Daily Mirror* 13/07/2017. Available at: ▶ https://www.mirror.co.uk/tv/tv-news/broadchurch-viewers-uproar-david-tennants-10022861 (Accessed 10/04/2023).

Montoro, R. 2011. Multimodal Realisation of Mind Style in Enduring Love. In *Telecinematic Discourse: Approaches to the Language of Films and Television Series*, eds. R. Piazza, M. Bednarek, R. Rossi, 69–84. Amsterdam and Philedephia: John Benjamins.

Moore, L. 1991. *Like Life*. New York: Plume.

Mukařovsk, J. 1958. Standard Language and Poetic Language. In *A Prague School Reader on Aesthetics, Literary Structure and Style*, ed. Trans. P. L. Garvin. Washington, DC: Georgetown University Press.

Müller, W. G. 2018. Irony in Jane Austen: A Cognitive-Narratalogical Approach. In *How to Do Things with Narrative: Cognitive and Diachronic Perspectives*, eds. J. Alber and G. Olsen, 43–64. Berlin: Mouton DeGruyter.

Nabokov, V. 1955. *Lolita*. New York: Vintage International.

Nash, W. 1985. *The Language of Humour*. London and New York: Longman.

Neary, C. 2014. Stylistics, Point of View and Modality. In *The Routledge Handbook of Stylistics*, ed. M. Burke, 175–190. London: Routledge.
Nobokov, V. 1955. *Lolita*. New York: Vintage International.
Nørgaard, N. 2018. *Multimodal Stylistics of the Novel: More than Words*. Abingdon and New York: Routledge.
Nørgaard, N. 2014. Multimodality and Stylistics. In *The Routledge Handbook of Stylistics*, ed. M. Burke, 471–484. Routledge: Abingdon and New York.
Nørgaard, N. 2011. Multimodal Stylistics: The Happy Marriage of Stylistics and Semiotics. In *Semiotics: Theory and Applications*, ed. S.C. Hamel, 255–260. New York: Nova, pp255–260. Available at: ▶ http://www.nslbooks.com/arts/semiotics-theory-an-applications.pdf#page=271
Nørgaard, N. 2010. Multimodality: Extending the Stylistic Tool-Kit. In *Language and Style*, eds. D. McIntyre and B. Busse, 433–448. Houndmills Basingstoke: Palgrave Macmillan.
Nørgaard, N. 2003. Systemic Functional Linguistics and Literary Analysis. A Hallidayan Approach to Joyce. A Joycean Approach to Halliday. Odense: University Press of Southern Denmark.
Nünning, V., ed. 2015a. Unreliable Narration and Trustworthiness: Intermedial and Interdisciplinary Perspectives. Berlin: DeGruyter.
Nünning, V. 2015b. Conceptualising (Un)reliable Narration and (Un)trustworthiness. In *Unreliable Narration and Trustworthiness: Intermedial and Interdisciplinary Perspectives*, ed. V. Nünning, 1–30. Berlin: DeGruyter.
Nünning, V. 2015c. Reconceptualising Fictional (Un)reliability and (Un)trustworthiness from a Multidisciplinary Perspective: Categories, Typology and Functions. In *Unreliable Narration and Trustworthiness: Intermedial and Interdisciplinary Perspectives*, ed. V. Nünning, 83–108. Berlin: DeGruyter.
Nuttall, L. 2015. Attributing Minds to Vampires in Richard Matheson's I Am Legend. *Language and Literature* 24, 1: 23–39.
Nuttall, L. 2018. *Mind Style and Cognitive Grammar: Language and World View in Speculative Fiction*. London and New York: Bloomsbury.
Nuttall, L. 2019. Transitivity, Agency, Mind Style: What's the Lowest Common Denominator?. *Language and Literature* 28, 2: 159–179.
Nuyts, J. 2005. Modality: Overview and Linguistic Issues. In *The Expression of Modality*, ed. W. Frawley, 1–26. Berlin: Mouton DeGruyter.
O'Brien, F. 2007. *The Complete Novels*. New York: Knopf.
O'Halloran, K. 2007. The Subconscious in James Joyce's 'Eveline': A Corpus Stylistic Analysis that Chews on the 'Fish Hook'. *Language and Literature* 1, 3: 227–244.
Omori, A. 2008. Emotion as a Huge Mass of Moving Water, *Metaphor and Symbol* 23, 2: 130–146.
O'Neill, P. 1994. *Fictions of Discourse: Reading Narrative Theory*. University of Toronto Press.
Oring, E. 2003. *Engaging Humor*. Urbana and Chicago: University of Illinois Press.
O'Rourke, J. 1987. Persona and Voice in Keats' Ode to a Grecian Urn. *Studies in Romanticism* 26, 1: 27–48.
Ortony, A., (Ed.). 1979. *Metaphor and Thought*. Cambridge, England: Cambridge University Press.
Ortony, A., (Ed.). 1993. *Metaphor and Thought*. 2nd ed. Cambridge: Cambridge University Press.
Page, R. 2014. Saying 'Sorry': Corporate Apologies Posted to Twitter. *Journal of Pragmatics*, 62, 30–45.
Palmer, A. 2002. The Construction of Fictional Minds. *Narrative* 10, 1: 28–46.
Palmer, A. 2003. The Mind Beyond the Skin. In *Narrative Theory and the Cognitive Sciences*, ed. D. Herman, 322–348. Chicago IL: CSLI Publications.
Palmer, A. 2004. *Fictional Minds*. Lincoln, NE: University of Nebraska Press.
Palmer, A. 2007. Universal Minds. *Semiotica* 165: 205–225.
Palmer, F. R. 1990. *Modality and the English Modals*. 2nd ed. New York and London: Routledge.
Partington, A. 2017. Corpus-assisted Studies of Laughter and Humor-Talk. In *The Routledge Handbook of Language and Humor*, ed. S Attardo, 322–339. London and New York: Routledge.
Partington, A. 2006. The Linguistics of Laughter: A Corpus-Assisted Study of Laughter-Talk. London: Routledge.
Partington, A. 2008. From Wodehouse to the White House: A Corpus-Assisted Study of Play Fantasy and Dramatic Incongruity in Comic Writing and Laughter-Talk. *Lodz Papers in Pragmatics* 4, 2: 189–213. ▶ https://doi.org/10.2478/v10016-008-0013-3.

References

Partington, A. 1995. Kicking the Habit: The Exploitation of Collocation in Literature and Humour. In *Linguistic Approaches to Literature*, ed. J. Payne, 25–44. University of Birmingham, UK: English Language Research.

Peplow, D., Swann, J., Trimarco, P., Whiteley, S. 2016. *The Discourse of Reading Groups: Integrating Cognitive and Sociocultural Perspectives*. London: Routledge.

Pfister, M. 1988. *The Theory and Analysis of Drama*. Cambridge and new York: Cambridge University Press.

Phelan, J. 2017. Somebody Telling Somebody Else: A Rhetorical Poetics of Narrative. Columbus, OH: Ohio State University Press.

Phelan, J. 2007. Estranging Unreliability, Bonding Unreliability and the Ethics of Lolita. *Narrative* 15, 2: 222–238.

Phelan, J. 2001. Why Narrators can be Focalizers and Why it Matters. In *New Perspectives on Narrative Perspective*, eds. W. van Peer, S. Chatman, 51-64. New York: State University of New York Press.

Phelan, J. 1996. Narrative as Rhetoric: Techniques, Audiences, Ethics, Ideology. Columbus: Ohio State University Press.

Piazza, R., Bednarek, M. and Rossi, F., (Eds.). 2011. *Telecinematic Discourse: Approaches to the Language of Films and Television*. Amsterdam and Philadelphia: John Benjamins.

Popper, K. R. 1959. *The Logic of Scientific Discovery*. London: Hutchinson & Co. Ltd.

Prince, G. 1981. Understanding Narrative. *Studies in 20th Century Literature* 6, 1: 37–50.

Prince, G. 2001. A Point of View on Point of View or Refocusing Focalization. In *New Perspectives on Narrative Perspective*, eds. W. van Peer and S. Chatman, 43–50. State University of New York Press: New York.

Rayson, P. 2003. *Matrix: A Statistical Method and Software Tool for Linguistic Analysis through Corpus Comparison*. Ph.D. thesis, Lancaster University.

Rayson, P. 2008. From Key Words to Key Semantic Domains. *International Journal of Corpus Linguistics*. 13:4, 519–549.

Rayson, P. 2009. *Wmatrix: A Web-Based Corpus Processing Environment*. Computing Department, Lancaster University. ▶ http://ucrel.lancs.ac.uk/wmatrix/

Raskin, V. 1985. *Semantic Mechanisms of Humour*. Dordrecht: D. Reidel.

Rescher, N. 1979. The Ontology of the Possible. In *The Possible and the Actual*, ed. M. J. Loux, 166–181. Ithaca, NY and London: Cornell University Press.

Richards, I. A. 1936. *The Philosophy of Rhetoric*. Oxford: Oxford University Press.

Rimmon-Kenan, S. 2002. *Narrative Fiction*. London: Methuen.

Ringrow, H. and Pihlaja, S., (Eds.). 2020. *Contemporary Media Stylistics*. London and New York: Bloomsbury.

Rimmon-Kenan, S. 1983. *Narrative Fiction*. London: Methuen.

Ritchie, G. 2004. *The Linguistic Analysis of Jokes*. London: Routledge.

Ritche, G. 2010. Linguistic Factors in Humour. In *Translation, Humour and Literature. Volume 1 'Translation and Humour'*, ed. D. Chiaro, 33–48. London and New York: Continuum.

Romero Trillo, J. (Ed.) (2008). *Pragmatics and corpus linguistics: A mutualistic entente*. Berlin: Mouton.

Ronan, P. 2022. Directives and Politeness in SPICE-Ireland. *Corpus Pragmatics* 6, 175–199.

Ross, S.M. and Polk, N. 1996. *Reading Faulkner: The Sound and the Fury*. Jackson: University Press of Mississipi.

Ritchie, D. L. 2013. *Metaphor*. Edinburgh: Edinburgh University Press.

Ruano, P. 2018. A Corpus-Based Approach to Charles Dickens's use of Direct Thought Presentation. *Corpora* 13, 3: 319–345.

Rühlemann, C. 2017. Integrating Corpus-Linguistic and Conversation-Analytic Transcription in XML: The Case of Backchannels and Overlap in Storytelling Interaction. *Corpus Pragmatics* 1, 201–232.

Rundquist, E. 2020. The Cognitive Grammar of Drunkenness: Consciousness representation in Under the Volcano. *Language and Literature* 29, 1: 39–56.

Rundquist, E. 2014. How is Mrs Ramsay thinking? The Semantic Effects of Consciousness Presentation Categories Within Free Indirect Style. *Language and Literature* 23, 2: 159–174.

Russell, B. 1905. On Denoting. *Mind* XIV, 4: 479–493.

Ryan, M. L. 1980. Fiction, Non-Factuals, and the Principle of Minimal Departure. *Poetics* 403–422.

Ryan, M. L. 1991a. Possible Worlds and Accessibility Relations: A Semantic Typology of Fiction. *Poetics Today* 12, 3: 553–576.

Ryan, M. L. 1991b. *Possible Worlds, Artificial Intelligence and Narrative Theory*. Bloomington: University of Indiana Press.

Ryan, M. L. 2012. 'Possible worlds'. In Hühn, Peter et al., eds. *The Living Handbook of Narratology*. ► http://www.lhn.uni-hamburg.de/article/possible-worlds (Last accessed: 2nd October 2017)

Schank, R. C. 1986. *Explanation Patterns: Understanding Mechanically and Creatively*. Hillsdale, NJ: Erlbaum.

Schank, R. C. and Abelson, R. P. 1977. Scripts, Plans, Goals and Understanding: An Inquiry into Human Knowledge Structures. Hillsdale, NJ: Lawrence Erlbaum.

Schneider, R. 2001. Towards a Cognitive Theory of Literary Character: The Dynamics of Mental-Model Construction. *Style* 35, 4: 607–633.

Scott, M. 2020. *WordSmith Tools version 8*. Stroud: Lexical Analysis Software.

Scott, M. and Tribble, C. 2006. *Key Words and Corpus Analysis in Language Education*. Amsterdam and Philadelphia: John Benjamins.

Semino, E. 1997. Language and World Creation in Poems and Other Texts. London and New York: Longman.

Semino, E. 2002. A Cognitive Stylistic Approach to Mind Style in Narrative Fiction. In *Cognitive Stylistics: Language and Cognition in Text Analysis*, eds. E. Semino and J. Culpeper, 95–122. Amsterdam and Philadelphia: John Benjamins.

Semino, E. 2007. Mind Style 25 years on. *Style* 41, 2: 153–203.

Semino, E. 2010. Descriptions of Pain, Metaphor and Embodied Simulation. *Metaphor and Symbol* 25: 205–226.

Semino, E. and Culpeper, J., (Eds.). 2002. Foreward. *Cognitive Stylistics: Language and cognition in text analysis*, ix–xvi. Amsterdam and Philadelphia: John Benjamins.

Semino, E. 2014a. Pragmatic Failure, Mind Style and Characterisation in Fiction about Autism. *Language and Literature* 23, 2: 141–158.

Semino, E. 2014b. Language, Mind and Autism in Mark Haddon's The Curious Incident of the Dog in the Night-Time. In *Linguistics and Literary Studies*, eds. M. Fludernik and D. Jacob, 279–303. Berlin: De Gruyter.

Semino, E. 2015. Deixis and Fictional Minds. *Mind and Text. Style* 45, 3: 418–440.

Semino, E., Heywood, J., Short, M. 2004. Methodological Problems in the Analysis of Metaphors in a Corpus of Conversations About Cancer. *Journal of Pragmatics* 36, 7: 1271–1294.

Semino, E. and Swindlehurst, K. 1996. Metaphor and Mind Style in Ken Kesey's One Flew over the Cuckoo's Nest. *Style* 30, 10: 143–166.

Semino, E. and Short, M. 2004. *Corpus Stylistics: Speech, Writing and Thought Presentation in a Corpus of English Writing*. London: Routledge.

Shen, D. 2013. Unreliability. In *The Living Handbook of Narratology*, ed. P. Hühn. Hamburg: Hamburg University. ► http://www.lhn.uni-hamburg.de/article/unreliability (Last accessed 4th February 2019)

Shen, D. 1988. Stylistics, Objectivity and Convention. *Poetics* 17, 3: 221–228.

Sherzer, D. 1978. Dialogic Incongruities in the Theater of the Absurd. *Semiotica* 22, 3-4: 269–86.

Shklovsky, V. 1917/2016. Art as Device. In *Viktor Shklovsky: A Reader*, ed. A. Berlina, 73–96. London and New York: Bloomsbury Academic.

Shklovsky, V. 1919/1973. On the Connection Between Devices of Syuzhet Construction and General Stylistic Devices. In *Russian Formalism: A collection of Articles and Texts in Translation*, eds. S. Bann and J. E. Bowlt, 48–53. Edinburgh: Scottish Academic Press.

Short, M. 1988. Speech Presentation, the Novel and the Press. In *The Taming of the Text*, ed. W. van Peer. London: Routledge.

Short, M. 1994. Mind Style. In *Encyclopaedia of Language and Linguistics*, ed. Roger E. Asher, 2504–2505. Oxford: Pergamon.

Short, M. 1996. *Exploring the Language of Poems, Plays and Prose*. Harlow: Longman.

Short, M. 2007. Thought Presentation Twenty-five years on. *Style* 41, 2: 227–257.

Short, M. 2012. Discourse Presentation of Speech (and writing but not thought) Summary. *Language and Literature* 21, 1: 18–32.

References

Short, M., Semino, E. and Wynne, M. 2002. Revisiting the Notion of Faithfulness in Discourse Presentation Using a Corpus Approach. *Language and Literature* 11, 4: 325–355.

Short, M., Freeman, D. C., van Peer, W. and Simpson, P. 1998. Stylistics, Criticism and Mythrepresentation Again: Squaring the Circle with Ray Mackay's Subjective Solution for all Problems. *Language and Literature* 7, 1: 39–50.

Short M, McIntyre D, Jeffries L and Bousfield D. 2011. Processes of Interpretation: Using Meta-Analysis to Inform Pedagogic Practice. In *Teaching Stylistics*, ed. L. Jeffries L and D McIntyre, 69–94. Basingstoke: Palgrave.

Short, M. and Van Peer, W. 1999. A Reply to Mackay. *Language and Literature* 8, 3: 269–275.

Short, M. and Van Peer, W. 1989/2017. Accident! Stylisticians Evaluate: Aims and Methods of Stylistic Analysis. In *Stylistics* Vol 1: Theory, Method and History, ed. M Burke, 134–171. Abingdon and New York: Routledge.

Shultz, T. R. 1972. The Role of Incongruity and Resolution in Children's Appreciation of Cartoon Humor. *Journal of Experimental Child Psychology* 13, 3: 456–477.

Simpson, P. 1993. *Language, Ideology and Point of View*. London and New York: Routledge.

Simpson, P. 1997. The Interactive World of The Third Policeman. In *Conjuring Complexities: Essays on Flann O'Brien*, eds. A. Clune and T. Hurson, 73–81. Belfast: Institute of Irish Studies.

Simpson, P. 2002. Odd Talk: Discovering Discourses of Incongruity. In *Exploring the Language of Drama: From Text to Context*, eds. J. Culpeper, M. Short and P. Verdonk, 34–53. London: Routledge.

Simpson, P. 2003. On the Discourse of Satire: Towards a Stylistic Model of Satirical Humour. Amsterdam and Philadelphia: John Benjamins.

Simpson, P. 2006. Humor: Stylistic Approaches. In *Encyclopedia of Language and Linguistics*, ed. K Brown, 426–429. Amsterdam and London: Elsevier.

Simpson, P. 2011. 'That's Not Ironic, that's just Stupid!': Towards an Eclectic Account of the Discourse of Irony. In *The Pragmatics of Humour Across Discourse Domains*, ed. M. Dynel, 33–350. Amsterdam and Philadelphia: John Benjamins Publishing.

Simpson, P. 2004. *Stylistics: A Resource Book for Students*. London and New York: Routledge.

Simpson, P. and Bousfield, D. 2017. Humor and Stylistics. In *The Routledge Handbook of Language and Humor*, ed. S Attardo, 158–173. London and New York: Routledge.

Simpson, P. and Canning, P. 2014. Action and Event. In *The Cambridge Handbook of Stylistics*, eds. P. Stockwell and S. Whiteley, 281–299. Cambridge: Cambridge University Press.

Simpson, P., Mayr, A. and Statham, S. 2018. *Language and Power: A Resource Book for Students*. 2nd ed. London and New York: Routledge.

Sinclair, J. 2004. *Trust the Text: Language, Corpus and Discourse*. London: Routledge.

Sinkeviciute, V. 2013. Decoding Encoded (im)politeness: "Cause on My Teasing you can Depend". In *Developments in Linguistic Humour Theory*, ed. M. Dynel, 263–287. Amsterdam and Philadelphia: John Benjamins.

Sotirova, V. 2016. Introduction: The Discipline of Stylistics. In *The Bloomsbury Companion to Stylistics*, ed V. Sotirova, 3–18. London and New York: Bloomsbury.

Sotirova, V. 2004. Connectives in Free Indirect Style: Continuity or Shift?. *Language and Literature* 13, 3: 216–234.

Spark, M. 1972. You should have seen the Mess. In *The Second Penguin Book of English Short Stories*, ed. C. Dolley, 301–307. London: Penguin Books.

Sperber, D. and Wilson, D. 1981. Irony and the Use-Mention Distinction. In *Radical Pragmatics*, ed. Peter Cole, 295–318. New York: Academic Press.

Steen, G. 1999a. From Linguistic to Conceptual Metaphor in Five Steps. In *Metaphor in Cognitive Linguistics: Selected papers from the 5th International Cognitive Linguistics Conference, Amsterdam, 1997*, eds. R. W. Gibbs, and G. J. Steen, John Benjamins Publishing: Amsterdam, NL.

Steen, G. 1999b. Analyzing Metaphor in Literature: With Examples from William Wordsworth's "I Wandered Lonely as a Cloud". *Poetics Today* 20, 3: 499–522.

Steen, G. 2007. Finding Metaphor in Grammar and Usage: A Methodological Analysis of Theory and Research. Amsterdam and Philadelphia: John Benjamins.

Steen, G. 2009. From Linguistic form to Conceptual Structure in Five Steps: Analyzing Metaphor in Poetry. In *Cognitive poetics: Goals, gains and gaps*, eds. G. Brône and J. Vandaele, 197–226. Berlin: Mouton de Gruyter.

Steen, G. J., Dorst, A. G., Herrmann, J. B., Kaal, A. A., & Krennmayr, T. 2010. Metaphor in Usage. *Cognitive Linguistics* 21, 4: 765–796.
Steen, G. J., Dorst, A. G., Herrmann, J. B., Kaal, A., Krennmayr, T. and Pasma, T. 2010b. *Method for Linguistic Metaphor Identification: From MIP to MIPVU*. Amsterdam: John Benjamins Publishing Company.
Stefanowitsch, A. 2006. Words and their Metaphors: A Corpus-Based Approach. In *Corpora in cognitive linguistics: Corpus-based approaches to syntax and lexis*, eds. S. Gries and A. Stefanowitsch, 63–104. Berlin: Mouton de Gruyter.
Sternberg, M. 1982. Proteus in Quotation-Land: Mimesis and the Forms of Reported Discourse. *Poetics Today* 3, 2: 107–156.
Stockwell, P. 2015. Cognitive Stylistics. In *The Routledge Handbook of Language and Creativity*, ed. R. H. Jones. London: Routledge.
Stockwell, P. 2010. The Eleventh Checksheet of the Apocalypse. In *Language and Style*, eds. D. McIntyre and B. Busse, 419–432. Basingstoke: Palgrave Macmillan.
Stockwell, P. 2009. *Texture: A Cognitive Aesthetics of Reading*. Edinburgh: Edinburgh University Press.
Stockwell, P. 2002. *Cognitive Poetics: An Introduction*. London and New York: Routledge.
Stockwell, P. and Mahlberg, M. 2015. Mind-Modelling with Corpus Stylistics in David Copperfield. *Language and Literature* 24, 2: 129–147.
Stockwell, P. and Whiteley, S. 2014. Coda: The Practice of Stylistics. In *The Cambridge Handbook of Stylistics*, eds. Stockwell, P. and Whiteley, S., 607–615. Cambridge: Cambridge University Press.
Su, H. 2017. Local Grammars of Speech Acts: An Exploratory Study. *Journal of Pragmatics* 111, 72–83
Suls, J. 1972. A Two-Stage Model for the Appreciation of Jokes and Cartoons: An Information Processing Analysis. In *The Psychology of Humor*, eds. J. Goldstein and P. McGhee, 81–100. New York: Academic Press.
Suls, J. 1983. Cognitive Processes in Humor Appreciation. In *Handbook of Humor Research, vol. 1*, eds. P McGhee and J Goldstein, 39–57. New York: Springer Verlag.
Swann, J. and Allington, D. 2009. Literary Reading as Social Practice. *Language and Literature*, 18, 3: 217–344.
Synge, J. M. 1911 [1907]. *The Playboy of the Western World*. Dublin: Maunsel and Company LTD.
Talmy, L. 1996. Fictive Motion in Language and "Ception". In *Language and space*, eds. P. Bloom, M. A. Peterson, L. Nadel, & M. F. Garrett, 211–276. Cambridge, MA: MIT Press.
Taylor, J. R. 2002. *Cognitive Grammar*. Oxford: Oxford University Press.
Thomas, J. 1995. *Meaning in Interaction: An Introduction to Pragmatics*. London: Routledge
Thompson, G. 1996. Voices in the Text: Discourse Perspectives on Language Reports. *Applied Linguistics* 17, 4: 501–530.
Toddington, R. 2008. (Im)politeness in Dramatic Dialogue: Understanding Face-Attack in Shakespeare's Othello. In *The State of Stylistics*, ed. W. Greg, 427–450. New York: Rodopi.
Todorov, T. 1966. Les Catégories du récit littéraire. *Communications* 8: 125–151.
Toolan, M. 2001. *Narrative: A Critical Linguistic Introduction*. 2nd ed. London: Routledge.
Toolan, M. 2014a. The Theory and Philosophy of Stylistics. In *The Cambridge Handbook of Stylistics*, eds. P. Stockwell and S. Whiteley, 13–31. Cambridge: Cambridge University Press.
Toolan, M. 2014b. Stylistics and Film. In *The Routledge Handbook of Stylistics*, ed. M. Burke, 455–470. London and New York: Routledge.
Toolan, M. 1990/1996. Stylistics and its Discontents: Or, Getting off the Fish 'Hook'. In *The Stylistics Reader: From Roman Jakobson to the Present*, ed. J.J. Weber, 117–135. London and New York: Arnold.
Tsur, R. 2002. Aspects of Cognitive Poetics. In *Cognitive Stylistics: Language and Cognition in Text Analysis*, eds. E. Semino and J. Culpeper, 279–318. Amsterdam and Philadelphia: John Benjamins.
Uspensky, B. 1973. *A Poetics of Composition: The Structure of the Artistic Text and Typology of a Compositional Form*. In Trans. V. Zavarin and S. Wittig. Berkeley: University of California Press.
van Peer, W. 1986. Stylistics and Psychology: Investigations of Foregrounding. London: CroomHelm.
van Peer, W. 2001. Justice in Perspective. In *New Perspectives on Narrative Perspective*, eds. W. van Peer, and S. Chatman, 325–338. New York: State University of New York Press.
van Peer, W., Hakemulder, J., and Zyngier, S. 2007. Lines on feeling: Foregrounding, aesthetics and meaning. *Language and Literature*, 16, 2: 197–213.

References

Van Zyl, M. and Botha, Y. 2016. Stylometry and Characterisation in *The Big Bang Theory*, *Literator* 37:2, a1282.
Vassilopoulou, K. 2008. Possible Worlds in the Theatre of the Absurd. In *The State of Stylistics*, ed. G. Watson, 157–76. Amsterdam and New York: Rodopi.
Veale, T. 2013. Strategies and Tactics for Ironic Subversion. In *Developments in Linguistic Humour Theory*, ed. M. Dynel, 321–339. Amsterdam and Philadelphia: John Benjamins.
Veale, T. 2009. Hiding in Plain Sight: Figure-Ground Reversals in Humour. In *Cognitive Poetics: Goals, Gains and Gaps*, eds. G. Brôle and J Vandaele, 279–288. Berlin and New York: Mouton de Gruyter.
Veale, T. and Hao, Y. 2007a. Learning to Understand Figurative Language: From Similes to Metaphors to Irony. In *Proceedings of CogSci, The 29th Annual Meeting of the Cognitive Science Society*, 683–688. Mashville, USA.
Veale, T. and Hao, Y. 2007b. A Context-Sensitive Framework for Lexical Ontologies. *The Knowledge Engineering Review* 23, 1: 101–115.
Veragen, A. 2007. Construal and Perspectivization. In *The Oxford Handbook of Cognitive Linguistics*, eds. D. Geeraerts and H. Cuyckens, 48–81. Oxford: Oxford University Press.
Verhagen, A. 2007. Construal and perspectivization. In *The Oxford Handbook of Cognitive Linguistics*, eds. D. Geeraerts and H. Cuyckens, 48–81. Oxford: Oxford University Press.
Wales, K. 2011. *A Dictionary of Stylistics*. Harlow, UK: Pearson Education Ltd.
Wales, K. 2014. The Stylistic Tool-Kit: Methods and Sub-Disciplines. In *The Cambridge Handbook of Stylistics*, P. Stockwell and S. Whiteley, 32–45. Cambridge: Cambridge University Press.
Walker, B. 2010. WMatrix, Key Concepts and the Narrators in Julian Barnes's Talking It Over. In *Language and Style*, eds. D. McIntyre and B. Busse, 364–87. Basingstoke: Palgrave.
Walker, B. 2012. *Character and Characterisation in Julian Barnes's Talking It Over: A Corpus Stylistic Analysis*. Unpublished PhD thesis: Lancaster University.
Walker, B. and Karpenko-Seccombe, T. 2017. Speech Presentation and Summary in the BBC News Online Coverage of a Russian TV Interview with Vladimir Putin. *CADAAD Journal* 9, 2: 79–96.
Walker, B., and McIntyre, D. 2015. Thinking About the News: Thought Presentation in Early Modern English news writing. In *Corpora and Discourse Studies*, eds. P. Baker and T. McEnery, 175–191. Basingstoke: Palgrave.
Warner, C. 2014. Literary Pragmatics and Stylistics. In *The Routledge Handbook of Stylistics*, ed. M Burke, 362–377. London and New York: Routledge.
Waugh, E. 1967. Mr. Loveday's Little Outing. In *The Penguin Book of English Short Stories*, ed. C. Dolley, 293–301. Harmondsworth, Middlesex, England: Penguin Books Ltd.
Weber, J. J. 1992. Critical Analysis of Fiction: Essays in Discourse Stylistics. Amsterdam and Georgia: Rodopi.
Weber, J. J., (Ed.). 1996. The Stylistics Reader: From Roman Jakobson to the Present. London: Arnold.
Weinsheimer, J. 1979. *Theory of Character*. Poetics Today 1,1-2:185-211
Weisser, M. 2015. Speech Act Annotation. In *Corpus Pragmatics: A Handbook*, Eds. K. Aijmer & C. Rühlemann, 84–113. Cambridge: Cambridge University Press.
Weisser, M. 2016. DART: The Dialogue Annotation and Research Tool. *Corpus Linguistics and Linguistic Theory*, 12:2, 355–388.
Weisser, M. 2018. *How to Do Corpus Pragmatics on Pragmatically Annotated Data: Speech Acts and Beyond*. Amsterdam: John Benjamins.
Werth, P. 1995. How to build a world (in a lot less than six days, using only what's in your head). In *New Essays in Deixis: Discourse, Narrative, Literature*, ed. K. Green, 49-80. Amsterdam: Rodopi.
Werth, P. 1999. *Text Worlds: Representing Conceptual Space in Discourse*. London: Longman.
Werth, P. 1999. *Text Worlds: Representing Conceptual Space in Discourse*. London: Longman.
West, D., (Ed.). 2019. *Language and Literature*, Special Issue: Song Lyrics, 28: 1.
West, D. 2013. *I. A. Richards and the Rise of Cognitive Stylistics*. London: Bloomsbury.
Whiteley, S. 2016. Building Resonant Worlds: Experiencing the Text-Worlds of *The Unconsoled*. In *World Building: Discourse in the Mind*, eds. J. Gavins and E. Lahey, 165–182. London and New York: Bloomsbury.
Whiteley, S. 2011. Text World Theory, Real Readers and Emotional Responses to *The Remains of the Day*. *Language and Literature* 20, 1: 23–41.

Whiteley, S. and P. Canning (Eds.). 2017. Special Issue: Stylistic Approaches to Reader Response Research. *Language and Literature*. 26, 2: 71–187.

Widdowson, P. 1999. Hardy and Critical Theory. In *The Cambridge Companion to Thomas Hardy*, ed. D. Kramer, 73–92. Cambridge: Cambridge University Press.

Widdowson, H. G. 2008. The Novel Features of Text. Corpus Analysis and Stylistics. In *Language, People, Numbers: Corpus Stylistics and Society*, eds. A. Gerbig and O. Mason, 293–304. Amsterdam: Rodopi.

Wilson, D. and Sperber, D. 1992. On Verbal Irony. *Lingua* 87: 53–76.

Wilson, A. and Thomas, J. A. 1997. Semantic Annotation. In *Corpus Annotation: Linguistic Information from Computer Text Corpora*, eds. R. Garside, G. Leech, and A. McEnery, 53–65. Longman, London.

Zubin, S. A. and Hewitt, L. E. 1995. The Deictic Center: A Theory of Deixis in Narrative. In *Deixis in Narrative: A Cognitive Science Perspective*, eds. J. F. Duchan, G. A. Bruder, and L. E. Hewitt, 129–155. Hillside NJ: Lawrence Erlbaum Associates.

Zunshine, L., (Ed.). 2015. *The Oxford Handbook of Cognitive Literary Studies*. Oxford: Oxford University Press.

Zunshine, L. 2006. *Why We Read Fiction: Theory of Mind and the Novel*. Columbus, OH: Ohio State University press.

Zupan, S. 2008. Mind Style, Modality and Poe's 'The Fall of the House of Usher'. In *The State of Stylistics.*, ed. G. Watson, 451–471. Amsterdam and New York: Rodopi.

Index

A

Absurd(ism) 34, 36, 208, 231, 233, 239, 245
Accessibility (relations) 32, 33, 35
Action chains 204, 219–222
Adjacency pair 125, 126, 242
Ambiguity 4, 99, 192, 228–231, 233, 243, 246
AntConc 138, 163, 164, 215
Antonymy 233
Artistic function 3, 26

B

Banter 133, 240
Bathos 231

C

Categories
- group membership 149
- peripheral vs. prototypical 149
- personal 149
- social role 149

Centrality 233
Character 40, 146–148, 153, 155, 157, 161–163, 166
Characterisation 238
- and mind style 211, 213, 215
- explicit and implicit characterisation cues 158
- implicit characterisation cues 160, 211
- other-presentation 156, 160
- self-presentation 156, 157

Circumlocution 206
Cognitive Grammar 14, 69, 202, 204, 215, 218, 222
Cognitive semantics 14
Collocation 20, 21
Concepts 173, 174
Conceptual domains. *See* Domains
Conceptual Metaphor (Theory) 175, 179, 196, 211, 213
Concordance(s) 20–22, 80, 81, 139, 140, 164, 193–195, 218, 245
Construal 14, 219

Context vs co-text 176, 181, 236, 246
Conversational implicature 121, 123, 154. *See also* Cooperative Principle
Conversational maxims
- flouting 123
- infringement/infringing 210
- maxim of manner 122
- maxim of Quality 123, 210, 241
- maxim of Quantity 123, 210
- maxim of Relation 123, 127, 210
- violation 123

Cooperative Principle 121, 140, 210
Corpus (corpora) 2, 18
Corpus annotation 103, 105, 136
Co-text 20, 104, 135, 194
Counterpart 50
Cues. *See* Characterisation

D

Defamiliarisation 3, 4, 8
Deictic centre 39, 41, 67, 69, 92, 95, 98
Deictic projection. *See* Deictic shift theory
Deictic shift. *See* Deictic shift theory
Deictic shift theory 67, 71
Deixis 39, 41, 46, 63, 67, 91
'Deviant' mind styles 202, 207
Deviation 5, 8, 253
- external deviation 5
- internal deviation 5, 8, 76

Dialect 152, 167
- eye dialect 152

Direct Speech 46
Direct speech and thought presentation 153
Discourse, anterior vs. posterior 88, 89, 96
Discourse markers 98, 154
Discourse participants 10, 38–40, 47, 51, 62, 66, 95, 240, 246, 264
Discourse presentation 88–97, 99–107, 110, 111, 255
- free direct speech 206

Discourse structure 10–12, 57, 62, 140, 213, 255
Discourse worlds. *See* Worlds
Dispreferred response 126, 127, 132, 138

Domains
- source domain 175, 177, 190
- target domain 175, 177, 190

E

Empathy. *See* Narrative empathy
Enactors 40, 41, 44
Encyclopaedic Knowledge (EK) 173, 174, 176, 177, 182, 191, 192, 196
Eye dialect 152

F

Face
- negative face 129, 132
- positive face 128, 129
Face Threatening Act 129, 130, 156, 211
- mitigation 137
Facework 128
Felicity conditions 120
Figure/ground (in cognition) 237, 247
Figure/ground (in metaphor) 193
Figures of speech 172, 246. *See also* Tropes
Focalisation 65
Foregrounding 4, 5, 8, 24, 25, 149, 253
Free Indirect. *See* Speech and Thought Presentation
Function-advancing propositions 42

G

Given and new information 71
Graphology 94, 152
Ground 177

H

Halliday, M.A.K. 41, 43, 203–205
Homographs 229
Homonymy 229
Homophones 229
Honorific 48
Humorous world 228, 231, 238
Humour
- in general 228
- referential humour 228
- register humour 244
- verbal humour 229
- visual humour 228
Hyperbole 241, 246

I

Illocutionary force/acts 118
Illocutionary Force Indicating Devices 120, 137
Imperative 121, 122
Impoliteness 132, 154, 239. *See also* Politeness
- in characterisation 155
Incongruence/incongruity 228, 231, 232, 236
Incongruent . *See* Incongruence/incongruity
Incongruous 181
in media res 41, 71
Irony 229
- dramatic 240
- echoic 241
- in general 240
- oppositional 233, 241
- referential 240
- verbal 240

K

Keyness 24, 25, 165
Key-Word-In-Context (KWIC) 194
Keywords (positive/negative) 24, 216
Knowledge Resources (KRs) 234, 246

L

Levels of language 4, 6, 8
Literal language vs. Figurative language 172, 191

M

Maxims. *See* Conversational maxims
Metafunctions (of language)
- ideational 203
- interpersonal 203
- textual 203
Metaphor 172, 175. *See also* Conceptual Metaphor (Theory)
- conventional, creative and dead metaphors 185
- explicit metaphor 175, 176
- non-explicit metaphor 180
Metonymy 172, 185
Mind modelling 148, 213
Mind style 202, 203, 207, 209
- underlexicalisation 212
Modality (epistemic, deontic, boulomaic)
- epistemic 44, 51, 72
Modal worlds 45

Index

N

Narration 46, 47, 62, 63, 65, 68, 69, 73–75, 81, 106, 107, 158, 160, 213, 215, 216, 221, 234, 256
Narrative 8, 11, 16, 33, 46, 49, 51, 62, 64, 67, 71, 72, 74–76, 81, 82, 88, 94, 95, 105, 166, 203, 208, 211, 216, 232, 246, 255
Narrative empathy 214
Narrator
- heterodiegetic 64, 74, 158, 203, 204
- homodiegetic 64, 69, 71, 73, 158, 160, 188, 203
- omniscient 65
- unreliable 73

Negative face. *See* Face
N-grams 82, 138–140

O

Omniscient narrator. *See* Narrator
Ontology/ontological status 146
Other-presentation. *See* Characterisation

P

Paralinguistic features 152, 167
Parallelism 5, 6, 8, 236, 237
Passive voice 204
Patient 219, 221, 222
Perlocutionary effect 119, 121
Poetic function 3, 8, 26
Point-of-view 203
Politeness 128. *See also* Impoliteness
- in characterisation 156
- in mind style 210
- on-record, vs off-record (im)politeness 133, 240
Polysemy 229
Positive face. *See* Face
Possible world 32
POS tagger 79
Pragmatics 202, 209, 210
Principle of minimal departure 32, 36
Principle of non-contradiction and excluded middle 34, 36
Principle of text-driveness 40
Processes. *See* Transitivity processes
Processing
- bottom-up 15, 148
- top-down 15, 148
Puns
- homographic 229, 230
- homonymic 229

- homophonic 8, 229, 230

R

Reader response research 264, 265, 269
Reference corpus 24, 72, 78, 108, 111, 215, 243, 244
Reference
- definite reference 17, 40, 41, 71, 210
- deictic reference. *See* Deixis
- indefinite reference 71, 72
Reported clauses 92, 96
Reporting clauses 92–98, 104, 106, 109, 153, 234
Resolution 231–234
Rhetoric 9
Rhetorical function 26

S

Sampler corpus 79
Sarcasm 231, 234, 235, 240, 242, 243
Schema-refreshing 149, 161, 208, 236
Schemas 232, 264
- schemata 149
- social 149, 152
Schema Theory 212
Schematic knowledge 16, 70, 149, 212
Script opposition 233
Scripts 231–234
Scrotum. *See* Humour
Self-presentation. *See* Characterisation
Semantic prosody 22, 245
Sequential scanning 69, 70, 75
Simile 172, 189, 190
Source domain. *See* Domains
Speech acts 118, 153
Speech and Thought Presentation 153, 214
Stage directions 158, 164, 167, 255
Standard deviation 52, 53
Story 11, 33, 36, 62, 65, 75, 111, 157, 158, 229, 230, 234, 244, 255, 258
Style 2, 20–22
Stylistics 3, 9, 17, 26, 257, 263
Surge features 154, 164, 166
Synecdoche 189
Systemic Functional Linguistics 203

T

Tagging. *See* Corpus annotation
Tags, semantic 195
Tags (start vs. end) 106

Tagset 52
Target corpus 24
Target domain. *See* Domains
Target (of humour) 234–236
Tenor 197
Text 2, 9, 26
Text internal norm 52. *See also* Deviation, internal
Text-world 32, 36
Text World Theory 32, 36, 94, 95, 111, 221, 228, 236, 247, 255, 264
- function-advancing 221
- World-building 221
Theory of Mind 209, 210, 214
Topic control 125, 154
Topic elicitation 125
Topic initiation 125
Topic nomination 125
Transactional vs. interactional language 117
Transitivity 41, 203, 204, 212
Transitivity processes 43, 204
- material processes 49
- relational process 48
Tropes 172, 196
Truth value 32
Turn allocation 124, 125, 127, 154
Turn-taking 124, 154

U

Underlexicalisation 205, 206, 212
Unreliable narrator. *See* Narrator

V

Verba. *See* Verba sentiendi
Verba sentiendi 70, 73, 76, 78
Viewpoint 203. *See also* Point-of-view
Viewpoint indicators 79

W

Wmatrix 24, 79, 195
Word list 140
Words of estrangement 72
World-building 39, 41, 47
World-building information 40–42, 46, 49, 111
Worlds 32
- modal-worlds 51
World switch 48

www.ingramcontent.com/pod-product-compliance
Ingram Content Group UK Ltd.
Pitfield, Milton Keynes, MK11 3LW, UK
UKHW030609310125
454325UK00014B/219